THE CRISIS OF MODERN TIMES

WITHDRAWN

The Review of Politics Series

A. James McAdams and Catherine H. Zuckert
Series Editors

T H E

Crisis

O F

Modern Times

Perspectives from *The Review of Politics,*
1939 – 1962

A. JAMES McADAMS

University of Notre Dame Press
Notre Dame, Indiana

Copyright © 2007 by University of Notre Dame
Notre Dame, Indiana 46556
www.undpress.nd.edu
All Rights Reserved

Designed by Wendy McMillen
Set in 10.4/13.8 Stone Print by Four Star Books
Printed on 50# Williamsburg Recycled Paper by Sheridan Books, Inc.

Library of Congress Cataloging-in-Publication Data

The crisis of modern times : perspectives from the Review of politics,
1939–1962 / edited by A. James McAdams.
    p.   cm. — (The Review of politics series)
  ISBN-13: 978-0-268-03505-1 (cloth : alk. paper)
  ISBN-10: 0-268-03505-9 (cloth : alk. paper)
  ISBN-13: 978-0-268-03506-8 (pbk. : alk. paper)
  ISBN-10: 0-268-03506-7 (pbk. : alk. paper)
  1. Political science.   2. World politics—20th century.
I. McAdams, A. James. II. Review of politics.
  JA71.C737   2007
  320.01—dc22

                                2007019492

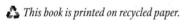 *This book is printed on recycled paper.*

Let us think of the human being, not in an abstract and general way,
but in the most concrete possible, the most *personal* fashion. Let us think
of this certain old man we have known for years in the country—this old
farmer with his wrinkled face, his keen eyes which have beheld so many
harvests and so many earthly horizons, his long habits of patience and
suffering, courage, poverty and noble labor, a man perhaps like those
parents of a great living American statesman whose photographs
appeared some months ago in a particularly moving copy of a weekly
magazine. Or let us think of this certain boy or this girl who are our
relatives or our friends, whose everyday life we well know, and whose
loved appearance, whose soft or husky voice is enough to rejoice our
hearts. . . . We perceive intuitively, in an indescribable not inescapable
flash, that nothing in the world is more precious than one single
human being.

—Jacques Maritain, "The Immortality of Man" (1941)

Contents

Preface

The Review of Politics is one of those rare academic journals that has survived the test of time. In fact, it continues to thrive. Since its first issue in January 1939, the *Review* has outlasted America's involvement in several major wars, the Cold War, the bankruptcy of multiple ideological movements, and the rise and fall of scores of trends in the study of politics. More importantly, the journal is unusual in that the core elements of its identity have remained largely unchanged over these years. Far from shifting from one intellectual trend to the next, the *Review*'s editors have adhered to a set of common themes and a scholarly style that have attracted a broad range of sympathetic authors and readers. For some, the journal's appeal has resided in the fact that its approach to political theory is more traditional than other journals of its kind. For others, the *Review*'s attraction is due to its suggestion that the vocation of philosophy should never be far removed from the everyday world. Yet, whatever the particular interests of its readers, there seem to be at least two factors that have consistently drawn them together. The first is the conviction that despite the ebb and flow of historical events, certain fundamental questions about the human condition have still to be answered. The second is that thinking people can draw upon their natural ability to reason or their religious faith, or both, to make responsible judgments about what these answers might be.

This volume, which focuses on the origins of *The Review of Politics*, is the first in a series that Catherine H. Zuckert and I will edit over the coming years. The goal of our project is not simply to gather together the works of the *Review*'s most noteworthy contributors, of which there are many. Rather, by focusing on some of the defining themes of the journal's history, we hope to demonstrate that there are alternative ways of addressing the major issues of political theory than those offered by currently popular approaches, such as utilitarianism, postmodernism, and rational choice theory. The next volume in this series will be concerned with theories about the origins of political conflict and war, a topic on which *Review* authors had a major influence.

In this volume, I focus on the exceptional group of theorists and intellectuals who were associated with the *Review* and its eccentrically charismatic editor, Waldemar Gurian, in the roughly two decades between the advent of World War II and the height of the Cold War. In looking back on these writers' involvement in the journal, one wonders why their collective contributions have not as yet received greater attention. In a period in which the human capacity to commit evil seemed to expand with relentless fury, these thinkers from different philosophical traditions and religious or nonreligious backgrounds came together to provide hard-nosed but still hopeful answers to humanity's woes. In light of the human dilemmas of our own time, their essays have retained a freshness and poignancy that simultaneously uplifts and challenges the contemporary reader.

The task of organizing this volume and writing the introduction has been time-consuming and labor intensive. I could not have accomplished either objective on my own. Thankfully, I have been in the position to draw upon the advice and generous assistance of a number of individuals. I am especially grateful to Dennis W. M. Moran, whose knowledge about the journal has proved invaluable. Dennis joined the *Review*'s staff in 1971 and has the distinction of being one of only two designated managing editors in the journal's history (the other was Frank O'Malley). Along the way, I have had the pleasure of getting to know Anthony O. Simon, son of the Notre Dame and Chicago philosopher Yves Simon, who has enlivened my understanding of the *Review of Politics* community with recollections of the colorful personalities who interacted with his father—the ever-cantankerous but brilliant Waldemar Gurian, the nervous, chain-smoking Hannah Arendt, the saintly Jacques Maritain, and the gracious and cultured John U. Nef.

I have been fortunate to benefit from the knowledge and experiences of many friends and colleagues at Notre Dame, including four of the *Review*'s seven editors since its founding: Fred Crosson (editor, 1977–1981); Edward Goerner; Rev. Theodore Hesburgh, C.S.C.; Donald Kommers (editor, 1982–1994); Ralph McInerny; John McGreevy; Walter Nicgorski (editor, 1994–2004); and Michael Zuckert. In particular, my co-editor Catherine H. Zuckert (editor, 2005–present) has been an unfailing source of encouragement throughout the project. Over the past few years, I have also benefited in countless ways from the research assistance provided by Elizabeth L'Arrivee, Joshua Bandoch, Brian Klein, Emma Cohen de Lara, and Timothy Webster. They have all had a tangible impact on the organization and tenor of both this volume and *The Review of Politics* series.

Special acknowledgment is given to the following for permission to include the photographs appearing in this volume: the Hannah Arendt Bluecher Literary Trust; Lester Embree, Center for Advanced Research in Phenomenlogy, Florida Atlantic University; Paul Friedrich; Annette Kirk; Mrs. John U. Nef; Ellis Sandoz, Eric Voegelin Institute; Anthony O. Simon; Glenn Tinder; the University of Chicago Library; the University of Münster Library; and the University of Notre Dame Archives.

Finally, I would like to thank everyone at the University of Notre Dame Press for their generous assistance in editing, producing, and promoting this book: Rebecca DeBoer, Lowell Francis, Margaret Gloster, Barbara Hanrahan, Katie Lehman, Wendy McMillen, and Kathryn Pitts.

A. James McAdams

Notre Dame

February 1, 2007

Introduction

The Origins of *The Review of Politics*

A. James McAdams

"*The Review of Politics*, without neglecting the analysis of institutions and techniques, is primarily interested in the philosophical and historical approach to political realities."

This brief statement of purpose by Frank O'Malley, a professor of English literature at the University of Notre Dame, has adorned the opening pages of *The Review of Politics* since the publication of the journal's first issue in January 1939. O'Malley's distinction between these two approaches, the institutional and the philosophical, will undoubtedly sound arcane, even banal to the contemporary reader. In 1939, however, it corresponded with the desire of a diverse group of classically trained thinkers to preserve an approach to the study of politics that emphasized the big picture and posed big questions about the human condition. For them, the emergence of qualitatively new types of dictatorial regimes in Germany and Russia and the looming threat of another, even more devastating European war meant that world affairs could not be approached dispassionately. The authors who congregated around the new journal, including its founding editor, Waldemar Gurian, his co-editors, O'Malley, F. A. Hermens, and Rev. Thomas McAvoy, C.S.C., and an extraordinary assemblage of American and European émigré writers, such as Jacques Maritain, Hannah Arendt, and Yves Simon, were intent upon wrestling with the meaning of these events and their moral consequences. They were also attracted to the idea of sharing their convictions with other like-minded thinkers. Given the times, a retreat into their ivory towers would have been impermissible. For the *Review*'s founders and many of its contributors, this commitment was grounded in religious belief. But, the journal also

had a great number of nonreligious authors who were just as convinced that issues of right and wrong could not be excluded from any inquiry into the nature
and purposes of politics.[1]

For many political and social theorists today, these writers' attraction to a
value-driven approach to the events of the modern age may seem foreign. At the
beginning of the 1990s, it was popular for scholars and political commentators to
suggest that the weighty existential conflicts of the past had been, if not resolved,
dramatically reduced in the post–Cold War world. The last of the great ideological challenges to liberalism and laissez-faire capitalism, Marxism-Leninism, ex-
pired with the fall of the Berlin Wall in 1989. Thanks to a proliferation of fledg-
ling democracies in Latin America, eastern Europe, and Asia and the explosive
growth of communications technologies around them, the twenty-first century
opened with widespread optimism that the threat of both internal disruption and
global war had diminished. As a result, many contemporary theorists believe
that their primary task is not to cast doubt upon people's choices but rather to
use sophisticated analytical approaches to clarify them.

Considering the eclectic spirit of the founders of the *Review*, there is no reason to think that they would have dismissed these methods out of hand. Personally immersed as they were in the tragedies of the "hot" and "cold" war, they liked
to characterize themselves as realists rather than, as they would have put it,
starry-eyed romantics. But, they would not have agreed that the truly challenging questions they posed about humanity needed to be revised or updated. In fact,
given the emergence of numerous new dangers to western society in the form of
Islamic terrorism, biomedical experimentation, and biological warfare, it seems
strange that scholars should put so much faith in the possibility of true human
progress.[2] Instead, as I shall suggest in the following pages, the *Review*'s writers
presented viable alternatives to this way of thinking. From this standpoint, the
essential questions about the human experience remain as relevant to our age
as they were in the 1940s and 1950s. They only need to be raised anew: What is
the nature of human existence? What can we really know about our lives? How
should we act in a world populated by people just like ourselves?

This volume, which is comprised of some of the most important articles to
appear in *The Review of Politics* between 1939 and 1962, provides a variety of ideas
about how these questions can be approached in our day. As we shall see, although the early contributors did not need to be persuaded about the importance of their undertaking, they were by no means agreed about the concrete
form it should take. Some of their political differences were far-reaching. Al-

though none would have adhered to extremist positions, their personal enthusiasms ranged across the political spectrum, from Christian Democracy to social progressivism, agrarianism, and Burkean conservatism. For these reasons, had the editors insisted upon uniformity, or worse, had they demanded that the *Review* function as the mouthpiece of the Roman Catholic university where it was published, the University of Notre Dame, the journal would have failed. Its editors would never have caught the attention of many of the era's greatest thinkers, let alone persuaded them to publish some of their most influential essays in its pages. In retrospect, the *Review* succeeded because its writers welcomed the existence of a forum where they could bring different philosophies to bear on matters that troubled them all.

One has only has to consider a few of the contributors over the period covered by this volume to appreciate the unusual intellectual chemistry that was required to meet this challenge. Simon (Notre Dame), Josef Pieper (Münster), Aron Gurwitsch (Brandeis University), Glenn Tinder (Massachusetts), Msgr. Louis de Raeymaeker (Louvain), Denis de Rougement (Geneva), and Leo Strauss (Chicago) were among the philosophers; Rev. John Courtney Murray, S.J. (Woodstock), the theologians; and Hans Kohn (Smith College), Herbert Butterfield (Cambridge), Stephen Kertesz (Notre Dame), and Christopher Dawson were among the historians. Other contributors were at the forefront of the emerging social sciences, Hermens (Notre Dame), Carl J. Friedrich (Harvard), Clinton Rossiter (Cornell), Robert Strausz-Hupé (Pennsylvania), and Hans Morgenthau (Chicago). Economics and economic history were represented by John U. Nef (Chicago), John Kenneth Galbraith (Harvard), and Peter Drucker. Some of the best-known names defy easy classification because of the breadth of their writings, among them Arendt, Jacques Maritain, Robert M. Hutchins, Mortimer Adler, and Eric Voegelin. Finally, the *Review* published articles by political practitioners as well. An older generation was represented by such figures as Desmond Fitzgerald (Ireland's first Minister of External Affairs) and Rev. Luigi Sturzo (co-founder of Italy's Christian Democratic Party); a younger generation of public servants included American policymakers like George Kennan and Paul Nitze.

These names alone will grab the attention of any reader. But, to provide the reader with insight into the substance of the following chapters, I propose to address two questions. First, why was the *Review*, literally from its first issue onward, able to attract to its pages so many prominent writers with such diverse disciplinary and philosophical perspectives? I shall argue that despite the authors' differences, three factors helped to make their association more substantial than haphazard: an inspirational editor, the political historian Waldemar Gurian; an indescribably tumultuous time in world affairs; and finally, a happy confluence of different approaches to the era. Second, and just as important, why should one read these essays today? The easy answer to this question would be that they were written by learned individuals who made thoughtful observations about their times. Yet if one wants something more than a recounting of the spirit of an age, this answer is unlikely to be satisfactory. I will therefore suggest a few respects in which the *Review*'s agendas in the 1940s and 1950s have continuing currency in the scholarly debates of the contemporary world. Finally, in the last section of this introduction, I will briefly explain how I selected the particular essays that appear in this volume.

The Foundations of *The Review of Politics*

Historians frequently argue about the extent to which outcomes can be attributed to the influence of specific persons. Was it the individual who shaped the agenda or did the conditions of the time make the individual's success possible? Let us consider the first possibility. Among the many different factors that gave life to the *Review*, one must start with its founder, Gurian. In many ways, Gurian's personal credibility was grounded in the fact that he shared the life experiences of many of the thinkers whom he brought to the *Review*. He was born in St. Petersburg in 1902, the son of Russian Jews. Shortly before the outbreak of the First World War, his parents' marriage dissolved and Gurian's mother took him and his sister to Berlin. There, she converted the family to Catholicism. Gurian studied philosophy, politics, and law at the University of Berlin under two of the most eminent thinkers of the day: the early phenomenologist Max Scheler and the constitutional theorist Carl Schmitt, with whom he later broke after the latter's turn to National Socialism.[3] In 1934, fearing political persecution, Gurian fled to Switzerland, where he co-edited a small, fiercely anti-Nazi weekly, *Die deutsche Briefe*. Finally in 1937, Notre Dame's president, Fr. John O'Hara, recruited Gurian, along with numerous other European émigrés, to a professorship at the university.

Gurian had the ineffable personal qualities that are essential in attracting innovative thinkers to one's company. Before his arrival in the United States, he was well known in European intellectual circles both for his extraordinary command of multiple academic disciplines, from philosophy and history to literature and the arts, and for his obsession with world affairs. For example, Gurian seems to have been the first scholar to write about the institutional similarities between fascism and Stalinism, a judgment that would later be treated as received doctrine by many political scientists. Additionally, the *Review* provided him with a personal forum to expound upon a host of topics such as "The Sources of Hitler's Power," "Perpetual Peace?," "The Study of International Relations," and "Lamannais." Hannah Arendt was among many thinkers to be impressed by the unusual breadth of his interests. Gurian's curiosity, she later recounted in the *Review*, "was like his appetite, not at all the sometimes rather lifeless curiosity of the scholar and expert but concerned with nearly everything that mattered in the strictly human world."[4] In short, as the editor of a journal of opinion, Gurian had the instincts and charisma to persuade authors that their often solitary occupation, the life of the mind, should be applied to the events around them.

Gurian's understanding of his editorial vocation was rooted in an engaging idea. A journal devoted to the weighty philosophical and normative questions of the age, he reasoned, could play an active role in bringing together diverse perspectives on the world, religious and nonreligious, politically progressive and conservative, to serve a common cause—the good of humanity. Thanks to Notre Dame's geographical isolation from Rome and its administration's desire to build the university's academic reputation, as well as his location in the United States, Gurian undoubtedly enjoyed much greater editorial license than he would have in Europe. In fact, he seems to have relished the opportunities that arose to steer the *Review* away from even his Church's more egregious errors, including the all-too-frequent tendency of some clerical authorities to make their peace with authoritarian movements, such as the Action Française, and with dubious personalities, such as General Francisco Franco.[5] In his characteristically irreverent fashion, Gurian routinely mocked the great thinkers of the Catholic past who, in his view, bore responsibility for the Church's rigidity and intolerance. Indeed, in 1941 he is said to have advised that "if St. Thomas were alive today, he would be for Franco, for Tiso, for Pétain . . . St. Thomas, that's Garrigou today."[6]

Because most of Gurian's publications over his years at Notre Dame were focused on current events—the war, the threat of Hitlerism and Stalinism, and the prospects for a democratic peace in Europe—one must look back before his arrival in the United States to find an exposition of his personal journalistic philosophy. This position is nowhere better represented than in a 1931 lecture, "The Catholic Publicist" (chapter 16 of this volume), which was published in the *Review* shortly after his death in 1954. The article is noteworthy because much of the case Gurian makes for the responsibility of a Catholic editor like himself is reflected in the journal's character.

In Gurian's view during the 1930s, the prevailing model of professional journalism is represented by the "liberal publicist." This editor, he informs us, is a well-intentioned product of the Enlightenment, someone who sees himself as the agent for conveying all that is good and just about modern society. As such, his job is to shape public opinion by availing himself of the freedom and objectivity that come with the rejection of all that is old and outmoded. Nevertheless, Gurian argues, the liberal publicist's shortcoming is that his beliefs have no solid foundations. As a result of this deficiency, he is easily co-opted in the business of conducting his trade into supporting whatever ideological forces and cultural mores happen to govern society at any given moment. Moreover, this journalist does not even realize what has happened. Basically, he becomes an unknowing victim of his own naïveté. In Gurian's words, "The journalist [has] turned against the powers of tradition in order to be free, to be able to express his opinion without restraint—and he [has thereby become] a servant, a functionary, a slave of the power which he himself had at first promoted."

These observations are curiously reminiscent of Karl Marx's and Friedrich Engels' depiction in the *Communist Manifesto* of the fate of the industrial bourgeoisie. Despite the role of this revolutionary class in laying the foundations for a transformation of its society, it ended up becoming enslaved to the very productive forces and ways of thinking that it unleashed. Yet, unlike his Marxist predecessors and their authoritarian epigone who proposed to overturn the old world, Gurian's objective was to promote an attitude that was respectful of tradition, although not necessarily bound to it. For this purpose, he offers the alternative model of the "Catholic publicist." This editor's responsibility, Gurian explains, is to play a leading role in "the confrontation of the contemporary crisis of the European mind and [to possess] an alert understanding of its travail." In this case, Gurian reveals, the Catholic publicist has a distinct advantage over the liberal publicist. He can appeal to universal truths to gain insight into these conditions.

From this point, Gurian's interpretation of the religious elements of this vocation sheds light on why the *Review* would be attractive even to contributors who did not share his faith. For him, Catholicism provided the foundations for his personal objectives, but in no way was it to become an obstacle to free thought. In Gurian's depiction, no matter how great the Catholic editor's devotion, his faith should not require him to fulfill his duties with dogmatic rigidity. Quite the contrary, the Catholic publicist should seek guidance in the fact that no one can claim to know God's message with certainty. Thus, while this editor tries to provide his readers with some sense of common direction, he is obliged to act with the humility that comes from recognizing his human limitations. "In the pathos of life's present struggle," Gurian concludes, "he senses the peace of eternity, knowing that he is not the savior of the world." As a consequence, it is the Catholic publicist, and not his "liberal" counterparts, who really promotes freedom of thought.

We will never know how Gurian's personal perspectives would have been received at a more tranquil juncture in history. There can be no doubt, however, that a second factor in the *Review*'s success was the specter of war and dictatorship in Europe in the 1940s. In the absence of these conditions, the Notre Dame historian Thomas Stritch has written, the prospects for an intellectually viable journal coming out of a Catholic university would have been problematic.[7] Even in the late 1920s, European elites still held out hope that some form of representative government could take hold in their region. Also, many persisted in the belief that reasoned dialogue with one's enemies would be an effective antidote to the allure of yet another attempt to remake the map of Europe. The futility of World War I was fresh in these leaders' minds. Nonetheless, the tumult unleashed by Hitler's rise to power in Germany, Mussolini's invasion of Ethiopia, the outbreak of civil war in Spain, and the absorption of Austria into the Third Reich destroyed these dreams. Revelations about the extent of Stalin's bloody purges in the Soviet Union also demonstrated that the conditions in Europe were more dire than even many pessimists feared.

These events led to a resurgence of interest in finding alternative approaches to the opportunistic and fundamentally naïve attitudes of many politicians. For example, in an influential article in the inaugural issue of the *Review*, "Integral Humanism and the Crisis of Modern Times" (chapter 1 of this volume), Jacques Maritain bewailed the fact that many opinion leaders refused to recognize the complicity of some of Europe's greatest thinkers in the barbaric acts that one encountered all-too-regularly in the streets. In this essay, Maritain singled out Friedrich Nietzsche's writings as proof that wrong ideas can be even more dangerous than political or economic might. Nietzsche's fantasy of a Dionysian superman had emboldened the worst elements of mankind to assert themselves. "The newspapers and radio give us news of him [Dionysius] every morning," Maritain vividly observes in the article, "and [they] inform us as he leads his dance through the concentration camps, and the new ghettos where thousands of Jews are condemned to a slow death, through the cities of China and

Spain eviscerated by bombs, through Europe maddened in an armament race and feverishly preparing for suicide."

Maritain's reference to the concentration camps is striking in itself. Not only in Germany but throughout the continent, countless politicians and, to employ Gurian's terminology, "liberal publicists" would take years to admit to the reality of the Holocaust. Even more compelling, both for Maritain and other authors, was the prospect of using an open-minded Catholic opinion journal to condemn such atrocities and, in the process, to introduce alternative perspectives on current affairs. The *Review* could call attention to the horrifying events in Europe while simultaneously persuading scholars and other thinkers that a natural bond existed between their professional vocations and their responsibilities as thinking human beings. In contrast to the modern political scientist's aspirations to conduct his research *sine ira et studio,* there was nothing value-free about this approach.

To these convictions, one must add the fact that some of the *Review*'s editors and many of its writers were European émigrés.[8] They had direct and, in many cases, devastating personal encounters with the power of totalitarian movements. National Socialism was especially disconcerting because it had arisen in Germany, a country whose poets and philosophers had played a central role in the growth of the humanistic traditions that their successors cherished. That a culture central to the West's intellectual life could be seduced to the radical idea of the total state suggested that the supremacy of the western values in which they were imbued was no longer self-evident. In their eyes, the acclamation with which the German people greeted Hitler's ascent to power was not an historical accident. Ordinary Germans, it appeared, had lost the moral conviction to resist the temptations of dictatorship, and thus, they cast their votes for tyranny in mass numbers. In the same way, the fact that millions of other people were swayed by Marxism-Leninism's promise to create a paradise on earth was also a sign of the decreasing influence of transcendent values and humanistic sensitivities in the modern world. According to the communist catechism, one only needed to allow those enlightened in the true dynamics of world history to guide the way. Like Nazism, Marxism filled the state with quasi-religious meaning. It treated human beings as infinitely malleable, and it prevented any other voices from being heard.

Just as disturbing to the *Review*'s writers were the appalling weakness and complacency of the western democracies in resisting these threats. In the second half of the 1930s, they had seen politicians in England and France watch calmly as fascist regimes rose to power. It was only when Nazi Germany and its allies began to tear the continent apart that these politicians mustered the courage to defend their populations. Later, the victorious western powers took nearly as long to come fully to terms with the dangers represented by communist totalitarianism. Both during and immediately after World War II, many of these governments were steeped in denial about the enormity of Stalin's crimes. For a time, they tried to convince themselves that the Soviet Union could become a responsible ally. Only after Moscow's brutal suppression of the fragile democracies of eastern Europe and its emergence as a global threat did they fully grasp the necessity of containing Soviet expansionism.

For these reasons, the editors of the *Review* chose to make the education of democratic leaders one of the journal's primary functions. Writing in 1940, Gurian emphasized that the problem with these figures was that they lacked the understanding and the stamina to fight for their ideals. These leaders assumed that all one had to do to win the battle against totalitarianism was to assert the moral superiority of their values. For Gurian, this attitude was worse than simplistic. It increased the confidence of the anti-democratic forces. Even "superior civilizations," he lectures in the article, "disappear if they lack vital power and if their leaders are no longer able or willing to fight." Without these virtues, their claims to truth are empty. It does not matter, Gurian adds, that the fascist and communist regimes were hated by much of the world, including their own citizens. He concludes: "A living lie—and that is the tragedy of human life—is superior, as force, to a dead truth."[9]

In these respects, the *Review* was unmistakably a product of its times. Nevertheless, aside from the impact of these conditions and of Gurian's personal editorial role, there was a final and long-lasting factor in the journal's success. In its formative decades, the *Review* was much more than a convenient platform for disaffected intellectuals. In accord with Gurian's desires, its authors were drawn to a way of thinking that corresponded, in one way or another, to both their ideals and their anxieties. The *Review* allowed them to give voice to their personal assessments of the world while also calling their attention to their common interests. The challenge is to identify how this sense of common values could have crystallized when, as the reader will see throughout this volume, these writers came from many different philosophical and political traditions. Notwithstanding the ever-present risks of making generalizations, I shall suggest that at least four different ways of approaching the trials of the twentieth century contributed to this confluence of interests: critical Catholicism, traditionalism, the emerging discipline of political science, and phenomenology.

A self-evident starting point is with the Catholic agenda of the *Review*'s editors. This was not just any kind of Catholic temperament, but rather a critical mindset that rejected much of their Church's dogmatic thinking and intolerance of dissenting views. On one level, writers like Gurian found their religious faith to offer a useful perspective on the West's inability to stand up to totalitarianism. From this vantage point, the western powers' weakness of will was caused by more profound factors than strategic miscalculations. The real danger lay in the modern world's rejection of God and its replacement of the thirst for eternal truth with the crass philosophical dispositions of the age—materialism, utilitarianism, pragmatism, and positivism. Under these conditions, with little to believe in, democratic leaders had little to fight for. Yet importantly, Gurian and other Catholic contributors rejected the idea that there could be an easy solution to this dilemma. Although they agreed that a return to religious belief could reinvigorate the West's determination to defend its cultural values, they were skeptical that this ideal could be attained merely by dictating it. Given the extent of human devastation during their times, religious faith could not simply be proclaimed from a holy citadel on high. It was incumbent upon Catholic leaders to take this campaign into the real world.

Maritain, with whom Gurian had regularly corresponded since 1931 and later brought to Notre Dame, was arguably the most articulate proponent of this view. As one of the major figures in the neo-Thomistic revival of the first half of the twentieth century, he occasionally crossed swords with the journal's founder about the most appropriate way to judge the "Angelic Doctor." But like Gurian, he too seemed determined to frame his arguments in ways that challenged establishment thinking, not least within the Vatican hierarchy.

Church officials had good reason to be concerned. In one of his best-known essays, "Integral Humanism" (chapter 1 of this volume), Maritain comes close to accusing the Holy See of losing track of its earthly responsibilities at an historical juncture when humanity was most in need of direction. In the opening section of the article, this critique is philosophical and oblique. In Maritain's view, the Church's primary approach should not be to assert its discipline over its believers but should instead focus on *integrating* two axes of the human personality into a unified whole. One element of this activity, he advises, is the "vertical movement" of faith, the identification of the essential nature of all human beings as children of God. Through this supra-rational bond with his creator, every individual encounters the meaning of life and learns to act upon his personal capacity for reason. The other element, "horizontal movement," represents the need for believers to relate to each other. This is the direction, Maritain tells the reader, "whereby the substance and creative forces of man are progressively revealed in history." The mandate of integral humanism is to pursue both of these goals simultaneously—a deeper bond with God and a greater understanding of human interaction. Otherwise, Maritain contends, in a clear reference to the burgeoning chaos of the late 1930s, people will either reduce their lives to "materialistic nonsense" or, conversely, contribute to their own "destruction."

These observations will undoubtedly seem outdated if we consider them from the vantage point of the Catholic Church after the meetings of the Second Vatican Council. Yet in 1939, the Church was still twenty three years away from endorsing this way of thinking on an official basis; ironically when it finally did so, it was influenced by many of Maritain's views. In fact, it is telling that in making his case, Maritain managed to alienate groups on each side of the religious spectrum. Sharing many of the *Review*'s writers' distaste for the self-indulgent spirit of bourgeois society, especially the widespread belief that the Church should adapt itself to the moral and technological imperatives of modernity, Maritain chided Catholics who used pro forma professions of faith as vehicles for rationalizing their acquisitive instincts and appeasing their guilty consciences. In his view, their only hope for returning to the right path to salvation lay in giving greater attention to the spiritual side of their personalities ("vertical movement"). But Maritain also antagonized conservative Church officials by emphasizing that one's belief in God should not be limited to the observance of Catholic rituals. True believers, he insisted, knew that their convictions had to be tested through action.

Had Maritain stopped at this point and only offered the concept of integral humanism as an alternative to the secular religions of fascism and Marxism, his critics probably would have been mollified. But in this *Review* article in particular, Maritain takes his argument one step further by, in effect, advising his readers that good Christians had gotten off track in the first place. Christianity, he contends, can never be allowed to become an abstraction or a lifeless dogma. It is a living spirit which should inspire the faithful to work for the good of all humanity. But the groundwork for this faith had not been laid. One of the major failures of the Catholic Church in Europe after World War I, Maritain asserts, is that its leaders did not attend to believers' needs for spiritual guidance. They provided a "universe of formulas and words," but they allowed themselves to remain blissfully ignorant of the fact that the living conditions of those to whom they ministered were growing more and more unbearable. As a result, Maritain concludes, the Church stayed on the sidelines, while the emotions of ordinary people were left open to exploitation by extremists and demagogues.

It does not take much imagination to see why these observations would have been interpreted as an indictment of the Church establishment. If average people had succumbed to the allure of totalitarianism, then the political aspirations of megalomaniacs like Hitler and Stalin represented something more substantial than the earthly manifestation of evil. It signaled a continuing failure of leadership on the part of those who allowed these figures to come to power. Still, it is significant that Maritain did not treat this condition as irremediable. The most important response, he argues in "Integral Humanism," is to recognize that the rectification of injustice and inhumanity is a basic duty of all Christians, wherever they find themselves. For this reason, when one seeks alternatives to modern forms of extremism, it is foolhardy to look for solutions in formal institutions. They will always come up short. Rather, all Christians should be encouraged to work together of their own volition to lay the foundations for a more just and humane society. Naturally, Maritain stresses, their goal can never be worldly salvation. Instead, their actions should be a manifestation of God's spirit on earth "through which would stream," as he expresses it, "a temporal refraction of the truths of the Gospel."

Against this background, it is useful to ask which aspects of Maritain's writings, or those of similar Catholic thinkers, would have been appealing to other contributors to the *Review*. Since many were not Catholics or, for that matter, were not religious at all, there had to be other points of commonality. Among these, a second group of thinkers can be loosely referred to as traditionalists. For many of these writers, there was much to be admired about the high quality of daily life and the scientific and technological achievements of the twentieth century. But in their view, humanity had also paid a heavy price for this progress. Ordinary citizens had lost their moorings; they had become alienated from the normal course of social and political events; and they had thereby become susceptible to the appeal of ideological movements. One way to counter these self-destructive tendencies, the traditionalists felt, was through a selective appreciation of the virtues of past civilizations.

One scholar who embraced this way of thinking was John U. Nef, a founding member of the University of Chicago's humanistically-inclined Committee on Social Thought and a frequent host of the *Review*'s authors in his home.[10] Let us consider his 1943 article, "Philosophical Values and the Future of Civilization" (chapter 7 of this volume), which in many respects mirrors the ambivalent feelings about modernity held by other contributors to the *Review*. Thanks to the spread of machines and other technologies, Nef maintains, as well as the disruption of traditional norms of behavior during the Industrial Revolution, modern society has lost sight of the beauty and simplicity that once provided comfort to its members. The technician has been elevated over the artist, and the desire for material comforts has taken precedence over the cultivation of higher values. As a result, Nef argues, human beings have largely abandoned the search for universal principles that once occupied earlier generations. While this situation is harmful to each individual, it is potentially fatal for democracy. If ordinary citizens are disinclined to abide by the moral standards that are required for living together peacefully, they will be even less open to the principles of moderation and compromise that undergird a free society.

What, then, should be done? According to Nef, the sensible approach is to reconsider those earlier eras of human development when people were, as he assures the reader, more confident about what they knew, that "truth is preferable to falsehood, discussion to force, loyalty to faithlessness . . . humility to pride, temperance to gluttony, justice to power." Nef admits that these attitudes cannot be easily recaptured. Furthermore, he concedes that one cannot afford to approach the wisdom of past civilizations uncritically. But here, Nef parts ways with his religious counterparts. In his analysis, centuries of conflict have made it increasingly difficult for human beings to find consolation in the hope for a life to come. In fact, one of the lessons of the past century is that individuals will continue to rebel against this belief, feeling that they have justifiably earned the right to free themselves "from the heavier burdens which [the doctrine of Christ] placed on men's shoulders." The cold truth, Nef tells his reader, is that religion, as it is generally understood, is no longer available to provide the world with a sense of purpose. The only realistic alternative is for humanity to place its hope in what remains, in Nef's words, a "Kingdom of God" on earth.

At this point, it would be easy to jump to the conclusion that there is an anti-Christian element in Nef's thinking. Whatever his personal feelings about religion might have been, however, this assertion would be beside the point. As he emphasizes, Christianity may no longer have the power over believers that it once had, but its historical imprint is still available for them to learn from its example. If they want to join others in leading more productive lives and minimizing future conflicts, Nef advises, they do not have far to look. They only need to emulate "those very virtues which Christ set forth in his teachings, and which all the wisest and most saintly men and the most inspired artists before and since His time, have accepted as the highest ideals for human conduct." In fact, Nef emphasizes, an informed understanding of the limits of the human condition and a measure of hope for the future are by no means incompatible. If the transcendent principles embodied in Christianity "could be even partially translated into something approaching reality in the United States," he declares, "this country might lead mankind out of the blood and the darkness that are now working themselves across the globe."

In addition to traditionalists like Nef, the *Review* attracted a third group of scholars with yet another agenda. These thinkers were interested in expanding the study of politics to include social scientific approaches to human behavior. For them, an advantage of the journal was that writers like Gurian had brought a coolly objective approach to the analysis of totalitarianism which contrasted sharply with the utopian fantasies of other circles. Although some of these early political scientists may have been put off by the fact that the *Review*'s editors also had normative agendas, others such as the constitutional theorist Carl J. Friedrich maintained that the systematic study of political events and institutions did not have to be incompatible with the ideals of the humanist. One simply needed to approach the world as it really is with a reasonable amount of analytical rigor. In fact, Friedrich thought that political theory could be enriched by political science by bringing its enthusiasts out of their ivory confines: "It was not enough to expound Plato, Kant and Hegel, but, like Henry David Thoreau, who he also expounded, [Friedrich] felt that there were many professors of philosophy but few philosophers in the sense of putting their ideas on the line in life in the so-called real world."[11]

In "The Deification of the State" (chapter 3 of this volume), which appeared alongside Maritain's case for integral humanism in the *Review*'s inaugural issue, Friedrich provides a good example of this position. In the essay's opening pages, he presents himself to the reader as nothing more than a dispassionate observer of political events. His objective, he writes, is to identify that historical moment at which the state emerged as humanity's primary form of political organization. Like other commentators, Friedrich locates the most dangerous expression of this development in the rise of right-wing and left-wing dictatorships in the period after World War I. But he goes further, arguing that the seeds of these regimes were planted centuries earlier.

In Friedrich's assessment, the pivotal moment for humanity can be found in the waning years of the Roman Empire. This juncture was marked by the rejection of the Aristotelian notion that the *polis* was the highest form of political community and the emergence of the idea that religious forms of authority were distinct from and even superior to governmental power: "Government stood in need of [the Church's] blessing in order to acquire the halo which would give its commands authority." For centuries, Friedrich cautions, this arrangement worked well because Christian authorities could appeal to the highest possible good, God, as a way of holding political institutions up to high moral standards and, when necessary, restraining their leaders. Yet as the power of the Church declined and as its theologians, in Friedrich's view, perverted its original message, religious institutions were replaced by a new form of political organization, the modern state. Because people had little else to believe in, they gradually attributed God-like characteristics to it. Totalitarianism was the most brutal and morally unfettered expression of this development.[12]

From a social-scientific standpoint, Friedrich's assessment of the rise of the "deified state" is straightforward. However, it is revealing that he expresses ambivalence about embracing the use of formal comparative categories—an approach now regarded as integral to discipline—to make this claim. Should the study of politics be reduced solely to the generation of abstract typologies ("the logomachy of the acute nominalists"), Friedrich wonders, what is to keep observers from confusing the existence of a host of different types of states—fascist, communist, democratic—with their desirability? In his judgment, this problem is already evident in the state's deification. There really is no such thing as "the state," Friedrich insists, "there are [only] governments, peoples, countries, there are kings, parliaments, dictators, parties and concentration camps." He adds, "there is no evidence in support of the idea that some sort of holy unity, some mystical transcendence need be attributed to them."

At this point in the article, Friedrich's humanistic sympathies emerge. The trouble with relying upon abstract concepts to make sense of the world, he suggests, is that this approach prevents those who need to know the most about political realities (i.e., the leaders of western democracies) from "looking at the world in terms of a common humanity." The only way out of this dilemma is through a "radical change" in humanity's conception of politics. For this reorientation to work, Friedrich insists, human beings must consciously reject the idea that any kind of government can improve upon the human condition. In place of this assumption, they should consider the "achievement of good government the result of a perpetual struggle of the better against the worse elements of humanity and hence beyond all patent solutions." Thus, Friedrich concludes, all the individual needs to do to serve his best interests is to abandon the fiction of the holy state. Humanity can then return to the early Christian notion—but not the faith—that there are "higher standards involved which do not originate in the government, but must be imposed upon it."[13]

Friedrich's approach to politics brings us to the last and, in many ways, the most demanding group of contributors to the *Review*, those using phenomenological methods to study politics. Up to this point, we have focused upon three scholarly approaches that converge around a common mission. The Catholic theorists, traditionalists, and many of the early political scientists all sought to link a hard-edged assessment of their times with the aspiration to look for answers rooted in humanistic sensibilities. The adherents of phenomenological approaches had similar motivations. They, too, thought that the individual's alienation from his fellow human beings—or, depending on the writer, his alienation from God—was at the center of the European crisis. But they differed in one significant respect from the other theorists. They resolved to look for humanistic goals within the phenomena they were assessing, rather than, as they would have put it, imposing them from without.

Phenomenology was hardly an unknown way of thinking for the *Review*'s editors. Beginning well before the journal's founding, such approaches had won favor in Catholic intellectual circles, attracting such figures as Scheler, Edith Stein, a convert from Judaism, and no less a personality than Pope Pius XII (who would, in turn, shape the thinking of a later pontiff, John Paul II). Yet of equal import, many of the theorists from this tradition were not religious at all. Hannah Arendt, a secular Jew and, like Gurian, a German émigré who also fled Nazism, was among them.

The key to understanding Arendt's special relationship with the *Review* is her distinctive interpretation of fascism and Stalinism. While writers like Maritain, Nef, and Friedrich urged their readers to focus their attention on the concrete threats of totalitarian movements, Arendt's method was to begin from a purely philosophical standpoint by identifying the essence of these phenomena. Although this angle meant that her premises were at variance with theirs, she ended up reaching many of the same conclusions.

We can see what distinguished Arendt's approach by examining a position on which she, Gurian, and Maritain, although not Friedrich, appeared to be in complete agreement. This was the view that the totalitarian movements of the day were not refined versions of earlier dictatorships but qualitatively new phenomena.[14] The issue arose in an exchange of views between Arendt and the Austrian philosopher Eric Voegelin, who reviewed her book, *The Origins of Totalitarianism*, in 1953 (see chapter 13 of this volume for his review). Although generally an acerbic critic of others' scholarship, Voegelin's critique of the work was unusually respectful. But, he had reservations. Among other things, he found fault with the idea that totalitarianism was as new as she (and others) wanted to believe. In Voegelin's judgment, the roots of the fascist and Stalinist dictatorships were to be found in the sectarian heresies of the Middle Ages. True to form, Arendt framed her response to this position in philosophical terms (see "A Reply," also in chapter 13 of this volume).

The methodological challenge for all students of politics, Arendt argues in her rebuttal, is to identify what things are in themselves. Yet, she notes, with an apparent eye to Voegelin's own works, scholars have typically failed to live up to this task because they have repeatedly, if unconsciously, looked for the similarities among political phenomena. Unfortunately, this search for "sameness" is pointless. The search cannot be completed because the essence of something, as she puts it, "did not exist before it had . . . come into being." Arendt finds the appearance of totalitarianism to be a good demonstration of this fact. This phenomenon, she argues, is not only compromised of new elements. It is new in all respects. The result, Arendt emphasizes, is that everything has changed. Society no longer consists of "multitudes" of human beings. Under totalitarianism, there are only "masses." These masses are distinguished by the fact that it is impossible for them to share anything in common because they no longer have individual interests: "They are self-less." In much the same way, the totalitarian state is distinguished not by the fact that it imposes severe restrictions on people's freedoms. The issue of freedom does not arise because the concept as such has ceased to exist.

At first glance, it might appear as though Arendt is simply restating the *Review*'s expression of concern about the gravity of these threats. But there is a telling difference. Where some writers were seeking a remedy to the world's dilemmas in a revitalization of humanity's relationship with its Creator (Maritain) and others were hoping to find comfort in the rediscovery of the estimable traditions and mores of past generations (Nef), Arendt explicitly rejects the romanticization of any of the defining features of previous societies. The implications of her argument are that the past cannot be idealized because it no longer exists. In standing up to totalitarianism, therefore, one cannot call for a return to God because there is no "metaphysical place for God" in such a society. This space, it seems, is "empty."

Given this position, one cannot help wondering why Arendt does not ultimately diverge from her fellow contributors' hopes of creating a more humane society. But, in her debate with Voegelin, she arrives at the same point as they do via the phenomenological path. Arendt begins by agreeing with the principle that the philosopher has a responsibility to confront inhumanity wherever it is found. Yet rather than searching for an external standard to justify this attitude, she contends that this obligation inheres within the injustice itself. To want to destroy something, which Arendt admits is her personal stance on dealing with totalitarianism, is not to pretend that one can do so dispassionately. Rather, the appropriate gesture is to acknowledge that one's feelings are a part of what constitutes the subject matter.

To explicate the point, Arendt asks us in "A Reply" to consider the impoverished English working class at the beginning of the industrial revolution. "The natural human reaction to such conditions," she writes, "is one of anger and indignation because these conditions are against the dignity of man." She continues:

> If I describe these conditions without permitting my indignation to interfere, I have lifted this particular phenomenon out of its context in human society and have thereby robbed it of part of its nature, deprived it of one of its important inherent qualities. For to arouse indignation is one of the qualities of excessive poverty insofar as poverty occurs among human beings.

The same argument, Arendt stresses, must be made about the Nazi's persecution of the Jews. "To describe the concentration camps *sine ira*," she argues, "is not to be 'objective,' but to condone them; and such condoning cannot be changed by a condemnation which the author may feel duty bound to add but without which remains unrelated to the description itself." In this spirit, she and at least Gurian and Maritain would converge. An authentically realistic approach, Arendt concludes, is "to describe the totalitarian phenomenon as occurring, not on the moon, but in the midst of human society." It is not surprising that she would take this stand. For all three writers as well as many émigrés, fascism and communism were not merely topics of abstract, academic speculation. They were concrete movements that exercised a direct impact on their lives.

The Significance of *The Review of Politics*

Looking back at the array of personalities who added their voices, to the essays by Gurian, Maritain, Nef, Friedrich, and Arendt over the first two decades of *The*

Review of Politics' existence, it is striking that the journal achieved something to which many periodicals aspire but few are able to realize, let alone sustain. This accomplishment was the sense for many contributors that despite their differences, they shared certain core values that required enunciation. Among these were a sensitivity to the collective wisdom of past civilizations, a critical appreciation of the search for absolute standards to guide human behavior, and a common hope that the western democracies have the fortitude to withstand the ideological challenges of their enemies. Nevertheless, by the late 1950s, this spirit was dissipating.

Undoubtedly, the death of the *Review*'s founder provides part of the explanation. Waldemar Gurian passed away on May 26, 1954, after years of inattention to his health. Gurian's intense presence and his network of intimate personal relationships with scholars in Europe and the United States departed with him. Of equal consequence, two of the driving factors behind the *Review*'s original mission underwent major changes. The first was a shift in the constellation of world politics. In the late 1930s, the journal's founders had good reason for concern about the western democracies' lack of military and moral wherewithal to stand up to Nazi Germany and its fascist allies, sentiments which were then revived after the West's alliance with the Soviet Union. By the 1950s, however, it had become clear that the same democracies, and especially the United States, no longer had any problem defending their interests and ideals against the threat of Soviet power. At the height of the Cuban crisis, in October 1962, an American president, John F. Kennedy, himself a practicing Catholic, demonstrated that his country was willing to risk nuclear war to prove this point.[15]

Second, in literally the same month, the Second Vatican Council convened in Rome to give its imprimatur to an historic shift in the Church's character. In the pronouncements that came out of these meetings, the council endorsed the more open and less dogmatic image of the faith that certain of the *Review*'s writers had considered essential for reinvigorating the Church's religious and moral authority. Paradoxically, as this dream came to fruition, another factor in the journal's founding slipped away.

Fortunately, the quality of the *Review*'s articles did not suffer as a result of these developments. The journal continued to publish significant essays, each bearing the scholarly imprint of its successive editors. Nevertheless, the *Review*'s early authors would have agreed that the convergence of perspectives that filled its pages during the 1940s and 1950s would be difficult to repeat. However, they would *not* have agreed with anyone who suggested that the underlying reasons for their positions had been affected. After all, a majority of the contributors perceived themselves to be writing about universal questions that could be posed about any civilization at any time.

In this light, were these authors around today, we can imagine that they could identify cases in which the mistaken judgments of their age have been passed on to the present. One of these would be the common assumption among policymakers and public intellectuals that one can make judgments about matters of good and evil, life and death, without reference to any of the higher principles that bind humanity together. The other problem would be the widespread belief, already implicit in the weakness of western democracies in their times, that this capacity for judgment cannot be extended to the behavior of other persons.

The *Review*'s contributors could find evidence of the first fallacy in society's steadily growing confidence that the human condition should not be treated as a constant but rather as a subject of continuing modification and improvement. On one level, this attitude can be found in the notion that the primary function of the democratic state is to satisfy citizens' desires for social concord and material well-being. In this circumstance, it is logical for the position's advocates to contend that the study of politics should not be focused on the search for ultimate principles but instead upon analytical problems, such as the fair and efficient distribution of resources.

On a more fundamental level, this approach is reflected in the proposition that the identity of the individual person is malleable, even to the point of perfectibility. Without denying that the last century saw significant progress in, among other things, overcoming infectious diseases and raising living standards (at least in the West), some commentators have argued that this "progress" has not all been for the good. Whereas advances in fields such as cosmetic surgery, pharmacology, and bioengineering have provided welcome opportunities for ordinary people to improve the quality of their lives, others have been seduced by the possibility of taking these achievements one step further. They are attracted to the idea of a new type of human being, someone who aspires to live in a world without pain, blemishes, imperfections, and anxiety.

The *Review*'s authors were already concerned in the 1940s about such naïve conceptions of the malleability—and perfectibility—of human nature. For example, in "On Contemporary Nihilism" (chapter 8 of this volume), the Swiss phenomenologist, Aron Gurwitsch, takes a stand that practically anticipated developments like an excessive faith in the power of technology and personal consumption to provide happiness, even self-realization. In his view, one of the most profound symptoms of the pathologies of modernity is that philosophers have deprived the human person of his or her essential traits as a thinking, reasoning being, "an animal rationale." In their place, they have transformed the individual into an isolated "creature of appetites and passions," an animal pure, whose primary pursuit is self-gratification. Under this circumstance, there is little about human existence that remains unique or intrinsically defensible. "In the final analysis," Gurwitsch underscores, "man [becomes] a vital being who, in principle, does not differ greatly from the other animals."

To be sure, Gurwitsch would have had no difficulty accepting the scientific and technological achievements of the postwar era. His concern, writing in 1945, was that people's immediate desires not be conflated with their ultimate needs. There were already signs, in Gurwitsch's view, that the road to be taken by most democratic governments in the postwar reconstruction of the continent would not be to recover a common spiritual and moral foundation for humanity. Instead, they were aiming only to build efficient social-market economies and to meet their populations' demand to return to high levels of personal consumption. Western politicians reasoned that the more one maximized the happiness of each of society's members, the easier it would be to reduce the propensity for conflict among them. Yet for Gurwitsch, this is where they were going awry. If one abandons the proposition, he writes in "On Contemporary Nihilism," that moral action should be governed by an overarching truth that sets human beings apart from other animals, then society will be deprived of the organizing principles that allow human beings to lead good lives.

Eighteen years later, in the context of the West's complete economic and political recovery, a similar perspective was advanced in the *Review* by a young political theorist Glenn Tinder. In "Human Estrangement and the Failure of Political Imagination" (chapter 20 of this volume), Tinder laments the fact that "the contemporary political imagination lies in its insensibility to the ultimate questions of political life." The study of politics, he emphasizes, is not merely about "who gets what, when, and how" or "the apportionment of means" but instead with the "good life . . . [and] the discovery and pursuit of valid ends." Lacking this perspective, people may be better off, but they have no way of regaining their connections with the past; their personal relationships are attenuated; and they have become separated from each other. "Estranged men are not reconciled merely by the equalization of economic and social status," Tinder concludes, "their need is for a rediscovery of meaning, and for a restoration of integrity to a 'broken world.'"

On first inspection, Gurwitsch's and Tinder's concerns will seem like a far cry from the earlier acts of human depravity that their contemporaries found to be rooted in spiritual and moral disintegration of their age. In a 1941 article, "The Immortality of Man" (chapter 5 of this volume), Maritain grimly attributes "the present-day transportations of populations, concentration camps, [and] wars of enslavement" to a loss of belief in what makes human existence special, the immortality of the individual. Only an appreciation of this factor, Maritain counsels, raises society over the "heartless bestiality" and "cowardly delicacy" of modernity. Yet Gurwitsch and Tinder, too, were attuned to the connection between the individual's loss of identity and the collapse of European civilization. For Gurwitsch, the cause was to be found in the emergence of totalitarian ideologies which were, in his view, "the culmination of nihilism." For Tinder, it was the equally grave danger presented "by the capacity of [estranged individuals] to be moved by a will to total destruction," not least during the escalating arms race between the United States and the Soviet Union.

Viewed from this perspective, all three writers would have had no reason to be surprised by the fate of many observers' judgments about the prospects for moral progress and world peace in the 1990s. The decade had opened with breathless optimism. But before the century closed, a host of events testified to the fact that human beings were not so malleable as to allow their impulses to be governed by rational calculations alone. The fall of the Soviet empire did not lead, as many hoped, to the creation of a harmonious network of independent republics but rather to the outbreak of intense ethnic and political violence between Russians and Chechens, Azeris and Armenians, Georgians, Ossetians, and Abkhazians, and countless other peoples. The outbreak of military conflict among the former member states of communist Yugoslavia, Serbia, Croatia, and Bosnia-Herzegovina led to widespread human rights abuses and calculated acts of ethnic cleansing. Notably, these countries' western European neighbors were quick to condemn these atrocities, but their actions were more revealing than their words. As in the period surrounding the *Review*'s founding, they took years before agreeing that intervention was required to put an end to the violence.

Likewise, the world has not become safer, only different. The risks of nuclear proliferation and the refinement of other technologies of death, including chemical and biological weapons, have escalated as states like Iraq, Iran, and North Korea have sought to match the military power of their rivals. In most cases, as the *Review*'s authors would have predicted, international organizations, such as the United Nations, have turned out to be incapable of moderating, let alone preventing, world conflicts. Above all, the terrorist attacks on the United States in September 2001, Spain in March 2004, and Great Britain in July 2005 have signified the emergence of a new form of armed conflict.

Here, too, the *Review*'s writers would not have been surprised. As the Swiss philosopher Denis de Rougement observed in his 1941 article, "Passion and the Origin of Hitlerism" (chapter 4 of this volume), notably before the Japanese attack on Pearl Harbor, the West's lack of preparedness for the rise of fascist militarism and the outbreak of World War II was due to the striking naïveté of many democratic leaders about those who wished them ill. They badly underestimated their enemies' fanatical hatred of Western values and commitments. About Europe's leaders, de Rougement notes, they "persisted in believing that they could discuss matters objectively and come to terms . . . with men who have immured themselves in the dream of the millennium autarchy." As a result, he adds, one could consistently predict "their failures, delays, and perpetual state of surprise."

The abiding question is why, despite these experiences, democracies continue to be slow in responding to such threats. Contemporary political science provides a variety of explanations, including the restraining influence of interparty competition for risk-averse voters and the culture of complacency fostered by high standards of living. However, the *Review*'s authors would insist that the weakness of democracies raises questions for political theorists as well. Are democratic leaders sufficiently committed to defending the ideals and values on which their societies are based? Or, in times of uncertainty, is their belief in the rightness of their views so tenuous that they continually fall prey to pragmatic and utilitarian solutions to problems that are deeper than they appear on the surface?

In considering this point, we need to keep the obvious in mind. Philosophers cannot be held responsible for a state's failure to defend itself. Nonetheless, one can take philosophical concerns into account, as the *Review*'s contributors demanded, by recognizing that they can illuminate the temperament of a society and the spirit of an age. Interestingly, this subject arose in the early 2000s in capitals from Washington to London and Berlin to Paris when policymakers deliberated over ways to respond to the threat of Islamic terrorism. Some argued that although the form of the threat was new, the remedy to such dangers was the same as it had ever been. The western world needed to meet force with force. In contrast, others found their response in the fact that the conflict was driven by more fundamental issues, including rival conceptions of truth and justice. For the position's advocates, it was not enough to rely upon traditional forms of statecraft and organized violence. Right ideas needed to be squared off against bad ones.[16]

This second perspective would have been familiar to the *Review*'s writers. When one looks back on the journal's first two decades, these authors were demanding a great deal of their leaders. They were saying that the major political and military challenges of the modern age could not be properly understood unless they were approached in terms of searching questions about the human condition. At the same time, however, it was equally important to them that the diverse answers that were offered never be transformed into fixed and frozen dogmas. To allow this development would be to abandon a distinctive attribute of the democratic state.

In this light, Gurian's image of the "Catholic publicist" is enlightening. When this ideal-typical personality is judged from a purely philosophical perspective, he clearly embodied the *Review*'s purpose. Gurian was intent upon having this figure draw upon deeply-felt convictions in holding his society and its politicians up to close scrutiny. But in a restrictive climate, such as that represented by pre-Vatican II Catholicism, the *Review*'s founder also insisted that his publicist act of his own volition. To paraphrase Gurian's remarks earlier in this chapter, he could not be allowed to follow the path of the servant, functionary, and slave of established opinion. By rejecting this temptation, he could "sustain his lot as a man in ceaseless search for the real meaning of his age without surrendering to relativism and despair or growing torpid and stiff in an objectivism that only appears to transcend the temporal flux."

We can see why Gurian's engaging interpretation of this mission appealed to so many different authors. In a time of growing skepticism about western values and institutions, he was defending the idea that the quest for overarching principles to guide human behavior was an essential part of the philosophical enterprise. But in the same breath, he was leaving open the possibility that different approaches could be taken to realize this objective. In this sense, for the inspired collection of thinkers who congregated around a journal of political thought run out of a Catholic university in the American heartland—a place of "life and calm at the center of the black whirlpool in which we are now roaring"[17]—the *Review* was an inspiring undertaking. Its editors did not tell them that they had to make a choice between searching for the truth and maintaining their critical edge. Instead, the *Review* provided the intriguing possibility that they could pursue both goals simultaneously. This model of intellectual honesty seems as appropriate today as it was over a half-century ago.

ABOUT THE READINGS

In selecting the articles for this volume, I have emphasized those essays that say the most about the editorial philosophy behind *The Review of Politics* and, at the same time, have the greatest potential to speak to issues in our own times and beyond. As the reader will discern, it is much easier to express these twin objectives than to live up to them. For one thing, as my list of contributors at the beginning of this introduction suggests, there are so many significant essays in the first two decades of the *Review*'s publication that it would be impossible to include them in a single volume. This problem is compounded by the fact that the authors were, of their own accord, routinely seeking to live up to the criteria I have identified. It was part of the journal's culture that they self-consciously addressed themes with the potential, to quote Jacob Burckhardt's admonition, "to last for all time." Another, perhaps less self-evident selection problem involves the issue of quantity. What does one do, for example, when there are too many substantial articles by Gurian (at least 12, not counting those penned under "The Editors"); Simon (4); Arendt (7); Maritain (6); and Nef (8)? One could publish an entire book of each author's essays alone.

My way of responding to these dilemmas has been necessarily and regrettably imperfect. First, I have attempted to choose articles which best fit into the four groups of contributors that I have outlined above. Accordingly, I have included authors such as Josef Pieper, Louis de Raeymaeker, and Frank O'Malley because their essays bear similarities to Maritain's critical Catholicism. Likewise, political theorists such as Russell Kirk, Leo Strauss, and Tinder seem to share affinities with Nef's traditionalist approach. But, the shortcomings of this approach are manifest. There is enough overlap among the four categories that one could easily contest the inclusion of an author in one group when he or she might better fit into another. Is Nef primarily a traditionalist or is he much more a social scientist? The greater dilemma, however, is that many of these authors would resist the idea of being put into categories at all. For example, if Voegelin were writing today, he would undoubtedly refuse to accept any such designation.

Second, there is no happy solution to the otherwise fortunate dilemma of having too many high-quality articles from which to choose. For this reason, some of my choices may appear ad hoc. I have selected the greatest number of articles (4) for Maritain, though I could easily have been persuaded to use all six, given their groundbreaking quality. I have chosen two of Arendt's articles because I felt that these particular pieces represent the clearest articulation of her views on totalitarianism; all of the other foundational articles for her famous book on this subject can be found in the *Review*'s pages.[18] In a couple cases, I have selected an article that turned out to be especially important to an intellectual biography, even though that author only published once in the *Review*. This is the case with Strauss's "Natural Right and the Historical Approach."

As I have noted in the preface to this book, the most satisfying approach to resolving the problem of abundance will be to produce a second collection of essays. This future volume will include articles by the many contributors to the journal who were instrumental in developing the field of international relations theory, among them names like Morgenthau, Butterfield, Kennan, and Nitze.

There is one issue I have not been able to resolve, but it should not go unmentioned. The *Review* has a long tradition of publishing review essays that go beyond the standard evaluations of recent books to address broader historical, philosophical, and moral questions. In the journal's first two decades, these reviews are notable for a number of reasons. Some speak to the editors' eclectic interests. For example, there are reviews of both Kant's essay on "Perpetual Peace" and Hitler's *Mein Kampf*. Others are notable because their authors are not usually associated with penning book reviews (e.g., Voegelin, Arendt, and even the priest/politician Sturzo). On one specific note, these reviews testify to the inexhaustible intellectual curiosity of the *Review*'s founder. Up to his death in 1954, Gurian wrote one hundred forty reviews, give or take a few, and this figure includes only the ones that identify him by name. Although space limitations have prevented me from including any of these reviews, I recommend them to anyone interested in the *Review*'s authors and their times.

Overall, my goal in editing the essays in this volume has been to make each of them as accessible and useful as possible. For the reader's convenience, I introduce each chapter with a short biography of the author. These paragraphs are not intended to provide extensive details about the writer's life but instead to locate his or her essays within their respective political and intellectual contexts. I have corrected and clarified some of the authors' references. In many cases, to compensate for the passage of time, I have added short notes (in brackets) to provide background information about historical actors and schools of thought. Finally, on a limited basis, I have quietly removed extraneous material and toned down stylistic idiosyncrasies and archaisms which, in my judgment, detracted from the author's message. Of course, should the reader want to consider these emendations or resolve any other questions about this volume, he or she can readily turn to the original versions of the articles in the *Review*.

NOTES

1. For useful accounts of the *Review*'s history, see Frank O'Malley, "The Image of Man: Ten Years of the *Review of Politics*," *The Review of Politics* 10, no. 4 (1948): 395–98; Thomas Stritch, "After Forty Years: Notre Dame and the *Review of Politics*," *The Review of Politics* 50, no. 4 (Fall 1988): 520–29; Donald P. Kommers, "Fifty Years," *The Review of Politics* 50, no. 4 (Fall 1988): 515–19; M. A. Fitzsimons, "The Human Prospect as Seen in the *Review of Politics*, 1939–1992: A Sesquicentennial Reflection," *The Review of Politics* 54, no. 4 (Fall 1992): 509–49.

2. For a contemporary, Catholic interpretation of the concept of "progress" that would have been welcomed by many of the *Review*'s religious contributors, see William Pfaff, "Progress," *World Policy Journal* 12, no. 4 (Winter 1995/96): 41–49.

3. "With an intensity greater than any other Catholic in the 1930s," M. Dalheimer writes, "Waldemar Gurian went to battle against the theories, political activities, and the person of Carl Schmitt." See "Carl Schmitt und der deutsche Katholizismus 1888–1936," in *Veröffentlichungen der Kommission für Zeitgeschichte*, Series B, vol. 83 (1998): 556.

4. Hannah Arendt, "The Personality of Waldemar Gurian," *The Review of Politics* 17, no. 1 (January 1955): 37. Also see Robert E. Burns, *Being Catholic, Being American* (Notre Dame: University of Notre Dame Press, 2000), 21–25; Heinz Hürten, *Waldemar Gurian* (Mainz: Matthias-Grünewald-Verlag, 1972), 149–70; and Hans Kohn, "Waldemar Gurian: Witness of the Twentieth Century," *The Review of Politics* 17, no. 1 (January 1955): 73–79.

5. On this subject, see John Hellman, "The Anti-Democratic Impulse in Catholicism: Jacques Maritain, Yves Simon, and Charles de Gaulle during World War II," *Journal of Church and State* 33 (Summer 1991): 453–72.

6. Msgr. Jozef Tiso was president of Slovakia from 1939–1945, during the country's alliance with Nazi Germany. Marshall Philippe Pétain headed France's Vichy government from 1940 to 1944. Fr. Reginald Garrigou-LaGrange, O.P., a leading neo-Thomist theologian and antagonist of Jacques Maritain, was a Vichy sympathizer. Gurian's remarks are paraphrased by Yves Simon in a letter to Maritain on July 16, 1941. Speaking for himself to a man who wanted to rescue Aquinas for the modern age, Simon added: "To try to make practical politics with Aquinas in 1941 is silly." From the archives of the Yves R. Simon Institute, South Bend, IN. John T. McGreevy discusses the context of this letter in his authoritative study of Catholic intellectual life in the U.S., *Catholicism and American Freedom* (New York: W. W. Norton, 2003), 198.

7. Stritch, "After Forty Years," 520.

8. For a useful study of five prominent Catholic émigrés, Gurian, Maritain, Yves Simon, F. A. Hermens, and Don Luigi Sturzo, all of whom were contributors to the *Review*, see Kathleen Mary Connelly, S. C. L., "Catholic Witness: The Political Activities of Five European Christian Democratic Scholars While in Exile in the United States, 1938–1945," PhD dissertation, Department of History, Boston College, December 1995.

9. Waldemar Gurian, "Trends in Modern Politics," *The Review of Politics* 2, no. 3 (July 1940): 336.

10. In a tribute to Gurian after his death, "The Significance of the *Review of Politics*," Nef points out that the Committee on Social Thought tried to found its own journal in 1949, but this publication met an early demise, unlike the *Review* which thrived. See *The Review of Politics* 17, no. 1 (January 1955): 24–32.

11. In the words of his son, the anthropologist Paul Friedrich. Unpublished lecture given to the Director's Conference of the Newspaper Association of America, April 1, 2006.

12. Somewhat like Gurian, Friedrich attributed some of the responsibility for Christianity's decline to religious thinkers like Aquinas who, in his view, mistakenly helped to give the state legitimacy.

13. This stance was not based upon any religious faith on Friedrich's part. According to Paul Friedrich (see note 11 above), his father stated during his naturalization procedures that his religion was "Homer."

14. For background, see Dana Villa, "Introduction: The development of Arendt's political thought" and Margaret Canovan, "Arendt's theory of totalitarianism: A reassessment" in Dana Villa, ed., *The Cambridge Companion to Hannah Arendt* (Cambridge, U. K.: Cambridge University Press, 2000), 1–24 and 25–43, respectively.

15. The year 1962 also marks the publication date of the last article in this volume (chapter 22), John U. Nef's "Is the Intellectual Life an End in Itself?" *The Review of Politics* 24, no. 1 (January 1962): 3–18.

16. Although the subject is not as new as some think, the political scientist Samuel Huntington engaged this issue in 1993 with a controversial statement about the coming "clash of civilizations." See his full treatment of the topic in *The Clash of Civilizations and the Remaking of World Order* (New York: Simon and Schuster, 2006). Roger Scruton has presented a similar, but more differentiated view (which could easily have appeared in *The Review of Politics*) in *The West and the Rest* (Wilmington, DE: Institute of Intercollegiate Studies Books, 2002).

17. The Editors, "The Hundred Years of Notre Dame," *The Review of Politics* 4, no. 4 (October 1942): 378.

18. I am referring to Arendt's *The Origins of Totalitarianism* (New York: Harcourt, Brace & World, 1973).

CHAPTER 1

Integral Humanism and the Crisis of Modern Times

JACQUES MARITAIN

Jacques Maritain (1882–1973) was born in Paris and studied philosophy at the Sorbonne and the University of Heidelberg. His thinking was heavily influenced by his conversion to Catholicism. Before World War II, he moved to America where he taught philosophy and Catholic theology at Columbia and Princeton, and frequently lectured at universities such as the University of Chicago and the University of Notre Dame. Maritain understood himself to be a "critical realist," emphasizing metaphysics over epistemology and rejecting rationalist and positivist accounts of knowledge. As a so-called neo-Thomist, he argued against a rigid and unreflective understanding of scholasticism. But like Aquinas, he maintained that reason and revelation are not fundamentally in opposition, and that philosophy can demonstrate the truth of certain religious beliefs, for example the existence of God. Maritain sought to ground human rights and duties in a conception of natural law which derived its purpose from the divine. At the same time, he held that Catholic teachings were fully compatible with modern science and democracy.

I. THE CRISIS OF MODERN TIMES

To avoid misunderstanding, I should note at once that my point of view is here not that of the mere logic of ideas and doctrines, but that of the *concrete logic of the events of history.*

From the first point of view, that of the mere logic of ideas and doctrines, it is evident that there are many possible positions other than the "pure" positions which I shall examine. One might ask theoretically and in the abstract, what value these various positions have. That is not what I plan to do. In a word, my point of view is that of the philosophy of culture, and not that of metaphysics.

From this point of view, that of the concrete logic of the events of human history, I think that we may be satisfied with a rather general definition of humanism, such as the following:

To leave the discussion quite open, let us say that humanism (and such a definition may itself be developed along quite divergent lines) tends essentially to make man more truly human, and to manifest his original grandeur by enabling him to participate in everything which can enrich him in nature and history (by concentrating the world in man, almost in Max Scheler's words, and by making man as large as the world). It demands that man develop his powers, his creative energies and the life of reason, and at the same time labor to make the forces of the physical world instruments of his freedom. Certainly the pagan's great wisdom, which, according to the author of the *Eudemian Ethics,* aimed to link itself to "that which is better than reason, being the source of reason," cannot be cut off from the humanistic tradition; and we are also warned never to *define* humanism by excluding all reference to the superhuman and by foreswearing all transcendence.

What is it that I call the concrete logic of the events of history? It is a concrete development determined on the one hand by the internal logic of ideas and doctrines, and on the other hand by the human milieu within which these ideas operate and by the contingencies of history as well as by the acts of liberty produced in history. Necessity and contingence are quite remarkably adjusted in this concrete logic, and to designate this logic we may use the word "dialectic" in the sense I have just expressed, a sense neither Hegelian nor Marxist.

And because in this discussion we are in the practical and existential order of human life, with the exigencies of the universe of desire and of its concrete ends, of passion and action, this dialectic implies a movement much swifter and much more violent than that of abstract logic. Positions theoretically tenable, rightly or not, are swept aside, because practically they appear at once *unlivable.* I do not say for such and such individual, but for the common consciousness.

Here we see the peculiar vice of classical humanism. This vice, in my judgment, concerns not so much what this humanism affirms, as what it negates, denies and divides. It is what we may call an *anthropocentric* conception of man and of culture. I am aware that this word is not too felicitous, but I have used it for want of a better. We might say the error in question is the idea of nature as self-enclosed or self-sufficient.

Instead of an open human nature and an open reason, and this is real nature and real reason, people make out that there exists a nature and a reason isolated by themselves and *shut up* in themselves, and exclusive of everything not themselves.

Instead of a human and rational development in continuity with the Gospel, people demand such a development as replacing the Gospel.

And for human life, for the concrete movement of history, this means real and serious amputations.

Prayer, miracle, suprarational truths, the idea of sin and of grace, the evangelical beatitudes, the necessity of asceticism, of contemplation, of the means of the Cross—all this is either put in parenthesis or is once for all denied. In the concrete government of human life, reason is isolated from the suprarational.

It is isolated also from all that is irrational in man, or it denies this—always in virtue of the very sophism that what is "non-rational," in the sense of not reducible to reason itself, would be "non-rational" in the sense of antirational or incompatible with reason. On the one hand, the life proper to the universe of will is ignored. And the non-rational in the very world of knowledge is equally ignored. On the other hand, the whole world of the infra-rational, of instincts, of obscure tendencies, of the unconscious, along with that which it includes of malicious and indeed of demonic, but also of fecund reserves, is put in parentheses and modestly forgotten.

Thus, little by little, will spring up the man conformable to the pattern of *bourgeois pharisaism,* this respectable conventional man in whom the nineteenth century long believed, and in whose unmasking Marx, Nietzsche and Freud will glory; and they really have unmasked him, while in the very act disfiguring man himself.

And at the same time, there have been made to man, ever since the days of Descartes, enormous promises. Automatically the progress of the luminaries will bring about a complete felicity of release and repose, an earthly beatitude.

Very well, but *that will not do,* as the continuation of the story of history has shown. Having given up God so as to be self-sufficient, now man is losing track of his soul, he looks in vain for himself, he turns the universe upside-down, trying to find himself, he finds masks, and behind the masks death.

And then there comes a spectacle which we witness: an *irrational* tidal wave. It is the awakening of a tragic opposition between life and intelligence.

This opposition was begun by Luther, and carried on by Rousseau. But certain phenomena of symbiosis, which I have not time to analyze here, took place later.[1] Today this opposition appears sometimes in servile forms, for example in the form of the philosophy of Klages, or in the form of racism, or in the greatly simplified form of certain military men who shout: "Death to intelligence." I shall return to this point in a moment.

It appears also in noble and very noble forms—I am thinking of Nietzsche, of Kierkegaard, of Karl Barth, of Chestov. But even here, no matter with what intelligence should be developed the theme that intelligence comes from the serpent, and no matter with what generosity they try to salvage human values, this position unmistakably gives way to what one may call a *counter-humanism*. I am not blind to the fact that one might raise objections here and ask whether a humanism defending man against reason is not conceivable. But precisely what I think is that if we set out to defend man, not against a certain use of reason, but against reason itself, and against knowledge, the result—fatally and in spite of everything—will be a counter-humanism.

Here it is evident that reason has been imperiled by rationalism, and humanism by anthropocentric humanism. Terrible voices rise up in man, crying out: We've had enough of lying optimism and illusory moralities, enough of hypocritical justice and hypocritical right, enough of liberty which starves workmen and burns the stacks of grain, enough of idealism which does us to death, which denies evil and unhappiness and robs us of the means of struggling against them; take us back to the great spiritual fruitfulness of the abyss, and the absurd, and the ethics of despair.

The lofty counter-humanism of a Kierkegaard or a Barth may be regarded as a mistaken Christian position. In Barth particularly it is a reactional and archaic position, in as much as it signifies a will of absolute purification by a reversion to the past—in fact, a return to primitive Lutheranism. In Nietzsche it was rather a thunderstruck Christianity: no longer able to adore, he denied and blasphemed, and nevertheless he still sought and still loved. And all these lofty forms of counter-humanism—because in them is a spirit which protests against itself and destroys itself with a kind of Promethean generosity—still preserve admirable values of humanity and spirituality. But they are only of the passing moment, for they give way fatally to the servile forms of which I spoke a moment ago. Poor Nietzsche! The truly terrifying voice, the fatal voice is not the voice of Nietzsche, it is the voice of this mediocre and base multitude whose mediocrity and baseness themselves appear as apocalyptic signs, a voice which scatters to the four winds of humanity the gospel of the hatred of reason, in the form of the cult of the fecundity of war or in that of the cult of race and blood.

When love and holiness do not transform our human condition and change slaves into sons of God, the Law makes many victims. Nietzsche could not bear the sight of the lame and halt of Christianity; more even than Goethe, he rebelled against the cross. He dreamed of a Dionysian superman, who was a fiction. Dionysius—the newspapers and radio give us news of him every morning and inform us as he leads his dance through the concentration camps, and the new ghettos where thousands of Jews are condemned to a slow death, through the cities of China and Spain eviscerated by bombs, through Europe maddened in an armament race and feverishly preparing for suicide. Nietzsche could not see that men can choose only between two ways: the way of Calvary and the way of slaughter. The irrational tidal wave is in reality the tragic wheel of rationalistic humanism; it reacts against a humanism of reason closed up in itself, but it does so by leaving man open to lower powers, shutting off from him higher communications and the spirit which frees, and walling the creature up in the gulf of animal vitality.

This is another spectacle which we attend, a spectacle quite the contrary of a continuation, aggravation, and exasperation of anthropocentric humanism in the direction which it had followed from its origin, in the direction of rationalistic hopes, founded no longer solely on philosophical religion, but on a lived religion.

This returns to take all the consequences of the principle that *man alone and through himself alone, works out his salvation.*

This unadulterated instance which we now face is that of Marxism. No matter how strong some of the pessimistic aspects of Marxism may be, it remains attached to this postulate. Marx brought back Hegelianism; he remained nevertheless rationalistic, so much so that for him the movement proper to matter is a *dialectical* movement. In Marxist materialism, it is not irrational instinct or biological mysticism, but reason which decapitates reason.

Man alone and through himself alone works out his salvation. Hence this salvation is purely and exclusively temporal. This salvation is accomplished naturally *without God*, since man is truly alone and acts truly alone only if God does not exist; and even *against God*, I mean against whatever in man and the human milieu is the image of God, that is to say, from this point of view, the image of heteronomy. This salvation demands the organization of humanity into one body whose supreme destiny is not to see God but to gain supreme dominion in history. It is a position which still declares itself humanistic, but it is radically atheistic and it thereby destroys in reality the humanism which it professes in theory. It is well known that dialectical materialism claims to be heir to classical humanism, and Engels used to write that the revolutionary proletariat was the heir to classical German philosophy. If it is true that this is the most pure and therefore the most active form of the spiritual impulse which appeared earlier in the quite different form of rationalistic humanism, we understand that the god of rationalism does not count in the presence of this atheism, and that what remained of disaffected Christianity in classical rationalism is like a cake of starch in alcohol. As for the humanism to which it invites us, the way in which revolutionary materialistic dialectic, as lived for twenty years in the country it conquered, has devoured its leaders, reduced their morality to that of the end justifies the means, and put to death or persecuted thousands of suspected men. This is sufficient to edify us on that subject.

There is finally a position removed as far from anthropocentric humanism as from anti-humanist irrationalism. This is the Christian humanistic position, according to which the misfortune of classical humanism was not to have been humanism but to have been anthropocentric; not to have hoped in reason, but to have isolated reason and to have left it to dry out; not to have sought liberty, but to have orientated itself toward the myth of the democracy of the individual, instead of toward the historical ideal of the democracy of the person.

In short, in this view the modern world has sought good things by bad ways; it has thus compromised the search for authentic human values, which men must save now by an intellectual grasp of a profounder truth, by a substantial recasting of humanism. In my opinion, we have today to make a considerable liquidation— a liquidation of four centuries of classical culture—the culture in question being a brilliant dissolution (in which new creative forces appear) of medieval civilization. It is the merit of Irving Babbitt and Paul Elmer More to have called attention to the historical necessity of a new humanism, and to the responsibilities of Rousseau in the tragedy of modern humanism. What I wanted to indicate in the preceding analysis is the breadth of this tragedy, the double responsibility of the rationalist current and the irrationalist current (the latter nevertheless depending on the former, as reaction on action), and the breadth with which we have as a consequence to conceive a new humanism. A new humanism ought then to be new in a singularly profound sense. It ought to evolve within the movement of history and create something new in relation to these four centuries that are behind us; if it has not such power to renew, it is nothing.

The new humanism must reassume in a purified climate all the work of the classical age. It must remake anthropology, find the rehabilitation and the "dignification" of the creature not in isolation, in a closed-in-ness of the creature on itself, but in its openness to the world of the divine and super-rational. This implies in practice a work of sanctification of the profane and temporal. This means, in the spiritual order, the discovery of the *ways of childhood* whereby the "humanity of God our Savior," as Saint Paul says, finds, with fewer human trappings, a readier way into man, and causes more souls to enter into this hidden task of suffering and vivifying. It implies, in the moral and social order, the discovery of a deeper and fuller sense of the dignity of the human person, so that man would re-find himself in God refound, and would direct social work toward an heroic ideal of brotherly love, itself conceived not as a spontaneous return of emotions to some illusory primitive condition but as a difficult and painful conquest of the spirit, a work of grace and virtue.

Such a humanism, which considers man in the wholeness of his natural and supernatural being, and which sets no a priori limit to the descent of the divine into man, we may call the *humanism of the Incarnation.* It is an "integral" and "progressive" Christian position which I believe conforms to representative principles of the genuine spirit of Thomism. I am happy to find in agreement with it, not all theologians (that would be too much, and is never the case) but some theologians such as Père Chenu, l'Abbé Journet, and many others.

In the perspectives of this integral humanism, there is no occasion to choose, so as to sacrifice one or the other, between the vertical movement toward eternal life (present and actually begun here below) and the horizontal movement whereby the substance and creative forces of man are progressively revealed in history. These two movements should be pursued at the same time. To claim to sacrifice the second to the first is a sin of Manichaeism. But to claim to sacrifice the first to the second is materialistic nonsense. And the second, unless it is to turn to the destruction of man, is effected only when vitally joined to the first, because this second movement, having its own proper and properly temporal finalities, and tending to better man's condition here below, prepares in history the Kingdom of God, which, for each individual person and for the whole of humanity, is something metahistorical.

II. Some Problems

To examine all the problems raised by the preceding considerations would try the patience of the reader; these problems are in fact infinite. Let us eliminate first of all the problem of the *chances of realization,* near or remote, of an integral humanism such as I have tried to characterize. It is clear that the barbarism of the world which passes before our eyes at an accelerated speed seems singularly unfavorable to such an occurrence. But the essential thing, if not for our dearest human interest, at least for our philosophy, is to know whether this true human-ism answers to the tendencies of the creative forces which act in history simul-taneously with the forces of degradation and disintegration, and which act more or less masked by them. If so, it will be necessary that the true humanism have its day, even though it be after a night of several centuries comparable to the night of the later middle ages.

Next, it is proper to remark that the crisis of civilization, as it appears today in the concrete, is very far from being reduced to an opposition between the "pure" forms and tendencies of which I spoke in the first part of my exposé.

Moreover, if we consider that complex ensemble of forces which we may call, in a general sense, totalitarian, we used to make a very neat distinction between their principle in the pure state and the realizations which it has or will produce in this or that place, and in which the contingency, resistance and germination of life occasion all sorts of mixtures and sometimes of attenuations.

Then, finally, it is just to say that in many aspects communist totalitarianism on the one hand (totalitarianism of the social community), and on the other hand, fascist totalitarianism (of the political State) or National Socialism (of the racial community), these two opposed species of totalitarianism present pro-found analogies and even phenomena of osmosis. This is not only in the order of political techniques, but in the order of principles themselves. Yet between these principles and these philosophical roots, there are profound differences.

In spite of the combative pessimism imprinted on it by Marxism, commu-nism has as metaphysical root an absolutely optimistic philosophy of man, that great optimistic mysticism which began with rationalism and was continued by the Encyclopedics, then by Jean-Jacques Rousseau, then by utopian socialism on the one hand and Hegelian philosophy on the other. Practically, it denies that man is a creature of God, because it is unwilling to recognize in man that which comes from nothingness. Because of this optimistic basis, it does not profess to be totalitarian; the totalitarian principle is immanent in it as a vice and fatality, which one does not profess.

Fascism, on the contrary, has as a metaphysical root an absolute pessimism of a rather voluntaristic and Machiavellian sort. Practically, it denies that man comes from the hand of God, and that he maintains within him in spite of every-thing, the grandeur and dignity of such an origin. This pessimism, which invokes incontestable empiric truths, turns these truths into ontological lies, because the fact that man comes from God does not matter to it. Then it despairs of man—I mean of the human person, the individual person—in favor of the State. Not God but the State will create man. The State by its constraints will oblige man to come forth from the nothingness of the anarchy of the passions, and lead an upright and even an heroic life.

As for National Socialism, it also makes the most fundamental mistake about the nature of man. This is in the sense that in practice it basically refuses to see in man the creature and image of God, and it uses man as zoological material. Man must become the apotheosis of the telluric, primitive and divine (demonic) element which is developed in him and by him, that is to say in the blood and by the predestinated blood, in such a way that a quite apparently combative optimism, which is trust in force, is added to a fundamentally pessimistic conception of human nature.

Because of this pessimism, National Socialism and fascism proclaim themselves totalitarian, and the totalitarian principle is raised up by them as a shield and standard.

In a word, looking at these two opposed totalitarian species, we might say that practically, existentially, we have here an atheism which declares that God does not exist and yet makes its own god of an idol. It is an atheism which declares indeed that God does exist, but makes of God himself an idol, because it denies in act if not in word the nature and transcendence of God. It invokes God, but as a spirit-protector attached to the glory of a people or a State, or as the demon of the race.

These remarks are made to avoid confusion. I will return now to the purely anti-Christian position of which I spoke at the outset, and which it would be better to call "anti-Christ," because it is less a question of doctrinal opposition to Christianity than of an existential opposition to the presence and action of Christ at the center of human history. To be brief, it is on the problems of the religious significance of racism and communism that I would say a few words. In this section I shall not speak of fascism, because, for various reasons on which I have not space to insist, the religious or mystical dynamism of fascism is feeble. On the one hand the resistance of the Catholic Church puts a considerable check on the pagan mysticism of Empire; on the other, the idea of the State lends itself less readily to serve as substitute for the religious bond than does the idea of racial community. However, because of that, it is difficult for it not to submit, in this domain, to forms that are more virulent.

Let us consider first the racial principle in the pure state. From the point of view of the nexus of ideas, it appears that racism is, as we said, above all an irrational reaction. Think of the actual status of scholars in the country which seemed to have vowed to them forever its veneration—racism is a protest of the man in the street against the scholar! More profoundly, it is a pathological protest, nourishing itself on the most absurd pedantry; though, in such case, the more absurd the pedantry, the more efficacious it is. It is a pathological protest of nature with all its forces of vitality and ferocity rising out of the depths of mother-earth, with its needs of euphoria and power and physical beauty, with the implacable rage which can exalt instinct when the spirit betrays itself and becomes engulfed in animalism, a protest against the messengers of the absolute and transcendent who had not sufficiently shared the miseries of human kind.

We should recognize the chastisement exercised here against this primacy of the ideal unfaithful to itself, and, so far, artificial and hypocritical, which was the great vice of the Kantian nineteenth century and which we may call a clericalism of the reason. This is a world of many characteristics: of elementary values in nature, of physical courage, of simplicity, no matter if brutal and gross; of that sort of natural, if cynical, candor by which the animal is not ashamed to exist nor has need to justify existence; a world of primitive feelings, of pacts such as exist even in the horde, of the instinct of physical solidarity such as exists among robbers, of the need of being together and feeling together such as exists even in the great herds on the prairies. This world can indeed be disciplined by true wisdom, which does not despise it and which turns it toward transformations of the spirit. But against false wisdom which humiliates and deceives it, some day or other, it takes terrible revenge.

A mystic hatred of all intellectual or moral subtlety, of wisdom and all asceticism is thus developed; and at the same time a powerful religiosity, the natural religiosity inherent in the human substance down to its elementary physical fibers. God is invoked, but only in virtue of the testimony, if I may say so, of these elementary fibers and of the desire of nature written in the biological elements of the human being. Because of the basic reactive process which I indicated, He is invoked *against* the god of the spirit, of intelligence and love, excluding and hating this God. For an extraordinary spiritual phenomenon, then, here you are. People believe in God, and yet do not know God. The idea of God is affirmed, and at the same time disfigured and perverted. A God who will end by being identified with an invincible force at work in the blood is set up against the God of Sinai and against the God of Calvary, against transcendent Being, *He who is* and who dwells in inaccessible glory, against the Word who was at the beginning, against the God of whom it is said that He is Love. We are facing, not a pseudoscientific atheism, but, if I may speak thus, a demonic paratheism which while declining wisdom, is open to every kind of occultism, and which is not less anti-Christian than is atheism.

Of course, if it were not perverted thus, the testimony I just spoke of, that of the natural desire of God inherent in the elementary physical fibers of the human being, is in itself authentic and valid. Will it some day be able to free itself from the unregulated affective forces which set it against the testimony of the spirit? If so, on what conditions? And by what processes? Well, in any case, racism as it exists and acts in reality today and in the minds of today will have been evacuated.

This is because, if we take the point of view not only of the nexus of ideas but of society in the concrete, we see that racism is existentially bound to this demonic paratheism. Because in its reaction against individualism and its thirst for a communion, it seeks this communion in human animalism, which, separated from the spirit, is no more than a biological inferno. In the metaphysics of society in the concrete, the god of the community of the blood can only be the demon of the blood. Racial neo-paganism is thus lower than the paganism of classical antiquity, which was faithful to eternal laws and to the supreme Divinity. It brings into existence again the lowest elements of paganism.

The account of atheism and communism calls for a like discussion. From the point of view of the connection of ideas, one sees that the genesis of communism in Marx is of the philosophical order. It proceeds from impulses from the Hegelian left and from Feuerbach. In Marx the theory of the alienation of work by private property presupposes *de facto*, before becoming first *de jure*, the Feuerbachian theory of the alienation of conscience by the idea of God.

More profoundly, the discovery of historical materialism as Marx conceived it, implies an absolutely atheistic position; because it implies a universal process of substitution of the dialectic of history for all transcendent causality, and for the universe of Christianity in general; it implies consequently an absolute realistic and naturalistic immanentism, by hypothesis exclusive of all divine transcendence.

For Marx, then, the historical and sociological action of religion works *necessarily* against the emancipation of the proletariat, because it is the action of a factor of the super-structure which is originally determined only by the need of justifying the economic exploitation of man by man.

If the master-idea of historical materialism can be purified, so as to designate
henceforth only the essential (but not principal) importance of material causality
in history, it is on condition that it break with Marxism, and replace the outlook
of Hegelian dialectic by that of the fourfold causality of Aristotle.

This basic atheistic principle explains why the *existence* of class struggle (resulting from the capitalistic structure of economics) gave rise in Marx to a theoretical
and practical *conceptualization* turning the class struggle into a gesture of atheism.
I mean a moral secession fully accepted by the dispossessed class, by the accursed
of the earth, from the political community, which, no matter how oppressive and
inhuman its economic structure might be, holds its natural value from God. This
same basic atheistic principle explains also why, as the Webbs[2] report, one of the
deepest features of the new civilization worked out in the Soviet Republics is anti-
godism; and why, as they also report, a formal pledge of atheism and of repudiation of every form of the supernatural is required in Russia of every adherent to
the communist party, and even of every candidate for that party.

Are there yet other potentialities in Marxism? Because in Marx, as I have just
tried to explain by reason of a presupposed atheism, the social problem of the
emancipation of the proletariat has in fact the priority over the metaphysical and
religious problem, the class war over the anti-religious war, can we conceive within
Marxism a development allowing a clearly affirmed dissociation between social
theory and a materialistic conception of the world, and, on the other hand, a revision of the naïve atheism which Marx held in the nineteenth century? If so, on
what conditions? And by what processes? Well, in any case, communism as it exists and acts in reality today and in the minds of today would have to be evacuated.

This is because, if we take the point of view not only of the connection of ideas
but of society in the concrete, we see that communism is existentially bound to
atheism. For if it reacts against individualism, if it thirsts for communion, it does
so without finding a principle superior to anthropocentric humanism; quite on
the contrary it aggravates the latter and seeks this communion in economic activity, in pure productivity, which considered as the proper place and homeland
of human activity, is only a world of a beheaded reason, of reason without God.
In the metaphysics of concrete social fact, the god of the industrial community
can only be human reason as demiurgic manufacturer, the titanism of industry.
Communism thus transforms Christian communion into another, a quite temporal communion, which is achieved by the abolition of private property.

Under this heading of communism and racism, we may make a concluding
remark. If it is true that in the dialectic of culture, communism is the final state

of anthropocentric rationalism, we see that in virtue of the universality inherent in reason, even in reason gone mad, communism is all-embracing, and sets itself against Christianity by pretending to substitute for the universalism of the Mystic body of Christ its own earthly universalism. In contrast, racism, on its irrational and biological basis, sets itself against Christianity by rejecting all universalism and by breaking even the natural unity of the human family, so as to impose the hegemony of a so-called higher racial essence.

We see also that communism tends, quite in the line of industrial rationalism and of capitalistic materialism, toward a transformation of economics by annihilating the ultimate cadres of bourgeois society. Its directive elements are furnished to communism especially by a working population whose thought a century of socialistic tradition has disciplined in a revolutionary direction. Racism on the contrary and fascism, do indeed exert on the energies of bourgeois society a high revolutionary pressure, and they do detest capitalism. But being above all reactive processes, they do not go on to a social transformation destructive of the ultimate machinery of capitalistic society. By another road, preferably by war, do they threaten its destruction. The masses on whom they depend belong especially to the middle classes on the path to proletarianism, classes whose affective mobility is very great. The personal magnetism of the leaders plays a main part; but the leaders could not make their enterprise succeed without the aid given them by strong privileged interests anxious to safeguard their own position.

III. THE WORLD AND CHRISTIAN CONSCIENCE

A characteristic of the humanism which I call integral would be that, far from being limited to the elite, it would care for the masses, for their right to work and to a spiritual life, and for the movement which historically brings them, we may say, to an historically full age. On the social significance of such a humanism, I will simply say that in my opinion it should assume the task of radically transforming the temporal order. This task would tend to substitute for bourgeois civilization, and for an economic system based on the fecundity of money—not a collectivist economy, but "personalistic" civilization and a "personalistic" economy—through which would stream a temporal refraction of the truths of the Gospel.

This task is joined to a thorough awakening of the religious conscience, and I wish to insist on this point. One of the worst vices of the modern world is the dualism, the dissociation between the things of God and the things of the world. The latter, the things of the social, economic and political life, have been abandoned to their own carnal law, removed from the exigencies of the Gospel. The result is that they have become more and more unlivable. At the same time, Christian ethics, not really carried out in the social life of peoples, became in this connection—I do not say in itself or in the Church, I say in the world, in the general cultural behavior—a universe of formulas and words; and this universe of formulas and words was in effect, vassalized, in practical cultural behavior, by the real energies of this same temporal world existentially detached from Christ. Such a disorder can be remedied only by a renewal of the profoundest energies of the religious conscience arising into the temporal existence.

On the other hand, modern civilization, which pays dearly today for the past, seems as if it were pushed by the very contradictions and fatalities suffered by it, toward contrasting forms of misery and intensified materialism. To rise above these fatalities we need an awakening of liberty and of its creative forces, we need the energies of spiritual and social resurrection of which man does not become capable by favor of the State or any partisan pedagogy, but by a love which fixes the center of his life infinitely above the world and temporal history. In particular, the general paganization of our civilization has resulted in man's placing his hope in force alone and in the efficacy of hate, whereas in the eyes of an integral humanism, a political ideal of brotherly love alone can direct the work of authentic social regeneration. It follows that to prepare a new age of the world, martyrs of love of neighbor may first be necessary. And this also shows how all depends here on a profound renewal of the interior energies of conscience.

Granted what I said just now about the pathological process of vassalization, in the behavior of contemporary civilization, of religious formulas by worldly energies, we see that the renewal we speak of should be a kind of Copernican revolution, which would in no way affect doctrine, not even an iota of it, but would make a great change in the relative importance of the elements in the universe of action. It would consist in a general and bold acknowledgment of the primacy of the vital and the real (even the implicitly or virtually real) over matters of appearance and external formulation—let us say—for I am primarily their King of the Christian conscience—of the primacy of the practically or vitally Christian over the nominally or decoratively Christian. Such a Copernican revolution would have notable consequences for the question of the ways and means of political action.

Truly speaking, it is the idea of the primacy of the spiritual which here dominates the debate. To say that Christianity will remake itself through Christian means or that it will unmake itself completely; to say that no good is to be expected from the enterprises of violence and constraint—with no compunction of heart and no interior reform or inner creative principle—enterprises animated by the same spirit which is at the elemental source of the evils actually suffered by civilization; to say that the witness and the patient and persevering action of the Christian spirit in the world is more important than the outer apparel of a Christian order, especially when those who pretend to save this order bind themselves, and also the order, either to established injustice or even to the immense pagan energies sweeping away one part of the actual world—this is simply to affirm that the principle of the primacy of the spiritual demands respect in the very mode in which men work to give it reality; it is simply to affirm that the primacy of the spiritual cannot be realized while denying itself.

I add that if it is true that the leaven of the Pharisees, against which Christ put us on our guard, represents, as Père Fessard, a Jesuit well known in Paris has said in one of his books, a standing temptation for the religious conscience. And if it is true that this leaven will not be totally expelled from the world till the end of time, then we must say that the renewal of the religious conscience of which I speak would be a step in the right direction. It would be a signal victory in the never-ending struggle of the religious conscience against Phariseeism.

At the same time, it seems clear to me that in the temporal order an attitude corresponding to what has always been called the liberty of the Christian before the world and the powers of the flesh, is the only one to safeguard, tomorrow and the day after, either as a favorable solution of the present crisis or as a dawn after a long night. This is the hope of men in the terrestrial efficacy of the Gospel, and of reason.

Translator unknown

NOTES

Reprinted from *The Review of Politics* 1, no. 1 (January 1939): 1–17.

1. Notably in France, the Rousseauian current was swept away by the counter-current, the current of rationalistic humanism, which it has at last reinforced by its strong sentimental dynamism.

2. [Sidney (1859–1947) and Beatrice (1858–1943) Webb were leading members in the socialist Fabian Society. Ed.]

CHAPTER 2

Problems Facing Catholic Rulers

DESMOND FITZGERALD

Desmond Fitzgerald (1888–1947) was born in London, and was briefly associated with a group of young English poets known as the "imagists." He moved to Ireland in 1913 where he became active in the revolutionary politics of Irish nationalism. He participated in the Easter Rising of 1916, and was one of the editors of the underground Catholic Bulletin. *He later served in the Irish Free State as its first Minister for External Affairs, Minister for Defence, and senator in the Seanad Éireann. A devout Roman Catholic, Fitzgerald frequently gave lectures on Thomism in the United States, and was a visiting scholar at the University of Notre Dame, where he taught political philosophy. Fitzgerald considered the Catholic ruler's central problem to be the question of how to promote the common good without impeding greater good or creating evil. His solution was to advocate political moderation and practical wisdom in statecraft.*

When a ruler inherits authority he inherits a responsibility for ordering the relations of living people whom he has not created himself, and therefore has not formed with a view to the order that he conceives as most suitable. Moreover he inherits an existing order in which the relations of the members of that society operate. That order, the result of a long historical process, has itself conditioned the people who live within it to suit its requirements, and those people have themselves given to it a certain mode which they, wittingly or unconsciously, have evolved as best suited to give them the conditions that they desire.

Let us note the peculiar complexity that this implies. Society is a living thing differing from all other organisms in this respect—the parts of which it is composed are intelligent autonomous beings each directed to a personal end that transcends the end of society itself. Those autonomous beings are ordained to live here in time, to live human lives for which society is necessary. Their outlook on things, their way of life, their needs have been determined to some extent by an historical development. They and those who went before them have made society as it is, and society, through its development and as it is, has to a large extent made them to be as they are; for it has determined the conditions in which they live. And the ruler inherits the responsibilities for the ordering of that society in such a way that its members will be able to live the good human life. But he cannot change the people who form that society except through the order that he imposes upon that society. But that order is a most complex interrelationship between society and its members, between those members and society and between those members among themselves.

He sees that his work to create conditions that will be favorable to their leading the good human life requires a change in the totality of society including a change in those who constitute it. But he knows that when he exercises his authority to bring about a change directed to the elimination of certain obvious evils, he must also take responsibility for any other effects that may flow from his action by repercussion, and those other effects may more than counter-balance the good that he anticipated—they may even be disastrous. The existing evils may be obvious for the very reason that they are evils, just as a pain may make us aware of some abnormality in our body. But if that abnormality has developed through slow growth, it may well be that the organ involved has adapted itself to that abnormality, and now its drastic and sudden removal would affect the whole body adversely.

If the order in which we live, or those elements of it that we are conscious of as evil, as detrimental to the true human good, had been suddenly imposed in one bloc and immediately observed to be so detrimental, then it might be possible to bring about a simple solution by merely removing what had been so imposed. But that is not the case. If we look over the development that the flux of time has brought about during the last four hundred years, say, we can see that in a general way, each change was welcomed in its aspect of good. After the decay of scholasticism the new learning was ushered in as calculated to enrich the lives of men. Scientific discoveries were also such an enrichment, and when these gave man a control over the forces of nature, so that they could be harnessed to his service, that also could be seen as an enrichment of man. Indeed it might reasonably have been conceived as a means to provide for his material needs with a minimum of labor, so that he would have greater opportunity to develop his intellectual and moral being. Again it might be said that to condemn man to long hours of dreary labor for the production of some thing that might be produced in a tithe of the time with the aid of machines would be a wanton condemnation to slavery.

But now when we see men huddled together in vast industrial towns spending their hours of labor ministering to the machine, we cry out against it. We see the evil, but we accept what it produces as necessities of our daily life. What we want is that we should be able to reap all the material benefits that the developments of the last few centuries have produced without any of the concomitant evils. And even if we were prepared to forego some of those benefits we should still require to act with caution. We might find that the decision to do without certain things that we now have would promote a certain disorganization, as for instance the disemployment without prospect of reemployment in any other sphere.

Thus it sometimes seems that the modern ruler inherits a race of deformed men subsisting in an order made to the image of their deformity. But that order is undermined by a grave and growing discontent, for in spite of his deformity human man still persists. His specifically human nature cries out against that order, and yet he is only inclined to listen to promises that appeal to his deformity.

It is more than two thousand years now since Socrates said that his sole business in going about the streets was persuading old and young not to be preoccupied with their body or with their fortune as passionately as with their soul; to make it as good as possible: "Yes," he said, "my task is to tell you that fortune does not make virtue, but that from virtue comes fortune and all that is advantageous whether to private persons or to the state."

May we not assume that even at that time, if his message had been different, if he had been explaining how to add to fortune, how to multiply the creation of goods for the satisfaction of men's desires, he would not have been brought before the court, and would not have received the sentence to death.

It will be noted that he did not condemn the desire for fortune *per se,* but rather a wrong ratio between the preoccupation with external goods and the concern with the soul.

I have no time even to attempt to disentangle the forces that have operated in our later history and their interplay in the life of man. But we may observe that alongside the development of the multiplication of goods proceeds the decay and rejection of religious affirmation. The great discoverers, the great inventors gave new continents for man's exploitation, and new modes of production. We cannot say that they were the enemies of man—quite the contrary. But these new spheres for man's activity, this enrichment of his temporal life, required more than ever that he should maintain the proper ratio between the things of the body and the things of the soul. But they coincided with a progressive denial of the soul. So that the new things offered to men were, as one might say, seized upon to fill a void. If man were a purely temporal being, or even if he merely assumed that his temporal life were dissociated from, and autonomous with regard to, his spiritual life, then all that his life in time had to offer to him were the things of time. But as a spiritual being his thirst was for the infinite, and could be assuaged by no multiplicity of finite things. But the ever increasing multitude of things made available to him created a conviction that it was indeed possible to satisfy his desires to the full out of his mastery over nature and the things she provides. Thus he tended to look for the coming of Utopia.

But that hope for Utopia is rooted in a deep-seated despair. It is nearly a hundred years since Kierkegaard observed that the marks of life outside religion are doubt, sensuality, and despair. Despairing man must needs believe that all the good things that the modern world makes available to him can be multiplied indefinitely and no man be enslaved in the process. His very acceptance of society is to some extent conditioned by his assumption that it can provide him with what he desires—that it can bring him about the promised Utopia and make it acceptable and utterly satisfying to him. But to do that society would have to destroy him as a human person. It has, at the command of man, to some extent dehumanized him. But his human personality persists operating like a revolutionary leaven. Man directs society to minister to him as an individual, to use the distinction so beautifully elaborated by Jacques Maritain. He demands that it shall use all the forces at its command to that end. But the forces it commands are seated in the human beings that form it. Society becomes non-human directed to a non-human, or only partly human end and subordinates man to the requirements of that end. And the human being revolts because the life allocated to him outrages him as a human person while at the same time it fails to satisfy the demands he makes as an individual.

I have suggested that one of the most powerful elements operating in the development of the form of man's life has been the decay of religion. But it by no means follows that those in whom decay has not taken place have remained completely unaffected. They necessarily live in society and adapt their lives to its conditions. They have to live their physical lives and must needs draw upon society and be part of it. And its effect upon them does not remain superficial. It affects their very mode of thought. Generally they live as isolated individual persons, or as small groups, mere units in the social mass. Their numbers offer them no proximate likelihood that they will be able to determine the action of the state authority.

In such a position a man is far from being without responsibility. He knows that each member of society is like an abyss out of which action flows informing the totality. He knows that each man is master of his act and therefore determines as it were the leaven that he will pour into the social body. But he also knows that he is master of his own act only. In the complex interplay of social relations he must order his own mode of life so that it will conform to the order in which it has to be lived. Truth may live in his own heart, and as a man he may accept in the most integral fashion the command of justice, and regulate his personal acts according to that command. He knows that by council and example he must endeavor to communicate that truth and that mode of action to those with whom he is in contact, and even to society itself. But when his conscience is thus satisfied he can regard things objectively and condemn in one relationship and commend in another. He rightly feels that he, one unit among many millions, cannot be justly condemned for failing to impose his own rectitude upon the mass of his fellows, or to impose upon the unity of society the form that his mind has declared to be good, as being in harmony with the reality of man, and such as would procure the good human life for the multitude. But when it is so abundantly clear that there is so much wrong with the world, the very impotence of, or restricted power of efficacious action in the one so placed tempts him to seek to assess blame. He may indeed be able to point to a visible and concrete evil which he can attribute to a visible and contemporary cause. And he marvels that those vested with authority should permit this thing to continue. But even in such a case I think it would be well for him to be very sure that he has examined the matter carefully before he condemns. What appears to be a contemporary cause may in fact have evolved through an historical development, and be so closely knit in the very fabric of society that the change that seems to be so obviously good might also bring about certain evils of greater magnitude than those that will be removed. The ruler who is responsible for the right ordering of society is also responsible for all the results that flow from his acts. And what, considered *in abstracto*, may seem to be entirely good, may, when it is incorporated into the social organism turn out to be productive of certain evils.

I should like to give an instance that I have heard of, but about which I cannot guarantee the exact truth. The civic authorities of a great city in order to remove a slum evil built what amounted to a small town outside the city area. In this new town which was composed of modern houses with modern equipment it was soon observed that there was an epidemic of suicides amongst the women who had been summoned from the slums and who found the tedium of life in the new town with its modern houses unbearable.

In such a case we see that the persons concerned had been so molded by their pitiful conditions during their own lives that they were unsuited to a more normal condition. They were like the caged bird that has become so inured to its captivity that release would be disastrous: it would leave its cage to face death from starvation or from other birds.

But I think that we can also say that the historical process that has made despair the keynote of modern man had also left its mark upon those poor souls. The millionaire who committed suicide when he lost his wealth in the great slump of ten years ago was akin to them in that. He could conceive of no happiness, no purpose in life when the external things that vast wealth could procure were no longer available to him. Both in the case of the extreme rich and the extreme poor the significance of life had been centered in those things and those circumstances external to the self. Their eyes looked outward to them, and were thereby prevented from looking inward to the dead despair that resided within. Let us give our pity to those poor millionaires as well as to those poor women, for charity must flow up the social ladder as well as down it, though that is a doctrine that one does not often hear preached.

The objective observer of society might well have decided that it was unfortunate for those people to live in slums, and for those others to be millionaires. And, considering the matter *in abstracto,* he might decide that it would be well to provide such houses for the first and remove the wealth from the second. But the ruler is required to be responsible for all that flows from his acts. If he wishes to provide greater services he must also recognize that he may be required to impose greater taxation, and therefore he must take into account what the effect of the greater taxation may be on the general well-being. And in relation to the people he governs he must realize that they are concrete human beings, not dead things. He has received authority to govern them for the right ordering of their society and of their relations together. And to that end he is also invested with coercive power. But he has always to remember that those human beings for whom he is responsible have been formed by an historical process, by heredity, by their own internal and external acts, by national tradition. No matter how much he may regret their imperfections it would be to sin against prudence if he were to act as though they were other than they are. He has a certain perfection in mind that he hopes to give to the society that he rules. But that perfection is to be brought about by a harmonious action in which he and his people cooperate together. They are intelligent beings who receive communication from him as the mason receives communication from the architect with regard to the complete building. But the architect leaves to the mason what belongs to the specific art of masonry. And yet the perfection of the building cannot be attained unless the mason fulfils his function properly. If, in fact, the masons are inadequate as masons, that fact will be revealed in the complete structure.

St. Thomas reminds us that the human government derives from the divine government and should imitate it. But God, although He is all powerful and sovereignly good, allows evils that He could prevent to happen in the world, lest in suppressing them greater goods should also be suppressed or worse evil come about. Thus in the government of men those who are in power should tolerate certain evils in order not to prevent certain goods or not to give place to worse evils.

If the ruler overlooks this fact, conceiving in his mind a perfection or order as attainable if only men were different and more perfect, he may well seek, as it were, to take the place of the reason in the human person and to usurp the function of the personal will, and so establish a totalitarian regime of the most extreme form. He may hope thus to create the perfection of order that we find in the ant hill. But the very end for which that order is required is the perfection of the human beings who are incorporated within it. But the effect of such an usurpation is a mutilation of their humanity. I cannot say the destruction of their humanity, for it cannot be completely destroyed. It remains in its mutilated form to breed further evils in an order thus established and maintained.

I am well aware that to stress difficulties unduly tends to discourage all activity, but on the other hand I also know that if we desire (as we must desire) to bring about a change that penetrates into the very depths of society and to change the whole movement of historical development, then an oversimplification of the task may easily result in disaster. We cannot force a man to be happy, or to be free, or to be a person. "The end of the multitude gathered together in society is to live according to virtue." But you cannot force a man to be virtuous by external constraint. For the movement towards virtue is rooted in what is most intimately the man himself. You can remove obstacles to virtue. But even in this the ruler can only advance a very short distance unless there is a corresponding movement in the persons who form the society that he rules. He must seek to foster a new evolutionary process in the public thing that he controls. But the individual may assist that evolution by a revolution in his own self.

Deep-seated in the revolutionary ferment that stirs in men's hearts today is a revolt against the limitations innate in human life itself. The ruler has to distinguish between that discontent and the discontent that flows from a hunger and thirst for a justice that is being withheld or distorted. His task might appear to be simplified if he chose to favor one class of the community and disregard the just rights of another. But the essence of his problem is one of real justice. The appetite for gain, that deadly cupidity that is perverted love, and that flows from an interior despair is not the peculiarity of one section of the community; it is general.

He may impose mild restraints in one direction, and try to inject certain stimulants to encourage a movement in another direction. But even in this he is aware that he must move with extreme prudence. And meanwhile a vast stream is pouring into society from the press, from the films, from popular novelists and from other and similar sources that are all informing the very society that he is trying to reform in a new or more perfectly human image. If, moved by impatience, or by his own zeal, conscious of the purity of his own intention and of the desirability of his preconceived image, he seeks to obstruct or destroy all other forces so that state action shall be the sole informing element, he is already embarked upon the course of totalitarianism. And this has its own natural dialectic that is almost certain to overcome the purity of his original intention. An exact justice may be received with a universal tepidity, while it may be clear that by sacrificing the few to the many, powerful and enthusiastic cooperation will be obtained. The end can only be achieved by communal action. To outrage some of the most intense desires and strongest passions in men is not an apt means for securing this. There are passions latent in all men at all times, and others that have been developed historically, bearing certain aspects of good, that seem to clamor to be invoked and harnessed to the work in hand. It is so easy to stress that aspect of good, to the point where it seems mere madness not to allow them to be subservient to the good that is to be attained.

I recognize that implicit in what I have said is the suggestion that in the earnest man who is deeply wounded by the present order there is an impetus towards a dictatorial tendency which requires to be governed by a most exact prudence. And it is natural that Catholics should be even more earnest than others. They are aware of the tragedy in its innermost reality. Therefore, their judgment should be controlled by the most careful prudence.

And yet how often we meet those who speak as though a simple expedient, a simple panacea, only needs to be applied and the face of the earth will be changed. They seem to forget that what they recognize as hideous in that face derived from the hearts of men. And that the most that any external agency can do is to make it less difficult for a man to change his own heart.

There are those who seem to think that nothing more is required than that rulers should enact papal encyclicals as civil law, and that then every problem is solved. The assumption seems to be that certain encyclicals are proposals directed to governments so that those governments may give them the force of law. How simple it would be for Catholic rulers if that were the case. How they would welcome it.

Dollfuss was a man for whom I felt something of affection.[1] His sincerity I considered to be above question. When it was announced that he was going to govern according to the papal encyclicals I heard many Catholics rejoice at this as a triumph for the Church. I was far from rejoicing. The very circumstances of his country were such as to suggest that she must face more than the average amount of human difficulties. And the means to face them must be chosen according to the judgment of poor defectible human minds. Even if the means were well-chosen they would depend for their effect upon the cooperation of citizens, and of powers outside the state. And yet upon the concrete results of government under those circumstances the teaching of the Church might be judged.

I do not know Salazar of Portugal, but all that I know of him suggests a great integrity, selflessness of purpose, an informed mind, and wise prudence.[2] Nevertheless I am oppressed when I hear it said that his policy also is the implementation of papal teaching. We have no divine promise that economic misery can be avoided. The material resources of a state are the results of the productive energies of its citizens. The interior conditions of a country benefit and suffer according to changes in world conditions. And a thousand other forces operate that cannot be completely controlled by an individual ruler. And yet a divine institution may be judged by the concrete results of that ruler's government. His own integrity of mind and will count for little in the balance used by the world when it weighs up.

The government with which I was associated was singularly fortunate in this that the vast majority of those we ruled were sincere Catholics. We did not describe ourselves formally as a Catholic government. Perhaps we were to some extent conscious of our own inadequacy. We also knew that apart from the ills that are natural to mankind at all times, our people could not entirely escape from certain ills that were peculiar to those post war years. Also there were other things that had grown out of our own particular history and that could only be eliminated or reduced with the process of time. We thought that much could be done, but we knew that even though we acted with the most complete integrity of mind and will the technique of means would not permit the creation of such a material utopia as the world demands as proof of the spiritual truths of the religion that we affirm.

Even in certain matters where it might be thought that the Catholicism of our people would facilitate action on certain lines, there are difficulties. Thus the corporative formation of society which seems to have the strength of papal commendation might appear for that reason to be a simple matter to create. But our society has the form that it received from its historical process. We adopted trades unions from England and on the English model. In the past they have certainly benefited town workers. Anything that might even interfere with their functioning exactly as they now do would be represented as an insidious attempt to rob workers of their rights and to impose upon them a Fascist rule. The corporative form can only come about, as far as one can judge at present, from within the body of society itself. One can do no more than try to stimulate its development, and even that must be prudently done.

Maritain's proposed pluralism already exists in a certain way with regard to the control of our education. It may be that at some later time that pluralist arrangement might be extended. There is considerable social and economic injustice. But minor attempts at remedy reveal a danger of creating greater evils. Thus the fixing of conditions of industrial labor in towns, brings out in high relief, the disparity between those conditions and the conditions of workers on the land. By repercussion they increase the cost of what the land worker buys and, to that extent, depress his condition. The fixing of wages on the land is delimited by the prices received for agricultural produce, which itself is determined by world forces. The combination of these effects tends to lure the people from the land to the towns where the conditions are so much more favorable, and it can easily be seen that if that were to go on unchecked, new social evils would develop.

I could indeed go on with a list of reforms that seem to be as simple as they are desirable, but even if they are instituted with a most careful prudence and advertence to the parallel effects that they are likely to produce, they may very well bring about more bad effects than good.

I have merely referred to these things, because I have met with so many Catholics who seem to think that so much can be achieved by a simple stroke of the government pen. If we are to face up to and to overcome the crisis of the modern world, we must realize that it cannot be done by over-simplification. The effects of an historical process that has proceeded for four or five hundred years cannot be reversed over night. The society of man that has received its form from that process cannot be changed by external action. For it is fed by roots that lie in the deeps of society, and in the hearts of men. When certain organs of a human body have streptococcus as one of their elements, we do not marvel that the body itself should be unhealthy. We know that the organs of that body must first be freed of their infection. How then shall we demand a healthy society when we who compose it, as a result of historical formation and personal act, have not the true form of men?

A short time ago I visited two old people, both over eighty, peasants, living in dire poverty. They had lived all their lives in conditions that were certainly unjust. Their forebears had suffered persecution for generations. And yet I think that I could describe them as persons. Generations of social injustice and of government tyranny had failed to destroy personality in them and others of their like. And it is much easier to destroy than to create.

As I have said before, I think that we should aim at revolution in the man himself, and at no more than a slow evolution in society, though at the same time we should also work for that evolution. Let us remember when we think that encyclicals are addressed to the rulers of states that they are generally addressed to all men. And each one of us falls within that category. Therefore, before we cry out against the ruler and society itself, we should first be satisfied that we have fulfilled the command that was addressed to us in our sphere as well as to the rulers of men.

NOTES

Reprinted from *The Review of Politics* 1, no. 3 (July 1939): 307–19.

1. [Engelbert Dollfuss (1892–1934), an Austrian statesman, became chancellor of his country in 1932. His efforts to establish a Right-wing Roman Catholic regime contributed to the fall of the Austrian Republic. Ed.]

2. [António de Oliveira Salazar (1889–1979) became prime minister of Portugal in 1932. His promulgation of a new constitution in 1933 led to Portugal's transformation into a crypto-fascist dictatorship. Ed.]

CHAPTER 3

The Deification of the State

C. J. FRIEDRICH

Carl J. Friedrich (1901–1984) was born in Leipzig, in the German state of Saxony. He studied philosophy and the natural sciences, and received a PhD in history and economics from the University of Heidelberg. He was hired by Harvard University's Department of Government in 1926, and taught there for over fifty years. Friedrich was virulently opposed to National Socialism, and helped many German Jews to escape from their country in the late 1930s. After the war, he was actively involved with the German reconstruction effort, and contributed to the composition of the new German constitution. Friedrich published on a wide array of topics in political thought and played an important role in the development of modern political science, writing about the role of leadership and bureaucracy in government, public administration, and American foreign policy. His later works concentrated on law, constitutionalism, and comparative totalitarianism. Along with Zbigniew Brzezinski, Friedrich authored one of the basic texts on the latter subject, which built directly on Waldemar Gurian's arguments.

It is a common heritage of English and American liberals to denounce state absolutism, to deny it as regimentation, paternalism, etc. Indeed, Englishmen and Americans have always been inclined to adopt a condescending attitude towards other traditions which seemed to exalt state power. French and German, Russian and Italian tendencies have in turn been pictured as "naturally" inclined toward state "absolutism," and when anyone in rebuttal mentioned Hobbes or Bentham or Austin, the "exceptional" position of these thinkers has been emphasized. Still, can there be any question that the idea of the state as an ultimate source of authority has been as strong in Great Britain as anywhere? For reasons which will become plainer in the course of the argument, English-writing thinkers have accordingly been in the vanguard of those who sought to construct the "state" as the "highest" of all human communities, thus following out the Aristotelian heritage. In spite of all the titter-tatter about national character, muddling through and the rest, the fact remains that Britain has provided us with the most radical, deep-laid expositions of an "absolute" state. This much admitted, one might add that the limited state also has found eloquent and epoch-making exponents in English-speaking lands. In short, the whole gamut of modern political philosophy has been most thoroughly expounded in English.

A telling illustration of British "sublimation" has recently been provided by Bertrand Russell who in his clearly Hobbesian book on *Power* discussed only Hegel, Fichte and Nietzsche when he came to "philosophies of power," with not a word on Hobbes or Spinoza. In truth, the three Germans mentioned are, as concerns their ideas on power, rather shallow replicas of the two great seventeenth century exponents of the "power drive," as the *ultima ratio rerum*. Indeed Hobbes and Spinoza rather than the three Germans were truly inclined towards the deification of the state, Spinoza through his pantheistic optimism.

It appears to be paradoxical, but is not really, that the English-speaking tradition should also have given rise to anarchist views. This has been, no doubt, a persistent minority trend. In England the strand runs from Wycliff through the Levellers to Ricardo and Malthus. It has always been, except in limited areas like academic economics, a minority view. In America it has acquired greater strength, and often been dominant in an inchoate, pioneering way. Jefferson and Emerson, the I. W. W.[1] and Albert Jay Nock[2] are different facets of this common tendency. It has lately become a favorite hunting ground of reactionaries (strange as it may seem—even the jungle of our contemporary industrial society has its "back to nature" prophets). But if the state is chided as "our enemy," this is in fact only the reverse side of the same medal—for it amounts in fact to a devil theory of the State. Now the State as Satan is still the State as Leviathan, only looked at with disapprobation. While the disapprobation is an improvement from one viewpoint, the satanic view is nevertheless objectionable, because of its exaggeration of the modern state's place in man's life.

General disapproval of the state as political community is deeply linked to our Christian heritage. We are in fact striking here a persistent vein of Western political philosophy. It was sloganized at an early date by St. Augustine who dubbed the state "a robber-band," or, as a contemporary American might say, "a bunch of gangsters." This piratical view of the state is coming more and more into favor amongst those who study the political reality of contemporary dictatorships. G. A. Borgese,[3] in a moving indictment of Mussolini's *Goliath*, pictured *Il Duce* as the Evil One who, an anarchist at large, seeks to destroy contemporary civilization with Satanic glee. The book, which is full of profound political criticism, develops with striking eloquence the kinship between anarchism and absolutism, their common preoccupation with power as the *ultima ratio rerum,* and of the political community as transcending *all* others. But any such conception presupposes a fixed standard, by which to judge finally this earthly God, the Hobbesian Leviathan. For if it takes courage to pronounce government a godlike creature, it takes no less boldness to denounce it as the opposite. In fact, if the state is essentially a *gang,* it does not yet follow that those composing the gang are gangsters. Nor must we conclude that because the state is essentially dealing with paramount issues and values, and has great power, it therefore is entitled to our adoration and awed reverence.

The trouble with all this fuss over the "state" is due to the inclination of the human mind to soar into questionable abstractions. Essential as is the capacity to reason theoretically, it is forever threatened by the danger that folks, under the influence of emotional thinkers, transform these abstracts into concrete realities. Every time Moses looked away, the Jewish people made themselves a golden calf before which to render homage to a deity the abstract grandeur of which they could not endure. Likewise the contemporary mind has made the "state" into a golden calf of misplaced concreteness. The next step is to make it into an absolute. Indeed, the concrete symbol in front of which the intellectuals indulge their hapless desire to fall on their bellies before some mysterious something, may even take the more extreme form of a "constitution." Thus a constitution drafted by men who had no illusion about "the State" can become a step on the road toward the "deification of the state." This has certainly happened in the United States in recent years. It is the more interesting since the word "state" had not until very recently acquired any currency in this country. To the American, "state" still meant one of the component units of the Federation. The word "state" stems, admittedly, from "estate"—indeed in French *état* designates both. Since the juristic doctrine of Jean Bodin is of central importance for the spread of the modern state concept, his use of *état* is characteristic. While medieval constitutionalism recognized only a government of "estates," of which the King was one, the rise of royal absolutism led to the claim that the king was the foremost, and finally that his was the only estate = *état* = state. Later constitutional forces challenged the royal pretensions. Indeed, in England they never gave way and Sir Edward Coke significantly claimed that sovereignty and the rule of law were incompatible (strange bedfellows). But instead of questioning the conception of the state and of sovereignty altogether, they followed the lead of Althusius and Rousseau by developing the idea of popular sovereignty and of the constitutional state (*Rechtsstaat*). But all the logomachy of acute nominalists could never overcome the inherent contradictions of the two terms. In the United States, however, neither of these antithetical notions really took root—since the theses never had, the antitheses were of no importance. The people were never envisaged as some mystical whole which could make "ultimate decisions," nor was the government, admittedly organized according to and limited by a constitution, ever given a mystical transcendence and all-inclusiveness. The people were seen as containing both those governing and those governed, divided into changing groups which were fighting for temporary ascendancy and predominance. Outside of purely academic circles, the folk speech of America talked about the people, the country, the government, the law, the constitution—sovereignty and the state were "hifalutin." Only the advent of Marxism has changed that a bit.

The "state" as some kind of neutral god charged with looking after the national interest is so central in all dictatorial ideologies, that a reconsideration of its philosophical origins has become one of the most urgent concerns of all those who still appreciate that human action is vitally related to ideas, the pictures in the minds of the actors. Now the state as an institutional device for achieving the "highest" good traces clearly to the political doctrines of Plato and Aristotle. Both thinkers, pagan in their political background, are of course merely the culmination of a long line of men who sought to express in abstract and general language what constituted the essence of Greek, as distinguished from barbaric, politics. When Aristotle talks about the *polis* as the highest community and hence organized for the highest good, he has in mind a political community built upon the principle of group solidarity, not only in matters of politics, but of religion and all the rest. Each of these *polei* had its own local gods or goddesses, and the struggles between the *polei* were mythologically symbolized through quarrels between their "Gods." Everyone knows, of course, the Homeric legends, the fight between Athene, Hera and Aphrodite. But ideas of this kind permeated the entire tradition of the *polis* in which religion and politics were so intricately intermingled that the *polis* cannot adequately be described unless one joins together again two words which the whole development of Western Christianity has tended to dissociate, and speaks of a state-church, or church-state organization. Mixed in with this pagan idea of the state-church, of the *polis*, and constituting an essential aspect of it, is the conception of the blood-clan. No reader of Aristotle's discussion of the development of the Constitution of Athens can fail to see how the whole organization of the *polis* rests upon the idea that in the last analysis all the members of the polis are and ought to be "relatives"—indeed their most distinguished families will cheerfully trace their descent from the local deities, even if it has to be done in terms not highly flattering to the family, from a moral standpoint. One is reminded here of the delight with which French snobs trace their ancestry to a royal concubine.[4]

What matters here is the emphasis upon blood kinship as a decisive element in bringing about the politico-religious community. Of course, we must remember that these people had the excuse of their complete ignorance concerning even the elementary data of genetics which their present-day imitators cannot offer. But though "blood" be "bloody" nonsense, we have to admit that the Aristotelian *polis* is seen as built upon this basis. Now, it is precisely this linking of the clan, of the common blood descent with religion which Christ most uncompromisingly rejected. For in emphasizing common blood descent the Jewish tradition was not very different from the rest of the Mediterranean world, and nothing more profoundly agitated their priesthood than the denial of any significant difference between Jews and Gentiles, when it came to the question of religion. Hence we can say that the Greek *polis* conception as expounded by Plato and Aristotle is incompatible indeed with the Christian idea of man as fundamentally alike and equal in the face of his Creator. Hence the *polis* is *not at all* the highest or most comprehensive community, nor is it instituted to realize the highest good. Since this, however, is the central conception of Aristotle's "state-church," any compromise must in the end prove fatal to the Christian way of life.

There is, then, a breadth to the *polis* conception of the Greeks which the modern idea of the state does not adequately reflect. Precisely because religious life has become the concern of the church, a separate institution, the state lacks spiritual significance. In their development, the concept of church and state go together, but of the two the church was the first offspring of the *polis*, the Roman *Civitas.* But whereas the *civitas* had been a clan, and even the Roman Empire had never succeeded in shaking off the fetters of this conception, the church was built on faith and dogma. It was as such profoundly different, and could truly claim for its faithful that it is the highest and most comprehensive community, and that it was instituted to realize the highest good, namely the salvation of the immortal soul. Thus the pagan *polis* became the bride of Christ. The Church challenged and eventually superseded the Roman emperors who had persecuted it with such ferocity in the correct realization of the fact that the Christian faith in the equality and equal dignity of all men meant death to the pagan *polis* of which the Emperor was the divine head, a mortal God.

Of course, the disappearance of the Roman Empire and the emergence of the Roman Church did not eliminate the need for secular government. But since the church was from now on charged with the religious tasks, the government stood in need of its blessing in order to acquire the halo which would give its commands authority. The Christian faith with its emphasis upon the value of the individual and upon the crucial significance of personal salvation demanded that all such government be conducted according to law, the divine law most of all. A first attempt at realizing this task was medieval constitutionalism. It rested upon the faith in a higher law, fixed and immutable; in doubtful cases, the clergy played a decisive role in interpreting it. Governmental authority was divided between the King and the "estates"; together they expounded the meaning of the law through the high court of parliament.

A multitude of factors gradually tapped the strength of this system, as it broke up into its national constituents. But the ensuing period of absolutism led to a new, secular form of constitutionalism. The rule of law, though never completely abandoned as the natural law school held sway, once more issued into constitutionalism—our modern type, whether monarchial or republican. Resting upon the belief in reason and property, it has lately been declining rapidly, as both pillars were disintegrating under the impact of irrationalist psychology and materialist sociology.

It is important at this point to call attention to a common confusion in the United States as regards the relation between constitutional government and democracy. For the term, as currently understood in the United States, does not denote the rule of the majority, but constitutional government of the kind traditional in the United States. To be sure, the rule of the people is implied, but not the people in the Rousseauian sense of a mass of equal atoms, welded by a mystical general will into some sort of living organism. Rather it is the people as divided into certain orders, such as the several states, and guided in all their actions not only by *their* will, but by the will of those who preceded them—the manifest expression or symbol of this traditionalism being the constitution. And again not merely the written document, but whatever happens to have grown up under it. Democracy then, is not only the rule of the many, but a political order in which legitimacy and authority can only be claimed as a part of the constitutional pattern. This conception means a complete abandonment of Aristotelian terms, just as our conception of monarchy does. For monarchy in our Western sense designates a peculiar type of legitimacy resting upon the idea that kingship is divinely instituted. The monarch, no matter how limited may be the extent of his governing functions is enabled to represent the people through belonging to a certain family by hereditary descent. What made France a monarchy in the time of Richelieu was not the rule of one man—for that man was certainly Richelieu—but the fact that there existed "by divine grace" an hereditary being from whom Richelieu derived his authority and legitimate powers.

As contrasted with these conceptions which are essentially Christian in that they subject the exercise of all power to some sort of higher law, Stalinism, Hitlerism and Fascism are different variants of a pagan approach, similar in general conception to the view of Greek political philosophy. They, like Aristotle, maintain that some secular community, either the proletariat, the nation or the state, is the highest community and that it serves the highest good. To put it another way, Aristotle's *polis* is variously represented by the proletariat, the nation, or the state. And since in actual practice neither the proletariat nor the nation can operate without some sort of political organization, they all end up in an apotheosis of the government, which means themselves.

Here, then, we have arrived at the core of the trend toward the deification of the state, but the roots of these ideas reach back into Aristotle and Plato. Inasmuch as this exaltation of the political community is not an accidental, but an integral part of the Aristotelian political philosophy, a critical examination of its entire pattern becomes necessary. Unhappily St. Thomas Aquinas, in undertaking to work out the relationship between Aristotle and the Christian faith failed to realize this basic incompatibility. He suggested the danger more by implication. In his commentaries upon the *Ethics* and *Politics* of Aristotle, he imperceptibly shifted the emphasis. He did not openly protest the suggestion that the *polis* is organized to achieve the highest good. Accepting the Aristotelian teleology, Aquinas reiterates Aristotle's argument that each community is organized for some good, that every *civitas* is a community, and that therefore every *civitas* is constituted for some good. So far so good. But then the premise of the all inclusiveness of the *civitas* which forms so essential a part of Aristotle's and other Greek political thought is reiterated by St. Thomas. This is startling, because such a premise is manifestly out of keeping with the reality of the church in medieval society, even if the *civitas* be considered as coextensive with the Holy Roman Empire (which does violence to other parts of Aristotle's premises). St. Augustine's doctrine of the invisible church quite apart, the church was certainly not considered as comprehended within the *civitas*. Still, St. Thomas claimed that it is manifest that the *civitas* is the *communitas principalissima*. Now how can that be maintained in view of the Christian ideas concerning the overwhelming importance of the human personality and its immortal soul? St. Thomas, in paraphrasing Aristotle's assertion about the highest good, had slipped in a more decisive qualification. St. Thomas speaks of it as the highest amongst human goods, i.e., goods to be realized in this world! But the distinction here implied between *human* and divine values is quite alien to Aristotle's whole way of thinking. Once accepted, this distinction dissolves all of Aristotle's political philosophy, inasmuch as there may then be a community like the church, serving higher values, and hence entitled to the primary allegiance of men. As this community, too, is composed of human beings it transcends the *civitas*.

The Scholastics failed to perceive that this point is so crucial that in the last analysis it must lead to a rejection of the Aristotelian philosophy, at least his political and moral philosophy. Perhaps this could best be corroborated by examining the manner in which St. Thomas deals with Aristotle's well-known doctrine of the highest life, the contemplative life. St. Thomas, in keeping with the ideas of medieval Christianity, approves of course Aristotle's doctrine, as expounded in the *Nicomachean Ethics*, Book X. Yet, in spite of an apparent coincidence of the Aristotelian and the Christian view, there is a world of difference. For whereas Aristotle sees this contemplative life of the scientific philosopher as the most intense embodiment of the spirit of the *polis*, the *civitas* or folk-community to which the philosopher belongs, St. Thomas points out that the "justification" of the political community is to be found in making this contemplative life possible. What a complete contrast! For Aristotle the *polis* finds its fulfillment in the creative thinker, for St. Thomas the *civitas* (state) maintains the order without which the truly good life would be impossible. "*Si enim per vitam politicam quaesimus eam quasi alteram existentem ab ipsa. Haec est enim felicitas speculativa, ad quam tota vita politica ordinata; dum per pacem, quae per ordinationem vitae politicae statuitur et conservatur, datum hominibus facultas contemplandi veritatem.*"

Can it possibly be maintained that those who founded the political community, did it in order to realize this end? Yet, in commenting upon Aristotle's *Politics*, St. Thomas had accepted the idea of a subjectivist purpose as essential to the *polis*. All men, he said in paraphrasing Aristotle, are doing everything they do because of what seems to them good, every community is instituted by somebody, and all communities therefore seek to realize some good. Here the gap is yawning between Aristotle and St. Thomas. The decisive passage in which Aristotle states that men, in order to become moral, must live under laws which are backed by force is accepted by Aquinas. He adds that a father's teaching or any other persuasion will not do it, but only a law which is promulgated by a king. Only such a law is a "*sermo procedens ab aliqua prudentia et intellectu diligente ad bonum.*" This view simply fails to perceive the problem around which all modern constitutionalism revolves, namely: how to discover what this *rectus ordo* is and how to find ways and means of realizing it. So by accepting the hidden premises of Aristotle's pagan conception of the *civitas* as the all-inclusive, and the highest community, St. Thomas and the scholastics allowed Western political philosophy to become encumbered with the idea which stood at the center of the Greek tyrannies and the Deification of the Roman Emperors, the political idea against which the Christian faith had most explicitly revolted.

Far be it from me to suggest that St. Thomas had any thought of deifying the state. But as the Christian faith declined, men proceeded to stress exclusively those *bona humana* of which St. Thomas had admitted that they were realized by the *civitas*. The Renaissance as this movement was later called hence culminated very naturally in the political doctrine of Machiavelli. The great Florentine, far from being the faithless cynic as which he is frequently depicted, asserted that the state, the *civitas*, was the highest of all values. In doing so, he went beyond Aristotle's ideas by far. Where Aristotle, with the life of the Greek city behind him had simply seen the *polis* as the framework within which the fulfillment of man's destiny had to be achieved, had described the *polis* as nature's most admirable product, Machiavelli looking at the *condottiere*, the gangster of the Italian city-state, and knowing that the cultural life was quite independent of whatever these governments did, asserted that the state was the highest, the most remarkable work of art. The state, like other works of art had to be created by man. Only the most skillful use of all the known techniques of warfare, military as well as civilian, could bring results. Here, then, was the first and most uncompromising conception of the state as *God*. It is clear why the views of Machiavelli, though derived from Aristotle, are totally different in their emphasis.

If Machiavelli's pagan deification of the state, his unchristian doctrine of the "reason of State" as a set of principles of action transcending all "higher law" codes, stands as the complete antithesis of the medieval conception, the same cannot be said of the views of the Reformers. Although they, too, objected to the universal church and its claim to be the guardian of the higher law, they absorbed the Aristotelian tradition of scholasticism, in regard to moral and political fundamentals. Though Luther presumably derived some of his inspirations from St. Augustine, he failed to follow St. Augustine in the realm of politics. Instead of maintaining that the government is a "bunch of gangsters," he attributed to the prince the function of heading the church, thus moving closer to the Greek idea of the church-state. By doing so (and the point was further elaborated by his Aristotelian friend Melancthon), Luther prepared the ground for the secular papalism of a James I. Hence Luther, and with him the entire Lutheran and Anglican tradition in political philosophy from Hooker on, is bound to lead to a more uncompromising deification of the state: the philosophy of Hegel. All that was required was a gradual weakening of its ecclesiastical and moral moorings. After they were gone, the state remained as the only focal point of human allegiance. Was it not headed by the head of the church anyway?

Calvinism seemed at first decidedly opposed to these aspects of Luther's teaching. Calvin's own leanings were hierocratic (*theocratic* is a misnomer, as it is not God but the priests who rule). Where Luther had been content to teach and preach and to write letters of spiritual, if at times, fierce advice for his prince, Calvin established himself as a ruler (in Geneva), and together with his elders he dominated the government of the city no less thoroughly than the Pope the papal state. Nevertheless, the Aristotelian roots remained powerful, and they gained the upper hand once more in the Arminian and Erastian variants. Hugo Grotius, an ardent Arminian, became an almost equally ardent exponent of the state and its sovereignty.

For the idea of sovereignty became from the sixteenth century onward an important part of the growing exaltation and adoration of the state. The most radical expounder of the absolute state concept prior to Hegel was Thomas Hobbes. There is no need here for giving an analysis or even a summary of his well-known system. Its mechanistic psychology, its materialistic sociology have been expounded and criticized a hundred fold. In spite of it all, the essence of Hobbes' political ideas persists. Bentham, Rousseau and Hegel, Austin and Marx, Stalin and Hitler, they all have followed in his footsteps in broadening the government into the state and then looking upon this state as an earthly god, a Leviathan beyond good and evil, a tool for all purposes, a panacea for all ills. Underlying all the many arguments and disagreements between these modern thinkers we find a common core of worship for the secular political community and its organization—a deification of the state. The only radical opposition has, in recent times, come from anarchists who, denying the ethical value of the political community, have insisted that it is the devil incarnate which stands in the way of all that is desirable. Marx's skillful fusion of this attitude and the *civitas* worship, by drawing an absolute distinction between the *civitas* dominated by the capitalists and the *civitas* dominated by the proletariat, has had its enormous quasi-religious appeal precisely because it utilized the common trend towards exaggerating the role of the *civitas* by reconstructing its conception in terms of both a devil and a God.

Is there any escape from this pseudo-theological claptrap? Can we hope to get away from the specter which haunts our thinking on man and society, as we have distorted the Aristotelian heritage (which as such is not only beyond our deepest convictions, but also contrary to our most obvious experience)? Not only is it inherently contrary to the Christian view, but it stands in the way of creative innovation both at home and abroad. At home it prevents our progressing beyond the present impasse between labor and its employers; abroad it keeps us from looking at the world in terms of a common humanity and its emerging common ends. There is no answer to these questions except in terms of radical change. We must recognize the purely functional nature of such concepts as order and the state. Indeed, we may go so far as to assert that *the state does not exist.* There are governments, peoples, countries, there are kings, parliaments, dictators, parties and concentration camps, but there is no evidence in support of the idea that some sort of holy unity, some mystical transcendence need be attributed to them, that they indeed should be seen as a whole. This idea, propagated by governing gangs who wished to see themselves identified with the community, in the last analysis appears to be a perfectionist ideal for the realization of which man would have to be something different than he actually appears to be. There lurks the danger of a *petitio principii,* if we delude ourselves into thinking that through the coercive power of government men can be made better. For can we assume that this coercive power is exercised by those who are best? By implication, all worshippers make such an assumption. Let us, instead, consider the achievement of good government the result of a perpetual struggle of the better against the worse elements of humanity and hence beyond all patent solutions. There are higher standards involved which do not originate in the government, but must be imposed upon it. Where do they come from? A vast and crucial issue, transcending all politics. Hobbes, prophet of state worship, asserted that justice is what the state says it is. In rejecting this view, one destroys the concept of the state, false God of the modern world.

Notes

Reprinted from *The Review of Politics* 1, no. 1 (January 1939): 18–30.

    1. [Industrial Workers of the World, an international trade union with socialist goals founded in 1905. Ed.]

    2. [Albert Jay Nock (1870 or 1872–1945), a well-known American individualist-libertarian author and theorist of education. Ed.]

    3. [Giuseppe Antonio Borgese (1882–1952), an Italian historian and author of *Goliath: The March of Fascism*. Ed.]

    4. A very interesting side issue, transcending the scope of this essay, is that of slavery. Aristotle's discussion is most revealing.

CHAPTER 4

Passion and the Origin of Hitlerism

DENIS DE ROUGEMONT

Denis de Rougemont (1906–1985) was born in Naissance à Couvet, Switzerland. He studied psychology under Jean Piaget at the University of Neuchâtel, and German and Latin at the Universities of Vienna and Geneva. De Rougemont then moved to Paris, where he became associated with the Christian philosopher Emmanuel Mounier who sought to affirm the value of the human person in the face of modern materialism. As a result of regular contributions to French literary magazines, his connection to Mounier's school of "personalists," and his publications of the works of Christian philosophers and theologians, such as Søren Kierkegaard and Karl Barth, de Rougemont became convinced about the power of European culture and ideals to bring his divided continent together. After a sojourn in the United States during World War II, he returned to Europe to promote the cause of European unity. As both philosopher and promoter of unification, de Rougemont was instrumental in founding several centers devoted to European studies, including the Bureau of European Studies in Geneva, the European Cultural Studies Center, and the Association Écologique Européenne. In a highly influential work, Love in the Western World, *Rougemont explored the passion of love in relation to different myths of love and the mystery of the person. He believed that there was a direct relationship between the highest levels of human passion and the rise of totalitarian movements.*

Hitlerism is not the creation of a single individual, the personal creation of Hitler: it is a mass phenomenon. Nor is it the necessary result of a determined economic system, since we see individuals in the most dissimilar countries, who are "converted": rich and poor, industrialists and farmers, intellectuals and army men.

The enumeration of the more or less immediate historical causes of Hitler's success, such as Eternal Germanism, the Versailles Treaty, inflation, the fear of Bolshevism, the Dictator's personality, the defects of the democracies, the complicity of big business, does not suffice to explain why they have all converged to the same result. Viewing the breadth and depth of the phenomenon, these heterogeneous "causes" seem to play the part of mere pretexts, of catalyzing agents determined, orientated and carried along by the phenomenon itself which, therefore, still remains to be explained.

What then is the cohesive principle of the Hitler movement? What is the secret of its contagious power? This principle and this secret seem to me to reside in the two following facts: (1) Hitlerism comes as an answer to the communitarian aspiration of modern times, as a remedy for the individualistic decomposition of modern society. (2) Hitlerism effects a gigantic transfer of individualistic passions to the Nation, represented by the Party and its Führer.

The following essay is intended to examine this second thesis.

I. Passion in the Western World

Almost all our sociology, as a science, rests on rationalistic or materialistic presuppositions. Let it suffice to mention its ancestors: Hegel, Auguste Comte, and Marx. Since Levy-Bruhl, it is true, we have attempted to describe and interpret certain collective phenomena of a non-rational nature. Curiously, however, we have sought to localize them among so-called "primitive" peoples. The study of passion in the bosom of civilized societies has hardly been started by such marksmen as Georges Sorel, Le Bon, or Keyserling. Valuable elements would be found in the psychoanalysis of the collective Unconscious, as conceived by C. G. Jung. To me, such a study alone, systematically pursued, would appear capable of explaining the mass phenomena that dominate our times. For a mass does not react as an ensemble of reasonable individuals. A mass reacts according to the dialectic of the Unconscious, and, in particular, of passion in a pure state.

Therefore the phenomenon of *passion in itself* is to be first of all examined. I shall here use certain results of a study which I conducted on the evolution of the love-passion and mystical passion in the Western world, from the Middle Ages to our own times.[1]

We are aware that the twelfth century witnessed what I shall not hesitate to call an affective revolution: that century in truth saw the almost simultaneous apparition of the first Christian mystic of Divine Love, Saint Bernard of Clairvaux; the first story of passionate love, *Tristan et Iseult*; the first lyrics of pure love, the Troubadours; and the first love couple famous for their despairing passion, Abélard and Heloise.

The consequences of this sentimental revolution have been so numerous and monumental, in the most varied fields, that we are hardly able today to measure them, or even to conceive their extent. Passion having become second nature to the people of the Western world (including Americans), they find a quasi-instinctive difficulty in considering it as a specific phenomenon, limited in time, since it has appeared as such only since the twelfth century, and limited in space, since it is almost entirely unknown in the Eastern world. The peoples of Antiquity and of the Orient have undoubtedly known certain forms of passion. But they have never admitted, cultivated and admired passion in itself as do those of the West. They saw in it either a morbid (Plutarch) or ridiculous (Menander) excess. It can therefore be stated that passion is one of the characteristics of the modern Western world. To analyze it, as it finds its original expression in the *Tristan et Iseult* myth, is to analyze at the same stroke certain aspects of the recent evolution of the Western world, those which belong to the collective Unconscious and which are intimately linked with the totalitarian phenomenon.

The narrative of the love of Tristan and Iseult is the first known description of passion wholly triumphant. Likewise it is the model universally admired and forever repeated, of all love stories. It treats, it is true, of only one form of passion, passion concentrated in the love of man for woman. It characterizes it with truly exemplary forcefulness, and has become the classic illustration of the constant traits of passion in general. Let us enumerate them briefly.

It is recalled that Tristan's love for Iseult is shown as a *fatality,* in all the meanings of the term. The lovers love each other because they drank the love-potion by mistake. Their love therefore arises by virtue of a power outside themselves, independent of their wills and their individual qualities. Their love is not a choice, but a destiny overpowering them, and depriving them of all feeling of responsibility.

Now, he who is no longer responsible for the acts of his feelings feels freed for that very reason from the sense of guilt. Destiny led the lovers to drink the love-potion. The magic power of the love-potion forces them to commit adultery. They live thereafter in a state of soul in which the categories of good and evil lose their reality. In those who experience intense passion, the first result is a beclouding of the sense of truth in itself. Soon this intensity itself becomes the proof of the "truth" of their love.

Not only does passion transport the lovers beyond good and evil, it also immures them in a quasi-transcendent world in relation to everyday life. They can no longer explain themselves. Soon they will no longer want to. They live in a kind of *psychological autarchy*. They no longer feel obliged to explain their conduct. Others can never understand.

This state of bliss and denial of norms does not obtain without creating increasing torments. But the *obstacles* erected against their passion by the laws of God and man, far from repressing it, only strengthen it. It may be said that love thrives on obstacles (e.g., separations, various trials, the existence of the legal husband: King Marc). It invents them when they no longer exist, as in the episode of the unsheathed sword placed by Tristan between himself and his beloved, while they are alone in the forest. As their love becomes greater, the obstacles increase. Finally, life itself, with all its natural limitations, physical and moral, becomes the only obstacle to the infinite yearning of their passion. Passion gives the lie to life. Hence the desire for death, characteristic of pure passion. Wagner understood this so well that he made it the very subject of his *Tristan*. In death, the supreme obstacle, the lovers see the final and deifying emancipation from all the hindrances of the created world. In death, as the German philosopher Karl Jaspers has so well said, the Passion of Night triumphs over all the Norms of Day.

The essence of passion therefore appears as a choice of intense and even mortal torment, in preference to the happiness and sorrows of daily life. Moreover, passion acts precisely as a *hypnosis*. It deprives the individual of his free will and encloses him in a world without contact with the outside, beyond moral, legal and rational categories.

II. EVOLUTION OF PASSION IN THE WESTERN WORLD

Why did passion erupt in the Western world in the twelfth century? To examine this subject would lead me too far afield.[2] I shall here take passion as an historical point of departure, merely pointing out that it undoubtedly results from an heretical and paganizing deviation from primitive Christian aspiration: love for things Eternal, the Pauline belief that "for me . . . to die is gain." Passion and Christianity are bound together in the same manner as heresy and orthodoxy.

One might define passion in general as a reaction of a pagan soul against Christianity. In fact, it developed in the twelfth century in zones of heresy lying between Christian gnosticism and platonizing paganism. However, we are here interested in the sociological evolution of this passion, once "broken out" (like a sickness, which after passing through a period of incubation, breaks out one fine day).

The mystique of a Saint Bernard or a Saint Francis of Assisi "canalises" nascent passion in the categories of Christian orthodoxy. It realigns it with Revelation and evangelical morality, while retaining its vocabulary, which was created by the troubadours and the trouvères. The Romanesque literature begotten by *Tristan* canalizes passion in the erotic domain. It furnishes it with the rules, rhetoric and ordinary means of expression which are applicable only to love stories. Wherefore this literature becomes society's means of defense against anarchical and antisocial passion. It restricts the damage to a domain apparently the least dangerous for the public weal, that of individual sentiment. On the other hand, the laws of chivalry prescribe at the same time the form to be observed in the passion for arms. In reality, we are meeting with a single and unique reaction of social self-protection, since we know that courtly love (*cortezia*) determines at one and the same time, love ritual, the poetry idealizing it, and military art in its minutest details.

The great merit of the Middle Ages, as J. Huizinga has shown,[3] is that it set the form for love and raised it to the rank of a rite, in order to sublimate the overwhelming violence of passion. However, this very success involved certain risks. The literature of courtly love idealized passion, it is true, but at the same time prolonged its tradition and infused thousands of listeners, later readers, with a nostalgia for its enjoyment. The following centuries of classical thought attempted the rational analysis of passion (Corneille, Racine). The eighteenth century even carried this analysis to an almost complete dissociation of the affective and irrational elements in our conscious life. (In the time of Voltaire, love loses its tragic or sentimental halo. Warfare loses its savage violence and becomes a "war in lace.") But this repression was making way for the fearsome explosions that were already visible embryonically in Rousseau's work as well as in the Marquis de Sade's. The French Revolution exploded like a destructive blast of passion. Being both sentimental and bloody—Rousseauistic and sadistic—it immediately destroyed the entire framework of norms and conventions within which the Middle Ages had endeavored to encompass passion, and which rationalism had been imprudently undermining for a full century. Beginning now, we see passion overflowing its dykes into the social domain. *Nationalism* appears together with romanticism. Nationalism is the collective expression of this resurgence of passion too long repressed in the unconscious, the individual aspects of which are described by romanticism.

During the whole nineteenth century, the decadence of those conventions created by medieval courtliness will grow with increasing velocity. Meeting fewer and fewer serious obstacles in the domain of individual morals, passion will be popularized, sink into sentimentality, and meet with no real intensity save on the collective level. This is so true that in the twentieth century, in the behavior of the masses rather than in the psychology of lovers, we will find the original and virulent characteristics of passion.

III. THE MASSES AND THE UNCONSCIOUS

The twentieth century has become *conscious of the unconscious.* Meanwhile it has seen the *organization of the masses.* These two facts are more than mere coincidence.

The behavior of a mass has nothing in common with that of a reasonable individual. But, in my mind, it resembles sufficiently the behavior of the unconscious in an individual. A mass precisely is made up of individuals deprived momentarily of their rational judgment and their normal consciousness. The eruption of the masses as such on the political plane and in the social life of our times resembles the eruption of the unconscious in the life of an individual: it is a kind of collective neurosis.

As is known, a neurotic is a man who is suddenly attacked by certain psychic realities long repressed or ignored by his reason. In a sane mind, these attacks of the unconscious usually take place during sleep, in the form of nightmares. The eruption of the Proletariat in modern life is a phenomenon of the same order: the "lowly and obscure" levels of the population, which we would not or dared not look at, touch, or take into consideration—which we therefore "repressed" socially in the "depths" of the collective unconscious—now suddenly arise and make themselves heard with terrifying violence. The Proletariat, therefore, is really and not merely metaphorically, the "nightmare" of the bourgeoisie. The demands of the masses, made "conscious and organized" by Marxism, are formally like those compensations of the unconscious which strive to overthrow the superficial equilibrium of a man who is too narrowly reasonable. And when they are established in the social body and the political consciousness as a permanent unbalance, they become properly a neurosis of society.

Let us point out that the rational content of these demands is much less important than the dynamic form in which they are expressed. Programs are only pretexts in modern revolutions. They can be as different or opposed as, let us say, Hitler's and Lenin's, without the dynamic scheme of arousing the masses being measurably changed. *Now, this unchanging technique of arousing the masses is the very one that the examination of the passion myth revealed to us.*

C. G. Jung[4] studied a certain number of psychic symbols and schemes which reappear, identical, sometimes in the consciousness of an epoch, and in its religious rites, sometimes in the unconscious of individuals of an entirely different epoch and entirely different region. There is no need, may we note, for such or such an individual to have heard of these symbols to have them appear in his dreams: symbols are not "transmitted," they are permanent in the human psyche, and when they are repressed by the conscious, they live on in the collective unconscious, until they break forth anew. The passion myth, expressed long ago in the *Tristan* story, seems to me to furnish an excellent illustration of Jung's theory. Repressed by rationalistic consciousness, depressed by modern immorality, it has little by little gone down into the unconscious, and actually it rules the behavior of collectivisms, insofar as they are based on the loss of consciousness in individuals, therefore insofar as they constitute the *masses.*

Because they did not take this all-important phenomenon of our era seriously, most of the democratic statesmen during these last ten years have found themselves in a position of psychological inferiority in their dealings with dictators. For the whole success of dictators has consisted precisely in their skill to feel and to utilize cynically in Jung's phrase, "the energetic of the collective soul" that is to say, the latent forces of the unconscious. Modern masses have chosen veritable "directors of the unconscious." Hitler is, in my opinion, the most gifted of all. As early as 1924, he gave surprisingly accurate descriptions of the awakening of the subterranean powers that he proposed to manipulate. Now, what interests us here, is that these descriptions correspond exactly to what we said above about *passion.* If a man intends to create a dynamic force, the whole problem is to arouse passion, Hitler repeats twenty times, "hysterical passion, and not reflection." To designate this process in its fullness, Hitler has recourse to the expression "nationalization of the masses," and he does not err, if we recall that nationalism is the most living and virulent form of passion in the Western world.

IV. "THE NATIONALIZATION OF THE MASSES"
ACCORDING TO "*MEIN KAMPF*"

All great movements are movements of the people, are volcanic eruptions of human passions and spiritual sensations (sic!), stirred either by the cruel Goddess of Misery or by the torch of the world thrown into the masses, and are not the lemonade-like pourings of aestheticizing literati and drawingroom heroes. Only a storm of burning passion can turn people's destinies, but only who harbors passion in himself can arouse passion. . . . Every movement with great aims has anxiously to watch that it may not lose connection with the great masses. It has to examine every question primarily from this point of view and to make decisions in this direction. (*Mein Kampf,* pp. 136–37)[5]

The rationalization of the great masses can never take place . . . by a weak emphasis upon the so-called objective viewpoint, but be a ruthless and fanatically one-sided orientation as to the goal to be aimed at. . . . The great mass of people consists neither of professors nor of diplomats. The small abstract knowledge it possesses direct its sentiments rather to the world of feeling. . . . It is more difficult to undermine faith than knowledge, love succumbs to change less than to respect, hatred is more durable than aversion, and at all times, the driving force of the most important changes in this world has been found less in scientific knowledge animating the masses, but rather in a fanaticism dominating them and in a hysteria which drove them forward. (pp. 467–68)

To arrive at this hysteria, one must first annihilate the objections of the mind, then the opposition of the feelings. This second operation is by far the more important and difficult: "Here solely an appeal to these mysterious forces themselves can be effective" (p. 707).

What will be the technique of this appeal to the mysterious forces? The technique of collective hypnosis. For the mass meeting, the most favorable hour will be set, that is to say, the time at which the individual will offer the least conscious resistance. The leader will also choose a place where a receptive atmosphere has the greatest chance of being created (Cf. pp. 709–10).

All these cases involve *encroachments upon man's freedom of will.* . . . It seems that in the morning and even during the day men's power revolts with highest energy against an attempt at being *forced* under another's will and another's opinion. In the evening, however, they succumb more easily to the dominating force of a stronger will. (pp. 710–11. My italics)

No one should attempt to convince a crowd intellectually, rather he should endeavor to deprive them of their means of reflection, and should present them with an affective *fait accompli* (p. 714). For as the members of a crowd are deprived of all feeling of responsibility, they are reduced to the state of a "mass." Now, a mass "is only a part of nature" (p. 469), that is to say, it has no other reactions than those determined by the dialectic of the unconscious.

We know how successfully Herr Goebbels perfected the technique of collective hypnosis; at times when the Führer delivers his more important discourses, he creates a new genre of stage-setting, a veritable theater of the masses. We have seen above that the passion-hypnos (produced in *Tristan* by the love-potion), by depriving man of his free will, frees him simultaneously from his sense of guilt. Hitler was well aware that he would hasten the hypnotic action by fighting the guilt complex of the German people during the aftermath of the war. To hypnotize a subject, the agent on the one hand *forces* his will, on the other, *seduces* his emotions. Now, nothing is more seductive then the prospect of being freed from a guilty conscience. Whoever promises this freedom will have every chance on his side to be "believed."

> It was clear to myself at that time that for the small basic stock that at first formed the movement, the question of the war *guilt* had to be cleared up. . . . In those days, when everybody still looked upon this peace (The Versailles Treaty) as a success of democracy, one had to stand up against it and to dig oneself in the brains of the people forever as the enemy of this treaty, so that later . . . the memory of our attitude of those days would win us their confidence. (p. 697–98)

The Treaty of Versailles, a new Medusa (". . . *our people, which, under the thousand eyes of the Treaty of Versailles,* has to live disarmed . . .") (p. 463), must symbolize all the individual and collective guilt of the Germans, and must be described as the most monstrous and inhuman cruelty of all times, in contrast to the treaty of Brest-Litovsk, described as an act of limitless humaneness (p. 472).

Thus, the irresponsible and washed-as-white-as-snow mass, is ready to accept the final process of passion. It will henceforth accept as "truth" whatever "intensifies" its passion:

In the ruthless attack upon an adversary the people see at all times a *proof of its own right,* and it perceives the renunciation of his destruction as an uncertainty as regards its own right, if not as a sign of its own wrong.

The frenzied masses will give the lie to all the "norms of Day": to Roman law, for instance, which Hitler proposes to suppress, to Christian morals, to "intellectuality," and to reflection in general. The mass will shut itself up in a *psychological autarchy,* which will prepare for and condition in part the economic autarchy ahead. Hitler wages a polemic against every thing which would enable the German mass to communicate with the outside, against every universal-minded concept: against the Jews, the Marxists, the intellectuals, the Churches.

> The nationalization of our mass will only be successful if along with all positive fighting for the soul of our people, its international prisoners are extirpated. (p. 469)

Hence, racism and the exalting of pure Germanism: the German community must be made impervious to all "reason," to all exchange with and to all understanding of the outside world which would threaten to weaken its passion. Now, racism is the most impervious of religions, *since no one can be converted to it.* (If you are not born a German, you can never understand the creative mysteries of the German mind. . . .)

Another characteristic of passion is: *the need of forever-recurring obstacles and of ends that are more and more inaccessible:*

> Yes, one can even say that the strength of a movement and with it its justification of its existence increases only so long as it acknowledges the principle of fight as the presumption of its development, and that it has passed the climax of its strength in the moment when the complete victory is on its side. Thus it is only useful for a movement to aspire to this victory in a form which does not lead to a momentary victory, but which gives it a long period of growth, due to the long duration of the struggle caused by absolute intolerance. (p. 486)

Thereafter, as is known, Hitler adopted the tactics of systematically multiplying obstacles. Every time he obtained a victory that he himself had previously qualified as signifying "the final abolition of the shameful Diktat," he would immediately discover new articles in the treaty against which the fight had to carry on. It was likewise with territorial demands. For the essence of passion is to feed on obstacles, and to aspire not to such or such a concrete realization, but to some objective infinitely distant—to an aspiration always more intense—even though the end, when all is said and done, is beyond all material or human possibility, beyond life and its laws, in warfare, which is held up as glorious, that is to say, in death *which makes men gods.*

A reasonable people, finding themselves in Germany's position after the First World War, would have chosen for their objective the concrete reconstruction of their country: work. This is what we see in France today. But an impassioned people must have some other objective than work: revolt, affective demands, indefinite conquest. They know no obligation to reestablish a certain standard of conduct, rather, they feel an obligation to seek and to prefer the hardships in place of the pleasures and woes of daily life.

In one of Somerset Maugham's comedies, a woman deeply in love wavers between her husband and her lover. The husband offers her happiness and material advantages. The lover simply says: "All I can promise you is drama and the torments of the heart." The woman immediately throws herself into the arms of her lover. This elemental reaction of passion explains the plebiscite of the Saar; by an overwhelming majority, the Saar inhabitants in 1935 preferred the misfortune of becoming Nazis to the happiness of being free men. Hitler had succeeded in inflaming their "passions."

Let us leave the summation to Hitler himself: "The astounding development of our movement . . . must be attributed to the constant remembrance and application of these observations" (p. 713).

V. The Transfer of the Passions to the Nation

The "nationalization of the masses" is a *fait accompli* in many countries of Europe, and is even now in preparation in the rest of the world, although at an infinitely slower pace. It has been more radical in Germany than in other totalitarian countries.

A few remarks on these last two facts must be made.

The general evolution of our times favors the depersonalization of individuals. Modern man lives more and more in a world of collective bewilderment, in a world in which he participates in forms of living foreign to his individual experience. The cinema offers a good example of this. There everybody can "by proxy" live adventures which never happen to him. The radio, the press, the monster mass-meetings likewise allow the individual to join through his imagination and his emotions in the great events going on between Nations which are personified with their rulers, and in Revolutions which are identified with their leaders. All this contributes to the removal of the individual from his own environment, wherein nothing similar could ever happen. The inconveniences of this life, formerly considered normal, become more and more unacceptable as the notions of unlimited Progress, comfort and rapid success spread and as transcendental ideals disappear—those which formerly enabled the individual patiently to accept his lot. On the one hand, the individual is infuriated to the point of seeking escape from his petty existence, on the other hand, he is inflamed by collective emotionalism. This repulsion and attraction work the same way: they lead men to seek the opportunity *to escape from themselves.* They predispose us all for collective hypnosis, ready victims of mass passion.

The Germans in general, and those of the between-the-two-wars in particular, have shown special disposition for this kind of collective escapism, or selfsurrender. Let it be sufficient to recall the existence of their perpetual inferiority complex, aggravated by their keen sense of guilt and belittlement after Versailles. The makers of the Treaty forgot that the Germans are much more sensitive than other peoples to the symbolic humiliation of being disarmed: it is, for them, a kind of castration. To be without weapons, in the Germanic world, is to cease being a free man. For this reason, the Nuremberg celebration for the reestablishment of the Reichswehr was christened by Hitler: *Tag der Freiheit.*

The Nazis have distinguished with keen insight these general factors of depersonalization, common to all men of our times, and those factors more specifically German, and far from thwarting, have intentionally and cynically exploited them. And this in two ways:

1. The National-Socialist *Weltanschauung* teaches that the individual is entitled to existence only as a part of the *Volkstum.* Let us look closer. "Every German by race," says Hitler, "has the right to live freely." Let us translate this into Nazi terminology: "Every German must accept completely the law of the totalitarian Party, alone capable of guaranteeing Germany its freedom." Let us translate again, this time into democratic terms: "Every German has the right to live, but only in so far as he ceases to be himself, and collaborates blindly in the impassioned effort of the Party to achieve on conquest world-wide hegemony." The whole morale, the whole ideology of the Nazi party tends to suppress in the individual the aspect of his *person* (of his irreducible and transcendental calling)

to hand him over, well-disciplined and enthusiastic, to obscure forces manipulated by the Führer.

2. That the demoralization of German youth, in the sexual domain, was far advanced after the war, is well known. Now, with the lowering of moral and social barriers, there necessarily ensues a degradation of passion in love. To put an end to the anarchy in morals, the Nazis evidently did not attempt to restore Christian morality and bourgeois conventions. (This would have meant, implicitly, the rebirth of individual passions.) They decreed a certain number of State measures concerning marriage and eugenics. They removed the last vestige of the romantic halo from woman, and reduced her to the role of procreatrix of citizen–soldiers, and of housewife. They founded compulsory "schools for fiancées" for the prospective wives of the S.S., the elite troops of the Party. They tend more and more to authorize marriages only on the basis of pseudo-scientific and racial selection. This means that marriage ceases to be a personal and emotional affair for German youth. It tends to become only a civic act, a kind of service to society. Once again, we see that bourgeois demoralization and totalitarian moralization move in the same direction: they deny and discountenance the need of individual passion; they destroy its more intimate motivations. But the need of passion subsists in the heart of the Western man, and especially in the heart of the German. If he no longer finds satisfaction in his private life, he will go elsewhere to seek means of exaltation. This is precisely what Hitler offers him on the national scale. And thus, Nazi propaganda, morals and legislation transpose individual passions to the level of the collective being. Whatever totalitarian training denies isolated individuals, it transposes to the Nation. The Nation (or Party) has passions. The Nation henceforth will adopt the dialectic of the exalting obstacle (e.g., territorial demands, never satisfied); the Nation will want autarchy; it will prefer hardship to happiness (e.g., no butter but guns); in fine, it will keep alive an indefinite aspiration to expansion and eventually to death—in war. All the tensions loosed in individuals who are at the base, are concentrated at the pinnacle of the totalitarian edifice. On this pinnacle stands the Führer. He personally polarizes the whole German passion, and nationizes it.

The relationship of the Führer to the German mass has always seemed to me to arise from a kind of sexualization of collectivism. The mass plays the part of the feminine element, and its femininity is particularly German. Hitler does not attempt its seduction by overwhelming it with flattering terms, as French politicians did when they courted the electoral assembly in the French fashion. Hitler strives "to force" the mass, naturally inert, or even hostile to his personality. He rages and pleads in turn. He never tries to win over his hearers; he casts a spell over them. He finally invokes Destiny, and states that he himself is that Destiny. . . . Then the crowd surrenders, ("succumbs," as he has written). It surrenders because it suddenly feels freed by this Destiny from the responsibility of its acts. It surrenders to the terrible Savior, and hails him as its "liberator" at the very moment he is enslaving and taking possession of it.

VI. HELPLESSNESS OF DEMOCRACIES

I realize that the type of sociological explanation I advance here gives rise to a certain amount of resistance among excellent minds. Some will say that I neglect too much the economic factors, or the great accidents of international politics, or the influence of Pan-Germanic doctrines, or the *Realpolitik.* My answer is that I am trying here to describe something deeper than all the analytic "causes," something that is anterior and underlying, and which has allowed them all to operate in the same direction. Some will perhaps believe that my explanation is too "romantic" to be really serious. Such an objection expresses and illustrates the capital error of our democracies. For Hitlerism *is* indeed a form of romanticism, and if we refuse to accept it as such, if we are unable to feel it, we are doomed to repeat the mistakes committed for more than fifteen years in the struggle against totalitarian movements. Herr Goebbels proclaimed at Danzig, on June 18, 1939: "Our policy is an artist's policy! The Führer is an artist in politics. Other statesmen are mere artisans. His State is the product of a genius's imagination."

An "artist's policy," a policy of collective romanticism—that is the nightmare the somnambulistic Third Reich is bringing into being before our eyes. Cheap romanticism, the romanticism adopted by its traditional enemies, the Philistines, but romanticism just the same, that is to say, *passion,* the taste for mortal exaltation.

The rationalistic incapacity of the democracies to understand the inner nature of this phenomenon explains only too well their failures, delays, and perpetual state of surprise. It explains why some of their leaders have persisted in believing that they could discuss matters objectively and come to terms—"as soldiers and with honor"—with men who have immured themselves in the dream of the millennium autarchy. It explains why these leaders have each time been disconcerted by the violence and size of the totalitarian achievements, rationally and technically impossible to foresee. It explains especially the failure of the thunderings of the democratic press against totalitarianism. This failure has two principal reasons:

1. Democratic propaganda exhausts its strength in showing that totalitarianism is barbarous, violent, warlike, Spartan, tyrannical, etc., whereas the democracies are civilized, refined, peaceful, prosperous, liberal, etc. Now, everybody knows this. The disciples of the dictators know it too. But *reasons,* however evident they may be, can do little against surging *passion.* Secondly, they can do little to prevent the spread of the contagion among masses predisposed by all of modern life to be contaminated.

2. Democratic propaganda consists mostly in a *refutation* of totalitarian doctrines. We ignore or forget that these doctrines only play a superficial part in the collective hypnotic process presented by Hitlerism. We ignore or forget also that when we stubbornly maintain a negative attitude, in a sterile criticism of totalitarian unreason, we run the risk of one day succumbing to its hypnotic influence. Nothing is more easily changed into a *Pro* than an *Anti* which is only that. I myself have followed closely the conversion to Hitlerism of a certain number of German Anti-Fascists. The best explanation I know on the subject was given by Thomas Mann, in a story entitled *Mario and the Magician.*

This story, probably symbolic, is simply the description of a public hypnotic séance held in a small watering place on the Adriatic. At a certain moment, the hypnotist invites a few spectators to pick some cards at random from a deck. Of course all of them select the cards already chosen by the will of the magician. A spectator then arises and states that he has decided to pick his own card, and to resist all psychic influence. Then the magician pronounces the following decisive words: "You are going to make my task slightly more difficult. Your opposition will however change the results in no fashion. Freedom does exist, the will also exists, but freedom of the will does not exist, *because* the will, *directed merely to its own freedom, strikes into the void.* You will choose the right card so much the more surely as you strive the harder to act freely." A little later in the evening, the magician compels another spectator to dance, although he had earlier insisted that he would not do so. "If I have understood correctly," the author of the tale comments, "the gentleman was conquered *because of the negative nature of his stand.* To all appearances, the soul cannot live on non-willing. Not to will for something is almost not to will anything—hence, to do eventually that which another will imposes."

There exists only one means (but infallible) to prevent being hypnotized: merely to will for something positive. To be satisfied with refusing totalitarianism, to will for "freedom" in general without any positive content polarizing the potencies of the person is to be defeated beforehand. Let us not forget: in the dramatic struggle between the Magicians of our times and the liberals deprived of *positive* faith, still so numerous in our democracies, the Magicians have a great advantage. They alone know the passionate nature of the struggle they are leading. They know they have nothing to fear from the right-minded, yet futile indignation of the liberals. On the contrary.

The democracies will resist the totalitarian contagion only if they give themselves positive objectives—to reform democracy and finally to achieve it on the economic level. The germs of totalitarian passion will be destroyed only in the souls of those individuals who recapture a taste to live their own lives. Where man seeks to be total, the State will never be totalitarian. The constitution of "nationalized masses" will be prevented only by the rebirth of true communities. But these communities must be founded on universal, not on narrowly nationalistic truth. Therefore, I can only conclude this essay with an appeal to the Churches.

Translated by Earl F. Langvell, Notre Dame, Indiana

NOTES

Reprinted from *The Review of Politics* 3, no. 1 (January 1941): 65–82.

1. *L'Amour et l'Occident* (Paris, 1939). Translated into English by Montgomery Belgion, under the title of *Passion and Society* (London, 1940), and *Love in the Western World* (New York: Harcourt Brace, 1940).

2. I refer the interested reader for this development to Books I and II of *Love in the Western World*, and particularly to Chapter V of Book II, for the theological aspect of the problem.

3. See J. Huizinga, *The Waning of the Middle Ages*, p. 96. [De Rougemont is probably referring to the first English translation of the book (London: E. Arnold & Co., 1924 or 1927). Ed.]

4. See C. S. Jung, *Psychologische Typen* and *Psychology and Religion*.

5. [De Rougemont is using a version of *Mein Kampf* (New York: Reynal & Hitchcock, 1939) which has among its "editorial sponsors" John Chamberlain, Sidney B. Fay, John Gunther, Carlton, J. H. Hayes, and various others, many of whom were active in the American Office of Strategic Services. Ed.]

CHAPTER 5

The Immortality of Man

JACQUES MARITAIN

I

Let us think of the human being, not in an abstract and general way, but in the most concrete possible, the most *personal* fashion. Let us think of this certain old man we have known for years in the country—this old farmer with his wrinkled face, his keen eyes which have beheld so many harvests and so many earthly horizons, his long habits of patience and suffering, courage, poverty and noble labor, a man perhaps like those parents of a great living American statesman whose photographs appeared some months ago in a particularly moving copy of a weekly magazine. Or let us think of this certain boy or this girl who are our relatives or our friends, whose everyday life we well know, and whose loved appearance, whose soft or husky voice is enough to rejoice our hearts. Let us remember— remember in our heart—a single gesture of the hand, or the smile in the eyes of one we love. What treasures on earth, what masterpieces of art or of science, could pay for the treasures of life, feeling, freedom and memory, of which this gesture, this smile is the fugitive expression? We perceive intuitively, in an indescribable not inescapable flash, that nothing in the world is more precious than one single human being. I am well aware how many difficult questions come to mind at the same time and I shall come back to these difficulties, but for the present I wish only to keep in mind this simple and decisive intuition, by means of which the incomparable value of the human person is revealed to us. Moreover, St. Thomas Aquinas warns us that the Person is what is noblest and most perfect in the whole of nature.

Nothing, however, nothing in the world is more squandered, more wasted than a human being. Nothing is spent with so prodigally, so heedlessly, as though a man were a bit of small change in the hand of careless Nature. Surely it is a crime to throw away human lives more cruelly and contemptuously than the lives of cattle, to submit them to the merciless will-to-power of totalitarian states or of insatiate conquerors. The present-day transportations of populations, concentration camps, wars of enslavement, are signs of a criminal contempt for mankind unheard of until now. Surely it is shameful as well to contemplate throughout the world the debasing standards of life imposed on so many human beings in their slums of distress and starvation. As Edmund Burke wrote a century and a half ago, "the blood of man should never be shed but to redeem the blood of man. It is well shed for our family, for our friends, for our God, for our country, for our kind. The rest is vanity; the rest is crime." Yet since the blood of man is well shed for our family, for our friends, for our country, for our kind, for our God, this very fact shows that many things are indeed worth a man's sacrifice of his earthly life. What things? Things of a truly human and divine value, things that involve and preserve that justice, that freedom, that sacred respect for truth and for the dignity of the spirit without which human existence becomes unlivable; things that a man may and should love more than his own flesh and blood, just because they pertain to the great task of redeeming the blood of man.

But what I should like to emphasize is the fact that in the obscure workings of the human species, in that immense network of solidarity each mesh of which is made of human effort and human risk, and advances in its small way the progression of the whole, there is an infinity of things, often of little things, for which men expose themselves to danger and self-sacrifice. Often the reasons for such lavish courage are not love or pure generosity, but only natural energy, or temerity, or longing for glory, or pleasure in confronting new difficulties, or desire for risk and adventure. All these, however, are carried away in that flood of superabundance and self-giving which springs from the sources of being, and which brings mankind towards its fulfillment. A scientist risks his life for a new discovery in the realm of matter, a pioneer to establish a new settlement, an aviator to improve our means of communication, a miner to extract coal from the earth, a pearl fisher to filch from the ocean an ornament for the beauty of some unknown woman, a traveler to contemplate new landscapes, a mountain climber to conquer a bit of earth. What comparison is there between the result to be obtained, be it momentous or slight, and the price of human life which is thus wagered, the value of that being, full of promise, endowed with so many gifts and whom many hearts may love? Well, at each corner of human activity death lies in ambush. Every day we trust our life and the lives of our beloved to the unknown driver of a subway train, of a plane, of a bus, or a taxi. Where there is no risk, there is no life. A wisdom or a civilization based on the avoidance of risk, by virtue of a misinterpretation of the value of the human being, would run the greatest of all risks, that of cowardice and of deadly stupidity. That perpetual risk which man takes is the very condition of his life. That squandering of the human being is a law of nature; it is also the proof of the confidence, the trust, and the elementary love we everyday give to the divine principle from which we proceed, and the very law of which is superabundance and generosity.

Now we face a paradox. On the one hand nothing in the world is more precious than one single human person. On the other hand nothing in the world is more squandered, more exposed to all kinds of dangers than the human being— and this condition must be. What is the meaning of this paradox? It is perfectly clear. We have here a sign that man knows very well that death is not an end, but a beginning. He knows very well, in the secret depths of his own being, that he can run all risks, spend his life, and scatter his possessions here below, because he is immortal. The chant of the Christian liturgy before the body of the deceased is significant: Life is changed, life is not taken away.

II

As I have just noted, there is in men a natural, an instinctive knowledge of his immortality. This knowledge is not inscribed in man's intelligence, rather it is inscribed in his ontological structure; it is not rooted in the principles of reasoning, but in our very substance. The intelligence may become aware of this knowledge in an indirect way, and through some reflection, some turning back of thought upon the recesses of human subjectivity. The intelligence may also ignore this instinctive knowledge, and remain unaware of it, for our intelligence is naturally turned or diverted towards the being of external things. It may even deny the soul and immortality, by virtue of any set whatsoever of ideas and reasonings; yet, when the intellect of a man denies immortality, this man continues living, despite his rational convictions, on the basis of an unconscious and, so to speak, biological assumption of this very immortality, though rationally denied. Although such discrepancies are not infrequent among us, introducing many troubles, deviations or weaknesses into our behavior, they cannot disturb or annihilate the basic prerequisites of that behavior.

The instinctive knowledge of which I speak is a common and obscure knowledge. When a man is not an "intellectual" man, that is to say, when his intelligence, rarely busy with ideas, science and philosophy, follows for guidance only the natural tendencies of our species, this instinctive knowledge naturally reverberates in his mind. He does not doubt that another life will come after the present one. The possibility of doubt and error about what is most natural in the basic strata of human existence is the price paid for the progress of our species toward its rational fulfillment. Sometimes it is a very high price! The only solution, however, is not to try some sort of return to purely instinctive life, as D. H. Lawrence and many others have dreamed it. This regression, moreover, is quite impossible, and could only lead, not to nature, but to a perversion of civilized life. The only solution worthy of man is not a backward flight towards instinct, but a flight ahead towards reason, towards a reason which at last is well equipped and knows the truth.

Of man's instinctive belief in his immortality, which is not a conceptual or philosophical knowledge, but a lived and practiced one, we have a striking sign in the behavior of primitive men. No matter how far back we look into the past, we always find the trace of funeral rites, of an extraordinary care about the dead and their life beyond the grave. What we know concerning the beliefs of primitive men shows us that their belief in immortality might assume the strangest and most aberrant forms. Sometimes, as in the old Chinese superstitions, the dead were terribly feared, and the living man was to take every precaution against their mischievousness. In any case, the ideas, the reasons and explanations by means of which primitive men sought to justify their belief and to imagine the survival of the dead seem to us very queer, often absurd. This oddness and absurdity of primitive mythologies, which Frazer emphasized with the naiveté of the civilized man, are easily explainable.[1] On the one hand the mental climate of the primitive man is not the climate of reason, but that of imagination. The intelligence of primitive men, a very acute and awakened one vitally immersed in nature, functions in a kind of dusk where the imagination rules. Their conceptions are regulated by the law of images. When this point is well understood, the myths of primitive men appear less absurd, much wiser even than some anthropologists believe. On the other hand, as regards belief in immortality, the conceptions of primitive man are not the result of any rational inquiry. On the contrary they only translate, according to the ebb and flow of the imaginative thought, a substantial—not intellectual—persuasion given him by nature. The more irrational and queer his myths of the soul and its survival appear, the more strikingly they give testimony to the fact that his certitude of survival is rooted in underground strata more profound and immovable, though less perfect and fertile, than the arable soil of reason.

How then can we explain the origin of the natural and instinctive knowledge of immortality? Here we must consider that the highest functions of the human mind, particularly the functions of judgment, are performed in the midst of a kind of consciousness which is vital and spontaneous and accompanies every achieved or perfected act of thought. This spontaneous or *concomitant* consciousness is to be carefully distinguished from the consecutive or *explicit* consciousness. The second one presupposes a special reflexive act, by means of which the mind comes back upon itself and produces special reflexive concepts, special reflexive judgments concerning what lies within itself. The concomitant consciousness does not do so. It only expresses the self-interiority, the self-involvement proper to the human mind; it is only the diffuse light of reflexivity—lived and practiced, not conceptualized reflexivity—within which every spiritual achievement is accomplished in the human soul. But such a spontaneous consciousness slips back to the very root and principle of our mental operations, attains this root as something unknown in itself, known only—and that is enough, moreover—as transcending all operations and psychic phenomena which proceed from it. The Self, the supraphenomenal Self, is thus obscurely but certainly attained by the spontaneous consciousness—in the night as regards every notion and conceptualization, with certainty as regards vital experience. This experience of a supraphenomenal Self, not conceptually formulated but practically lived by the intellect, is the basic datum, the rock of spontaneous consciousness. Our intelligence knows that before thinking of that, this obscure knowledge is involved in every achieved act of thought, dealing with any matter whatsoever. When philosophical reflection forms and elaborates the idea of the Self, it attains thereby an object which human intelligence already knew in a merely lived and unexpressed fashion and now recognizes.

Human intelligence also knows, in the same obscure fashion, that this supraphenomenal Self, vitally grasped by spontaneous consciousness cannot disappear. This is true precisely because it is grasped as a center which dominates all passing phenomena, the whole succession of temporal images. That is to say, the Self, the knower able to know its own existence, is superior to time. All perceptions and images which succeed one another, composing the fluent show of this world, may vanish, as happens when a man sleeps without dreaming. The Self cannot vanish, because death, as well as sleep, is an event in time, and the Self is above time. Even if it remains unformulated in the state of some intellectual feeling rather than of any conceptualized statement, this vivid perception is, I believe, the very origin of that instinctive knowledge of man's immortality which we are now considering.

Another point must be added, concerning the aspirations proper to the Self rather than the spontaneous consciousness of it. When philosophers look upon this metaphysical reality which is called Personality, they establish that a Person is essentially a spiritual totality, characterized by independence. A Person is a universe to itself, a universe of knowledge, love and freedom, a whole which cannot be subordinated as a part, except with regard to such wholes to which it can be related through the instrumentality of knowledge and of love. Personality is an analogical and transcendental perfection, which is fully realized only in God, the Pure Act. Then philosophers are led to distinguish in the human Person two different types of aspirations. Certain aspirations of the Person are connatural to man. These concern the human Person insofar as it possesses a determinate specific nature. Other aspirations may be called transnatural. And these concern the human Person precisely insofar as it is a person and participates in the transcendental perfection of personality. Now, among the aspirations of the Person, the most obvious one is the aspiration towards not-dying. Death, the destruction of Self, is for the human Self not so much a thing to be feared as it is first of all a thing incomprehensible, impossible, an offense, a scandal. Not to be is nonsense for the person. This is so true that although we meet death at every step, although we see our relatives, our friends die, although we attend their burial, still the most difficult thing for us, is to believe in the reality of death. Man sees death; he does not believe in it. Yet the human Person does not escape dying, so it may seem that his aspiration toward immortality is thus deceived. How is this possible? We know very well that an aspiration which expresses only the very structure of a being cannot be deceived. The only way is to distinguish, according to the distinction I indicated a moment ago, what is *connatural* and what is *transnatural* in the aspiration we are dealing with.

To the extent that it relates to the spiritual part of the human whole, to the soul, the aspiration toward not-dying is connatural to man, and cannot be deceived. To the extent that it relates to the whole itself, to the human Person made up of soul and body, this aspiration is a transnatural aspiration. It can be deceived. Yet, even when deceived, it remains within us, appealing to we know not what power, appealing to the very principle of being for we know not what kind of realization beyond death. This fact extends beyond the corruption of that body which is an essential part of the human whole and without which the individual soul is not, truly speaking, a Person; beyond every evidence of the disappearance of the Person scattered amidst the glamorous appearances of Nature and the seasons; beyond this very world the existence and duration of which is linked with the generation and corruption of material substances and is therefore a denial of the human Person's very claim to immortality.

III

I have spoken of the instinctive and natural, lived and practiced belief in man's immortality. Now I should like to pass to philosophical knowledge, to that kind of knowledge, no longer instinctive and natural, but rational and elaborated, by means of which the human mind can achieve perfectly tested or demonstrated certitudes.

The philosophical knowledge of which I speak is not positivism, because positivism seems to be a despair of philosophy rather than a philosophy; however, the father of all modern positivists, Auguste Comte, felt so strongly the inescapability of the problem of immortality that he tried to answer it according to his possibilities, and granted a major part, in his positivist religion of Humanity, to what he called the *subjective* immortality, the immortality of everyone, in the memory, thought and love of those who knew him and appreciated him. Naturally, as regards Auguste Comte himself, the immortality he would thus enjoy was to be the eternal gratitude of all mankind. I am very far from despising this subjective immortality. To be preserved within a mind, to endure in minds as something known and told in song and story is an enviable condition for material things, and precisely the kind of immortality they will enjoy. Events in human history groan after their epic and wait for their poet; this world will be immortal in the memories of immortal spirits, and in the stories they will tell one another about it. But if subjective immortality is something, it is precisely because there are immaterial minds which may receive in themselves the images of what is perishable. Subjective immortality would be nothing—or a derision—if objective immortality, genuine immortality did not exist.

The philosophical reasons which testify to immortality may be expounded in the following way. First, human intelligence is able to know whatever participates in being and truth; the whole universe can be inscribed in it; that is to say, the object it knows has been previously deprived, in order to be known, of any conditions of materiality: what is the weight and volume of my idea of man? Does man possess any dimension or perform any transmutation of energy within my mind?

Does the sun exert any heating action within my intellect? The objects known by human intelligence, taken not as things existing in themselves, but precisely as objects determining intelligence and united with it, are immaterial.

The second point: just as is the condition of the object, so is the condition of the act which bears on it and is determined or specified by it. The object of human intelligence is as such immaterial; the act of the human intelligence is also immaterial.

The third point: since the act of the intellectual power is immaterial, this power itself is also immaterial. Intelligence is in man an immaterial power. Doubtless it depends on the body, on the conditions of the brain. Its activity can be disturbed or hindered by physical trouble, by an outburst of anger, by a drink, a narcotic. But this dependence is an *extrinsic* one. It exists because our intelligence cannot act without the joint activity of memory and imagination, of internal senses and external senses, all of which are organic powers, residing in some material organ, in some special part of the body. As to intelligence itself, it is not *intrinsically* dependent on the body, since its activity is immaterial; human intelligence does not reside in any special part of the body. It uses the brain, since the organs of the internal senses are in the brain; yet the brain is not the organ of the intelligence, there is no part of the organism whose act is intellectual operation. The intelligence has no organ.

And the final point: since intellectual power is immaterial, its first substantial root, the very substance from which it emanates and which acts through its instrumentality is also immaterial. An immaterial soul must be the first substantial root of an immaterial psychic soul power. It is conceivable that such an immaterial soul have, besides immaterial faculties, other powers and activities which are organic and material. For this immaterial soul is not only a spirit, but also a spirit made for animating a body, in Aristotelian terms a "substantial form," an *entelechy* which by its union with matter constitutes a particular corporeal substance, the human being. But it would be perfectly inconceivable that a material soul, a soul which informs a body—as the souls of animals and plants do, according to the biological philosophy of Aristotle—but which is not a spirit and cannot exist without informing matter, should possess a power or faculty, that is, should act through an instrumentality, which is immaterial, intrinsically independent of any corporeal organ and physical structure.

Thus the human soul is both a soul—that is the first principle of life in a living body—and a spirit, able to exist and to live apart from matter. The human soul has its own immaterial existence and its own immaterial subsistence: and it is by virtue of this immaterial existence and subsistence of the human soul that each element of the human body is human and exists as such. The radical immateriality of the highest operations of the human soul, of intellectual knowledge, of contemplation, of suprasensuous love and desire and joy, of free will, is evidence that this soul is spiritual in itself, and cannot cease existing and living. It cannot be corrupted, since it has no matter, it cannot be disintegrated, since it has no substantial parts, it cannot lose its individual unity, since it is self-subsisting, nor its internal energy, since it contains within itself all the sources of its energies. The human soul cannot die. Once existing, it cannot disappear, it will necessarily exist always, endure without end.

Each one of us is inhabited. With what wonderful respect we would look upon every human being, if we thought of that invisible Psyche who dwells within him and who causes him to be what he is, and who will endure longer than the world, endure always, after these poor bones are reduced to dust! How can our eyes contemplate any human person without seeking anxiously after the eternal mystery which is living in him? The first Christians kissed the breasts of their children with awe and veneration, thinking of that eternal presence within them. They had some idea, some awareness, less fickle than ours, of the immortality of the human soul.

I have just considered the immortality of the human soul. All the certitudes which the wisdom of philosophers brings forth concerning immortality deal with the immortality of the human *soul*. Because non-cessation of being is the natural property of what is spiritual in us. But what of those aspirations of the human Person toward immortality that I emphasized a moment ago? These aspirations concern the very Person, Man himself, the natural whole made of flesh and spirit—not the human soul alone. About the aspiration of man to the immortality of *man*, not merely of the *human soul*, the philosophical reason has very little to say.

On the one hand, philosophical reason perceives that a separate soul is not a person, although it subsists in itself. It is not a person, because the notion of Person is essentially the notion of a complete and perfect whole. The body integrates the natural human totality, and the soul is only a part. What would be the life of separated souls, if they had to lead a merely natural life? They would live a truly pale life in a pallid paradise, like the Elysian fields of the Ancients, with their pallid asphodels. Separated souls in a merely natural condition would not see God face to face, which is a supernatural privilege. They would know God through that image of God which is themselves, and they would know themselves in an intuitive manner. They would be dazzled by their own beauty, the beauty of a spiritual substance, and they would know other things in a confused and imperfect way, through the instrumentality of their substance, in the measure in which the other things resemble them. But all this knowledge would remain in a kind of dusk, because of the natural weakness of human intellect. Moreover all the sensible powers of the human soul, sensible memory, imagination, instinct and passion, as well as external senses, remain asleep in a separated soul. In such a way that if there were not a supernatural compensation and supercompensation for such a soul, the happy life it would live, according to its natural condition, would be a half life in happiness.

On the other hand, philosophical reason understands that since the human soul is naturally made to animate a body, a kind of unfulfillment, incompleteness and substantial dissatisfaction must remain in the separated soul, as regards that other half of the human being which the soul, by virtue of its very being, tends to use for its own purpose and operations, while giving it ontological consistence and activity. In this way philosophical reason wonders whether such a desire for reunion with the body could not some day be fulfilled in the immortal soul? Yes, as regards God's omnipotence, there is no impossibility of some reembodiment of the soul into its flesh and bones, and some restoration of the human integrity. But human reason can only conceive of this possibility; it cannot go farther. Therefore, as concerns the supreme aspiration of the human Person toward immortality, toward the immortality of Man, human reason stops, remains silent, and dreams.

IV

Nevertheless, one must ask this question: Will this aspiration toward the immortality of the human Person remain forever unsatisfied? Such a question transcends the philosophical domain, the domain of human reason. The problem is a religious one, it engages and puts into play the deepest, the most crucial religious conceptions of mankind.

Two great conceptions here confront one another. They represent the two types of religious interpretation of human life which are alone possible. One conception is the Indian conception, the other is the Judeo-Christian one.

The Indian conception surrenders the immortality of the person, and teaches metempsychosis or transmigration. The soul is immortal, but the soul transmigrates. At the death of the body, the soul passes to another body, like a bird to a new cage, a more or less noble, more or less painful new cage, according to the merits or demerits gathered by the soul during its previous life. Thus there is for the same soul a succession of personalities as well as a succession of lives; each of these personalities slips away forever, will never appear again, like outworn coats that a man throws away from season to season. The unlimited flux, the irremediable disappearance of the successive personalities, is the ransom for the immortality of the soul.

There are very impressive and definite philosophical arguments against the idea of transmigration. The essential argument is the following: transmigration implies that each soul preserves its own individuality and yet passes from one body to another. But that is possible only if the soul is not substantially one with the body. The negation of the substantial unity of man, and the negation of the fact that soul and personality are inseparably joined—such a soul, such a personality; such a personality, such a soul—these two negations are inevitably involved in the doctrine of transmigration. That is to say, there is transmigration if man is not man; or, as Aristotle said, if the art of the flute player can descend into the harp and cause the harp to produce the sound of the flute. The basic truth concerning the human being, the substantial unity of man, is incompatible with the idea of transmigration.

But despite the strength of this philosophical evidence, the idea of transmigration remains a temptation for the religious consciousness of mankind. Why this temptation toward metempsychosis? In my opinion this temptation results from the conflict between the idea of the retribution for human acts and the idea of the brevity, distress and foolishness of human life. How is it possible that a man's unhappy life, with all its insignificance, its blundering, and its wretchedness should open suddenly out upon Eternity? How is it possible that an eternal retribution, an eternal and immutable end, may be fixed for us in virtue of some good or bad movements of so weak and queer, so dormant a free will as ours? The disproportion is too great between the End and the Means. I imagine that the mind of India was discouraged and frightened by such an idea, and therefore fell back, so to speak, into the infinity of time, as if a series of new lives offered to the same soul would somehow avail to attenuate the disproportion I just emphasized between the precariousness of the journey and the importance of its end.

Yes, but then there is no longer an end. Time continues always to be Time. The mind finds itself confronted with the horror of an endless series of reincarnations. The very law of transmigration becomes a terrible and intolerable law, of new suffering ceaselessly assumed, new trials, new pain amidst new vanishing and torturing appearances. The idea of Nirvana will then occur as a way of escape. But Nirvana is only a deliverance from Time. As it is conceived by Indian metaphysics (I do not say as it is lived in fact by such or such contemplative soul) Nirvana is only an escape, the self-annihilation of that very transmigration which was to bring about the immortality of the soul, and which now abolishes itself, and along with itself immortality. Transmigration was not a solution, it was an escape, a flight, and from which in turn escape must be sought.

The Judeo-Christian conception is a philosophy of the final end, and the philosophy of the final end is the exact contrary of the philosophy of transmigration. The pursuit of immortality through a horizontal movement all along a time without end, is quite different from, it is the exact opposite of, the vertical fulfillment of immortality by the attainment of an End which is eternal and infinite, just as Nirvana is quite different from, and in a sense is the exact opposite of, the passage to eternity and the possession of everlasting life. And what makes the Judeo-Christian solution possible is not only a true appreciation of the relationship between time and eternity: Lengthen time as much as you will, add years to years, hoard up lives upon lives, time will ever remain having no common measure with eternity; a thousand transmigrations are as little before eternity as is the short life of this particular poor little child; this short human life is as much before eternity as a thousand transmigrations. But what makes the Judeo-Christian solution possible is also and above all the fact that in it the philosophy of the last End is involved in the whole of the truths and mysteries of divine revelation. Let us understand that God is personal, Life and Truth and Love in Person; let us understand that there is a supernatural order, and that the least degree of grace, that is of participation in the inner life of God himself, is more valuable than all the splendor of this star strewn universe; let us understand that God has taken flesh in the womb of a virgin of Israel in order to die for mankind and to infuse in us the life of His own blood; let us understand that the free initiatives and resources, the patience and the ingenuity of the mercy of God are exceedingly greater than the weakness or the wickedness of our human free will. Then we understand that that disproportion between the precariousness of the journey and the importance of the end, which I emphasized a moment ago, is in reality counterbalanced, and even exceedingly compensated for, by the generosity and the *humanity*, as St. Paul put it, of our Savior God. Because man does not save himself through his own power. It is God and Christ who save man through the power of the Cross and of divine grace, by the instrumentality of Faith and Charity fructifying in good works.

But the Judeo-Christian conception is not only a philosophy of the last End; it is also, and by the same stroke, a philosophy of the immortality of Men. It asserts not only the immortality of the Soul, but also the immortality of the human Person, of the whole human subject. This is because grace perfects Nature and fulfills supereminently the aspirations of Nature, those aspirations of the human person which I have already called *transnatural*. What the sacred writings of the Jews constantly emphasized, what mattered most to them, was not so much the immortality of the soul as the resurrection of the body. It is the resurrection of the body that St. Paul preached in Athens, to the astonishment of the philosophers. It is the resurrection of the body that we Christians hope for. A resurrection which transcends all the powers of nature, and which is to be accomplished for the elect by virtue of the blood and resurrection of Christ, and by a miracle of justice for those who will have refused up to the end grace and redeeming life.

Such is the answer given not by philosophy alone, but by Faith and Revelation, to the question which we were led to ask a moment ago. In point of fact, will the aspiration of the human Person, of the entire man toward immortality remain forever unsatisfied? No, this aspiration will not remain unsatisfied, the soul and body will be reunited. This same Person, this identical human Person whom we knew and loved during our evanescent days is actually immortal, this undivided human totality that we designate by a man's name will perish for a while, yes, and will know putrefaction. Yet in reality and when all is said and done, he will triumph over death and endure without end. And this immortality of Man is inextricably engaged and involved in the drama of the Salvation and Redemption.

V

I have a few words to add in conclusion. I should like to come back to some considerations which I touched on at the beginning of this essay, concerning the value of human life. This value is greater than anything in the world, except things which are divine or concern what is divine in man, and serve, as Edmund Burke said, to redeem the blood of man. Such things, in truth, are not of the world, although they may be in the world.

Here we face a strange paradox, and that kind of assertion which may be, with the same words but according to diverse meanings, at the same time perfectly true and absolutely false. *Nothing in the world is more precious than human life.* If I think of the perishable life of man, this assertion is absolutely false. A single word is more precious than human life if in uttering this word a man braves a tyrant for the sake of truth or of liberty. *Nothing in the world is more precious than human life.* If I think of the imperishable life of man, of that life which will consist in seeing God face to face, this same assertion is perfectly true.

Human society can ask human persons to give and sacrifice their lives for it, as in the case of a just war. How is this possible? This is possible because the earthly common good of the earthly community is not a merely earthly good. Even this earthly common good involves suprahuman values, for it relates indirectly to the last end of men, to the eternal destiny of the persons who compose society. Human society must tend toward its earthly common good, toward a good and happy common life, in such a way that the pursuit of eternal happiness—which is more than happiness, for it is beatitude, and God himself—may be opened and made feasible for each human person in the community. If the common good of human society were only and exclusively a set of temporal advantages or achievements, as the common good of a bee hive or an ant hill, surely it would be nonsense for the life of a human person to be sacrificed to it.

As regards human civilizations, or pseudo-civilizations, two mortal errors are to be pointed out in this connection.

A civilization which despises death because it despises the human person and ignores the value of human life, a civilization which squanders the courage of men and wastes their lives for business profits or for satiating covetousness or hate or for the frenzy of domination or for the pagan pride of the state, is not a civilization, but barbarism. Its heroism is heartless bestiality.

But on the other hand a civilization which knows the price of human life but which sets up as its main values the perishable life of man, pleasure, money, selfishness, the possession of acquired commodities, and which therefore fears death as the supreme evil and avoids any risk of self-sacrifice and trembles thinking of death, under the pretext of respecting human life, such a civilization is not a civilization, but degeneration. Its humanism is cowardly delicacy.

True civilization knows the price of human life but makes the imperishable life of man its transcendent supreme value. It does not fear death, it confronts death, it accepts risk, it requires self-sacrifice, but for aims which are worthy of human life, for justice, for truth, for brotherly love. It does not despise human life and it does not brutally despise death, it welcomes death when death, as pioneers and free men see it, is the accomplishment of the dignity of the human person and a beginning of eternity. Let me recall in this connection the words of the late Greek statesman, Metaxas,[2] spoken to an American war correspondent.

"We Greeks," he said, "being Christians, know that after all death is only an episode." An episode on the road of the immortal life of man. Such is Christian civilization, true civilization. Its heroism is genuine heroism, a heroism integrally human, because divinely grounded in the immortality of man.

NOTES

Reprinted from *The Review of Politics* 3, no. 4 (October 1941): 411–27.

1. [Maritain is undoubtedly referring to Sir James George Frazer (1854–1941), the British anthropologist and author of *The Golden Bough*. Ed.]

2. [Ioannis Metaxas (1871–1941), a military officer and royalist, became Greece's prime minister in 1936 and imposed a right-wing authoritarian regime. He tried unsuccessfully to ally his country with Great Britain before Italy's invasion of Greece in 1940. Ed.]

CHAPTER 6

The End of Machiavellianism

JACQUES MARITAIN

I

My purpose is to consider Machiavellianism.[1] Regarding Machiavelli himself, some preliminary observations seem necessary. Innumerable studies, some of them very good, have been dedicated to Machiavelli. Jean Bodin, in the sixteenth century, criticized *The Prince* in a profound and wise manner. Later on Frederick the Great of Prussia was to write a refutation of Machiavelli in order to exercise his own hypocrisy in a hyper-Machiavellian fashion, and to shelter cynicism in virtue. During the nineteenth century, the leaders of the bourgeoisie, for instance the French political writer Charles Benoist, were thoroughly, naïvely and stupidly fascinated by the clever Florentine. As regards modern scholarship, I should like to note that the best historical commentary on Machiavelli has been written by an American scholar, Professor Allan H. Gilbert.[2] As regards more popular presentations, a remarkable edition of the *Prince* and the *Discourses* was recently issued by the Modern Library.

Max Lerner, in the stimulating, yet somewhat ambiguous Introduction he wrote for this edition of *The Prince* and *The Discourses,* rightly observes that Machiavelli was expressing the actual ethos of his time, and that "power politics existed before Machiavelli was ever heard of, it will exist long after his name is only a faint Memory."[3] This is perfectly obvious. But what matters in this connection, is just that Machiavelli *lifted into consciousness* this ethos of his time and this common practice of the power politicians of all times. Here we are confronted with the fundamental importance, which I have often emphasized, of the phenomenon of "prise de conscience," and with the risks of perversion which this phenomenon involves.

Before Machiavelli, princes and conquerors did not hesitate to apply on many occasions bad faith, perfidy, falsehood, cruelty, assassination, every kind of crime of which the flesh and blood man is capable, to the attainment of power and success and to the satisfaction of their greed and ambition. But in so doing they felt guilty, they had a bad conscience—to the extent that they had a conscience. Therefore a specific kind of unconscious and unhappy hypocrisy—that is, the shame of appearing to oneself such as one is—a certain amount of self restraint, and that deep and deeply human uneasiness which we experience in doing what we do not want to do and what is forbidden by a law that we know to be true, prevented the crimes in question from becoming a rule, and provided governed peoples with a limping accommodation between good and evil which, in broad outline, made their oppressed lives, after all, livable.

After Machiavelli, not only the princes and conquerors of the *cinquecento,* but the great leaders and makers of modern states and modern history, in employing injustice for establishing order, and every kind of useful evil for satisfying their will to power, will have a clear conscience and feel that they accomplish their duty as political heads. Suppose they are not merely skeptical in moral matters, and have some religious and ethical convictions in connection with man's personal behavior, then they will be obliged, in connection with the field of politics, to put aside these convictions, or to place them in a parenthesis, they will stoically immolate their personal morality on the altar of the political good. What was a simple matter of fact, with all the weaknesses and inconsistencies pertaining, even in the evil, to accidental and contingent things, has become, after Machiavelli, a matter of right, with all the firmness and steadiness proper to necessary things. A plain disregard of good and evil has been considered the rule, not of human morality—Machiavelli never pretended to be a moral philosopher—but of human politics.

For not only do we owe to Machiavelli our having become aware and conscious of the immorality displayed, in fact, by the mass of political men, but by the same stroke he taught us that this very immorality is the very law of politics. Here is that Machiavellian perversion of politics which was linked, in fact, with the Machiavellian "prise de conscience" of average political behavior in mankind. The historic responsibility of Machiavelli consists in having *accepted,* recognized, endorsed as a rule the fact of political immorality, and in having stated that good politics, politics conformable to its true nature and to its genuine aims, is by essence non-moral politics.

Machiavelli belongs to that series of minds, and some of them much greater than himself, which all through modern times have endeavored to unmask the human being. To have been the first in this lineage is the greatness of the narrow thinker eager to serve the Medici as well as the popular party in Florence, and deceived on both sides. Yet in unmasking the human being he maimed its very flesh, and wounded its eyes. To have thoroughly rejected ethics, metaphysics and theology from the realm of political knowledge and political prudence is his very own achievement, and it is also the most violent mutilation suffered by the human practical intellect and the organism of practical wisdom.

Radical pessimism regarding human nature is the basis of Machiavelli's thought. After having stated that "a prudent ruler ought not to keep faith when by so doing it would be against his interest, and when the reasons which made him bind himself no longer exist," he writes: "If men were all good, this precept would not be a good one; but *as they are bad,* and would not observe their faith with you, so you are not bound to keep faith with them." Machiavelli knows that they are bad. He does not know that this badness is not radical, that this leprosy cannot destroy man's original grandeur, that human nature remains good in its very essence and its root-tendencies, and that such a basic goodness joined to a swarming multiplication of particular evils is the very mystery and the very motive of struggle and progression in mankind. Just as his horizon is merely terrestrial, just as his crude empiricism cancels for him the indirect ordainment of political life toward the life of souls and immortality, so his concept of man is merely animal, and his crude empiricism cancels for him the image of God in man—a cancellation which is the metaphysical root of every power politics and every political totalitarianism. As to their common and most frequent behavior, Machiavelli thinks, men are beasts, guided by covetousness and fear. But the prince is a man, that is, an animal of prey endowed with intelligence and calculation. In order to govern men, that is, to enjoy power, the prince must be taught by Chiron the centaur, and learn to become both a fox and a lion. Fear, animal fear, and animal prudence translated into human art and awareness, are accordingly the supreme rulers of the political realm.

Yet the pessimism of Machiavelli is extremely removed from any heroic pessimism. To the evil that he sees everywhere, or believes he sees everywhere, he gives his consent. He consents, he aspires to become a clearsighted composite of fox and lion. "For how we live," he says, "is so far removed from how we ought to live, that he who abandons what is done for what ought to be done, will rather learn to bring about his own ruin than his preservation." Therefore we have to abandon what *ought to be done* for *what is done,* and it is necessary for the prince, he also says, "to learn how not to be good, and to use this knowledge and not use it, according to the necessity of the case." And this is perfectly logical if the end of ends is only present success. Yet such an abandonment, such a resignation would be logical also, not only for political life, but for the entire field of human life. Descartes, in the provisory rules of morality which he gave himself in the *Discours de la Méthode,* made up his mind to imitate the actual customs and doings of his fellow men, instead of practicing what they say we ought to do. He did not perceive that this was a good precept of immorality: for, as a matter of fact, men live more often by senses than by reason. It is easy to observe with Max Lerner that many Church princes, like the secular princes, and above all that Alexander VI whom Machiavelli gives often in example, were among the principal followers of Machiavelli's precepts. But never has any catechism taught that we must imitate the Church princes in our conduct, it is Christ that religion teaches us to imitate. The first step to be taken by everyone who wishes to act morally is to decide not to act according to the general customs and doings of his fellow men. This is a precept of the Gospel: "Do not ye after their works; for they say, and do not. . . ."[4]

The practical result of Machiavelli's teachings has been, for modern conscience, a profound split, an incurable division between politics and morality, and consequently an illusory but deadly antinomy between what they call *idealism* (wrongly confused with ethics) and what they call *realism* (wrongly confused with politics). Henceforth, as Max Lerner puts it, "the polar conflict between the ethical and the ruthlessly realistic." I shall come back to this point. For the present I wish to note two kinds of complications which arise in this connection in the case of Machiavelli himself.

The first complication comes from the fact that Machiavelli, like many great pessimists, had a somewhat rough and elementary idea of moral science, plainly disregarding its realist, experiential, and existential character, and lifting up to heaven, or rather up to the clouds, an altogether naïve morality which obviously cannot be practiced by the sad yet really living and laboring inhabitants of this earth. The man of ethics appears to him as a feeble-minded and disarmed victim, occasionally noxious, of the beautiful rules of some Platonist and separate world of perfection. On the other hand, and because such a morality is essentially a self-satisfying show of pure and lofty shapes—that is, a dreamed-up compensation for our muddy state—Machiavelli constantly slips from the idea of well-doing to the idea of what men admire as well-doing, from moral virtue to appearing and apparent moral virtue: his virtue is a virtue of opinion, self-satisfaction and glory. Accordingly, what he calls vice and evil, and considers to be contrary to virtue and morality, may sometimes be only the authentically moral behavior of a just man engaged in the complexities of human life and of true ethics: for instance, justice itself may call for relentless energy, which is neither vengeance nor cruelty, against wicked and false-hearted enemies. Or the toleration of some existing evil, if there is no furthering of or cooperating with the same, may be required for avoiding a greater evil or for slowing down and progressively reducing this very evil. Or even dissimulation is not always bad faith or knavery. It would not be moral, but foolish, to open up one's heart and inner thoughts to whatsoever dull or mischievous fellow. Stupidity is never moral, it is a vice. No doubt it is difficult to mark exactly the limits between cunning and lying, and even some great Saints of the Old Testament—I am thinking of Abraham—did not take great care of this distinction. This was a consequence of what may be called the twilight status of moral conscience in the dawn-ages of mankind.[5] Yet a certain amount of cunning, if it is intended to deceive evil-disposed persons, must not be considered fox's wiles, but intellect's legitimate weapon. Oriental peoples know that very well, and even evangelic candor has to use the prudence of the serpent, as well as the simplicity of the dove (the dove tames the serpent, but the lion does not tame the fox). The question is to use such cunning without the smallest bit of falsehood or imposture: this is exactly the affair of intelligence; and the use of lying—namely, the large-scale industrialization of lying, of which contemporary dictatorships offer us the spectacle—appears from this point of view, not only as moral baseness but also as vulgarity of mind and thorough degradation of intelligence.

The second complication arises from the fact that Machiavelli was a cynic operating on the given moral basis of civilized tradition, and whose cruel work of exposure took for granted the coherence and density of this deep-rooted tradition. Clear-sighted and intelligent as he was, he was perfectly aware of that fact; this is why he would pale at the sight of modern Machiavellianism. This commentator of Titus Livius was instructed by Latin tradition. He was a partaker as well as a squanderer of humanist learning, an inheritor as well as an opponent of the manifold treasure of knowledge prepared by Christian centuries, and degenerating in his day. He never negates the values of morality; he knows them and recognizes them as they have been established by ancient wisdom; he occasionally praises virtuous leaders (that is, whose virtues were made successful by circumstances); he knows that cruelty and faithlessness are shameful, and he never calls evil good or good evil. He simply denies to moral values—and this is largely sufficient to corrupt politics—any application in the political field. He teaches his prince to be cruel and faithless, according to the case, that is, to be evil according to the case, and when he writes that the prince must learn how not to be good, he is perfectly aware that not to be good is to be bad. Hence his difference from many of his disciples, and the special savor, the special power of intellectual stimulation of his cynicism. But hence also his special sophistry, and the mantle of civilized intelligence with which he unintentionally covered and veiled for a time the deepest meaning, the wild meaning, of his message.

Finally, the *"grammar of power"* and the recipes of success written by Machiavelli are the work of a pure artist, and of a pure artist of that Italian Renaissance where the great heritage of the antique and Christian mind, falling in jeopardy, blossomed into the most beautiful, delightful and poisonous flowers. What makes the study of Machiavelli extremely instructive for a philosopher, is the fact that nowhere is it possible to find a more purely artistic conception of politics.[6] And here is his chief philosophical fault, if it is true that politics belongs to the field of the "praktikon" (to do), not of the "poietikon" (to make), and is by essence a branch—the principal branch, according to Aristotle—of ethics. Politics is distinct from individual ethics as a branch from another branch on the same tree, it is a special and specific part of ethics, and it carries within itself an enormous amount of art, and technique is organically, vitally and intrinsically subordinated to the molding intelligence, and imagination is much greater in political than in individual or even familial ethics. But all this amount of art and technique, is organically vitally and intrinsically subordinated to the ethical energies which constitute politics, that is to say, art is there in no manner autonomous, art is there embodied in and encompassed with and lifted up by ethics, as the physico-chemical activities in our body are unsubstantiated in our living substance and superelevated by our vital energies. When these merely physico-chemical activities are liberated and become autonomous, there is no longer a living organism, but a corpse. Thus, merely artistic politics, liberated from ethics, that is, from the practical knowledge of man, from the science of human acts, from truly human finalities and truly human doings, is a corpse of political wisdom and political prudence.

Indeed, Machiavelli's very own genius has been to disentangle as perfectly as possible all the content of art carried along by politics from the ethical substance thereof. His position therefore is that of a separate artistic spirit contemplating from without the vast matter of human affairs, with all the ethical cargo, all the intercrossings of good and evil they involve, and to teach his disciple how to conquer and maintain power in handling this matter as a sculptor handles clay or marble. Ethics is here present, but in the matter to be shaped and dominated. We understand from this point of view how *The Prince* as well as *The Discourses* are rich in true observations and sometimes in true precepts, but perceived and stated in a false light and in a reversed or perverted perspective. For Machiavelli makes use of good as well as of evil, and is ready to succeed with virtue as well as with vice. That specific concept of *virtù*, that is, of brilliant, well-balanced and skilled strength, which was at the core of the morality of his time, as an aesthetic and artistic transposition of the Aristotelian concept of virtue, is always present in his work.[7] He knows that no political achievement is lasting if the prince has not the friendship of the people, but it is not the good of the people, it is only the power of the prince which matters to him in this truth perversely taught. The *Discourses*[8] eloquently emphasize the fundamental importance of religion in the state, but the truth or falsity of any religion whatsoever is here perfectly immaterial, even religion is offered as the best means of cheating the people, and what Machiavelli teaches is "the use of a national religion for state purposes," by virtue of "its power as a myth in unifying the masses and cementing their morale."[9] This perversion of religion is surely worse and more atheistic than crude atheism— the devastating effects of which the world may see and enjoy in the totalitarian plagues of today.

Here we are confronted with the paradox and the internal principle of instability of Machiavelli's Machiavellianism. It essentially supposes the complete eradication of moral values in the brain of the political artist as such, yet at the same time it also supposes the actual existence and actual vitality of moral values and moral beliefs in all others, in all the human matter that the prince is to handle and dominate. But it is impossible that the use of a supramoral, that is, a thoroughly immoral art of politics should not produce a progressive lowering and degeneration of moral values and moral beliefs in the common human life, a progressive disintegration of the inherited stock of stable structures and customs linked with these beliefs, and finally a progressive corruption of the ethical and social matter itself with which this supramoral politics deals. Thus, such an art wears away and destroys its very matter, and, by the same token, will degenerate itself. Hence Machiavelli could only have rare authentic disciples. During the classical centuries of Henry VIII and Elizabeth, Mazarin and Richelieu, Frederick,

Catherine of Russia and Talleyrand, the latter was perhaps the only perfect pupil of Machiavelli. Finally Machiavelli's teachings, which imply an essentially rational and well-measured, that is, an artistic use of evil, were to give place to that use of every kind of seemingly useful evil by great irrational and demonic forces and by an intelligence no longer artistic but vulgar and brutal and wild, and to that immersion of the rulers as well as of the ruled in a rotted ethics, calling good evil and evil good, which constitute the common Machiavellianism to today.

II

But so much for Machiavelli. It is this common Machiavellianism that I wish now to consider. In so doing, I should like briefly to touch the three following points: first, the notion of common good and the factual triumph of Machiavellianism; second, the crucial conflict which here constitutes the main problem, and its resolution; third, the roots and the more subtle implications of this resolution, which concern the specific structure of politics in its relationship with morality.

Now for my first point. For Machiavelli the end of politics is power's conquest and maintenance, which is a work of art to be performed. On the contrary, according to the nature of things, the end of politics is the common good of a united people; which end is essentially something concretely human, therefore something ethical. This common good consists of the good life—that is, a life comfortable to the essential exigencies and the essential dignity of human nature, a life both morally straight and happy—of the social whole as such, of the gathered multitude, in such a way that the increasing treasure and heritage of communicable good things involved in this good life of the whole be in some way spilled over and redistributed to each individual part of the community. This common good is at once material, intellectual and moral, and principally moral, as man himself is; it is a common good of human persons. Therefore, it is not only something useful, an ensemble of advantages and profits, it is essentially something good in itself. This is what the Ancients termed *bonum honestum.* Justice and civic friendship are its cement. Bad faith, perfidy, lying, cruelty, assassination, and all other procedures of this kind which may occasionally appear *useful* to the power of the ruling clique or to the prosperity of the state, are in themselves—insofar as political deeds, that is, deeds involving in some degree the common conduct—injurious to the common good and tend by themselves toward its corruption. Finally, because good life on earth is not the absolute ultimate end of man, and because the human person has a destiny superior to time, political common good involves an intrinsic though indirect reference to the absolutely ultimate end of the human members of society, which is eternal life, in such a way that the political community should temporally, and from below, help each human person in his human task of conquering his final freedom and fulfilling his final destiny.

Such is the basic political concept which Machiavellianism broke down and destroyed. If the aim of politics is common good, peace (i.e., a constructive peace struggling through time toward man's emancipation from any form of enslavement) is the health of the state; and the organs of justice, above all of distributive justice, are the chief power in the state. If the aim of politics is power, war is the health of the state, as Machiavelli put it, and military strength is the chief power in the state. If the aim of politics is common good, the ruler, having to take care of the temporal end of a community of human persons, and having to avoid in this task any lack of clear-sightedness and any slip of will, must learn to be, as St. Thomas taught, a man good in every respect, *bonus vir simpliciter.* If the aim of politics is power, the ruler must learn not to be good, as Machiavelli said.

The great rulers of modern times have well understood and conscientiously learned this lesson. Lord Acton was right in stating that "the authentic interpreter of Machiavelli is the whole of later history."[10] We have to distinguish, however, two kinds of common Machiavellianism. There was a kind of more or less attenuated, dignified, conservative Machiavellianism, using injustice within "reasonable" limits, if I may put it so; in the minds of its followers, what is called *Realpolitik* was obfuscated and more or less paralyzed, either by a personal pattern of moral scruples and moral rules, which they owed to the common heritage of our civilization, or by traditions of diplomatic good form and respectability, or even, in certain instances, by lack of imagination, of boldness, and of inclination to take risks. If I try to characterize more precisely these moderate Machiavellians, I should say that they preserved in some way, or believed they preserved, regarding the *end* of politics, the concept of common good. They were unfaithful to their master in this regard. And they frankly used Machiavellianism regarding the *means* of procuring this common good. Such an unnatural split and disproportion between means and ends was, moreover, inevitably to lead to a perversion of the idea of common good itself, which became more and more a set of material advantages and profits for the state, or territorial conquests, or prestige and glory. The greatest representative of moderate Machiavellianism was, in my opinion,

Richelieu. Bismarck was a transition from this first form of Machiavellianism to the second one, of which I shall now speak.

This second form of Machiavellianism is absolute Machiavellianism. It was intellectually prepared, during the nineteenth century, by the Positivist trend of mind, which considered politics to be, not a mere art, but a mere natural science, like astronomy or chemistry, and a mere application of so-called "scientific laws" to the struggle for life of human societies—a concept much less intelligent and still more inhuman than that of Machiavelli himself. Absolute Machiavellianism was also and principally prepared by the Romanticist German philosophy of Fichte and Hegel. It is well known that Fichte made an analysis of Machiavelli part of his *Address to the German Nation*. As to the Hegelian cult of the state, it is a metaphysical sublimation of Machiavelli's principles. Now the turn has been completed, ethics itself has been swallowed up into the political denial of ethics, power and success have become supreme moral criteria, "the course of world history stands apart from virtue, blame and justice," as Hegel put it, and at the same time "human history," he also said, "is God's judgment." Machiavellianism is no longer politics, it is metaphysics, it is a religion, a prophetical and mystical enthusiasm.

It sufficed for such an enthusiasm to enter into some desperados who were empty, as it were, of the usual characters of rational personality but open to the great collective forces of instinct, resentment and tellurian inspiration. In order for absolute Machiavellianism to arise in the world and in order for the unmasking Centaur to be unmasked in its turn, it sufficed for such leaders to give a full practical significance to the old infernal discovery of the endless reserves of evil when thoroughly accepted and utilized, and of the seemingly infinite power of that which negates, of the dissolving forces and of the corruption of human consciences.[11] Here we are confronted with that impetuous, irrational, revolutionary, wild, and demoniacal Machiavellianism, for which *boundless* injustice, *boundless* violence, *boundless* lying and immorality, are normal political means, and which draws from this very boundlessness of evil an abominable strength. And we may experience what kind of common good a power which knows perfectly how not to be good, and whose hypocrisy is a conscious and happy, ostentatious and gloriously promulgated hypocrisy, and whose cruelty wants to destroy souls as well as bodies, and whose lying is a thorough perversion of the very function of language, what kind of common good such a power is able to bring to mankind. Absolute Machiavellianism causes politics to be the art of bringing about the misfortune of men.

That's how it is. But absolute Machiavellianism succeeds, does it not? At least it has succeeded for many years. How could it not succeed, when everything has been sacrificed to the aim of success? Here is the ordeal and the scandal of contemporary conscience. Moreover it would be astonishing if a timid and limited Machiavellianism were not overcome and thrown away by a boundless and cynical Machiavellianism, stopping at nothing. If there is an answer to the deadly question which we are asked by the Sphinx of history, it can only lie in a thorough reversal of a century-old political thought. In the meantime, the peoples which stand against absolute Machiavellianism will be able to stop its triumphs and to overcome its standard-bearers only in wasting and sacrificing in this struggle their blood and their wealth and their dearest treasures of peaceful civilization, and in turning against this Machiavellianism its own material weapon, material techniques and gigantic means of destruction. But will they be obliged, in order to conquer it and to maintain themselves, to adopt not only its material weapons, but also its own spirit and philosophy? Will they yield to the temptation of losing for the sake of life their very reason for living and existing?

III

Here we arrive at the crucial conflict which I intend to discuss as my second point.

Confronted with any temptation of Machiavellianism, that is, of gaining success and power by means of evil, moral conscience answers and cannot keep from answering, just as when it is tempted by any profitable fault: it is never allowed to do evil for any good whatsoever. And Christian conscience in this case is strengthened by the very word of the Gospel. When the devil tempted Jesus by showing him all the kingdoms of the world, and the glory of them, and telling him "All these things will I give thee, if thou wilt fall down and worship me," Jesus answered: "Get thee hence, Satan." "For it is written, Thou shalt worship the Lord thy God, and him only shalt thou serve."[12]

Such is the answer that the human Person, looking up to his own destiny as a person, to his immortal soul, his ultimate end and everlasting life, to his God, gives to Politics when Politics offers him the kingdoms of the world at the price of his soul. This answer, and the personage to whom it was given, show us the root significance of Politics making itself absolutely autonomous, and claiming to be man's absolutely ultimate end. It shows us the transcendent meaning of the Pagan Empire, and of any paganized Empire, and of any self-styled Holy Em-

pire if its Cesar—be he a Christian Emperor or a Socialist Dictator, or any kind
of Great Inquisitor in the sense of Dostoyevsky's famous legend—wills to settle
and manage on earth the final kingdom of God or the final kingdom of Man,
which is the same final kingdom. "Get thee hence, Satan," answers Christ. State
and politics, when truly separated from ethics are the realm of those demoniacal
principalities which St. Paul spoke of, the Pagan Empire is the Empire of Man
making himself God, the diametrical opposite of the kingdom of Redemptive
Incarnation.

Yet the answer we are considering does not solve our conflict; on the contrary, it increases this conflict, it widens the tear to the infinite, it clamps down
on the Machiavellian temptation without appeasing the anguish and scandal of
our intellect. For it is an answer given by Personal ethics to a question asked by
Political ethics; it transcends the question, as the Person, with regard to his eternal destiny, transcends the state; it cuts short the question, it does not resolve it.
Obviously no assertion of the individual Ethics of the Person, as absolutely true,
absolutely decisive as it may be, can constitute a sufficiently adequate and relevant answer to a problem stated by the Ethics of the State. Exactly because it is
a transcendent answer, it is not a proper one. Machiavellianism succeeds, does it
not? Absolute Machiavellianism triumphs on earth, as our eyes have seen it for
years. Is Morality willing, is Christianity willing, is God willing that, of necessity, all our freedoms be conquered, our civilization destroyed, the very hope annihilated of seeing a little justice and brotherly amity raise our earthly life, willing that, of necessity, our lives be enslaved, our temples and institutions broken
down, our brethren persecuted and crushed, our children corrupted, our very
souls and intelligence delivered over to perversion by the great imperial standard-
bearers of Machiavellianism, because of the very fact that we adhere to justice
and refuse the devil, while they dare to use injustice and evil and accede to the
devil up to the end?

It is the true goal of the *Person* which is eternal, not that of the *State*. If a man
suffers martyrdom and enters paradise, his own soul enjoys bliss; but suppose all
the citizens of a tributary state of some Nero suffer martyrdom and enter paradise, it is not the soul of this state which will enjoy bliss; moreover, this state no
longer exists. The state has no immortal soul, nor has a nation, unless perhaps as
concerns a merely spiritual survival of its common moral heritage in the memory
of men or in the virtues of the immortal souls which animated its members long
ago, at the time when it existed. It is a joke to console Frenchmen and ask them to
accept the destruction or the enslavement of France in speaking to them of *la*

France éternelle. The soul of a nation is not immortal. The direct and specifying end, the common good of a nation is something temporal and terrestrial, something which can and should be superelevated by Gospel virtues in its own order, but whose own order is natural, not supernatural, and belongs to the realm of time. Therefore the very existence, temporal and terrestrial, the very improvement, temporal and terrestrial, the very prosperity of a nation, and that amount of happiness and glory which arises from the crises themselves and from the ordeals of history, really and essentially pertain to the common good of this nation.

No doubt, to imagine a thoroughly extreme example, a nation or a state could and should accept destruction, as did the legion of Mauritius, if its citizens were summoned to choose between martyrdom and apostasy. But such a case would not be a political case, it would be a case of sacrifice of political life itself to divine life, and a witnessing, in some way miraculous, of the superiority of the order of grace over the order of nature. But in political life itself, in the order of nature, in the framework of the temporal laws of human existence, is it not impossible that the first of the normal means of providing the common good of a state, that is, justice and political morality, should lead to the ruin and disaster of this state? Is it not impossible that the first of the means of corrupting the common good of a state, that is, injustice and political treachery, should lead to the triumph and prosperity of this state?

Yes, this is impossible.

Yet Machiavellianism succeeds in political history? Evil succeeds? What is then the answer?

The answer is that evil *does not* succeed. In reality Machiavellianism does not succeed. To destroy is not to succeed. Machiavellianism succeeds in bringing about the misfortune of man, which is the exact opposite of any genuinely political end. More or less bad Machiavellians have succeeded for centuries against other more or less bad Machiavellians, this is mere exchange of counterfeit coin. Absolute Machiavellianism succeeds against moderate or weak Machiavellianism, this also is normal. But if absolute Machiavellianism were to succeed absolutely and definitely in the world, this would simply mean that political life would have disappeared from the face of the earth, giving place to an entanglement and commixture of the life of the animals and the slaves, and of the life of the saints.

But in saying that evil and injustice do not succeed in politics, I mean a more profound philosophical truth. The endless reserves of evil, the seemingly infinite power of evil of which I spoke a moment ago, are only, in reality, the power of corruption, the squandering and dissipation of the substance and energy of Being and of Good. Such a power destroys itself in destroying that good which is its subject. The inner dialectic of the successes of evil condemn them not to be lasting. The true philosophical answer consists therefore in taking into account the dimension of time, the duration proper to the historical turns of nations and states, which considerably exceeds the duration of a man's life. According to this *political duration* of vital maturations and fructifications, I do not say that a just politics will, even in a distant future, always actually succeed, nor that Machiavellianism will, even in a distant future, always actually fail. For, with nations and states and civilizations we are in the order of nature, where mortality is natural and where life and death depend on physical as well as moral causes. I say that justice works through its own causality toward welfare and success in the future, as a healthy sap works toward the perfect fruit, and that Machiavellianism works through its own causality for ruin and bankruptcy, as poison in the sap works for the illness and death of the tree.

Now, what is the illusion proper to Machiavellianism? It is the illusion of *immediate success.* The duration of the life of a man, or rather the duration of the activity of the prince, of the political man, circumscribes the maximum length of time required by what I call *immediate success,* for immediate success is a success that our eyes may see. But what we are speaking of, what Machiavelli is speaking of, in saying that evil and injustice succeed in politics, is in reality *immediate success,* as I have defined it. Now immediate success is success for a man, it is not success for a state or a nation; it may be—it is, in the case of Machiavellian successes considered as to their inner causal law, a disaster according to the duration proper to state-vicissitudes and nation-vicissitudes. It is with regard to immediate success that evil and injustice enjoy a seemingly infinite power: a power which can be met and overcome only by a heroic tension of the antagonistic powers. But the more dreadful in intensity such a power of evil appears, the weaker in historic duration are the internal improvements, and the vigor of life, which have been gained by a state using this power.

As I have already put it in other studies, the good in which the state's justice bears fruit, the misfortune in which the state's injustice bears fruit, have nothing to do with the immediate and visible results; historic *duration* must be taken into account; the temporal good in which the state's justice fructifies, the temporal evil in which its iniquity bears its fruit, may be and are in fact quite different from the immediate results which the human mind might have expected and which the human eyes contemplate. It is as easy to disentangle these remote causations as to tell at a river's mouth which waters come from which glaciers and which tributaries. The achievements of the great Machiavellians seem durable to us, because our scale of duration-measurements is an exceedingly small one, with regard to the time proper to nations and human communities. We do not understand the fair play of God, who gives those who have freely chosen injustice the time to exhaust the benefits of it and the fullness of its energies. When disaster comes to these victors the eyes of the righteous who cried against them to God will have long putrefied under the earth, and men will not know the distant source of the catastrophe.

Thus it is true that politics being something intrinsically moral, the first political condition of good politics is that it be just. And it is true at the same time that justice and virtue do not, as a rule, lead us to success in this world. But the antinomy is solved, because on the one hand success in politics is not material power nor material wealth nor world-domination, but the achievement of the common good, with the conditions of material prosperity which it involves. And because, on the other hand, these very conditions of material prosperity, as terrible as the ordeals may be which the requirements of justice impose on a people, are not and cannot be put in jeopardy or to destruction by the use of justice itself, if historical duration is taken into account and if the specific effect of this use of justice is considered in itself, apart from the effect of the other factors at play.

I do not mean that God recompenses the just peoples by the blessings of military triumphs, territorial aggrandizements, accumulation of wealth, or infinite profit in business: such values are but secondary, sometimes even injurious to the political common good. Moreover, if it is true that the political life of peoples may be enveloped in its own order by Christian influences, it may be that a Christian nation has to undergo in a measure the very law of evangelic trials, and to pay for a certain abundance of spiritual or cultural improvements at the price of certain weaknesses and infirmities in worldly values; such was the case of Italy in the Middle Ages and the Renaissance; never did Italy know a more splendid civilization, than in those times when the power of the Popes brought her, as Machiavelli points out, weakness and pain regarding her political unity. Nor do I mean that a state using political justice is by this fact alone protected against ruin or destruction. What I mean is that in such a misfortune the very cause of ruin or destruction is never the use of justice. What I mean is that the very order of nature and of natural laws in moral matters, which is the natural justice of God, makes justice and political righteousness work towards fructifying, in the long run, as regards their own law of action, into an improvement of the true common good and the real values of civilization. Such was the case for the policy of St. Louis, although he was beaten in all his enterprises of crusade. Political injustices, on the other hand, political treacheries, political greed, selfishness or cowardice, exploitation of the poor and the weak, intoxication with power or glory or self-interest; or that kind of political cleverness which consists, as a professor in international policy told me candidly some years ago, in using flattery and leniency toward our enemy, because he is an enemy, and therefore is to be feared, and in forsaking our friend, because he is a friend, and therefore is not to be feared; or that kind of political firmness which consists in denouncing some predatory state which is attacking a weak nation, and in selling weapons and supplies to the same aggressor, because business must keep going—all this is always dearly paid for in the end. Wars, even just wars which must be waged against iniquitous aggressors, are often the payment thus exacted from a civilization.[13] Then war must be waged with unshaken resolution. But victory will be fruitful only on the condition of casting away the wrongdoings of the past, and of decidedly converting oneself toward justice and political righteousness.

The more I think of these things, the more I am convinced that the observations I proposed a moment ago on the dimension of time are the core of the question. To be lasting is an essential characteristic of the common good. A forester who would seek immediate visible success in planting plenty of big old trees in his forest, instead of preparing young saplings, would use a foolish forester policy. Machiavelli's prince is a bad political man, he perverts politics, because his chief aim is his own personal power and the satisfaction of his own personal ambition. But, in a much more profound and radical sense, the ruler who sacrifices everything to the desire of his own eyes to see the triumph of his policy is a bad ruler and perverts politics, even if he lacks personal ambition and loves his country disinterestedly: because he measures the time of maturation of the political good according to the short years of his own personal time of activity.

As regards the great representatives of contemporary Machiavellianism, with their mad lust for personal power, nothing is more instructive in this connection than the ferocious impatience of their general policy. They apply the law of war, which requires a series of immediate striking successes, but which is a supreme and abnormal crisis in the life of human societies, to the very development of the normal life of the state. In so doing, they appear, not as Empire-builders, but as mere squanderers of the heritage of their nations.

Yet a fructification which will come into existence in a distant future but which we do not see, is for us as immaterial as a fructification which would never exist on earth. To act with justice, without picking any fruit of justice, but only fruits of bitterness and sorrow and defeat, is difficult for a man. It is still more difficult for a man of politics. This is so even for a just and wise one who works at an earthly work that is the most arduous and the highest among temporal works— the common good of the multitude—and whose failures are the failures of an entire people and of a dear country. He must live on hope. Is it possible to live on hope without living on faith? Is it possible to rely on the unseen without relying on faith?

I do not believe that men in politics can escape the temptation of Machiavellianism if they do not believe that there exists a supreme government of the universe, which is, properly speaking, divine. For God, the head of the cosmos, is also the head of this particular order which is that of ethics. [They also cannot avoid this temptation][14] if they do not entrust the providence of God, by faith, with the care of all that supra-empirical, dark and mysterious disentanglement of the fructifications of good and evil which no human eye can perceive—thus closing their eyes, by faith, as regards the factual achievements in the distant future, while they open their eyes and display, by knowledge and prudence, more watchfulness than any fox or lion, as regards the preparations of these achievements and the seeds to be presently put into the earth.

A merely natural political morality is not enough to provide us with the means of putting its own rules into practice. Moral conscience does not suffice, if it is not at the same time religious conscience. What is able to face Machiavellianism, moderate Machiavellianism and absolute Machiavellianism, is not merely natural, as it were, just politics, it is Christian politics. For, in the existential context of the life of mankind, politics, because it belongs by its very essence to the ethical realm, demands consequently to be helped and strengthened, in order not to deviate and in order to attain a sufficiently perfect point of maturation, by everything man receives, in his social life itself, from religious belief and from the word of God working within him. This is what the authors of the Declaration of Independence and of the Constitution of this country understood and expressed in a form adapted to the philosophy of their time, and what makes their accomplishment so outstanding to the mind of everyone who believes Christianity to be efficacious not only for heaven but also for earth: among modern states, there is one state to whose political instinct and understanding Machiavellianism is basically repugnant, this one is the United States. Christian politics is neither theocratic nor clerical, nor yet a politics of pseudo-evangelical weakness and non-resistance to evil, but a genuinely political politics. It is ever aware that it is situated in the order of nature and must put into practice natural virtues; that it must be armed with real and concrete justice, with force, perspicacity and prudence. This politics would hold the sword that is the attribute of the state, but would also realize that peace is the work not only of justice but of love, and that love is also an essential part of political virtue. For it is never excess of love that fools political men, but without love and generosity there is regularly blindness and miscalculation. Such a politics would be mindful of the eternal destiny of man and of the truths of the Gospel, knowing in its proper order, in a measure adapted to its temporal ends, something of the spirits of love, and of forgiveness.

IV

We arrive now at the third consideration I indicated at the beginning, in which I should like to make clearer certain particular points concerning the relationship between Politics and Morality.

As I have previously pointed out, political reality, though principally moral, is by essence both moral and physical, as man himself, but in a different manner from man, because it does not have any substantial immortal soul. Societies are like ever-growing organisms, immense and long-living trees, or coral-flowers, which would lead at the same time a moral and human life. And in the order to which they belong, which is that of Time and Becoming, death is natural; human communities, nations, states and civilizations naturally die, and die for all time, as would these morally-living coral-flowers of which I just spoke. Their birth, growth and decay, their health, their diseases, their death, depend on basic physical conditions, in which the specific qualities of moral behavior are intermingled and play an essential part, but which are more primitive than these qualities. Similarly, imprudence or intemperance may hasten the death of a man, self control may defer this death, yet in any case this man will die.

Justice and moral virtues do not prevent the natural laws of senescence of human societies. They do not prevent physical catastrophes from destroying them. In what sense are they the chief forces of the preservation and duration of societies? In the sense that they compose the very soul of society, its internal and spiritual force of life. Such a force does not secure immortality to the society, no more than my immortal soul protects me from death. Such a force is not an immortal entelechy, because it is not substantial; yet, insofar as it is spiritual, it is by itself indestructible. Corrupt this force, and an internal principle of death is introduced into the core of the society. Maintain and improve this force, and the internal principle of life is strengthened in the society. Suppose a human community is hammered, crushed, overwhelmed by some natural calamity or some powerful enemy. As long as it still exists, if it preserves within itself justice and civic friendship and faith, there is actual hope of resurging within itself, there is a force within itself which tends by itself to make it live and get the upper hand and avail itself of disaster; because no hammer can destroy this immaterial force. If a human community loses these virtues, its internal principle of life is invaded by death.

What therefore must be said, is that justice and righteousness *tend by themselves* to the preservation of states, and to that real *success* at long range of which I spoke a moment ago. And that injustice and evil *tend by themselves* to the destruction of states, and to that real *failure* at long range of which I also spoke.

Such is the law of the fructification of human actions which is inscribed in the nature of things and which is but the natural justice of God in human history.

But if the normal fruit of success and prosperity called for by political justice and wisdom does not come into actual existence because the tree is too old or because some storm has broken its branches; or if the normal fruit of failure and destruction, called for by political wickedness and madness, does not come into actual existence because the physical conditions in the sap or in the environment have counterbalanced the internal principle of death—such an accident does not suppress that regularity inherent in the law which I emphasized in the previous part of this essay, and only bears witness to the fact that nations and civilizations are naturally mortal. As I pointed out some moments ago, justice may sometimes, even in a distant future, not actually succeed in preserving a state from ruin and destruction. But justice tends by itself to this preservation. It is not by virtue of justice, it is by virtue of physical conditions counterbalancing from without the very effects of justice that misfortune will then occur. Machiavellianism and political perversion may sometimes, even in a distant future, not actually break. They may triumph decisively over weak and innocent peoples. But they tend by themselves to self destruction. And it is not by virtue of Machiavellianism and political perversion, it is by virtue of other conditions counterbalancing from without the very effects of these, that success will then occur.

If a weak state is surrounded and threatened by Machiavellian enemies, it must desperately increase its physical power, but also its moral virtues. Suppose it delivers its own soul to Machiavellianism. Then it only adds a principle of death to its already existing weaknesses. If a civilization grown old and naturally bound to die, as the Roman Empire was at the time of St. Augustine, if a political state artificially and violently built up, and naturally bound to fail, as was the German *Reich* of Bismarck and Wilhelm, wished nonetheless to escape either death or failure by letting loose evil and perversion, then it would only poison centuries and prepare for itself a historical hell worse than death.

It seems not irrelevant to add the two following observations. First: innumerable are, in the history of mankind, the cases where the strong have triumphed over the weak; yet this was not always a triumph of strength over right, for most often right's sanctity was as immaterial to the conquered weak as it was to the conquering strong. Greece was conquered by Rome (and was to conquer intellectually Roman civilization); at that time Greece had lost its political soul.

Second: As to the lasting or seemingly lasting triumphs of political injustice over innocent people, they also are not rare, at least at first glance. They concern most often, however, the enslavement, sometimes the destruction, of populations or human groups not yet arrived at a truly political status by nations enjoying this very status. Of these, the most striking instance is to be found in the history of modern colonization. But it seems that in proportion as peoples arrive at a truly political status, and really constitute a *civitas*, a political house and community, in this proportion the immaterial internal force which abides in them and is made up of long-lived justice and love and moral energies, and of deep-rooted memories, and of a specific spiritual heritage, becomes a more and more *formed* and cohesive soul; and in this very proportion this soul takes precedence over the merely physical conditions of existence and tends to render such peoples unconquerable. If they are conquered and oppressed, they remain alive and keep on struggling under oppression. Then an instinct of prophecy develops among them, as in Poland at the time of Mickiewicz,[15] and their hopes naturally lift up toward the supernatural example of any historical perennity in the midst of oppression (e.g., the house of Israel) whose internal immaterial force and principle of communion is of a suprapolitical and supratemporal order.

Yet a final question arises now, which is of a rather metaphysical nature. I have said that the natural laws, according to which political justice fructifies by itself into the good and the preservation of a given human community, evil and political injustice into its destruction, are to be identified with the natural justice of

God in human history. But is not an essential tendency only connoted here? Did I not emphasize the fact that even at long range such normal fructifications may fail, that the fruit of evil for the unjust state, the fruit of good for the just one, may be marred, because of the physical factors and particularly because of the physical laws of senescence and death which interfere here with the moral factors? If this is the case, where is the natural justice of God? Justice does not deal with tendencies, as essential as they may be, whose factual result may fail to appear, it deals with sanctions which never fail.

The question we are facing here transcends the field of moral philosophy and historical experience, and deals with the knowledge we are able to stammer of the divine government of created things. The first answer which comes to the mind of a Christian metaphysician consists in affirming a priori that the natural fructifications of good and evil never fail. Also, the fruit of justice and the fruit of injustice are never marred, which seems self-evident, since the justice of God cannot be deceived. Because states and nations have no immortal destiny, the sanctions deserved by their deeds must not only reach men within time and upon the earth, but they must do so in an absolutely infallible manner.

In considering the problem more attentively, I believe, however, that this answer results from a kind of undue reverberation of considerations pertaining to theology upon metaphysical matters, which causes things which belong to time and history to be endowed with that absolute firmness which is proper to things relating to eternity.

It is perfectly true that God's justice cannot fail as regards the immortal destiny of each human person, which is accomplished in fact, according to Christianity's teachings, in the supernatural order. Yet it would be too hasty a procedure simply to conceive the divine justice which rules the historical fate of human societies, according to the pattern of that divine justice which rules the suprahistorical destiny of the human person. In these two cases justice applies to its subject matter in an analogical fashion. The suprahistorical justice cannot fail, because it reaches moral agents—the human persons—who attain their final state, above time. But the historical justice, dealing with human societies, reaches moral agents who do not attain any final state. There is no final sanction for them, sanctions are spread out for them all along time, and intermingled at each moment with their continuing and changing activity; often the fruit of ancient injustice starts up into existence at the very moment when a revival of justice occurs in a given society. Moreover, and by the same token, it appears that these sanctions *in the making* do not enjoy that absolute necessity which is linked with the immutability of some ultimate, eternal accomplishment. What seemed to us, a moment ago, to be self-evident, is not self-evident. It is possible that in the case of human societies the natural fructifications of good and evil be sometimes marred. The sanctions deserved by the deeds of nations and states must reach men within time and upon the earth, yet it is not necessary that they do so in a manner absolutely infallible and always realized.

Consider the civilization of the peoples which lived on legendary Atlantis. The good and bad political deeds of these peoples tended by themselves to bear fruit and to engender their natural sanctions. Yes, but when Atlantis was engulfed by the Ocean, all these fruits to come were cancelled from being as well as the peoples and the civilization from which they were to spring forth. The natural justice of God, as regards human societies, that is, moral agents immerged in time, may fail just as nature may fail in its physical fructifications. This is because this natural historical justice of God is nothing else than nature itself in its not physical but moral fructifications. God's justice is at work in time and history, it reigns only in heaven and in hell. The concept of perfect and infallible retribution for human deeds, with its absolute adamantine strength, is a religious concept relating to the eternal destiny of human Persons; it is not the ethico-philosophical concept which has to be shaped relating to the destiny of human communities in time and history.

Such is the answer which appears to me the true answer to be made to the question we are considering. But we must immediately add that these failures of historical justice are to occur in the fewest number of cases, just as do the failures of nature in the physical order, because they are accidents, in which the very laws of essences do not reach their own effect. There is, indeed, in nature an immense squandering of seeds in order that a few may have the chance of springing up, and still fewer the chance of bearing fruit. Even if the failures of natural historical justice were *abnormities as regards individual accomplishment,* as frequent as the failures of so many wasted seeds, the truth that I am pointing out throughout this essay would nonetheless remain unshaken: namely, that justice tends by itself toward the welfare and survival of the community, injustice toward its damage and dissolution, and that any long-range success of Machiavellianism is never due to Machiavellianism itself, but to other historical factors at play. Yet the abnormities which really occur *ut in paucioribus* in physical nature are *abnormities as regards specific accomplishment* as is the production of something deviating from the very essence of the species, the production of "freaks." And it is with such physical abnormities as regards specific accomplishment that the failures of the natural fructifications of good and evil, the failures in the accomplishment of the specific laws of moral essences, must rather be compared. We must therefore emphasize more strongly than ever the fact—which I have already stressed in a previous section—that the sanctions of historical justice fail much more rarely than our shortsighted experience might induce us to believe.

Here a new observation seems to me particularly noticeable. These sanctions, which have been deserved by the deeds of the social or political whole, must not necessarily reverberate on this political whole as such, on the state itself in its existence and power. They may concern the common cultural condition of men considered apart from the actual framework of this whole, yet in some kind of solidarity with the latter. This is so because the political whole is not a substantial or personal subject, but a community of human persons, and a community related to other communities through vital exchanges. Thus, during the life of a state the fruit of its just or perverted deeds may appear only in some particular improvement or plague of its internal strata. But still more, when a state, a nation, a civilization dies, it is normal that the fructifications of good and evil which its deeds had prepared pass over—in the cultural order and as regards such or such a feature of the common social or cultural status—to its remnants, to the scattered human elements which had been contained in its unity and to their descendants, or to the human communities which are its successors and inheritors.

Then a state or a civilization dissolves, but its good or bad works continue to bear fruit, not strictly political (for the word political, in its strictest sense, connotes the common life of a given state), yet political in a broader and still genuine sense, which relates to the cultural life and to the common cultural heritage of mankind. For there exists a genuine temporal community of mankind, a deep intersolidarity, from generation to generation, linking together the peoples of the earth. This is a common heritage and a common fate, which does not concern the building of a particular *civil society*, but of a *civilization;* not the prince, but the culture; not the perfect *civitas* in the Aristotelian sense, but that kind of *civitas*, in the Augustinian sense, which is imperfect and incomplete, made up of a fluid network of human communications, and more existential than formally organized, but all the more real and living and basically important. To ignore this non-political *civitas humani generis* is to atomize the basis of political reality, to fail in the very roots of political philosophy, as well as to disregard the progressive trend which naturally tends toward a more organic international structure of peoples.

Thus another fundamental consideration must be added to that of *historic duration*, which I emphasized some time ago: namely the consideration of the *human extension,* down through generations, of the fructifications of political deeds. Then we see in a complete manner the law which binds Machiavellianism to failure, as a rule and as regards the essential tendencies inscribed in nature. If, even at long range, political justice and political injustice do not ever fructify into the political success or disaster of the state itself which has practiced them, they may still produce their fruit according to the laws of human solidarity. By the same stroke we perceive Machiavellianism's mischievousness, weakness and absurdity in their full implications. It is not only for particular states that it prepares misfortune and scourges—first the victims of Machiavellian states, then the Machiavellian states themselves—it is also for the human race in general. It burdens mankind with an ever-growing burden of evil, unhappiness and disaster. By its own weight and its own internal law it brings about failure, not only with reference to given nations, but with reference to our common kind, with reference to the root community of nations. Just as every other sort of selfishness, this divinized selfishness is essentially blind.

To sum up all that I have stated, I would say the following. First, it suffices to be just in order to gain eternal life; this does not suffice in order to gain battles or immediate political successes.

Second, in order to gain battles or immediate political successes, it is not necessary to be just, it may occasionally be more advantageous to be unjust. Third, it is necessary, although it is not sufficient, to be just, in order to procure and further the political common good, and the lasting welfare of earthly communities.

The considerations I have developed in my essay are founded on the basic fact that Politics is a branch of Ethics but a branch specifically distinct from the other branches of the same generic stock. One decisive sign of this specificity of Political Ethics in contradistinction to Personal Ethics is that earthly communities are mortal as regards their very being and belong entirely to time. Another sign is that political virtues tend to a relatively ultimate end which is the earthly common good, and are only indirectly related to the absolutely ultimate end of man. Hence many features of Political Ethics which I can only allude to here, and which secure its truly realist quality; in such a way that many rules of political life, which the pessimists of Machiavellianism usurp to the benefit of immorality, like the political toleration of certain evils and the recognition of the *fait accompli* (the so-called "statute of limitations") which permits the retention of long ago ill-gotten gains, because new human ties and vital relationships have infused them with newborn rights, are in reality ethically grounded; and in such a way that Political Ethics is able to absorb and digest all the elements of truth contained in Machiavelli, namely, to the extent that power and immediate success are part of politics, but a subordinate part, not the principal part.

May I repeat that a certain hypermoralism, causing Political Ethics to be something impracticable and merely ideal, is as contrary to this very Ethics as Machiavellianism is, and finally plays the game of Machiavellianism, as conscientious objectors play the game of the conquerors. The purity of means consists in not using means morally bad in themselves, it does not consist in refusing pharisaically any exterior contact with the mud of human life, and it does not consist in waiting for a morally aseptic world before consenting to work in the world, nor does it consist in waiting, before saving one's neighbor, who is drowning, to become a saint, so as to escape any risk of false pride in such a generous act.

If this were the time to present a complete analysis of the particular causes of lasting success and welfare in politics, I should add two observations here. First, while political justice—which is destroyed both by the perversion, that is, by Machiavellianism, and by the distraction of Ethics, that is, by Hypermoralism—is the prime spiritual condition of lasting success and welfare for a nation as well as for a civilization, the prime *material* condition of this lasting success and welfare is on the one hand that heritage of accepted and unquestionable structures, fixed customs and deep-rooted common feelings which bring into social life itself something of the determined physical data of nature,[16] and of the vital unconscious strength proper to vegetative organisms; and on the other hand that common inherited experience and that set of moral and intellectual instincts which constitute a kind of empirical practical wisdom, much deeper and denser and much nearer the hidden complex dynamism of human life than any artificial construction of reason. And both this somewhat physical heritage and this inherited practical wisdom are intrinsically and essentially bound to and dependent upon moral and religious beliefs. As regards Political Ethics and political common good, the preservation of these common structures of life and of this common moral dynamism is more fundamental than any particular action of the prince, however serious and decisive this may be in itself. And the workings of such a vast, deep-seated, physico-moral energy are more basic and more important to the life of human societies than particular political good or bad calculations, they are for states the prime cause of historic success and welfare. The Roman Empire did not succeed by virtue of the stains, injustices and cruelties, which were intermingled in its policy, but by virtue of this internal physico-moral strength.

Now, and this is my second observation: what is in itself, even in the order of material causality, primarily and basically destructive of lasting historic success and welfare for a nation as well as for a civilization, is that which is destructive of the common stock and heritage I just described: that is, Machiavellianism on the one hand and Hypermoralism on the other. Both destroy, as do gnawing worms, the inner social and ethical living substance upon which depends any lasting success and welfare, of the commonwealth, as well as that political justice which constitutes the moral righteousness, the chief moral virtue and the very "soul" of human societies.

Thus the split, the deadly division created between Ethics and Politics both by Machiavellianists and by Hypermoralists, is overcome. This is because Politics is essentially ethical, and because Ethics is essentially realistic, not in the sense of any *Realpolitik* but in the sense of a real common good.

I am aware that if this antinomy, which has been the scourge of modern history, is to be practically, not only theoretically, overcome, it will be only on condition that a kind of revolution take place in our conscience. Machiavelli has made us conscious of what is in fact the average behavior of politics in mankind. In this he was right. It is a natural incline that the man who endeavors to overcome dissociation, the man of unity, has to climb up again. But inclines are made to be climbed. As Henri Bergson pointed out, a genuine democracy, by the very fact that it proceeds from an evangelic motive power, works against the grain of nature and therefore needs some heroic inspiration.

With whatever deficiencies human weakness may encumber the practical issue, the fact remains, in any case, that such an effort must be made, and the knowledge of what is true in these matters is of first and foremost importance. To keep Machiavelli's awareness, with reference to the factual conduct of most of the princes, and to know that this conduct is bad politics, and to clear our conscience from Machiavelli's rules, precepts and philosophy—this is the very end of Machiavellianism.

Here I emphasize anew what I pointed out at the beginning of this essay. Machiavellianism does not consist of this unhappy lot of particular evil and unjust political deeds which are taking place in fact by virtue of human weakness or wickedness. Machiavellianism is a philosophy of politics, stating that by rights good politics is supramoral or immoral politics and by essence must make use of evil. What I have discussed is this political philosophy. There will be no end to the occurrence of misdeeds and mistakes as long as humanity endures. To Machiavellianism there can and must be an end.

Let us conclude. Machiavellianism is an illusion, because it rests upon the power of evil, and because, metaphysically, evil as such has no power as a cause of being; practically, evil has no power as a cause of any lasting achievement. As to moral entities like peoples, states, and nations, which do not have any supratemporal destiny, it is within time that their deeds are sanctioned, it is upon earth that the entire charge of failure and nothingness with which is charged every evil action committed by the whole or by its heads, will normally be exhausted. This is a natural, a somewhat physical law in the moral order, although thwarted in some cases by the interference of the manifold other factors at play in human history. As a rule Machiavellianism and political injustice, if they gain immediate success, lead states and nations to misfortune or catastrophe in the long run. In cases where they seem to succeed even in the long run, this is not by virtue of evil and political injustice, but by virtue of some inner principle of misfortune already binding their victim to submission, even if the latter did not have to face such iniquitous enemies. One possibility is that the victims of power politics are primitive tribes which had been in a state of inexistence as to political life and therefore as to political justice. Their unjustly suffered misfortune, which cries out against heaven and makes God's justice more implacable with regard to the personal destiny of their executioners, does not reverberate upon the unjustly conquering state, unless in the form of some hidden and insidious, not openly political, self-poisoning process. The other possibility is that the victims of power politics are states and nations which were already condemned to death or enslavement by the natural laws of senescence of human societies or by their own internal corruption. And here also the very effect of the injustice which has been used against them is to introduce a hidden principle of self-destruction into the inner substance of their conquerors.

In truth the dialectic of injustice is unconquerable. Machiavellianism devours itself. Common Machiavellianism has devoured and annihilated Machiavelli's Machiavellianism; absolute Machiavellianism devours and annihilates moderate Machiavellianism. Weak or attenuated Machiavellianism is fatally destined to be vanquished by absolute and virulent Machiavellianism.

If someday absolute Machiavellianism triumphs over mankind, this will only be because all kinds of accepted iniquity, moral weakness and consent to evil, operating within a degenerating civilization, will previously have corrupted it, and prepared ready-made slaves for the lawless man. But if for the time being absolute Machiavellianism is to be crushed, and I hope so, it will only be because what remains of Christian civilization will have been able to oppose it with the principle of political justice integrally recognized, and to proclaim to the world the very end of Machiavellianism.

There is only one determining principle before which the principle of Machiavellianism finds itself spiritually reduced to impotence: that is the principle of real and absolutely unwavering political justice, as St. Louis understood it. Men will have to spring up to array against the knighthood of human degradation the true knighthood of justice.

The justice of which I speak is not an unarmed justice. It uses force when force is necessary. I believe in the effectiveness of the methods of Gandhi, but I think that they are suitable only in certain limited fields of political activity. Especially in the case of war, other means must be used. And when one considers the course of the wars waged by total Machiavellianism, one can but wonder to what extent aggressors, who respect nothing, force the rest of mankind to have recourse to the terrible law of just reprisals, or to put aside momentarily, if a superior concept of justice necessitates our doing so, certain juridical rules which the barbarous action of the adversary has rendered inefficacious in justice.

But the more forceful and even horrible the means required by justice, the more perfect should be the men who use them. The world requires, for the affirmation to the end, and the application without fear, of the terrible powers of justice, men truly resolved to suffer everything for justice, truly understanding the part to be played by the State as judge, the part which according to the great theologian Francisco de Vitoria, belligerent States assume in the absence of any international entity endowed with universal jurisdiction. These would be men truly certain of preserving within themselves, in the midst of the scourges of the Apocalypse, a flame of love stronger than death.

In his introduction to Machiavelli, Max Lerner emphasizes the dilemma with which democracies are now confronted. This dilemma seems to me perfectly clear. Either they perish by continuing to accept, more or less willingly, the principle of Machiavellianism, or they regenerate by consciously and decidedly rejecting this principle. For what we call democracy or the commonwealth of free men is by definition a political regime of men the spiritual basis of which is uniquely and exclusively law and right. Such a regime is by essence opposed to Machiavellianism and incompatible with it. Totalitarianism lives by Machiavellianism, freedom dies by it. The only Machiavellianism of which any democracy as such is capable is the attenuated and weak Machiavellianism. Facing absolute Machiavellianism, the democratic states, inheritors of the Ancien Régime and of its old Machiavellian policy, will therefore keep on using weak Machiavellianism and be destroyed from without, or they will decide to have recourse to absolute Machiavellianism, which is only possible with totalitarian rule and totalitarian spirit. Thus, they will destroy themselves from within. They will survive and take the upper hand only on condition that they break with every kind of Machiavellianism.

The end of Machiavellianism, that is the aim, that is the moral revolution to which, in the depth of human history, amidst savage wars which must be waged with inflexible determination, free men are now summoned.

NOTES

Reprinted from *The Review of Politics* 4, no. 1 (January 1942): 1–33.

1. This lecture was delivered in an abbreviated form at the symposium on "The Place of Ethics in Social Science," held in connection with the 50th Anniversary celebration at the University of Chicago, September 26, 1941. John U. Nef chaired the session, which included three other speakers, the university's president R. M. Hutchins, R. H. Tawney and C. H. McIlwain.

2. See Allan H. Gilbert, *Machiavelli's* Prince *and its Forerunners*; The Prince *as a Typical Book* De Regimine Principum (Durham: Duke University Press, 1938). I think that Professor Gilbert is right in locating *The Prince* in the series of the classical treatises *De Regimine Pricipum.* Yet *The Prince* marks the end of this series, not only because of the political changes in society, but because its inspiration utterly reverses and corrupts the medieval notion of government. It is a typical book *De Regimine Principum,* but which typically puts the series of these books to death.

3. Max Lerner, Introduction to *The Prince and the Discourses* by Niccolò Machiavelli (New York Modern Library, 1950), xxi and xlii.

4. Matt. 23:3.

5. Cf. Raissa Maritain, "Histoire d'Abraham ou la Sainteté dans l'état de nature," in *Nova et Vetera,* no. 3 (1935).

6. Allan H. Gilbert notes that "In these things lie the true originality of Machiavelli; all may be summed up in his conviction that government is an independent art in an imperfect world," *Machiavelli's* Prince *and Its Forerunners,* 235.

7. According to a very just remark by Friedrich Meinecke, the two concepts of *fortune* and *necessity* complete the trilogy of the leading ideas of Machiavelli: *Virtù, Fortuna, Necessità.* Cf. Meinecke, *Die Idee der Staatsräson* (Munich and Berlin: Oldenbourg, 1924), chapter 1.

8. Some authors magnify the divergences between the *Prince* and the *Discourses.* In my opinion these divergences, which are real, relate above all to the literary genus of the two works, and remain quite secondary. The *Discourses on the first ten Books of Titus Livius*

owed it to their own rhetorical and academic mood as well as to Roman antiquity to emphasize the republican spirit and some classical aspects of political virtue. In reality neither this virtue (in the sense of the Ancients) nor this spirit ever mattered to Machiavelli, and his own personal inspiration, his quite amoral art of using *virtù* to master fortune by means of occasion and necessity are as recognizable in the *Discourses* as in the *Prince*.

9. Lerner, Introduction, xxxvii.

10. [Acton's quote is to be found in *The History of Freedom, and Other Essays*, ed. John Neville Figgis and Reginald Vere Laurence (London: Macmillan and Co., 1922), n.p. Ed.]

11. "Hitler told me he had read and reread the *Prince* of the Great Florentine. To his mind, this book is indispensable to every political man. For a long time it did not leave Hitler's side. The reading of these unequalled pages, he said, was like a cleansing of the mind. It had disencumbered him from plenty of false ideas and prejudices. It is only after having read the *Prince* that Hitler understood what politics truly is." Hermann Rauschning, *Hitler m'a dit* (Paris: Coopération, 1939). [In 1985, Rudolf Haenel, a Swiss schoolteacher demonstrated that Rauschning's book was merely a compendium of others' accounts and not to be taken seriously. See *Der Spiegel* 37 (1985): 92–99. However, Maritain's point seems perfectly defensible. Ed.]

12. Matt. 4:10.

13. What Sir Norman Angell said in Boston in April, 1941, is true for all contemporary democracies. "If we applied," he said with great force,

ten years ago resolutely the policy of aiding the victim of aggression to defend himself, we should not now be at war at all.

It is a simple truth to say that because we in Britain were deaf to the cries rising from the homes of China smashed by the invader, we now have to witness the ruthless destruction by invaders of ancient English shrines.

Because we would not listen to the cries of Chinese children massacred by the invader we have now, overnight, to listen to the cries of English children, victims of that same invader's ally.

Because we were indifferent when Italian submarines sank the ships of republican Spain we must now listen to the cries of children from the torpedoed refugee ship going down in the tempest 600 miles from land.

But the remote responsibilities thus alluded to by Sir Norman Angell go back much farther than ten years. Western civilization is now paying a bill prepared by the faults of all modern history.

[Angell, an economist and Member of Parliament, was awarded the Nobel Peace Prize in 1933. Ed.]

14. [I have added these six words to make the sentence comprehensible. Ed.]

15. [Adam Mickiewicz was a Polish romantic poet and playwright who protested against Russian control of Poland and was arrested and exiled in 1823. Ed.]

16. See my "The Political Ideas of Pascal," in *Ransoming the Time* (New York: Charles Scribner's, 1941).

CHAPTER 7

Philosophical Values and the Future of Civilization

JOHN U. NEF

John U. Nef, Jr. (1899–1988) was born in Chicago, Illinois. He studied economic history at Harvard University and then joined the Economics Department at the University of Chicago. Nef quickly built a reputation as an eclectic or, as he put it, "unclassified" scholar, publishing on conventional topics like the British coal industry and the causes of war but also delving into other areas of Western civilization, including the history of architecture and the arts. For him, artistic expression was a prime vehicle for conveying the richness of the human experience. Along with Robert M. Hutchins, Nef was instrumental in founding the university's interdisciplinary Committee on Social Thought. His aim for the Committee was to educate students in the major texts of Western civilization and to dissuade them from falling prey to modern society's obsession with specialization. He aspired to build a bridge between the academy and the outside world that would enable graduates to contribute in original ways to resolving the great problems before humanity, above all its pointless recourse to war. Aside from being an institution-builder, Nef created an air of intellectual excitement at the university by hosting a stunning array of scholars, artists, and writers in his Chicago apartment, including such diverse personalities as Hannah Arendt, Waldemar Gurian, Marc Chagall, Igor Stravinsky, Arnold Schönberg, and Arnold Toynbee.

In an article published in the July 1942 number of *The Review of Politics*,[1] I suggested that contemporary learned men who deny the existence of truth, virtue, or beauty, are led into a dilemma. Either they must confine truth to positive science, where the results are always tentative and incomplete with respect to the universe in which human beings have to move, or else they must believe that people generally will be inclined towards good and wise actions even though learning refuses to admit the existence of standards, apart from the rules of conduct that can be derived from positive science. The second view, we suggested, involves the admission that impersonal standards do exist, independent of positive science. We might conclude that the nourishment of these standards by means of the intellect, and with the help of results obtained by science, ought to be the supreme task of learning.

I

Even when the existence of abstract standards is admitted, it is denied that abstract reasoning can give them meaning, or that schooling in reasoning can help men and women to conduct their lives in accordance with them. In the United States there is a group of learned men who admit that it is theoretically possible to distinguish good from bad, truth in the abstract from falsehood, beauty from ugliness, but who deny that philosophical and aesthetic training can do any more than scientific training to bring men nearer to the goals of human existence here on earth. Philosophy and theology had their innings down to the seventeenth or eighteenth centuries, these learned men tell us, and consider all the wars and horrors that took place in classical and medieval times. This proves that philosophy is no more able than science to make men better or wiser, or to teach them good taste.

This argument takes many forms and few of them are devoid of evasions. It would be impossible to treat all the forms adequately in brief compass. It would be foolish to try to treat all the evasions. The difficulty seems to arise, as we have already suggested, mainly because, in their higher reaches, truth, beauty, and virtuous conduct are not susceptible either to scientific proof, in the natural scientist's sense of experiment and observation, or to mathematical demonstration. The distinction between a Rembrandt and a Potts, between a play by Shakespeare and one by Thomas Nash, between a score of Johann Sebastian and one of Johann Michael Bach can be comprehended by only a trained and developed taste. Without any important exceptions, the great artists of recent generations and the critics who have established durable reputations have agreed as to the right choice between these pairs of artists. It does not follow that all great works of Western art have been recognized for what they are. It is quite possible that circumstances have prevented many masterworks from coming to the serious attention of the great artists and critics of modern times. Bach's work was practically unknown for many decades, before it found its impregnable place in musical literature. But the endowment and training of the true artist and the genuine critic have put them in a position to apply, to a work which circumstances oblige them seriously to contemplate, standards independent of their personal idiosyncrasies, independent of their tissues, standards which transcend science in the modern sense of the term. Their chances of making mistakes are much smaller than those of an untrained adolescent mechanic or an African tribesman.

It is frequently pointed out that these standards have not saved them from grievous errors concerning the works of artists who were their contemporaries. Their want of capacity for judging contemporary art has been exaggerated in recent times. That is because the opinions of the vulgar are more freely expressed, given greater prominence, and treated more seriously than ever in the past; and because vulgar men and narrow specialists alike find it convenient to emphasize the failings or the mediocrity of men of talent or of greatness. The public seldom has any way of distinguishing between good and bad critics, or of knowing whether there is a foundation for the criticisms they hear so freely expressed concerning the views of critics who are in fact entitled to make judgments. It remains true that among persons of genuine taste and judgment there is generally far less agreement concerning present than concerning past art. The explanation is simple. While it never breaks completely with tradition, a truly great work of art always contains a fresh conception. Its unique character makes it difficult to understand. John Maynard Keynes once confessed that his knowledge of German was elementary, and that in reading works in German he understood only what he already knew! A great work of art partakes in this respect of the character of a new language. That enhances the difficulty which even men of exceptional gifts, like Keynes, have in recognizing its quality and importance. Yet the gifted, disinterested, and audacious artist or artistic critic, who takes the existence of artistic standards for granted (elusive though those standards must remain), has a far better chance of recognizing true art than a person without native and cultivated taste.

When we say that art and science are distinct, we are not denying the value of either to man, or suggesting that no society could cultivate both at the same time, or that they have no elements in common. The point to understand is that the ends of the two are different, and that a recognition of the difference is fundamental to successful treatment of either. The aim of science is to find out about the universe—by analyzing matter, examining space, and so on—and to make generalizations concerning the body, the physical world in which we live, and the distant heavens. The aim of art is to use the materials about us to create with the mind a work of lasting beauty. Good technique is essential to both the artist and the scientist, but the technique appropriate to the tasks of each differs in *kind* as well as in detail, because the object for which it is used differs. While the technique of the modern machine shop and that of the hospital are close to the technique of the laboratory, they are more distant from the technique of the great artist's studio. There the object is to analyze and manipulate matter in relation to beautiful, permanent, and unique forms, lines, or colors. In the twelfth and thirteenth centuries the artist managed to create by *artistic* experiments and without power-driven machinery a species of glass, known as ruby glass, which formed an integral part of the jeweled mosaics in the windows of the cathedrals. Such color has never been recovered. The modern world, with its tons of glass, and all its elaborately appointed, mechanical workshops, is incapable of producing a genuine equivalent for medieval ruby glass.

There is a sharp conflict between the objectives of the modern industrial technician and those of the artist. Cézanne is reported to have remarked that the straight lines of modern industry were destroying the world of the arts. "Is there a straight line in nature?" he asked.

It is possible, of course, for a genuine artist to make an artistic use of the subject matter which modern industry provides. He may incorporate into his work factories, railroads, automobiles, and airplanes, or abstract lines and forms. But the purpose for which, and the spirit in which, most modern industrial structures are built is far more alien to a true artistic conception than the purpose and spirit embodied in medieval and even in Renaissance edifices. It is much more disastrous for an artistic result when a painter or sculptor adopts the attitude towards his subject matter which dominates in the construction of a factory, a motor car, or a permanent way, than when he adopts the attitude which dominated in the construction of chateaux like Langeais or Anet and churches like Brou at Bourg-en-Bresse, or in the making of the furniture and other decorations which adorned their interiors. This does not mean that art has ever been achieved merely by copying nature, or by copying nature as embroidered by human artistry in the wonderful landscapes of Provence and the Ile-de-France, which inspired Cézanne and Renoir. Steep hills—with castles, cottages, winding paths, and old stone bridges—have to be transmuted into art in the painter's mind no less than factories or mines. When Cézanne spoke of the damage done to the cause of beauty by the straight line of the railroad and the industrial plant, he did not mean that the old world presented the artist with his subjects ready-made. He is said to have been horrified by a cartoon in which he was represented as hugging a tree and exclaiming, "how I wish I could carry this on to my canvas." What he seems to have meant when he spoke as he did of straight lines, was that the older pre-industrialized world, with its highly sophisticated arts and crafts, its well-worn objects, and its natural blemishes, presented the artist with greater variety, greater humanity, than the clinical atmosphere and the shiny newness of the modern going concern, or the complete confusion and decadence of modern empty lots strewn with the disintegrating metal of once speedy automobiles. The spread of the methods of natural science and mechanical technology—together with the spread of the scientific and mechanical attitude towards workmanship into the institutes and schools ostensibly devoted to training artists—have placed great obstacles in the way of art that the artist of earlier generations escaped.

The new devices created by modern science for circulating sound and written matter have made it far easier than in the past to confuse with works of art stuff which masquerades as such. University professors confuse material comforts with culture, to which the comforts contribute only indirectly, if at all. As evidence of "cultural improvement" among the French Catholics in Canada, statistics are cited to show that their attendance at church has been decreasing while their attendance at motion pictures has been increasing. The specialization and departmentalization of functions which has characterized alike industrial development and the pursuit of knowledge, during the past two centuries or so, has permeated artistic work to the damage of art. Success in art depends, in part, upon thorough knowledge of all the materials and processes used. It depends, in addition, upon a conception of the whole in relation to which all the materials and processes must be ordered. It is easily possible for an essayist or historian to achieve almost perfect accuracy in detail and at the same time to obtain a total result which is entirely false, unless he is guided by a purpose which embraces all the particulars, but is something more than the sum of them. A great division of labor makes increasingly easy the production of cheap objects; it makes increasingly difficult the fashioning of beautiful and meaningful ones.

All these obstacles more than offset the advantages of greater wealth and leisure. They make art more difficult for the American than it has been for his European ancestors since at least the twelfth century.

Artistic purpose has become more not less important in the modern industrialized world than in Europe in the Gothic period and the Renaissance. We have been told often during the past fifty years or so that the artist can be successful only by adjusting himself to the environment created by industrialism, and drawing his inspiration from machinery, factories, and smoke. If we are concerned with his artistic success, it is far more important that the environment should be adjusted to art. The relation of art to the modern world of steel, steam, and electricity has been misunderstood. If modern man is to make a permanent contribution to art, he must labor to approach artistic standards even more than in the past. As there is a wider disposition to deny the existence of such standards than at any earlier period in the history of Western civilization, and as ignorant denials or misunderstandings, and the vulgarity that accompanies them, obtain through the radio, the newspapers, and the popular magazines a prominence unparalleled in the past, such concentration requires more effort. It requires more training and encouragement than ever before, at the very time when it is suggested that we can do nothing by education to increase beauty, truth, and virtue in the world. We can easily understand why men are discouraged from making the attempt. But the fact that the task has become more difficult than it was, is no excuse for evading it. For men of courage the difficulties constitute a challenge.

As personified in the great artist, artistic standards are made up of a very highly complicated mixture of qualities. Among these, a knowledge of the difficult technique of his art is indispensable but insufficient. So is an understanding of the qualities and possibilities of the materials that he uses. All this knowledge and skill must be combined with, and subordinated to, an intense need on the part of the artist to rise out of himself, because he has something important to say to mankind, because he has tremendous powers of observation and the wit to transmute his observations and experiences into a progression full of surprise and variety, yet perfect in its inevitability, once the surprise and variety are understood. The artist must have a profound conviction in the value of his art and in the value of what he is trying to express. The wit and charm, the capacity for disinterested statement, and the force of belief required to achieve the intensity without which there can be no great art are doubtless attained partly as a result of peculiarities in the cells of the human embryo, partly as a result of the circumstances of life into which the genius is thrown. But the nature of the cells and the character of the circumstances defy complete scientific analysis, as does still more the art which emerges from them. To reduce a work of art or a great artist to a scientific formula is to deny the very essence of art, which is independent of the individual, of time, and of place. Art is the possession of all human beings insofar as their heredity and their environment, including their *training* in art, enable them to appreciate it and to grasp something of its meaning.

Are we not now in a position to understand why the very reasons offered in the modern world against the existence of disinterested artistic standards are, philosophically considered, evidence of their existence? Are we not in a position to understand why it is only by drilling into human beings in the schools, colleges, and universities, in the churches, and through the periodicals, that such standards exist, that we can hope to strengthen or even to retain them? The artists make the standards. It is not for others to deny that these standards exist because they are not able fully to comprehend them. If it were possible to analyze, in terms of natural science, mechanics, and logic, the qualities that distinguish a great work of art, then there would be no such thing as art. The kind of standards which are demanded in the modern world as evidence of the possibility of distinguishing between good and bad are standards which art cannot supply.

The ultimate standards which give art a place of its own are transcendental. That does not make them dependent on the self. The transcendental is the common possession of human kind, far more than are the results of laboratory experiments and objective tests. It is concerned with universals; experiments and tests with particulars. The denial of the transcendental is a denial of the only realm where all human minds can meet. Such a denial throws men back on the self, and makes objectivity not less, as some pragmatists have assumed, but more difficult. The issue is confused because training in technique and a power to assimilate the sense experiences of the world are essential to art, while a knowledge of certain aspects of modern mechanics and of the results in the physical or biological sciences may be helpful. In themselves they all leave out the guiding purpose to which all of them need to be *ordered*. Without that purpose, all the rest is *artistically* nothing. It is that purpose—ever elusive, ever indefinable—that makes it possible for man to create *beauty*. The capacity to comprehend so much and subordinate all to a principle is exceedingly rare. Yet the product is universal. He who can achieve it has achieved a work that can be passed on to the future,

> For ever warm and still to be enjoy'd,
> For ever panting, and for ever young ... [2]

II

What has been said of beauty, should be said also of abstract truth and of virtue—the subject matter of metaphysics and moral philosophy. Philosophy is concerned with being; moral philosophy with what ought to be done; art with what is beautiful. The controlling principle in all can be found only in the realm of the transcendental, and, if that is not recognized, there can be no genuine metaphysics or moral philosophy, any more than there can be genuine art. This does not mean, as the vulgar suppose, that everyone can reason philosophically. The mere yearnings of the child, without knowledge or training, are no doubt excursions into the transcendental, the wonderful kingdom which can give a meaning to human life apparently denied to the animals. These yearnings are not to be confused with *philosophical reasoning*, though as felt by some human beings they are the stuff out of which it grows. Its development depends upon a profound and ordered knowledge of the world about us, of past learning, and of the philosophical tradition, together with training in objectivity, taught partly by logic, partly by insistence on humility and love of humanity. To be valuable, philosophy must be rooted in the experience of the age, as great art must be. Like great art, it must make use of the materials provided by the age. But a vast supply of knowledge is no more philosophy than a great number of documents and careful notes is a work of literature. Like great art, great philosophy can be achieved only when the man of genius manages to rise above his circumstances, his time, and himself.

The idea is prevalent in certain modern philosophical schools that any attempt at philosophical generalization must be either untrue or merely a verbal truism, valueless for either knowledge or moral conduct. But unless it is possible to reach with the mind—objectively—rough generalizations concerning what men ought to do, we are left with two alternatives. Either these generalizations will be derived exclusively from some "authority"—like the National Socialist leader—an authority that is treated as above human reason, or else everyone will be left free to do whatever his tissues prompt. In the realm of moral philosophy the choice will be between government by decree or anarchy. In either case the learned profession will have abdicated its share in determining the course of men's moral conduct or even the nature of the standards toward which men should aim.

The work of the moral philosopher, like that of the artist, has been rendered more rather than less difficult by the rise of modern industrialism. Just as the nature of industrial labor partakes less of artistry than before the general adoption of machinery, so the hail of publicity and advertising, made possible by modern science and industry, beats upon the public and even upon the learned man right through the University walls that are supposed to shield him. It interferes with disinterested, informed reasoning. Modern men respond less to the promptings of their tissues, than to the slogans and the half-baked advice hurled at them over the radio to drive their tissues into the kind of response that business or politics demands. The material of the modern world might be incorporated into true philosophy as well as into genuine art. But with philosophy as with art, it has become more rather than less necessary to cultivate a philosophical purpose independent of the world about us. The adjustment that we are all urged to make to this industrialized world is exactly what the moral philosopher must avoid.

If there is any truth in Aristotle's statement that man is a rational animal, that all men possess at least a spark of rationality, then the advantage of permitting wise men, with their minds, a share in the determination of standards of moral conduct is very great. If men are to live in societies of any kind, and especially in great societies like those of modern times, it is indispensable that there should be standards against which they can measure their day-to-day conduct. When these standards have been determined with the help of human reason, it is possible for all men and women, according to their intelligence and training, to recognize with their *minds* the soundness of these standards. They can get an inkling of the process by which these standards were arrived at. That is the only basis for true democracy, for government based ultimately not on fear but on assent. It is said that human beings generally are incapable of exercising such intelligence. This may be true. If it is, democracy is doomed. The natural scientist, with all his knowledge, cannot supply the principles that are necessary to establish a rational moral order, unless there are philosophers capable of absorbing, integrating, and relating his knowledge to moral purposes.

There is danger when the philosopher withdraws from the physical world and speculates without reference to new discoveries. Such a withdrawal is especially conspicuous when knowledge in the physical and biological sciences increases rapidly, as it has done during the past three or four centuries. It was partly a wholesome sense of the need for contact with the new discoveries in the natural sciences that prompted the best of the pragmatists in their teaching and writing. The philosopher must strive to comprehend, to order, and to integrate, the vast supply of fresh knowledge supplied by science, anthropology, and history in recent times. Aristotle was undoubtedly a greater philosopher than he would have been had he not acquired a complete knowledge of science. A great modern philosophy can hardly be built without an understanding of the science of our age comparable to that which Aristotle had of his. But the tendency in the universities in recent times has been to suggest that natural science, or still worse some particular natural science, can operate in the name of philosophy. The tendency has been to deny all objectivity to speculations in the realm of the transcendental.

It is speculations in that realm which must control philosophical activity, including the study of science, if we are to have philosophy, just as speculations in the same realm, but related to a different yet closely-allied purpose, must control all artistic activities if we are to have art. One has only to read the *Ethics* of Aristotle, in an objective way, to recognize that knowledge and wisdom in the philosophical sphere have a far greater permanence than has knowledge of biology, physics, or chemistry. These touch what are, in relation to the vast universe open to man's mind, only small, though important, segments of experience. In spite of modern science the secret of life still eludes us. It must always elude us, unless mankind should be merged into God. Why should it be necessary to lose the objectivity which comes from a recognition of the transcendental, and from the training of men to grope by reason towards transcendental truth, in order to gain the less comprehensive objectivity which is the fruit of experiments with, and observations of, the physical world? Knowledge in the kingdom of the transcendental and knowledge in the realm of the physical are generally treated as incompatible. They could coexist to their great mutual advantage, and to the advantage of mankind. To bring about their coexistence is the central problem of learning.

III

It is idle to argue that the attitude towards learning prevalent in the United States, or the structure of the modern university, is suited to the solution of this central problem. What is needed is philosophy nourished by the new knowledge which has been discovered and which will be discovered, but philosophy encouraged to use this knowledge for philosophical ends in the Platonic and Aristotelian sense. Philosophy would begin with a few very simple propositions, to which *as general propositions* there would be no serious dissent in either the humanist or the Christian traditions, as these have come to us across some 2,400 years of history. Among such general propositions, these would be prominent: Truth is preferable to falsehood, discussion to force, loyalty to faithlessness, knowledge to ignorance, love to hate, beauty to ugliness, skill to bungling, courage to cowardliness, humility to pride, temperance to gluttony, justice to power. The acceptance of such propositions as these as standards (call them prejudices if you will) has been essential to the conduct of civilization at its highest. They are in accord with the gospel of Christ. They have been reached independently of Christ's teaching by the disinterested human mind groping towards the truth. The more life on earth can, in fact, be ordered to such propositions, the better it will be for mankind. A wise friend,[3] who is regarded as a follower of the pragmatists, and who so regards himself, has written: "If the authority of human wisdom is ever and anywhere to be established, and if there is to be a knowledge of good and evil independently of the individual, there must be customs and traditions that are not only felt but are generally recognized to be binding upon all of us, at least all of us living in the same cultural unit. There can be no society, in the human sense of the term, except there be a generally recognized moral order."

The acceptance of such propositions as those we have set forth would have to be binding on philosophers. It is true that the propositions do not provide men with a rule of thumb guide to conduct. If they did they would not have general validity. One may appear to conflict with others. It is evident that in a world of some two thousand million souls the application of such principles to the human race as a whole, rather than to individuals, to institutions, to racial groups, or to nations, is an exceedingly complicated matter!

One of the tasks of a true philosophy of value, would be to give these simple propositions content and meaning, to resolve apparent conflicts between them, by showing how they are related to each other, and how one may be subordinated to others in the interest of the highest human good. Another of the tasks of a true philosophy of value would be to resolve the apparent conflicts between their application to individuals, to groups, to societies, and to the human race in general. In this last instance, it can be readily shown how a problem which might seem, at first sight, to be theoretically insoluble, is in fact less difficult than we would suppose. If we emphasize (in place of the *self-interest* and individual predilections which are now regarded as the only basis for action or thought) propositions that have universal human validity, we find that one of the gravest causes for conflict is removed. If, for example, a section of mankind, like the Negroes of the South, the Jews of New York, or the labor unionists in the mining and metallurgical industry, have as their sole principle of action, as at present, the betterment of the welfare of their group, and of themselves as individuals within their group, there is nothing specifically human in their objectives. Such a principle frequently conflicts both with the general welfare of the human race and with the welfare of the nation of which these groups form a part. But suppose these groups could be brought instead, under the influence of custom founded upon sound philosophy, to work for the establishment among themselves of truth, loyalty, knowledge, love, beauty, skill, courage, humility, temperance, and justice. Insofar as they abandoned their concern for advancing their own private interests or those of their group, in favor of the cultivation of these goods within it, they would add to the supply of them throughout the world. Unlike the scramble for material commodities, unlike the struggle for power, the search for the highest goods of the mind or spirit does nothing to deprive other persons or groups of these goods.

It becomes the duty, then, of the philosopher to set up these abstract propositions as the ultimate values for humanity, against which all other human and non-human values, economic and social and even racial and national, should be measured. The alternative values at their worst would probably result in the triumph over humankind of some super-race—the "Aryan" Germans or the Japanese. The alternative values at their best are better health, less toil, longer life, and more material wealth, as ultimate ends.

These are all excellent things, and it would be a part of the task of philosophy and of learning to show how wealth and health could be increased for the benefit of man. The point to grasp is that the material do not comprehend the ultimate values, and may be incompatible with them (as, for example, the removal of all need for toil removes purpose from life), while the ultimate values, when properly understood as they were by the greatest Greek and Christian philosophers, do comprehend the more limited material values. Pursued as ends, beauty, truth, and goodness include better health, longer life, and more material wealth for human societies. If properly ordered to the higher goods of the mind and spirit, and considered in its proper proportions, material improvement helps men to seek knowledge, skill, beauty, and love; it helps men to be courageous, humble, temperate, and just; it helps men to settle their differences by discussion rather than by force.

Yet if wealth, health, long life, and freedom from toil are pursued by individuals or societies for their own sake, regardless of the ends of moral philosophy, the objects which alone can justify human existence are bound to be lost sight of. As long as there is what my wise pragmatist friend calls a recognized moral order, as there was among the peoples of Western civilization in the eighteenth and nineteenth centuries, the dangers inherent in the pursuit of wealth, health, and long life are mitigated by the existence of other firm values to which individuals and groups subordinate, in some measure, their material objectives. As long as there is a recognized moral order, founded on reason and discussion, it is possible, as he says, to tolerate dissenters and people with quaint customs and beliefs, like the Mennonites of Pennsylvania or the African tribesmen. Superstition and false doctrine sometimes contain fragments of truth and these may, if there is a moral order based on rational thought, be assimilated into that order.

They may enrich it. Without a recognized moral order they do nothing more than provide ammunition for persons to demonstrate the futility for man of striving philosophically toward the good.

Much has been made by the totalitarian, and for more humane reasons also by the skeptic, of the irrational nature of men. Insofar as men are left to themselves—without the pressure of necessity and without coercion or effective appeals to their consciences—the great majority apparently prefer idleness to labor. The great majority are ignorant and stupid rather than well informed and intelligent. They defend a good cause so badly that they weaken the belief of the better endowed among them in the value of the cause itself. In view of the prevalence of ignorance, awkwardness, and even vice, there is a need for binding rules to train children. The difficulty is that in the case of adults the administration of the rules has to be in the hands of human beings subject to the same weaknesses as their fellows whom they govern. That is why everything should be done by education, by religious teaching, and by the strengthening of customs that are in accord with philosophical wisdom, to prevent the governors from forsaking abiding principles to govern in accordance with personal whims or with the transient fashions of the moment. That is why the rules to which the governors are subject should be based on the precepts that have come to us from the teachings of Christ and of the greatest philosophers and saints, who have owed their place in men's hearts and their influence on men's lives not to arbitrary authority gained by armed might, but to the force and elevation of their ideas. If these precepts are to gather sufficient strength to order the life of societies, if even they are to retain their importance for mankind, it is necessary that they should be continually reaffirmed and given content and concrete meaning in relation to the changing conditions which are a part of history. That is the only way of avoiding the rigidity and dogmatism to which enduring precepts and ideas are subject, when they are left at the mercy of the ordinary persons who predominate in society, and who manage the institutions necessary to the maintenance of civilized life. Rigidity leads to revolt. It makes sterile, principles that have been of benefit to man—as in the case of modern Puritan doctrine, which demanded a conformity beyond the human powers of most men or women, and forbade pleasures which are harmless and even refreshing to the mind and spirit when they are indulged in with good taste and moderation.

The remedy for dogmatism is not the abandonment of principles. It is their recovery and revival. The current disposition is to confuse principles with the attainable, when principles to be worth anything must be beyond our reach. Confronted with the lines from a sonnet (usually attributed to Shakespeare) which run, "Love is not love which alters when it alteration finds," most of our contemporaries would probably consign the statement to the realm of the absolutes, which they always regard with suspicion and frequently with alarm. Such a statement, they will say, is not true. The emotions which they and their associates are accustomed to identify with love *do* alter when they find alterations. They satisfy themselves that these emotions alter with all human beings. Even if that is so, it does not make the statement false. It simply means that no human being is capable of perfect love. Shakespeare's statement is not a description of human life, but of an abstract virtue which some human beings have the experience of participating in. Love is an ideal—and as such it does not alter because of the ravages of time upon the loved one, or because of the accentuation of blemishes in her character. Such an ideal has a practical purpose. The more steadfast is our emotion of affection—the more obstacles it is capable of surmounting—the more closely it approaches love.

It is self-evident that not all persons are equally capable of evoking or experiencing love in this sense. It should be evident also that a general belief in the truth contained in Shakespeare's line, and in the value of the love he describes, makes men and women more capable of experiencing it than a general denial of its truth and value. To endure, democracy demands a greater exercise of virtue among the people of a state than any other form of government. From the time of Machiavelli to that of Hitler, Machiavellianism has always justified itself on the ground that the citizens of every state are bound to be mainly evil and ignorant rather than good and wise. That is why the difficulty of maintaining the democratic form of government is increased by the denial of absolute principles, independent of individuals. Efforts to dethrone such principles have been made during recent decades in the name of democracy. Insofar as they are successful, such efforts help to dethrone democracy along with the principles. If the citizens are not bound by principles, why should the ruler be bound? If he is not bound, what is there ultimately save force or his personal inclinations to prevent him from exercising arbitrarily absolute authority?

Democracy rests on the assumption that human beings, in spite of their weaknesses and their ignorance, are more inclined towards good than towards evil, towards knowledge than towards falsehood, towards beauty than towards cheapness, when they have leaders and teachers capable of revealing—however imperfectly—the differences between them. It is the task of the intelligence to show the way. Democracy requires intellectual leadership directed towards the highest human ideals. Paradoxical though it may seem, the maintenance of democracy depends upon an aristocracy of the mind. It rests upon assent to enduring principles, and upon the ordering of conduct and thought—when a choice presents itself—in the direction of these principles.

IV

It is for these reasons that the ideal American university would set aside a special place for moral philosophy, whether or not persons could be found capable of occupying chairs in the subject. For the good of philosophy, for the good of the natural sciences and all the other disciplines which lend themselves to creative research, there should be continual interchange of ideas and scientific discoveries between philosophers and other learned men, or if no men worthy of philosophy are found, between philosophy in the ancient Aristotelian and Platonic sense—as derived from the works of Aristotle and Plato—and the professors. The learned men would no longer be divided, as at present, into a large number of separate and self-contained departments. The essential divisions would be two. First, there would be those learned men who were striving to relate their special disciplines—economics, politics, geography, chemistry, physics, or biology—to the philosophical objectives which the greatest ancient philosophers have emphasized and which modern philosophy should attempt to elaborate. As the various disciples and their subdivisions come to be related to common purposes, these learned men might find common ground for discussion—higher ground than is at present accessible to them. In time a universal universe of discourse might emerge, thought might be enriched, and a belief in the importance of general knowledge and wisdom in relation to transcendental values might be restored. The second, and far larger division would be for the learned men who were working to accumulate new knowledge, without direct relation to philosophical ends. The fruits of the researches of the second group would be at the disposal of the first. As they would not be concerned with philosophical problems, their views on philosophical issues would lie in the realm of opinion rather than of knowledge. Their province would be the one that has come in recent times to absorb the higher aspects of learning—that of trying to find the historical fact. The date of Christ's birth and death, for example, have a philosophical significance, but the historian with his chronological charts and calculations may establish these dates without being a philosopher.

Such a university might help the professors gradually to abandon their present prejudices in favor of intellectual chaos, fraternal departmentalism, and specialized research as the ultimate ends of scholarly endeavor, for prejudices in favor of philosophical values. There might emerge a plan for ordering society in the interest of those ultimate goals of which saints, philosophers, and artists have already offered us their visions. No doubt society would not accept such goals unless it were made over. But the war is already tearing down the old economic structure of society. Whatever happens, its structure after the war will be different from the one to which Americans became accustomed in the late nineteenth and early twentieth centuries. It might conceivably be reconstructed along the same lines as before. It might very easily be reconstructed along lines that were worse. It might disintegrate altogether. Is it not the duty of the American university—in a world where universities are disappearing almost every month—to offer the United States the pattern of a better society? To be worthy of the tradition of disinterested inquiry, which the universities have in their keeping, such a pattern would have to rest upon a philosophical theory of value.

The proper ends of scholarship ought to be clear. They are to consider, in connection with economics, how wealth can be produced and distributed, in order to strengthen justice, to encourage beauty, virtue, truth, and honor. They are to consider, in connection with history, the lessons that the past can teach about the failure of men and peoples to work steadily towards these goals of human endeavor. Political science, sociology, anthropology, and humanistic studies would all be ordered in a similar way to the ultimate objectives of worldly existence. The pursuit of such ends would mean that all social and humanistic disciplines would be gradually reformed and would find in philosophical purposes a common bond to unite them. The theoretical aspects of all these disciplines would be altered in the light of their new purposes. As a result of the research carried out during the last two hundred and especially the last hundred years, great masses of information are available. Much of this information could be utilized to advantage in building up the new theoretical structure behind social and humanistic studies. In the process new kinds of empty boxes would be found. To fill them, further factual knowledge would be required, and the research of the second group of learned men would be focused upon supplying such factual knowledge. In order to have research tell on behalf of the human race, it is necessary to ask the right questions. Today the questions asked are, at their best, more incomplete than they need to be. At their worst, they are trivial or useless. Philosophical purposes would help us to dispense with the trivial and useless questions, and to reformulate and amplify those which are incomplete. Ultimately research in the natural sciences might be brought under the influence of philosophical studies, so that scientific discoveries and technical inventions likely to benefit the human race would be encouraged and those likely to lead it, as has happened so frequently in the past, into self-destruction would be put out of the way by mutual agreement among the leading nations of the earth.

V

Our speculations concerning the higher learning and its functions seem to have led us into a world of make-believe. Scholars are to order their knowledge with a view to the establishment of a kingdom of heaven on earth! Even if they should prove capable of such disinterested labor, the human beings who would have to translate their plans into reality are made of flesh and blood. They have impulses towards the ideal, but they are weighed down with fleshly weaknesses and vices which prevent all of them from acting and thinking all of the time, and most of them most of the time, on behalf of the perfect good. The only intelligible explanation of these conditions, which have condemned mankind to suffer because of its failure to realize its possibilities here on earth, is the doctrine of Christ. The Western peoples in the nineteenth century—fortified by the unprecedented material progress—felt they were freeing themselves from the heavier burdens which that doctrine placed on men's shoulders, and which their medieval ancestors had accepted. Many of them felt that men should be released from the dogma of original sin, which in the hands of many Protestant pastors weighed them down farther than in the hands of Catholic priests. Mankind should be released from the fear of Hell, which blighted the spirit of young children and prevented elderly men and women from a tranquil enjoyment of old age. Eternal life ceased to inspire the people of an epoch in which, under the influence of natural science and pragmatic philosophy, men and women had stopped believing in any truth that could not be seen, analyzed, and explained in scientific terms. The ancient conception of Heaven did not provide them with a literal description—an outline of its hills, valleys, and streams, blueprints of sumptuous houses and yachts filled with the last word in modern conveniences—a description of a kind that medieval man, full of the transcendental and the supernatural, would never have asked for or expected. Three centuries of worship of worldly improvement have made it hard for men to seek consolation in the words, "My Kingdom is not of this world."

Mankind stands today at a parting of the ways. The Western peoples find it increasingly difficult, as the material hopes of the nineteenth century dissolve in warfare and hatred, to believe in the moral perfectibility of man. Yet the world which they were brought up to care about—the world they can see with their eyes and with the help of mechanical instruments and maps—could be won for them only by the practice here on earth of those very virtues which Christ set forth in his teachings, and which all the wisest and most saintly men and the most inspired artists before and since His time, have accepted as the highest ideals for human conduct. It is the worldly who have taken from man his hope in the life to come. The only thing left in its place is hope in the Kingdom of God on earth. If learning could provide a pattern of that Kingdom, if such a pattern could be even partially translated into something approaching reality in the United States, this country might lead mankind out of the blood and the darkness that are now working themselves across the globe. If the worldly cannot rise to these heights, if they cannot reform their higher learning and their institutions in the direction of the kingdom of God on earth, then where shall they look for that kingdom?

"What, at the time of the birth of Our Lord, at Christmastide,
Is there not peace upon earth, goodwill among men?
The peace of this world is always uncertain, unless men
    keep the peace of God.
And war among men defiles this world, but death in the
    Lord renews it. . . ."

NOTES

Reprinted from *The Review of Politics* 5, no. 2 (April 1943): 156–76.

1. See John U. Nef, "Philosophical Values and American Learning," *The Review of Politics* 4, no. 3 (July 1942): 257–70.
2. [John Keats, "Ode on a Grecian Urn." Ed.]
3. Robert E. Park. [Nef does not identify the location of this quotation. Park (1864–1944) was an influential American sociologist who contributed to the foundations of the field. Ed.]

CHAPTER 8

On Contemporary Nihilism

ARON GURWITSCH

Aron Gurwitsch (1901–1973) was born in Vilna, Lithuania. Under the advisement of Carl Stumpf, Gurwitsch studied mathematics, theoretical physics, philosophy and psychology, and he later went to Freiburg, Germany to study under Edmund Husserl. Husserl greatly influenced Gurwitsch, and he would spend his career continuing and expanding Husserl's phenomenological approach. With the rise of National Socialism, Gurwitsch moved to Paris where he lectured on Gestalt theory and phenomenology at the Sorbonne and interacted with prominent French thinkers including Maurice Merleau-Ponty. He then moved to the United States, continuing his work on phenomenology and Gestalt theory at such institutions as the American Philosophical Society and the New School for Social Research. Like Husserl, Gurwitsch's efforts in scholarship were directed towards grounding logic, mathematics, and the sciences in the structures of human consciousness by means of the phenomenological method. He believed that the achievement and promotion of human welfare in practice presupposed the acquisition of theoretical knowledge of the structures of human conditions.

I

At the present time, reason is not held in any too great esteem; "rationalism" is deprecated in most intellectual circles. "To believe in reason" is to be behind the times, to give evidence of a mode of thinking that is out of date, out of contact with what today is called "progress."

The "belief in reason" is now replaced by all sorts of psychological and sociological sciences: the psychology of the unconscious, of the subconscious, of behavior, of suppressed desires and conditioned reflexes. The variety of sociologies is no less disconcerting—not should we forget the sociological psychologies and the psychological sociologies. Formerly man was considered to be an *animal rationale*, a rational being; now he has become simply a vital being, not further qualified. Since man lives in community with his fellows, it was formerly the practice to inquire into the structure and organization which society ought to have in order to correspond to the rational and human nature of its members. But today no such question is raised; it is taken for granted that man, as a social animal, must adjust himself to his environment or suffer the consequence to his well-being and his happiness. It is no longer a question of whether one may or one should adjust oneself to certain social conditions: it is now only a question of what is the most effective means or technique of adjustment.

Let us look a little more closely into this naturalistic philosophy. We are told that man, like any other living being, comes into the world equipped with a certain organization; he has what are known as "instincts": primitive modes of behavior, elementary reactions. The human organization is more plastic than that of animals; this plasticity allows for the development of new reactions which are grafted upon the primitive modes of behavior. Depending upon the circumstances, the organization undergoes alteration and reconditioning; new modes of behavior make their appearance in increasing complexity. But, however great this complexity, every human action will forever be what it was in its most primitive form: simple reaction, behavior, produced by the functioning of the organism and conditioned by exterior stimulations. The psychological sciences are given up to the study of mechanisms which are set in motion by exterior stimulations and the action of which determines the whole life of man. At the same time, these sciences are concerned with discovering the means by which the functioning of the mechanisms can be influenced and modified, and, consequently, by which any reaction acquired by an individual in the course of his life may be supplanted by a different one. Of whatever sort these means may be, or the technique of their application, they can be reduced to a matter of reorganizing and reconditioning.

There are animals capable, in varying degrees, of being trained. From the point of view of the psychology we have described, man is the animal most susceptible to training. While we may not find this conception stated so explicitly or so crudely, it is, nevertheless, the basis of much that is done today, both in theory and practice.

As one consequence, it must follow that such things as beliefs, convictions and ideas are to be included among reactions. To have ideas, to form thoughts, to profess a belief, these, too, are among the ways in which one behaves, in which one reacts to his environment, to other human beings and to the circumstances surrounding him; these, too, are acts produced by the functioning of mechanisms. What else could they be? What else is there to man besides reactions and modes of behavior? In dealing with ideas and convictions one must always go back to these mechanisms: for example, to the satisfaction produced by a given idea. The whole value of any idea consists in answering the need for satisfaction. Therein lies the sole reason, necessary as well as sufficient, for preferring one idea to another. Thus, in studying an idea, the interest is directed to the mechanisms which have given rise to and which maintain the belief in this idea, rather than to the contents of the idea itself. The latter are almost entirely without significance; the only interest they can offer at best is concerned with their function of indicating the mechanism which has caused the individual to believe in the idea. This manner of approach to the spiritual life of man is common to many theories which differ among themselves in the methods employed and the explanations offered. And one cannot insist too much on the common nature of the "explanatory" and causal point of view: this is much more striking and much more important than are the differences of detail by which the various theories distinguish themselves from each other. That the adoption of the explanatory point of view has been possible, that it has come to be taken for granted, is due to the fact that, in a naturalistic interpretation of the whole of human activity, there can exist no intrinsic and essential difference between a corporeal reaction and the production of an idea. Both alike come about because a mechanism functions in a certain way, and both alike are the final effects of this functioning. In the face of a final effect derived from a causal chain, any question raised must bear only on this very causal chain and on the manner in which it is able to produce its effect.

Thus there does not exist with ideas, thoughts, and convictions that difference which the ancients designated by the terms "episteme" and "doxa," a fundamental distinction which through the centuries has dominated philosophical tradition, as well as tradition in general. In order to establish such a distinction, one must start, not from man but from the fact that there exists a truth: one, unchangeable and universal. Next, one may proceed to ascertain those natural capacities of man by means of which he can gain access to this truth; the question may be raised, as it has been in the religious tradition, whether the natural capacities of man are sufficient for attaining to truth, or whether there is not rather a need of divine aid, as for example, in the form of revelation.

All sorts of questions concerned with the search for truth and the possibilities of attaining it become possible; and, in fact, they have arisen. These differences, far-reaching though they may be, do not impair the common belief in truth, one and universal. It is not a matter of differences of doctrine or of method, or of different ways of propounding the problem, but of the point of departure: the recognition of a truth, one and unchangeable, to which the thoughts of man must conform, however differently this conformity may have been conceived by the different philosophical schools which succeeded each other in the course of centuries. But if, on the contrary, one starts from man considered purely as a vital being, one will never be able to reach the distinction between "episteme" and "doxa": one is faced with the fact that men exist and that they have ideas and maintain convictions. It is true that each man has his own and that each has them for different reasons, but all the reasons are purely causal. It is by psychological factors, such as historical circumstances and sociological constellations, that each man is brought where he is. Given the joint operation of all these factors, the individual in question cannot but think as he does—and the same is true of his neighbor. Each man is the product of the conditions in which he lives and one result of this conditioning is the fact that he holds to this particular idea and embraces this particular conviction. With this, we are in a world where only opinions (doxai) exist; in what way can the conviction of one man differ essentially from that of another? Are they not both opinions? Is not the one as good as the other, in that the one, as well as the other, is the outcome of certain causes which one can trace if one is curious enough? On such a basis there is possible a "tolerance" which, to be exact, would better be called complete indifference. You, my neighbor, have your opinion and I have mine. Yours is the expression of your personality as my opinion is of mine. And so, since we must live together, I will tolerate your opinion (unless I find it to my interest to make you change your mind) and, under the same condition, you shall tolerate mine. In order for a perfect harmony to be established between us, the best would be never to discuss our opinions. And indeed, why should we, since it is only a question of temperaments and since there is involved no question of truth—in which, of course, neither you nor I believe, we who are men of our time, children of progress. From all this it follows that if either of us finds it to his interest to convert the other to his own beliefs, this interest will be of a more "solid" and "real" nature than would be a purely academic interest in truth.

On this basis the attempt has been made to advance a new definition of truth. To arrive at this, however, the meaning of the term "truth" had to undergo a radical change. If man is considered as a vital being conditioned by various mechanisms, it is possible to examine his opinions in regard both to their antecedents (i.e., the causes by which they are brought about) and to their consequences (i.e., the effects which they contribute to produce). With this it becomes evident that certain opinions are useful while others are not. It is possible that, by acting on the basis of certain ideas, one will obtain results that bring him satisfaction; it is also possible that the very fact of entertaining certain opinions will bring about useful and agreeable consequences, particularly when it is a question of opinions sanctioned by society. And at this point there comes into play the various sociologies with their ethics of "adjustment to the milieu."

Today we are taught that the truth of an opinion consists in its functional and utilitarian value. It is possible, so we are told, to speak of the truth of an opinion only in consideration of the consequences produced by the very fact of trusting this opinion. It is not that an opinion *is* true: an opinion only *becomes* true to the extent to which it produces satisfaction and meets the deep need of mankind for compensation. And here, according to this philosophy, we have an authentic interpretation of the meaning itself of the term "truth," which does not and cannot have any other signification. All that has been taught and said about truth in the past is only chimera and mystification; today it is seen to be archaic and outmoded, surpassed by modern progress.

To this it must be objected that the "interpretation" of the term "truth" in question is neither authentic nor novel; it is, quite simply, a falsification. Truth is a rational system, the system of reason, however the nature thereof be conceived; it depends upon no human desires and has no connection with the need for compensation. It is one, unchangeable and universal and, consequently, the same for all men. This means that whoever seeks truth must adapt his thoughts to this rational system. Thus the endeavors to attain to truth insure respect even for abortive efforts, in virtue of which these efforts offer at least a historical interest. If, on the contrary, truth is conceived of in terms of salutary effects and useful consequences, there can no longer be any thought of its universality. The problem arises of determining which desires and which needs should be satisfied and, particularly, whose needs and desires; in speaking of utility and of salutary consequences, it is necessary to indicate the subject of reference to which these terms apply. And to this it will doubtless be answered that the subject of reference is the whole human race. But what, then, is the source of this "universalism," what its basis, in the conception in question? There is no evident reason why the human race—which means, of course, the most extensive group thereof—should arrogate to itself a privilege at the expense of more restricted groups, each one of which has its own specific interests, its particular desires and needs. Between these interests there are conflicts enough concerning what is useful and salutary. Instead of playing on words and attempting to save the situation by misrepresentation, it would be far better to state quite openly that we, men of the present day, no longer cling to such abstractions as "truth" (we could include here also "justice"). In their stead we have substituted things much more "concrete": biological advantages, satisfaction of desires and needs, utility, etc. Such a declaration would, of course, amount to a frank avowal of *nihilism*—which may be defined in effect by the substitution of "concrete" things for "abstractions."

Once the notion of "abstract" truth is abandoned, any effort on the part of the individual thinker to put his ideas in conformity with universal reason loses all sense. In the place of that conformity, we have conformism; to think like everybody else becomes almost a moral duty. Since everything is opinion, one opinion is as good as any other. Why not, then, prefer that one which is shared by everybody or, what amounts to the same, which is favored by public opinion? And this is all the more true since conformism will probably be accompanied by rewards on the part of society, while dissent might very well entail annoying consequences. If one is going to be a nihilist, there is, truly, not the slightest reason for not choosing the path along which one may expect to find a maximum of delights and advantages. Moreover, so long as the truth of an opinion is defined in terms of salutary effects, the rewards distributed by society among those who hold the sanctioned convictions, appear as proofs of the truth of these convictions. Thus conformism finds itself elevated to the rank of a criterion of truth.

We may not linger over the ravages caused by nihilism in the various domains of intellectual life; we shall only call attention to the extreme confusion which arises when questions of morality, particularly political morality, are involved. The soundness of moral views can be defined only by taking into account consequences and effects. But one is faced by the most diverse interests imaginable all in conflict with one another. Effects which seem salutary from the point of view of certain interests appear to be just the contrary from that of others. And, above this melee of particular interests, there is nothing towards which we may raise our eyes. What there might have been are precisely "abstractions" such as right and justice. But these "abstractions" have been abandoned or, more exactly, they have been conceived in "concrete" terms. And through the door thus left wide open to relativism, there enters upon the stage an array of hybrid monsters, such as truth-which-is-relative-to-a-social-class, justice-which-is-relative-to-a-race, etc. Is it not evident that only in a soil fertilized by relativism and nihilism could there take root, for example, the satanic conception that "right is what is profitable to the German people"? The world has been horrified, and rightly so, by this infamous proclamation—but on what grounds? For a rationalist there would exist here no difficulty at all. He knows that right, like all the other "abstractions," is an idea of reason, and that an idea, by virtue of its essential nature, is abstract and therefore universal. An act or an event belonging to the human sphere may be in conformity with the idea of right and justice, it may be in contradiction to it or, finally, it may be quite irrelevant to such a point of view. To decide which of these possibilities is realized in the case in question, it is necessary, so the rationalist will insist, to consider the nature of the act in question, without waiting upon consequences and effects to see whether they will be salutary and useful. In other words, the rationalist is able to make the distinction between success, on the one hand, and "abstractions" such as justice, truth, and right, on the other; and he will absolutely refuse to define the latter by the former. Unless one is a rationalist and clings to "abstractions," one will have great difficulty in opposing, to the infamy just mentioned as well as to many others, anything better than a simple aversion. The aversion may be rhetorical or highly emotional, but still it will be lacking in energy and forcefulness. The fact is that it is extremely difficult if not impossible to struggle against the products of nihilism when one is oneself imbued, if only slightly, with the spirit of nihilism.

II

Our analysis of contemporary psychological naturalism has led us along the path toward nihilism. And yet the logical order is the reverse of that which we have followed: nihilism is not a consequence of naturalism, but, on the contrary, the very basis thereof. To look upon man as a purely vital being means, as we have seen, the abandonment of the classical conception according to which man is an *animal rationale*. In the classical conception the combination of the terms *animal* and *rationale* indicates the profound duality of human nature and the highly problematic character of man's existence. Even though man is animal and thus subject to vital necessities and impulses, he is conceived as orienting himself toward the eternal universe of unchangeable reason. Thence comes that intrinsic duality, that tension, which appears to be the lot of human existence. In man's condition, all vital things, if we may use such an expression, are in relation with the idea, which finds its realization only when incorporated into life.

Ever since the second half of the nineteenth century there has been an ever-increasing skepticism in regard to all dualism, and even in regard to duality. The attempt was made to elaborate a conception of man in which all his activities would be reduced to a purely vital plane. In order for this tendency, which in our time has become still more evident, to be fully realized, it was first of all necessary to break the relationship existing between man and the universe of ideas, whether in denying the ideas or in disparaging the relationship. While it is admitted that man is endowed with reason, it is maintained that reason is of only secondary value to him or, more exactly, it is instrumental. Reason is in the service of vital functions; its role and its sole importance consist in serving the needs of existence. Doubtless man is a rational being, but he is, before all else, a vital being; and, if a rational being, he is so in the interest of his vitality. If, in the course of the evolution of the human race, reason has developed, this is because life has found it useful to forge this tool. However valuable reason may be, and however admirable the products thereof, one should never lose sight of the purpose to which reason is subordinated. This purpose has nothing to do with assuring man access to the universe of eternal and unchangeable ideas, but only with facilitating for him the struggle for existence; reason is to man what their organs of defense and attack are to animals of prey. And it is by reference to this relativity of reason that it must be judged. Thus the *animal rationale* gives way to the *animal* pure and simple who puts his powers of reason to use in the interest of his vitality—or, if we must say so, in the interests of his animality.

The biologistic and vitalistic theories that have flourished in abundance are all only products and symptoms of nihilism, which we have defined as a negation of "abstractions" or, at least as disbelief in the "abstract" ideas of reason. The same can be said of the immediate consequences of these theories: for example, the moral justification, by virtue of their origin, of all actions which are the product of vitality; the admiration of force and violence as expressions of vitality; activism in all its forms; aestheticism, etc. All these phenomena are so many morbid effects of the cause itself of morbidity. In our day we have seen the culmination of this biological and vitalistic approach in the racial theories of "blood and soil." It has been said that these theories have no "objective" basis; but they would never have been established if the way had not been prepared by the biological approach. The promoters of the racial theories merely brought to a climax the rather cautious attempts of those who first put forth a purely biological conception of man. By their very crudeness, these theories betray their nihilistic and anti-intellectual origin; nor do their proponents make any attempt to dissimulate this origin.

When man ceases to be defined in terms of his relationship with the universe of ideas, when he is reduced to the state of a purely vital being in whom reason plays only a servant role, the way is open for psychological naturalism. Every human activity, as we have seen, is considered only in the light of the vital functions, of which these activities appear as either the expression or the instrument. Accordingly, the psychological is the only approach possible to such things as thoughts and convictions; the question of their intrinsic value, that is to say, of their objective value, does not enter in: indeed, they have no such value, for this would presuppose a relation with "abstract" ideas such as truth or justice. The only question which can arise in regard to the spiritual activities of man is concerned with the utility of these activities, with the contribution they offer to the satisfaction of man's desires, including the desire for the approval with which society rewards the conformist. So long as the utilitarian value of a given activity is evident, no problem arises; nothing is more natural than that man should pursue what brings him satisfaction.

But a problem does indeed arise when the utilitarian value is not only not evident but seems to be entirely lacking; when, for example, a certain activity involves the individual in serious conflicts with his social environment, with possible unfortunate results. In such a case, an explanation is really in order; we have here to do with the fact of maladjustment and this can be explained only on a psychological basis. If we accept as axiomatic the fact that man does not and cannot seek anything except his own satisfaction, it becomes necessary, when the desire to be satisfied does not immediately reveal itself, to plunge into the "unconscious" in order to discover the dissimulated and repressed desires to which the activity in question might bring satisfaction. We are all acquainted with a certain type of contemporary psychological literature in which the great creative figures of the past—philosophers, scholars, artists, statesmen—are treated almost like psychopathics. Instead of concentrating on their work, in the attempt to understand what they have achieved, as was once the custom, today one looks to the "human side," to the personality preferably, to those strata of the personality which offer themselves less readily to view. This accounts for the many attempts to sound the "depths" of the unconscious, to search out puerile experiences in the great man's life—the resulting discoveries then being offered as explanation of a philosophical conception or a political idea. Even a slight familiarity with this type of literature is sufficient to recognize the model which, in the eyes of these psychologists, represents the human norm. This model is the Philistine who takes nothing seriously but his small personal happiness, who is in search of pleasures easily found and of satisfaction for his petty desires, who, in his thoughts as in his actions, scrupulously patterns himself upon his neighbor, a Philistine like himself, who is governed by no principle save that of avoiding friction with his environment, who takes the common opinion, that is to say, the common prejudices, as the guarantee of truth, and moderation at any cost and in all circumstances as the sum of wisdom—who, in a word, is a very model of adjustment to the milieu. Thus another result of nihilism and naturalism is the elevation of mediocrity as a measure of humanity. And it is not to be wondered at that so many personages of our time who have managed to pass for great men and representative figures, finally reveal themselves, upon closer inspection, as inflated mediocrities.

The very fact of being conceived in psychological or sociological terms seems, for many persons of today, to guarantee, to a certain extent, the validity of an interpretation of human phenomena; that psychological and sociological factors possess a major, if not an exclusive, efficacy is today a principle taken for granted. While the details of the explanations based upon this principle are open to discussion, the principle itself is not; to question it would be to expose oneself to the charge of absurdity, quite as if one should try to cast doubt upon an axiomatic truth. If the desire for satisfaction is accepted as representing the only or at least the principal motive of all human activity, it naturally follows that this motive must be seen everywhere in action: in every realm and at every period. Thus one reasons as if nihilism were a self-evident philosophy. The readiness to accept the aforementioned principle of the exclusive efficacy of psychological and sociological factors appears as one of the most striking symptoms of nihilism, a clear indication of the extent to which this philosophy has been able to penetrate. The fundamental error of the psychological and sociological theories consists precisely in the fact that nihilism is considered as a way of thinking natural to man, whereas it is, in fact, the perversion of a particular historical period.

We cannot enter here into a detailed discussion of the contemporary psychological trends from the point of view of the theory of knowledge. It may suffice to emphasize the fact that, in order to establish a scientific psychology, it is not at all necessary to adopt a conception of man according to which all his activities are reduced to the purely vital plane, i.e., explained exclusively in terms of the satisfaction of desires, as can be seen if we glance back over the history of this science. Long before our own time, indeed, long before the nineteenth century, a naturalistic psychology had been conceived. The beginnings of this may be found in the seventeenth century, particularly with the rationalistic thinkers Descartes and

Malebranche. But the psychological naturalism of today is separated by two fundamental differences from the psychological theories which were drawn from seventeenth-century rationalism.

1. Descartes and Malebranche offer naturalistic and even mechanistic explanations of perception, of imagination, of passions and propensities—in short, of those faculties which not only contribute nothing to the cognition of truth but even reveal themselves as obstacles to this end. But the naturalistic explanation of these philosophers stops short at reason—or, more exactly, at mathematical reason which, according to them, is the vehicle of cognition and the only natural capacity which assures man access to truth. Far from being weakened, the distinction between "episteme" and "doxa," reinterpreted with regard to the Aristotelian tradition, becomes thereby all the more accentuated; and this distinction serves to mark the limits of psychological naturalism. Everything not pertaining to mathematical reason falls into the domain of "doxa," with the exception, obviously, of religious revelation; it is only the domain of "doxa" that is abandoned to psychological naturalism—which may never encroach on that of "episteme." As a matter fact, neither Descartes nor Malebranche, nor any of their disciples, would have dreamed of offering a naturalistic explanation of the "*idées claires et distinctes*," that is to say, of mathematical reason. According to contemporary psychological naturalism, on the other hand, which does not recognize the distinction between "episteme" and "doxa," any conviction or doctrine or thesis is "doxa" and, consequently, no limit is imposed upon psychological, which is to say, naturalistic explanation. In this way it is possible to conceive reason itself as a purely biological function. And yet, it can be said that such a conception must lead to the destruction of the very idea of science itself. For scientific activity, according to this philosophy, can be considered only as a final effect of the functioning of certain psychological mechanisms set in motion by exterior stimuli; scientific activity cannot differ in principle from any mental activity whatever. Even when it is orientated in the direction of psychological naturalism, any scientific effort can be considered only as one mode of behavior among others, all of which alike are conditioned by psychological mechanisms. In every case it is simply a question of reactions. Psychological naturalism is robbed of such ideas of validity and objectivity by the very conception upon which it is based; by this conception it loses any special privilege in comparison with other activities, it is stripped of its scientific character and is made to appear as one of many possible reactions. This is a far cry from the psychological naturalism of the great rationalistic thinkers which, by virtue of the limitation mentioned, is not only quite com-

patible with the ideas of truth and true cognition, but follows directly from these ideas—as we shall show.

2. In order to establish the thesis that truth may be attained by mathematical reason alone, it is necessary that the other capacities, such as perception for example, be submitted to a critical examination by which they shall be made to appear as devoid of cognitional value. Moreover if, as the great rationalistic thinkers maintained, the world is in reality such as it is conceived in mathematical and physical constructions, and not as it appears to perception, then an explanation of the appearances, that is, of the "illusions" of perception, is necessary. Similarly, if no cognitional value may be attributed to any of the beliefs induced by imagination, natural tendencies, passion, etc., it is nonetheless necessary to explain the existence of these capacities, as well as the capacity of perception. It is this explanatory problem which psychological naturalism is intended to resolve.

According to the theories in question, the noncognitive capacities depend on the union of soul and body. There are interactions of a purely mechanical nature taking place between the human body and those bodies surrounding it, and it is from these interactions that are derived the data pertaining to the capacities in question. These capacities have, then, a function of their own, that of instructing us about the effects of the aforementioned interaction, that is, about the utility or harmfulness of that with which we are brought into contact. Now, it is precisely because of this biological function, which Descartes and Malebranche not only admit but even emphasize, that the capacities in question reveal themselves to be devoid of cognitive value—presenting objects to us not as these are in reality but from the perspective of their relation to our organisms; they serve the necessities of life, but contribute nothing to knowledge. Thus the explanation offered confirms the criticism whose aim it is to establish mathematical reason as the sole vehicle of knowledge. It is evident, then, that the idea of cognition is compatible with psychological naturalism—which, itself, is an integral part of the system of knowledge. The progressive realization of the idea of cognition leads to the naturalistic explanations whose principle derives from this same idea; and the same is true of the mechanistic explanations. As a matter of fact, the mechanistic conception, too, is a consequence of the idea of mathematical and physical cognition, as this idea was conceived in the seventeenth century. Accordingly, psychological naturalism is not to be considered as a simple superinduction upon the other sciences; on the contrary, it occupies a definite place in the body of sciences, and it is able to do so because of the function attributed to it by the idea of cognition itself.

If we have dwelt at such length on the psychological theories of the seventeenth century, it has been not so much because of their doctrinal content and, even less, because we would plead the revival of these theories. We have simply sought to show by this historical example how the idea of a psychological science was able to be conceived from the point of view of a certain ideal of cognition. It is by virtue of its connections with this ideal that the psychological science so conceived is justified. And it is only too obvious that no such justification exists for the naturalistic psychologism of today. Indeed, even the need thereof is scarcely felt.

It may be countered, from the point of view of present-day tendencies, that the scientific ideal of our epoch is quite different from that of the seventeenth century, which was marked by a boundless confidence in the powers of reason, the sciences being looked upon as the realization of reason: they appeared as an organized and coherent body of knowledge by means of which the rationalization of the universe was to be achieved. But today we are no longer rationalistic, we have ceased to "believe in reason." If we cultivate the sciences, it is not for the purpose of realizing a certain idea of cognition, or of penetrating into the intrinsic rationality of the universe; the sciences are considered from the point of view of the practical advantages offered by the technical exploitation of their results, advantages which, in truth, are considerable. Just as the scientific study of material bodies, both organic and inorganic, guarantees for man a mastery over nature and yields unquestionable advantages, so the scientific study of man, in which he is approached as a purely vital being and his behavior and reactions are studied according to this approach, will facilitate a better disposition of human capacities, making it possible to deal with man more or less as one deals with the other objects of nature. This mastery which man is thus to acquire over himself cannot fail, in the end, to be to his own advantage. We may not here enter upon a discussion of the many questions connected with the theory of knowledge which are concerned with the justification of science; we must limit ourselves to a consideration of the advantages which are to be expected from psychologistic naturalism. The promised advantages are indeed well worth a closer inspection.

III

To "handle" men is to induce them to certain actions and to persuade them to accept certain ideas, with little or no consideration of the rightness of the actions or the truth of the ideas. Indeed, such questions are no longer raised or, at least, they have lost the importance formerly attributed to them, either because one simply contests the existence of such "abstract" ideas as truth and justice, or because, disregarding all philosophical problems, one insists on the vital nature of the human being. Though man is endowed with reason, it is not this which determines his actions or his convictions; man is above all else a creature of appetites and passions. Underlying all his actions and all his opinions are desires, volitional tendencies, and impulses of all sorts; and it is the need to satisfy these which leads man toward certain actions and which makes certain ideas appear convincing to him. By understanding the play of the psychological mechanism one will be enabled to canalize and direct these forces, to appeal to this one or that among them, thereby making it possible to elicit any type of behavior, both in thought and in action, which it might seem opportune to provoke. And, given this power of influence over men, it becomes possible to contribute to their happiness and to aid them to adjust themselves better to their environment. The frictions between the individual and society will be thereby reduced, an advantage for both sides. It must be noted, however, that when there is some anxiety to influence men, this interest has no connection with truth, justice, or any such "abstract" ideas; in this regard there obtains that mutual tolerance which we have already denounced as tantamount to a consummate indifference. If there is anything to be gained from making men act and think in a certain manner, it will be, in the best of cases, subjective happiness and welfare of the individual or of society (or of both) which will be furthered. Never will there be any question of a cause transcending both the individual and the community. And, often enough, it is a question only of the interest of those who are adept at the art of managing men and who do not hesitate to use this art for their ends.

Thus, there has arisen in our time what may be called Neo-Sophism. The thinker gives way to the propagandist, to one who cares less for truth, for the objective basis of his position, than for the means necessary for making this position acceptable, of whatever sort it may be. It is no longer a question of suasion: of enlightening men, of dissipating prejudices and errors, of moving a step closer to truth. The whole interest is centered on ascertaining whether, given the prejudices and mental habits of a certain group, a certain proposition can be presented to this group with a fair chance of being believed; and when, for practical reasons, the propagation of this proposition becomes necessary, the question arises as to the best means to be employed for inducing men to accept it. A shift has taken place from objectivity toward subjectivity: what is important is the way in which men will probably react to what is offered them, the way in which this must be offered in order to make them react as desired. Presentation becomes a matter of greater concern than content, and intellectual responsibility becomes a lost virtue. The person who understands things is replaced by the psychological expert who understands "human nature," and who is a master of the art of managing and handling men, of playing on their desires and impulses, of exploiting their weaknesses. Intellectual probity is supplanted by propagandist efficiency. The importance attributed by contemporary society to the knowledge of "human nature," in its "scientific" and other forms, is highly revelatory of the role with which this society endows the man who creates "public opinion" and who is at home in it, that is to say, the propagandist and the demagogue. By comparison with the contemporary Neo-Sophists, the Sophists of antiquity appear as dilettantes in the art of managing men. The psychological sciences place at the disposal of whoever will use them, a store of methodical and systematic knowledge which, when used in conjunction with the technical and physical means of propaganda, is a charge of dynamite capable of blasting any moral order.

Our generation has seen, in its lifetime, the explosion of that dynamite. The practice of totalitarianism, in propaganda as well as in politics, has been inspired by the principle that men can be made to believe anything and can be led anywhere, if one only knows how to tackle them. Totalitarian literature is full of statements to the effect that intelligence plays only a minor role in the doings of men: the true motive forces are desires, impulses, passions, fear, greed and jealousy. In order to understand man and to guide him one must not count on reason and intelligence, which belong to the surface of his existence. On the contrary, it is necessary to descend to the depths of his nature, to the hidden strata of his being where all is seething confusion—and even beneath these strata, to the forces of "blood and soil."

If man does indeed correspond to the picture just sketched, why should not the forces determining his actions and his existence be made to serve certain goals? Why should man not be exploited—and condemned—in the bargain? How can this being command respect who is driven by obscure forces which can be released and directed at will, provided their mechanism be understood? To what dignity can he pretend? In the final analysis man is a vital being who, in principle, does not differ greatly from the other animals. Just as the forces and capacities of the latter are put to good use, so, with the aid of an adequate knowledge of "human nature," it should be possible to put man in the service of certain ends—for example, the ends of an "elite." There is nothing to prevent this "elite" from looking upon all those who do not belong to it as destined to serve its ends—provided the "elite" possesses the knowledge necessary for managing and directing men, has the power of applying these means, and, finally, is resolved to make use of this power. These are the three conditions by which the "elite" may be defined and by which it is constituted as such.

The first task facing this "elite" is that of putting to practical application its pretended knowledge of human nature. According to this it is taken for granted that reason and intelligence are of minor importance, are accidental, so to speak, their function consisting, at the most, in inhibiting the real motor forces. Now, it not infrequently happens that it is in the interests of the "elite" to release, rather than to restrain, these obscure forces, in order to canalize them in a certain direction; in such a case, it is necessary to reduce the activity of the checkrein of reason, perhaps to suppress it entirely. Accordingly, we find, in the literature of propaganda, the precept that one must never appeal to the intelligence of the public, much less arouse their intelligence: it is necessary to speak at the lowest possible intellectual level, and never to seek to raise this level; one should appeal to the "instincts" and passions, and should make use of stereotyped formulas which will strike home, will be retained and, by dint of repetition, will end by being believed—the formulas being measured not by their truth but by the effect they produce. These chapters of totalitarian literature are like a manual of applied psychology, a manual of the art of managing people; we find herein defined the various lies to be offered and the proper manner of their presentation; the means by which an atmosphere can be created in which the moral and intellectual level sinks to the point of producing a collective hysteria, which can be made to pass for the liberating release of forces arising from some mysterious, unfathomable depths. Here we have to do with an elaborate technique capable of bringing about (as it has brought about) the transformation of a people into a rabble which can be whipped into any shape and led anywhere.

No one can deny that this technique has given proof of its effectiveness; the success achieved by the totalitarian movements is due in part to their propaganda. Does it follow from this that man is indeed what he has been assumed to be in such movements? Before attempting to answer this question, let us consider another one. There have been moments in the recent past when a victory of totalitarianism was not beyond possibility; if this movement had prevailed, would such a success have vindicated the totalitarian forces and justified their ideologies? In the eventuality we are considering, the ideologies in question would have led to the most "useful and satisfactory" results possible—for those, that is, who had made use of the ideologies. And, in the circumstances in question, they would have been the only ones to decide what is useful and satisfactory. Would the fact of their having brought satisfaction, having produced the result desired, have proved the totaliarian ideologies to be true? In spite of its embarrassing implications, one can hardly refrain from raising this question, surrounded as one is by theories proclaiming that the truth of a conception should be defined in terms of the results obtainable by acting on the basis of this conception. For, to repeat what we learned above, it is believed that a conception cannot be said to *be* true: it only *becomes* true, to the extent that it helps bring about satisfactory results. If then totalitarianism had succeeded, would all its ideologies, by virtue of this fact, have *become* true and right?

In confronting totalitarian ideologies with modern philosophical and psychological doctrines, it is not our intention to declare that the former are derived, by direct affiliation, from the latter, as if the totalitarians had arrived at their ideologies by developing to their final consequences the doctrines just mentioned. Here we are hardly concerned with a question of literary history, and the problem of the relationship between totalitarianism on the one hand, and, on the other, of psychological naturalism and certain contemporary relativistic tendencies, is one which cannot be attacked with the methods of philological criticism. What should be stressed, however, *is the significant fact that the principles on which totalitarianism rests are the same as those which may be discovered at the base of psychological naturalism and relativistic philosophy.* It is obvious, of course, that the direction in which the principles have been developed, differs in the two cases since two different goals are involved. Moreover, it is quite possible, perhaps probable, that the totalitarian leaders have elaborated their ideology in complete ignorance of the philosophical, psychological and sociological tendencies of our times. Nevertheless, the identity of the basic principles, despite the different developments which they have received, is a fact which cannot fail to strike the analytical observer. By reason of the identity *it becomes possible, by starting from the basic principles of psychological naturalism and relativistic philosophy, to arrive at totalitarianism by a purely logical construction,* that is, by disengaging the virtualities comprehended in these principles. And the possibility of such a construction gives evidence of a basis or an origin which is common to totalitarianism and to the philosophical and psychological tendencies in question. *It is this common basis, rather than any eventual influence, with which we are concerned.* And this common basis, in our opinion, is nihilism. This is why it is so difficult to oppose a well-founded idea to the totalitarian ideologies, unless certain widely-accepted notions in modern philosophy and psychology are abandoned. The totalitarian movement is, so to speak, the culmination of nihilism; all its elements and all the tendencies originating therein may be found again in the totalitarian ideology. Moreover, they are found here in an extreme form; for with the totalitarians none of the traditional hesitations exist which have been able to prevent the extreme development of nihilism in a "pure" and radical form. Thus totalitarianism must be seen as the most representative phenomenon of nihilism which has found here its full expansion and the realization of all its potentialities.

While admitting the affinity, and perhaps even the identity, between the idea of man as conceived by totalitarianism and that advanced by psychological naturalism, the defenders of the latter may object that with totalitarianism the possibility of controlling man by means of a scientific knowledge of his modes of behavior, is abused. But, in order to distinguish between the abuse of techniques and their legitimate use, some principle is necessary by reference to which this distinction can be established, a principle which can never be derived from a technique as such. We learn, for example, from electrotechnics how to exploit electric forces for practical ends; but the question as to which practical use is legitimate and which is not, is no concern of electrotechnics: in order to answer this question one must go beyond electrotechnics. The same is true of psychotechnics in the larger sense. Because of the predominance in our time of nihilism and relativism, of which psychological naturalism is one expression, there is no longer any well-founded and justified principle on which the distinction in question may be established. And, indeed, if man is actually that purely vital being which our contemporaries would have him to be, and if the sole aim of any scientific effort is that of satisfying desires, tendencies and impulses, then the same applies as well to psychological science. To contribute to the happiness of the individual and to the welfare of the greatest possible number, is a practical goal toward which the exploitation of psychological sciences can be orientated; and the need felt by a certain group to set themselves up as masters to be served by those who do not belong to the "elite," determines another and quite different practical orientation of the scientific effort. From the point of view of psychological naturalism and relativistic philosophy, one must simply admit the actual existence of both orientations. At the most, one may seek to explain them, each alike, by reference to what is considered to be "human nature." But it is not easy to understand how, from the point of view of naturalism and relativism, it is possible to arrive at a well-grounded principle by reference to which the use of psychological sciences for a certain purpose can be judged legitimate, while, in another case, this would be an abuse—unless, of course, one depends on an attachment to traditional values for the sole reason that they are traditional: a rather frail basis. Now that the totalitarians, both in their ideology and in their practice, have questioned the Occidental tradition, it is no longer possible for this to survive by sheer inertia. It must be made to revive. But for this revival it is necessary to reactivate its fundamental motivating principles.

At the moment these pages are being written, it is certain that totalitarianism will succumb to the pressure of external forces. But, while rejoicing over that prospect, let us not forget that it is not enough to defeat totalitarianism: we must ask ourselves what can be opposed to this doctrine in order to make possible the reconstruction of the Western world. The very fact that such a movement could arise, that it could spread until it conquered so many nations, great and small, poses a problem which concerns every individual and every nation belonging to the Western world—those who have fallen victim to this movement as well as those who have been fortunate enough to escape. This problem involves our very existence as Occidentals.

The present war is being fought in order to prevent the reestablishment of the institution of slavery; it is being fought, that is, in the name of the principle of the *equality of all men and all nations.* But what, precisely, is the nature of this principle? Does it represent a simple statement of fact? If we stick to the facts, we must admit the existence of both similarities and dissimilarities among men. On what ground, then, may we accentuate similarities and hence insist on the principle of equality rather than emphasize the dissimilarities, and deduce from them the principle of inequality? The one conclusion appears no more justifiable, no less arbitrary than the other. Can it be said that the similarities exceed in number the dissimilarities? But the principle of the equality of men, in whatever form and on whatever grounds it has been proclaimed, has never been based on statistics— nor can one well imagine how such statistics could be established with any claim to completeness. But, even supposing for the sake of the argument that the way could be found to make such a statistical study, and that it would reveal a preponderance of similarities over dissimilarities; we should still have to decide between the conclusions that could be drawn from the results. One may easily imagine that the representatives of a certain group, while accepting the results of the statistics, would nevertheless insist on the distinctive traits characterizing their group. The fact, they would say, that the number of similarities is greater than that of the dissimilarities does not do away with the latter, and it is these that count. There are doubtless resemblances between man and the animals, and here, too, the resemblances may prevail. (This manner of reasoning is all the more to be expected from the totalitarians since they never tire of drawing upon data dealing with the animal kingdom in order to arrive at conclusions about the sphere of human affairs.) It is nonetheless true that the existence of similarities and their eventual preponderance has not prevented man from dominating the animals and exploiting them for his own ends; the fact is that, despite all the similarities, man does have a certain superiority over the animals, a superiority which is based precisely on the dissimilarities which distinguish him from them, whether these dissimilarities be many or few. Accordingly, so the representatives (or those who arrogate to themselves the right of representation) of a certain group will argue, even though it may be true that men have most of their qualities in common, still "our group" is distinguished by a certain characteristic trait (this trait may or may not be specified exactly), which is a sign of its superiority over all other human groups. Thus it could be said that the superiority in question has a basis in the facts.

Now, to give political expression to this superiority would be, according to their argument, to reestablish the natural state which had been corrupted by the influence of perverse ideologies. The equality of men at large thus becomes the equality of inferior men in respect to the "elite" group. And if this group seeks to restore its inferiors to their suitable place and to impose upon them the function for which they were destined by Nature, that is, to serve as slaves for the "elite" just as animals serve men, the group is merely acting in conformity with the "laws of nature"—and all the means used to this end find their justification. Again, we find ourselves stripped of our weapons before totalitarianism. It follows from all this that it is impossible to establish the principle of the equality of men and of nations so long as we base our arguments only on the facts of similarities and dissimilarities, etc. Even though we may succeed in defeating totalitarianism by force of arms, there still remains the problem of finding the idea by means of which it can be morally overcome.

For a man living at the time of the French Revolution, there was no such difficulty standing in the way of establishing the principle of human equality. For a man of the eighteenth century still relied on the classical definition of man as *animal rationale*. Man, though a vital being, is characterized and distinguished by the fact of being endowed with reason; it is the presence of reason which determines the specific nature of man and which constitutes him as such. In face of this essential and constitutive determination of man's nature, all the similarities and all the dissimilarities which do in fact exist among men and which can be ascertained empirically (though never *in toto*) sink into total insignificance. The

man of the eighteenth century, following the classical tradition, would surely
have invoked the conception of man in the form given by Descartes: that *"bon
sens"* or reason *"est la chose du monde la mieux partagée,"* so much so that *"elle est
toute entière en un chacun."* Thus, there is established within the human race a
unity and a solidarity (or "fraternity," to speak the language of the French Revolution) truly worthy of the name. This unity and this solidarity consist in the fact
that, in the words of Kant, every man is for every other man the representative of
the idea of humanity, an idea for which that of reason is constitutive. The postulate of political equality thus shows itself to be a consequence of this conception
of man. In fact, if man is distinguished from all other living being by his possession of reason, and if this attribute is the distinctive and constitutive sign of
human existence, then it is necessary to organize society into a society of rational
beings. In other words, it is necessary that public, which is to say political, institutions be such as to correspond to the essential and constitutive nature of man.
Now all men are equal in respect to reason, since this is to be found *"entière en un
chacun"*—who, in turn, owes to his possession of reason the fact of being a man.
Thus we have the equality of all men before the products of reason, hence before
the law, which is one of these products.

With a concept of political equality founded on such a basis, the man of the
eighteenth century would have been sure to insist (again, in accordance with the
doctrine of Descartes) upon the great and decisive difference between *"bon sens"*
and *"sens commun."* The first, which is synonymous with reason, is anything but
the totality of opinions (doxa) prevalent in a certain period or in a certain social
milieu; thus, using *"bon sens,"* this term being accepted in the specific sense given
it by Descartes, is a quite different matter from using *"sens commun,"* which means
to adopt the common opinions, to espouse the common prejudices, to think like
everyone else simply because everyone else thinks that way. If the essential and
constitutive determination of human nature consists in the presence of reason,
and if it is from this presence that man derives his dignity as a human being (and
from what other source could it be derived?), then this title of nobility imposes
certain obligations upon him. The fact of possessing reason obliges him to follow
its teachings, for otherwise he would bring himself into contradiction with his
human nature, with the very condition of his existence as a man. The fact that
man has, in principle, access to the truth binds him forever to the active pursuit
of truth; endowed with reason, man is obliged to develop and to realize it in himself. He is obliged, that is, not to follow *"le sens commun"* but, on the contrary, to
examine its expressions in the light of *"bon sens"* (in the Cartesian acceptation of

the word). It matters little whether the opinions to be submitted to the judgment of reason are those of an individual or whether they come from the social milieu, where, very often, they are circulated and reinforced by means of the artifices of propaganda. It is man's obligation to conform to reason which forbids and excludes "conformism." The fact that man owes his existence as a man to the reason he possesses entails for him the moral duty of intellectual integrity.

This is not to say that reason be considered solely as an organ of criticism. In contrast to modern views which hold that reason has only the function of inhibition and control, the tendency of the seventeenth and eighteenth centuries was to attribute to reason an importance of the first order for human productivity: it is to reason that man owes his creative forces, it is reason which is the source of his productivity. Bound to that which he possesses because he is defined thereby, man finds himself obliged to put this possession into active functioning, that is, to establish and develop the systems of reason: scientific reason, political reason, etc. Thus we may understand the noble and lofty enthusiasm for all scientific enterprises which marked the eighteenth century: science was not considered as an instrument in the service of vital functions and interests, its sole *raison d'être* consisting in its ability to bring satisfaction. In the Century of Enlightenment, science was seen as the realization of reason and, consequently, as the realization of human nature itself. According to this attitude, if science happens to yield useful results, these are made to serve in reforming human conditions so as to make them correspond to the state of man as a rational being. Underlying the delight which this epoch took in any sort of rational reform, there is the enthusiasm of man who has finally succeeded in rediscovering his true nature.

It is in the light of this rationalistic view of man that the importance of "discussion" is clearly seen. The fact that reason is constitutive to man's nature does not preserve the individual from the possible mishap of falling into error. In order to guard against this, the individual thinker will seek to compare the results attained by him with the conclusions of others. Discussion, so conceived, is an enterprise undertaken by rational beings for the purpose of corroborating or correcting each other; it presupposes that all who take part in it are oriented toward reason, towards truth, in short, towards "episteme" that their aim is the attainment of greater clarity and certitude about a problem rather than the vindication of their opinions. Discussion has no meaning unless the participants therein are disposed to enter fully into the arguments presented, to examine and analyze them, to sift out their implications and logical conclusions, and unless they are ready to submit their own arguments to the same criticism. The condition of discussion, then, is the willingness of the participants to convince and to be convinced by force of arguments—but, by force of arguments alone, and not by means of artifices of persuasion. Now, the philosophy of nihilistic relativism, according to which only opinions exist, entails that tolerance, or rather indifference, to which we have referred, the aim of which is to cover up all differences of opinion and to arrive at agreement, or at a pretense of agreement. In a discussion directed in the interests of truth and orientated toward "episteme," on the other hand, the differences between the various points of view appear in a highly accentuated light. Such a discussion, indeed, may be impassioned, but it will always be by the passion for truth that it is animated.

On this rationalist basis we may expect to find true tolerance, as opposed to the attitude of tolerant indifference. True tolerance is born out of the consciousness of being exposed to possible error. And yet it is much more than a measure of precaution. It is the expression of respect for that reason which is incorporated in the person of another, and which is the same as that by which oneself is constituted. In other words, tolerance worthy of the name is an expression of respect for the tendency towards "episteme" as a tendency thus orientated. Thus tolerance has its roots in self-respect, in one's awareness of oneself as a rational being inspired by the tendency towards "episteme." It is born from the consciousness of oneself as a representative of the idea of humanity. Consequently, tolerance always presupposes that the opinion to be tolerated is, indeed, orientated toward "episteme"; it does not apply to opinions *qua* opinions.

IV

Granted that the position of the eighteenth century was such as we have described, the objection could, perhaps, be made that we today are living in a very different period, and that our historical situation makes it impossible for us to return to the earlier position. And indeed there can be no doubt of the vast difference between our period and that preceding the French Revolution: it is precisely the difference between nihilism and rationalism. The general dissimilarity of "climate" between our age and the Age of Enlightenment should not, however, be deemed to constitute "progress." The last stages of the process which has led up to the point where we find ourselves today have been marked by a program, all too successfully executed, of exterminating whole nations and reducing others to slavery. Such a program was entirely unknown not only to the eighteenth century, but to all the centuries of Occidental history—a fact which should make us a little more cautious in speaking of "progress."

But if, leaving aside the question of progress, one still appeals to the existing historical situation as proof of the impossibility of returning to the rationalist position of the seventeenth and eighteenth centuries, it can be shown that such reasoning is fundamentally erroneous. An historical situation is a given fact; nihilism, too, is undoubtedly an historical fact, perhaps the most characteristic symptom of our period. Like any historical fact, nihilism has its particular origin; in the course of its development it has undergone certain phases, assuming a more and more positive shape; it has brought about certain results, etc. And the totality of these facts is a fit subject for historical research. It is possible to trace nihilism to its sources and to isolate the factors contributing to its origin and growth; the play of various mechanisms can be analyzed and the process of its development followed. And whatever discoveries may turn up in such a study— and there are surely many interesting ones to be made—there will not likely be discovered any fatality which has forced us into the abyss of nihilism. That same reason which is capable of comprehending historically a given situation is no less able to stimulate the will: it can guide and light men's actions, even an action tending to transform radically the given situation. To attribute to a historical situation forces of coercion, for no other reason save that the situation exists in fact, is pure mythology.

For the truth is that man does not correspond to the picture that nihilism presents of him. Man is not an impotent being driven by blind impulses, abandoned to the play of mechanical forces, subjected, with no means of defense, to conjunctions of historical forces, social forces, etc. On the contrary, man has the possibility of knowledge; he can put a distance between himself and the given historical situation; he can analyze the latter and is able to understand the functioning of the various mechanisms at work in the situation. In short, he can consider this situation in the light of a system of reason and rationality. It is untrue that man can do nothing but undergo the situation in which he is involved; on the contrary, he is capable of making it the object of knowledge. It is in this possibility of knowledge that man's liberty resides.

A being who must submit to whatever befalls him is indeed a victim. But a being who is capable of looking from a distance at what happens to him, that is to say, of looking upon it as if he were not concerned thereby—although, in fact, he is; who, instead of simply submitting to events is able to establish logical relationships between them, and to integrate them into a rational system constructed by him—such a being is no longer the victim of these events. Moreover, it is this attitude of contemplation at a distance, which constitutes objectivity—and not a mere accumulation of facts. Again, it is when man takes this attitude that he gains access to the universe of ideas, including the ideas of truth and justice, in their authentic, that is to say, their "abstract" form. Finally, this attitude is at the basis of scientific activity and its disinterestedness. When man objectifies the situation in which he finds himself, by considering it at a distance, by analyzing it into its component factors, by comprehending the functioning of these factors, by constructing rational systems to which the facts conform, he succeeds in freeing himself from the situation in question by making it appear under the perspective of possibilities so that it reveals itself simply as one possibility among others. Thus, man is led to conceive of states different from the one which actually exists; he can take his stand and form his decisions in regard to the actual situation; and, finally, he can act in accordance with these decisions. But this does not apply to a being who is incapable of putting a distance between himself and the happenings which befall him, who is reduced to accepting the actuality which imposes itself upon him. For such a being, nothing exists save the given reality in all its massiveness: he is incapable of taking possibilities into consideration or of conceiving a state of affairs different from what is given—or, more exactly, imposed. But, fortunately, this is not the condition of man. The doctrine of certain contemporary psychologists who hold that rationalization is an attitude of escape from reality and life, is basically false: it is indeed another symptom of nihilism. The contrary is true: rationalization is achieved when man faces the reality surrounding him (e.g., natural, political, social, etc.) and while facing and analyzing it, manifests his freedom and his spontaneity in respect to this reality. At once there appears the close connection between rationality and freedom, for the two are correlatives of each other. Only he is free who, instead of submitting to the actual, faces it from a certain distance and rationalizes it: and, conversely, it is just by bringing into play his capacities of reason that the rational being becomes aware of himself as a free being.

But there is a final objection which could be raised. Is it not true that the facts seem to bear out that conception of man which we have denounced as nihilistic? Surely, the efficacy of propaganda in every domain of life, including political life, is not to be denied. Is it not a fact, established by experience, that man can be made to behave and to react in any way desired, provided that one knows how to get at him? The totalitarian movements have based their propaganda on their so-called knowledge of human nature, and their methods have surely borne fruit.

Millions have rallied to the standard of totalitarianism, and with them the antici-pated effects have been achieved by playing upon the psychological mechanisms in the way described above. These millions, that is, have behaved in the way ex-pected of them by the totalitarians relying upon their conception of man. Must we not, then, conclude that this conception is exact, and that the rationalist con-ception, according to which man is defined by reason and by freedom, is only an "idealistic" dream?

What the facts in question prove is simply the historical reality of nihilism. Since it has been possible for nihilism to take root, it is hardly surprising that its logical consequences have been realized one after the other. Once man begins to follow the downward path of nihilism he becomes more and more similar to the picture of himself held up to him by nihilism. His moral as well as his intellec-tual level sink progressively lower. Instead of consulting reason and conscience, he takes his bearings from common opinion: *"le sens commun"* prevails over *"le bon sens."* The play of mechanisms released by exterior stimulations becomes in-creasingly important. The conception of man found in so many currents of con-temporary psychology is based on those aspects which man offers when in the state of decay. Significant in this regard is the great interest in the phenomena of morbidity. Consider also the varied and persistent attempts carried out in differ-ent schools of contemporary psychology to explain the nature of man in the full-ness of his existence, by starting from the phenomena which are produced in and are created by the state of decay. Even if we should grant (and this is not beyond dispute) that the theories in question are able to explain fully the phenomena of morbidity, there can be no doubt that they are utterly incapable of making understandable the nature of man in the fullness of his being. Without attempt-ing to go into the details of the very important question of methodology here involved, we must stress the point that, while it is quite possible to understand disintegration by starting from integrity (taking into account the modifications which disintegration produces), it is utterly impossible to understand man in the fullness of his nature if we start from the features which are observable in the state of disintegration and which exist only in this state.

The fact that nihilism was able to develop and that the consequences thereof have taken on a greater and greater historical reality, the fact that the experience seems to confirm conceptions which themselves are inspired by nihilism, all this proves only the corruptibility of man. But this corruptibility is not at all identi-cal with thoroughgoing degradation. By virtue of his full and authentic nature man is far from being in the state of decay, since he is an *animal rationale,* a free and rational being; he is, however, constantly exposed to the danger of decay. This corruptibility is the expression of the fragile and problematic condition of man, a finite and limited being; let us not forget that this *animal rationale* is also *animal* and is subject to all the dangers implied by this duality. For, if the nature of man is to be defined, essentially, in terms of rationality, this does not mean that man is so firmly bound to reason as to be unable to deviate. Man is free to abandon reason as well as to follow it. On the one hand, he may choose to endure conflict, to persist in his stand even in the face of circumstances stronger than himself, and that means to overcome defeat. In this case man has remained faithful to himself; he has realized his rational nature; he retains his liberty and increases in productivity. In short, he is man in the full sense of the word. But the other alternative exists also: man is free to give himself up to the world surrounding him—both the natural and the social world; he may succeed in adjusting himself to it by seeking and following the line of least resistance, ever ready to compromise in order to avoid conflicts as far as possible and to continue in a state of equilibrium with the surrounding world. In such a case he becomes increasingly dependent on his milieu; he develops into a passive being conditioned by the play of mechanisms which are set in motion by exterior stimulation and his responses become more and more stereotyped and unproductive. This path can lead only to a progressive alienation from oneself; when man takes this direction he is betraying both reason and his own essential nature; he loses thereby his freedom and his productivity. In a word, he falls into decay and comes more and more to correspond to that description which so many contemporary psychologists and sociologists endorse as representing the nature of man as such, though, in reality, it offers only some aspects of man characteristic of the state of decay.

These are the two alternatives which man must face. The choice between them is imposed by no exterior force, but depends entirely upon himself. The supreme decision awaiting man, whether to realize his essential nature or to alienate himself from it, casts a new light upon the fact of human freedom. Even if man allows himself to slip into decay he does so by an act of freedom: he is making a decision, if only passively, which he need not have made. There is nothing in the world which can force him to take a passive stand. Thus we have the paradox: man can lose his freedom by an act of freedom. It is only one of the many paradoxes with which man's existence is surrounded.

It is not, then, due to the pressure of any irresistible force that we have fallen into nihilism. We have drifted into this condition by our own consent—we have consented passively, perhaps, and tacitly, but nonetheless consented. But, just as it is true that no force has constrained us to fall into nihilism, so there is none which can constrain us to remain herein. If we were free to drift into this pitiful condition, we are still free to redress our condition. The whole responsibility for this rests upon the present generation of Western humanity; it depends on this generation whether we shall continue to remain in the infernal abyss of nihilism or whether, remembering that man by his essential nature is an *animal rationale* and reclaiming our rightful heritage, we shall become once more what we, the Occidentals, have been in the great moments of our history.

Translated from the French by Anna G. Hatcher

NOTE

Reprinted from *The Review of Politics* 7, no. 2 (April 1945): 170–98.

CHAPTER 9

The Person and the Common Good

JACQUES MARITAIN

Among the truths of which contemporary thought stands in particular need and from which it could draw substantial profit, is the doctrine of the distinction between individuality and personality. The essential importance of this distinction is revealed in the principles of St. Thomas. Unfortunately, a right understanding of it is difficult to achieve and requires an exercise of metaphysical insight to which the contemporary mind is hardly accustomed.

Does society exist for each one of us, or does each one of us exist for society? Does the parish exist for the parishioner or the parishioner for the parish? This question, we feel immediately, involves two aspects, in each of which there must be some element of truth. A unilateral answer would only plunge us into error. Hence, we must disengage the formal principles of a truly comprehensive answer and describe the precise hierarchies of values which it implies. The nineteenth century experienced the errors of individualism. We have witnessed the development of a totalitarian or exclusively communal conception of society which took place by way of reaction. It was natural, then, that in a simultaneous reaction against both totalitarian and individualistic errors the concept of the human person, incorporated as such into society, be opposed to both the idea of the totalitarian state and that of the sovereignty of the individual. In consequence, minds related to widely differing schools of philosophic thought and quite uneven in intellectual exactitude and precision have sensed in the notion and term of "person" the solution sought. Whence, the "personalist" current which has developed in our time. Yet nothing can be more remote from the facts than the belief that "personalism" is one school or one doctrine. It is rather a phenomenon of reaction against two opposite errors, which inevitably contains elements of very unequal merits. Not a personalist doctrine, but personalist aspirations confront us. There are, at least, a dozen personalist doctrines, which, at times, have nothing more in common than the term "person." Some of them incline variously to one or the other of the contrary errors between which they take their stand. Some contemporary personalisms are Nietzschean in slant, others Proudhonian; some tend toward dictatorship, while others incline toward anarchy. A principal concern of Thomistic personalism is to avoid both excesses.

Our desire is to make clear the personalism rooted in the doctrine of St. Thomas and to separate, at the very outset, a social philosophy centered in the dignity of the human person from every social philosophy centered in the primacy of the individual and the private good. Thomistic personalism stresses the metaphysical distinction between individuality and personality.

Schwalm[1] and Garrigou-Lagrange[2] not only called attention to this distinction but were, to my knowledge, the first to show its fecundity in relation to contemporary moral and social problems. Following them, other Thomists—including Eberhard Welty[3] and myself[4]—have tried to make explicit its meaning and develop its consequences in social and political philosophy.

The true sense of the distinction has not always been grasped. First, as indicated above, it is a difficult distinction (especially, perhaps, for sociologists, who are not always sensitive to the lures of the third degree of abstraction and wonder for what purpose they should first equip themselves as metaphysicians). Second, certain minds, despite their metaphysical inclination, prefer confusion to distinction. This holds especially true when they are engaged in polemics and find it expedient to fabricate monsters which for the lack of anything better, in particular for the lack of references, are indiscriminately attributed to a host of anonymous adversaries.

II

The Positions of St. Thomas on the Ordination of the Person to Its Ultimate End

The human person is ordained directly to God as to its absolute ultimate end. Its direct ordination to God transcends every created common good—both the common good of the political society and the intrinsic common good of the universe. Here is the fundamental truth governing the entire discussion—the truth in which nothing less than the very message of Christian wisdom in its triumph over Hellenic thought and every other pagan wisdom, henceforth toppled from their dominion, is involved. Here, too, St. Thomas Aquinas, following the precedent set by Albert the Great, did not take over the doctrine of Aristotle without correcting and transfiguring it.[5]

"The most essential and the dearest aim of Thomism is to make sure that the personal contact of all intellectual creatures with God, as well as their personal subordination to God, be in no way interrupted. Everything else, the whole universe and every social institution, must ultimately minister to this purpose; everything must foster and strengthen and protect the conversation of the soul, every soul, with God. It is characteristically Greek and pagan to interpose the universe between God and intellectual creatures."[6] It is to this essential concern for asserting and safeguarding the ordination, direct and personal, of each human soul to God that the principal points of doctrine, lying at the very heart of Thomism, are attached.

In the first place, there can be no question about the importance which St. Thomas unceasingly attributes to the consideration of the intrinsic order and "common good" of the cosmos—principally to establish the existence of Divine Providence against Greco-Arabian necessitarianism. Nonetheless, in comparing the intellectual substance and the universe, he emphasizes that intellectual creatures, though they, like all creatures, are ordained to the perfection of the created whole, are willed and governed for their own sakes. Divine Providence takes care of each one of them for its own sake and not at all as a mere cog in the machinery of the world—*ordinantur propter se a divina providentia.* Obviously, this does not prevent them from being related first to God and then to the order and perfection of the created universe, of which they are the most noble constitutive parts.[7]

"They alone in the universe are willed for their own sake."[8] In other words, before they are related to the immanent common good of the universe, they are related to an infinitely greater good—the separated common Good, the divine transcendent Whole.[9] In intellectual creatures alone, Aquinas teaches further, is found the image of God. In no other creature, not even in the universe as a whole, is this found. To be sure, *extensive et diffusive,* that is, with regard to the extension and variety according to which the divine attributes are manifested, there is more participated similitude of the divine perfections in the whole totality of creatures. But *intensive et collective,* that is, considering the degree of perfection with which each one approaches God according to its capacity, the intellectual creature, *quae est capax summi boni,* is more like unto the divine perfection than the whole universe in its entirety. For it alone is properly the image of God.[10]

Elsewhere, the Angelic Doctor writes that the good of grace of one person is worth more than the good of the whole universe of nature. For, precisely because it alone is capable of the supreme good, because it alone is the image of God, the intellectual creature alone is capable of grace. He also teaches that the natural knowledge of the angels does not extend to the secrets of the heart, even though it encompasses *de jure* all the things of this world. The reason is, as John of St. Thomas explained, because the free act of the human person, considered in its pure and secret intimacy as a free act, is not of this world. By its liberty, the human person transcends the stars and all the world of nature.

In the second place, concerning the possession itself of the ultimate end, St. Thomas teaches that in the beatific vision each blessed soul, knowing God *sicut est* and as it itself is known by Him,[11] grasps the Divine Essence and becomes God intentionally in the most immediate act conceivable. In this act, the Divine Essence itself assumes the role of *species impressa* in the human intellect. The *lumen gloriae* enables the intellect to know in a direct intuition, without any cre-ated intermediary, without even the mediation of an idea, the very Being whose intelligibility in pure act is *per se* proportionate only to the Intellect in pure act. The divine beatitude enjoys eternally the exhaustive knowledge of those uncre-ated depths. The beatific vision is therefore the supremely personal act by which the soul, transcending absolutely every sort of created common good, enters into the very bliss of God and draws its life from the uncreated Good, the divine es-sence itself, the uncreated common Good of the three Divine Persons.

Were there but a single soul to enjoy God thus, it would still be blessed, even though it would not have to share this beatitude with any other creature.[12] Or-dained to Him who is the Good by His essence and the Good *per essentiam*, it has, as the object of its vision and the substance of its beatitude, God as He is in Him-self. Together, God and the soul, are two in one; two natures in a single vision and a single love. The soul is filled with God. It is in society with God. With Him, it possesses a common good, the divine Good Itself. And thus the adage *"amicorum bona communia"* holds for it. *"Deus non tantum diligit creaturam sicut artifex opus, sed etiam quadam amicabili societate, sicut amicus amicum, inquantum trahit eos in societatem suae fruitionis, ut in hoc eorum sit gloria et beatitudo, quo Deus beatus est."*[13] The beatific vision, good so personal, knowledge so incommunicable that the soul of the blessed cannot even express it to itself in an interior word, is the most perfect, the most secret, and the most divine solitude with God.

Yet, it is the most open, most generous and most inhabited solitude. Because of it, another society is formed—the society of the multitude of blessed souls, each of which on its own account beholds the divine essence and enjoys the same uncreated Good. They love mutually in God. The uncreated common Good, in which they all participate, constitutes the common good of the celestial city in which they are congregated. It is this society of which St. Augustine writes: *societas fruendi Deo et invicem in Deo.*[14] According to St. Thomas, it is neither essential to nor necessarily required by perfect beatitude; this society accompanies it: *quasi concomitanter se habet amicitia ad perfectum beatitudinem.*[15]

Let us note further that, though God is the "separated common good" of the universe, the intellectual creature is related, *per se primo*, as to the object of its beatitude, not to God as the common good of the universe of nature and creation, but to God in the transcendence of his own mystery; to God as Deity, conceptually ineffable, expressible only in the Uncreated Word; to God as common good of the divine Persons and of the souls which have entered by participation into the universe of the Deity. It is only consequentially, because God is the common good of the multitude of beatified creatures which all communicate with Him, that they communicate in His love with one another, *extra visionem,* by all the created communications of mutual knowledge and mutual charity and common adoration, which flow from the vision; by those exchanges and that celestial conversation, those illuminations and that common praise of God, which render back unto each of them the goods which they have in common. The eminently personal act in which each beholds the divine essence at once transcends their blessed community and provides it with a foundation.

A third point of doctrine, concerning the superiority of the speculative over the practical intellect, likewise constitutes an essential thesis of Thomism and confirms what we have just observed. For St. Thomas, beatitude, which consists formally in the vision, pertains to the speculative and not to the practical intellect. The object of the practical intellect is a practical good, a good to be done, a good which, however lofty it may be, remains inferior to the truth to be known and the subsistent Good itself. In consequence, the resemblance to God is less in the practical than in the speculative intellect. "The asserted likeness of the practical intellect to God is one of proportion; that is to say, by reason of its standing in relation to what it knows (and brings into existence) as God does to what He knows (creatively). But the likeness of the speculative to God is one of union and information; which is a much greater likeness, *quae est multo major assimilatio.*"[16] Now this much more perfect similitude with God, characteristic of the speculative intellect, is accomplished by a personal and solitary act of each one's intellect.

The good and the end of the speculative intellect are of themselves superior to the good and the end of the practical intellect. Hence, they are superior to every created common good, however eminent it may be. For the highest object of the practical intellect is a common good to be realized.[17] "By the practical intellect," writes St. Thomas, "one directs oneself and others towards the end as it is exemplified in him who directs the multitude. But by the fact that a man contemplates, he directs himself alone towards the end of contemplation. The end itself of the speculative intellect surpasses as much the good of the practical intellect as the personal attainment of this speculative end, *singularis assecutio ejus,* transcends the common accomplishment of the good of the practical intellect, *excedit communam assecutionem boni intellectus practici.* For this reason, the most perfect beatitude resides in the speculative intellect."[18] These two texts, which we have just quoted and which yield, as has been noted, one of the keys to the "personalism" of a doctrine that also asserts, at each degree of the analogy of being, the primacy of the common good, introduce us to the second great Thomistic theme which we wish to recall in the first part of this study, namely, the preeminence of the contemplative over the political life.

This doctrine is so well known that a brief recollection will suffice here. Because of its perfect immanence and its high degree of immateriality, contemplative activity is the highest of human activities. It binds man to things divine. It is better than life *secundum hominem.* In supernatural contemplation it takes place according to a mode which is itself superhuman, through the connaturality of love with God and the action of the gifts of the Holy Spirit. It makes of the transfigured soul one spirit with God. It is supreme and active repose, activity essentially theological—received in its entirety from God, an imperfect and crucified beginning of beatitude. To it are ordained the moral virtues, which are at the service of wisdom as the valet is at the service of the king. It is from it, when the soul is perfect, that the works of the active life must overflow, at least as to the mode of their accomplishment. And if a man be called to abandon his contemplation to come to the aid of his brothers or to serve the good of the community, the reason for this call is not at all because the good of the practical order is of itself superior to his solitary contemplation. He must accept it only because the order of charity can require that an urgent necessity of a less elevated good, in the circumstances, be given priority. In truth, such a man if he has entered upon the pathways of the perfect life, would be abandoning rather the conditions and leisure of contemplation than contemplation itself, which would remain, in the recesses of the soul, the source from which his practical activity would descend *inter homines.*

Such is St. Thomas's doctrine on this crucial problem of action and contemplation—a problem at the very heart of social philosophy, a problem the solution of which is of prime importance to every civilization worthy of the name. With an incomparable incisiveness, it affirms the human person's vocation to contemplation. It is a doctrine of the primacy of the act, of the act *par excellence,* the act of the spirit; it is, for that very reason, a doctrine of the primacy of that which is spiritual and most eminently personal: "Just as that which is already perfect is superior to that which is practiced for perfection, so the life of the solitaries," of those who, in the words of Aristotle, are not as beasts but as gods, "is superior to life in society."[19] The contemplative life is better than the political life.

This doctrine is at the same time a doctrine of the primacy of the common good. No one more than St. Thomas has emphasized the primacy of the common good in the practical or political order of the life of the city, as in every order, where, in relation to a same category of good,[20] the distinction between the private and common good is found. At every opportunity, he repeats the maxim of Aristotle that the good of the whole is "more divine" than the good of the parts. Unceasingly he strives to preserve this *dictum authenticum,* applied according to the most diverse degrees of analogy. *A fortiori,* then, does he give it its full value in strictly social matters. Because the common good is the *human* common good,[21] it includes within its essence, as we shall see later, the service of the human person.[22] The adage of the superiority of the common good is understood in its true sense only in the measure that the common good itself implies a reference to the human person. As La Pira rightly observed, the worst errors concerning society are born of the confusion between the substantial whole of the biological organism and the collective whole, itself composed of persons, of society.[23] But to understand these things more profoundly, we must uncover the metaphysical roots of the question and engage in more subtle considerations about the individual and the person.

III

INDIVIDUALITY AND PERSONALITY

Is not the *person* the self? Is not *my person my self?* Let us consider the singular contradictions to which this term and notion of self give rise.

Pascal asserts that "the self is detestable." This expression is a commonplace of Pascalian literature. In everyday language when we represent someone as "self-assertive," do we not mean that he is self-centered, imperious and dominating, scarcely capable of friendship? A distinguished contemporary artist once remarked, "I do not like *others*"; a remark that reveals a strongly asserted personality. In this sense, we might construe personality to consist in self-realization achieved at the expense of others. So construed, personality would always imply a certain selfishness or imperviousness because no place remains for anything or anyone else in the man who is busy with himself.

On the other hand, is it not a serious reproach to assert of a man that he has no personality? Do not heroes and saints impress us as men who have reached the heights of personality as well as generosity? Nothing great is accomplished in the world save through a heroic fidelity to some truth which a man who says "I" sees and proclaims; a heroic fidelity to some mission which he, himself, a human person, must fulfill; of which, perhaps, he alone is aware and for which he lays down his life.

But let us turn to the Gospel; no personality is more magnificently asserted than that of Christ. Revealed dogma tells us that it is the personality itself of the Uncreated Word.

Here, in contrast to the expression of Pascal that "the self is detestable," the words of St. Thomas come to mind; "the person is that which is most noble and most perfect in all of nature."[24] Whereas Pascal teaches that "the self is detestable," St. Thomas teaches that whosoever loves God must love himself for the sake of God, must love his own soul and body with a love of charity. Concern for self, or what contemporary psychology calls introversion, can wreak much havoc. Those who have been reared in a strict Puritanism are said to complain of a suffering, a kind of interior paralysis, created by *self-consciousness*. On the other hand, philosophers, above all St. Augustine and in modern times Hegel, teach that self-knowledge is a privilege of the spirit; that much human progress consists in the progress of consciousness of self.

What do these contradictions mean? They mean that the human being is caught between two poles; a material pole, which, in reality, does not concern the true person but rather the shadow of personality or what, in the strict sense, is, called *individuality*, and a spiritual pole, which does concern *true personality*.

It is to the material pole, the individual become the center of all, that the expression of Pascal refers. St. Thomas' expression on the contrary refers to the spiritual pole, the person, source of liberty and bountifulness. Thus, we are confronted with the distinction between *individuality* and *personality*.

This is no new distinction but a classical distinction belonging to the intellectual heritage of mankind. In Hindu philosophy, it corresponds to the distinction between the *ego* and the *self*. It is fundamental in the doctrine of St. Thomas. Contemporary sociological and spiritual problems have made it particularly timely.

Widely different schools of thought appeal to it; the Thomists, certain disciples of Proudhon, Nicolas Berdiaeff and those philosophers who, prior to the invasion of the young existentialist group, already spoke of "existential philosophy." Hence it is all important to distinguish between the individual and the person. It is no less important to understand the distinction correctly.

Let us consider individuality first. Outside of the mind, only individual realities exist.[25] Only they are capable of exercising the act of existing. Individuality is opposed to the state of universality which things have in the mind. It designates that concrete state of unity and indivision, required by existence, in virtue of which every actually or possibly existing nature can posit itself in existence as distinct from other beings. The angels are individual essences; the Divine Essence, in Its sovereign unity and simplicity, is supremely individual. Pure forms or pure spirits are, of themselves or by reason of that which constitutes their substantial intelligibility, in the state of individuality. For this reason, St. Thomas says that each angel differs from any other as the whole species of lions differs from the whole species of horses or from the whole species of eagles. In other words, each angel differs specifically from every other; each is an individual by the very form (absolutely free from any matter) in which its being consists and which constitutes it in its species.

The situation of terrestrial things, material beings, is quite different. According to the Angelic Doctor, their individuality is rooted in matter in as much as matter requires the occupation in space of a position distinct from every other position. Matter itself is a kind of non-being, a mere potency or ability to receive forms and undergo substantial mutations; in short, an avidity for being. In every being made of matter, this pure potency bears the impress of a metaphysical energy—the "form" or "soul"—which constitutes with it a substantial unit and determines this unit to be that which it is. By the fact that it is ordained to inform matter, the form finds itself particularized in such and such a being which shares the same specific nature with other beings equally immersed in spatiality.

According to this doctrine, the human soul, together with the matter which it informs, constitutes one substance, which is both carnal and spiritual. The soul is not, as Descartes believed, a thing—thought—existing on its own as a complete being, and the body another thing—extension—existing on its own as a complete being. Soul and matter are the two substantial co-principles of the same being, of one and the same reality, called man. Because each soul is intended to animate a particular body, which receives its matter from the germinal cells, with all their hereditary content, from which it develops, and because, further, each soul has or *is* a substantial relation to a particular body, it has within its very substance the individual characteristics which differentiate it from every other human soul.

In man, as in all other corporeal beings, the atom, the molecule, the plant, the animal, individuality has its first ontological roots in matter. Such is St. Thomas' doctrine on the individuality of material things. This common characteristic of all existents, namely, that in order to exist they must be undivided and distinct from every other existent, does not in corporeal beings, as in pure spirits, derive from the form which constitutes them at such and such a degree of specific intelligibility. In them, this common characteristic is realized below the level of intelligibility in act which is proper to the separated form whether it is separated in real existence or by the abstractive operation of the mind. Corporeal beings are individual because of the *materia signata quantitate.* Their specific form and their essence are not individual by reason of their own entity but by reason of their transcendental relation to matter understood as implying position in space.

We have characterized matter as an avidity for being, having of itself no determination and deriving all of its determinations from form. In each of us, individuality, being that which excludes from oneself all that other men are, could be described as the narrowness of the ego, forever threatened and forever eager *to grasp for itself.* Such narrowness in flesh animated by a spirit derives from matter. As a material individuality, man has only a precarious unity, which tends to be scattered in a multiplicity. For of itself, matter is inclined to disintegration just as space is inclined to division. As an individual, each of us is a fragment of a species, a part of the universe, a unique point in the immense web of cosmic, ethnical, historical forces and influences and bound by their laws. Each of us is subject to the determinism of the physical world. Nonetheless, each of us is also a person and, as such, is not controlled by the stars. Our whole being subsists in virtue of the subsistence of the spiritual soul which is in us a principle of creative unity, independence and liberty.

We have sketched briefly the theory of individuality. Personality is a much deeper mystery, and to probe the depths of its meaning is considerably more difficult. Perhaps the most apposite approach to the philosophical discovery of personality is the study of the relation between personality and love.

"Not the person but only its qualities do we love," Pascal has said. This is a false statement, and exhibits in Pascal a trace of the very rationalism against which he strove to protect himself. Love is not concerned with qualities. They are not the object of our love. We love the deepest, most substantial and hidden, the most *existing* reality of the beloved being. This is a metaphysical center deeper than all the qualities and essences which we can find and enumerate in the beloved. The expressions of lovers are unending because their object is ineffable.

Love seeks out this center, not, to be sure, as separated from its qualities, but as one with them. This is a center inexhaustible, so to speak, of existence, bounty and action; capable of giving and of *giving itself;* capable of receiving not only this or that gift bestowed by another, but even another self as a gift, another self which bestows itself. This brief consideration of love's own law brings us to the metaphysical problem of the person. For love is not concerned with qualities or natures or essences but with persons.

"Thou art *thyself,*" says Juliet "though not a Montagu . . . Romeo, doff thy name, and for thy name, which is not part of thee, take all myself."

To bestow oneself, one must first exist; not indeed, as a sound, which passes through the air, or an idea, which crosses the mind, but as a thing, which subsists and exercises existence for itself. Such a being must exist not only as other things do, but eminently, in self-possession, holding itself in hand, master of itself. In short, it must be endowed with a spiritual existence, capable of containing itself thanks to the operations of the intellect and freedom, capable of superexisting by way of knowledge and of love. For this reason, the metaphysical tradition of the West defines the person in terms of independence, as a reality which, subsisting spiritually, constitutes a universe unto itself, a relatively independent whole within the great whole of the universe, facing the transcendent whole which is God. For the same reason, this tradition finds in God the sovereign Personality whose existence itself consists in a pure and absolute superexistence by way of intellection and love. Unlike the concept of the individuality of corporeal things, the concept of personality is related not to matter but to the deepest and highest dimensions of being. Its roots are in the spirit inasmuch as the spirit holds itself in existence and superabounds in existence. Metaphysically considered, personality is, as the Thomistic School rightly asserts,[26] "subsistence," the ultimate achievement by which the creative influx seals, within itself, a nature face to face with the whole order of existence so that the existence which it receives is *its own* existence and *its own* perfection. Personality is the subsistence of the spiritual soul communicated to the human composite. Because, in our substance, it is an imprint or seal which enables it to possess its existence, to perfect and give itself freely, personality testifies to the generosity or expansiveness in being which an incarnate spirit derives from its spiritual nature and which constitutes, within the secret depths of our ontological structure, a source of dynamic unity, of unification from within.

Personality, therefore, signifies interiority to self. And because it is the spirit in man which takes him, in contrast to the plant and animal, beyond the threshold of independence properly so called, and of interiority to oneself, the subjectivity of the person has nothing in common with the isolated unity, without doors or windows, of the Leibnizian monad. It requires the communications of knowledge and love. By the very fact that each of us is a person and expresses himself to himself, each of us requires communication with *other* and *the others* in the order of knowledge and love. Personality, of its essence, requires a dialogue in which souls really communicate. Such communication is rarely possible. For this reason, personality in man seems to be bound to the experience of affliction even more profoundly than to the experience of creative effort. The person is directly related to the absolute. For only in the absolute is it able to enjoy its full sufficiency. Its spiritual homeland is the whole universe of the absolute and of those indefectible goods which are as the pathways to the absolute Whole which transcends the world.

Finally, we turn to religious thought for the last word and find that the deepest layer of the human person's dignity consists in its property of resembling God—not in a general way after the manner of all creatures, but in a *proper* way. It is the *image of God.* For God is spirit and the human person proceeds from Him in having as principle of life a spiritual soul capable of knowing, loving and of being uplifted by grace to participation in the very life of God so that, in the end, it might know and love Him as He knows and loves Himself.

If our description is adequate, such are the two metaphysical aspects of the human being, individuality and personality, together with their proper ontological features. However evident it may seem, in order to avoid misunderstandings and nonsense, we must emphasize that they are not two separate things. There is not in me one reality, called my individual, and another reality, called my person. One and the same reality is, in a certain sense an individual, and, in another sense, a person. Our whole being is an individual by reason of that in us which derives from matter, and a person by reason of that in us which derives from spirit. Similarly, the whole of a painting is a physical-chemical mixture by reason of the coloring stuff of which it is made, and the whole of it is a work of beauty by reason of the painter's art.

Of course, material individuality is not something evil in itself. Obviously as the very condition of our existence, it is something good. But it is precisely as related to personality that individuality is good. Evil arises when, in our action, we give preponderance to the individual aspect of our being. For although each of our acts is simultaneously the act of ourselves as an individual and as a person, yet, by the very fact that it is free and involves our whole being, each act is linked in a movement towards the supreme center to which personality tends, or in a movement towards that dispersion into which, if left to itself, material individuality is inclined to fall.

It should be noted here that man must realize through his will that of which his nature is but the sketch. In terms of a commonplace—and a very profound one—which goes back to Pindar, man must become what he is. And this he must do at a sorrowful cost and with formidable risks. He himself, in the moral order, must win his liberty and his personality. In other words, as observed above, his action can follow the bent either of personality or of material individuality.[27] If the development occurs in the direction of material individuality, it will be orientated towards the detestable ego whose law is *to grasp* or absorb for itself. At the same time personality, as such, will tend to be adulterated and to dissolve. But if the development occurs in the direction of spiritual personality, man will be orientated towards the generous self of the heroes and saints. Thus, man will be truly a person only in so far as the life of the spirit and of liberty reigns over that of the senses and passions.

Here we are confronted with the crucial problem of the education of man. There are some who confound the person with the individual. To effectuate the development of personality and the freedom of expansion to which it aspires, they reject all asceticism; these would have the tree bear fruit without having been pruned. Instead of self-fulfillment, the man, thus educated, achieves only dispersion and disintegration. The heart becomes atrophied and the senses exacerbated, or else all that is most human in man recoils into a vacuum veiled in frivolity.

Others misunderstand the distinction between the individual and the person; they mistake it for a separation. These believe that there are two separate beings in each of us, the one—the individual, the other—the person. Their motto is: "Death to the individual, long live the person!" The pity is that, in killing the individual, they also kill the person. The *despotic* conception of the progress of the human being is no whit better than the *anarchistic* conception. Its ideal seems to be first, remove the heart, painlessly if possible, then replace it with the heart of an angel. The second is by far the more difficult operation, and succeeds more rarely. Instead of the authentic person, exhibiting the mysterious visage of the Creator, a mask appears, the austere mask of the Pharisee.

It is the interior principle, namely, nature and grace, which matters most in the education and progress of the human being, just as it is an inner principle which matters most in organic growth. Our instruments are simply the aids; our art is but the servant and cooperator of this interior principle. The whole function of this art is to prune and to trim—operations in which both the individual and the person are interested—in such wise that, within the intimacy of the human being, the gravity of individuality diminishes and that of true personality and its generosity increases. Such an art, to be sure, is difficult.

IV

THE PERSON AND SOCIETY

In our treatment of the characteristic features of the person, we noted that personality tends by nature to communion. This frequently misunderstood point should be emphasized. For the person requires membership in a society in virtue both of its dignity and its needs. Animal groups or colonies are called societies only in an improper sense. They are collective wholes constituted of mere individuals. Society in the proper sense, human society, is a society of persons. A city worthy of the name is a city of human persons. The social unit is the person.

But why is it that the person, as person, seeks to live in society? It does so, first, because of its very perfections, as person, and its inner urge to the communications of knowledge and love which require relationship with other persons. In its radical generosity, the human person tends to overflow into social communications in response to the law of superabundance inscribed in the depths of being, life, intelligence and love. It does so secondly because of its needs or deficiencies, which derive from its material individuality. In this respect, unless it is integrated in a body of social communications, it cannot attain the fullness of its life and accomplishment. Society appears, therefore, to provide the human person with just those conditions of existence and development which it needs. It is not by itself alone that it reaches its plenitude but by receiving essential goods from society.

Here the question is not only of his material needs, of bread, clothes and shelter, for which man requires the help of his fellowmen, but also, and above all, of the help which he ought to be given to do the work of reason and virtue, which responds to the specific feature of his being. To reach a certain degree of elevation in knowledge as well as a certain degree of perfection in moral life, man needs an education and the help of other men. In this sense, Aristotle's statement that man is by nature a political animal holds with great exactitude: man is a political animal because he is a rational animal, because reason requires development through character training, education and the cooperation of other men, and because society is thus indispensable to the accomplishment of human dignity.

There is a correlation between this notion of the *person* as a social unit and the notion of the *common good* as the end of the social whole. They imply one another. The common good is common because it is received in persons, each one of whom is as a mirror of the whole. Among the bees, there is a public good, namely, the good functioning of the hive, but not a common good, that is, a good received and communicated.[28] The end of society, therefore, is neither the individual good nor the collection of the individual goods of each of the persons who constitute it. Such a conception would dissolve society as such to the advantage of its parts, and would amount to either a frankly anarchistic conception, or the old disguised anarchistic conception of individualistic materialism in which the whole function of the city is to safeguard the liberty of each; thus giving to the strong full freedom to oppress the weak.

The end of society is the good of the community, of the social body. But if the good of the social body is not understood to be a common good of *human persons*, just as the social body itself is a whole of human persons, this conception also would lead to other errors of a totalitarian type. The common good of the city is neither the mere collection of private goods, nor the proper good of a whole which, like the species with respect to its individuals or the hive with respect to its bees, relates the parts to itself alone and sacrifices them to itself. It is the good *human* life of the multitude, of a multitude of persons; it is their communion in good living. It is therefore common to both *the whole and the parts* into which it flows back and which, in turn must benefit from it. Unless it would vitiate itself, it implies and requires recognition of the fundamental rights of persons and those of the domestic society in which the persons are more primitively engaged than in the political society. It includes within itself as principal value, the highest access, compatible with the good of the whole, of the persons to their life of person and liberty of expansion, as well as to the communications of generosity consequent upon such expansion. If, as we intend to emphasize later, the common good of the city implies an intrinsic ordination to something which transcends it, it is because it requires, by its very essence and within its proper sphere, communication or redistribution to the persons who constitute society. It presupposes the persons and flows back upon them, and, in this sense, is achieved in them.

Thus, that which constitutes the common good of political society is not only the collection of public commodities and services, the roads, ports, schools, etc., which the organization of common life presupposes; a sound fiscal condition of the state and its military power; the body of just laws, good customs and wise institutions, which provide the nation with its structure; the heritage of its great historical remembrances, its symbols and its glories, its living traditions and cultural treasures. The common good includes all of these and something much more besides, something more profound, more concrete and more human. For it includes also, and above all, the whole sum itself of these; a sum which is quite different from a simple collection of juxtaposed units. Even in the mathematical order, as Aristotle points out, "6" is not the same as 3 + 3. It includes the sum or sociological integration of all the civic conscience, political virtues and sense of right and liberty, of all the activity, material prosperity and spiritual riches, of unconsciously operative hereditary wisdom, of moral rectitude, justice, friendship, happiness, virtue and heroism in the individual lives of its members. For these things all are, in a certain measure, *communicable* and so revert to each member, helping him to perfect his life and liberty of person. They all constitute the good human life of the multitude.

Let us note in passing that the common good is not only a system of advantages and utilities but also a rectitude of life, an end, good in itself or, as the Ancients expressed it, a *bonum honestum*. For, on the one hand, to assure the existence of the multitude is something morally good in itself; on the other hand, the existence, thus assured, must be the just and morally good existence of the community. Only on condition that it is according to justice and moral goodness is the common good what it is, namely, the good of a people and a city, rather than of a mob of gangsters and murderers. For this reason, perfidy, the scorn of treaties and the sworn oath, political assassination and unjust war, even though they be *useful* to a government and procure some fleeting advantages for the peoples who make use of them, tend by their nature as political acts—acts involving in some degree the common action—to the destruction of the common good.

The common good is something ethically good. Included in it, as an essential element, is the maximum possible development, *hic et nunc,* of the persons making up the united multitude to the end of forming a people, organized not by force alone but by justice. Historical conditions and the still inferior development of humanity make difficult the full achievement of the end of social life. But the end to which it tends is to procure the common good of the multitude in such a way that the concrete person gains the greatest possible measure, compatible with the good of the whole, of real independence from the servitudes of nature. The economic guarantees of labor and capital, political rights, the moral virtues and the culture of the mind, all contribute to the realization of this independence.

A twofold observation is pertinent here. On the one hand, the common good of civil society implies that the whole man is engaged in it. Unlike a farmers' cooperative or a scientific association, which require the commitment of only part of the interests of the members, civil society requires the citizens to commit their lives, properties and honor. On the other hand, it should be noted that the idea of the *societas perfecta,* to which the idea of the common good of political society is linked, has experienced many adventures in the course of history; it may even be doubted whether it has ever been truly realized within the limits of any particular social group. Contemporary states are more remote from the ideal type of the *societas perfecta* than the city of Aristotle's day or the body politic in the time of Suarez. The common good in our day is certainty not just the common good of the nation and has not yet succeeded in becoming the common good of the civilized world community. It tends, however, unmistakably towards the latter. For this reason, it would seem appropriate to consider the common good of a state or nation as merely an area, among many similar areas, in which the common good of the whole civilized society achieves greater density.

We have emphasized the sociability of the person and the properly *human* nature of the common good. We have seen that it is a good according to the requirements of justice; that it must flow back upon persons, and that it includes, as its principal value, the access of persons to their liberty of expansion.

We have not yet considered what might be termed the typical paradox of social life. Here again we shall find the distinction of the individual and the person. For this paradox results from the fact, already noted, that each of us is in his entirety an individual and in his entirety a person.

At this point, a few metaphysical and also theological observations would help to assure the correct development of the discussion. Let us recall that the idea of person is an analogical idea which is realized fully and absolutely only in its supreme analogue, God, the Pure Act. Let us recall further that, for St. Thomas, the *ratio* or intelligible value of "whole," "totality," is indissolubly bound to that of person. It is a fundamental thesis of Thomism that the person as such is a whole. *"Ratio partis contrariatur personae."* The concept of part is opposed to that of person.[29]

To say, then, that society is a whole composed of persons is to say that society is a whole composed of wholes. Taken in its full sense, this expression leads us directly to the society of the Divine Persons (for the idea of society is also an analogical idea). In the Divine Trinity, there is a whole, the divine Essence, which is the common good of the three subsisting Relations. With respect to this whole, the Three who compose the trinitarian society are by no means parts, since they are perfectly identical to it. They are three wholes who are the Whole. "Among created things," St. Thomas writes, *"one* is part of *two,* and *two* of *three* (as one man is part of two men, and two men of three). But it is not thus in God. For the Father is as much as the whole Trinity: *quia tantus est Pater, quanta tota Trinitas."*[30]

We must be aware here of the irremediable deficiency of our language. Since our idea of society originates in and, as far as modes of conceptualization are concerned, is bound to our experience, the only possible way for us to express the fact that persons live in society is to say that they are parts of, or compose, society. But can it be said, except quite improperly, that the Divine Persons "are parts of" or "compose" the uncreated society? Here, precisely, where we are confronted with the society par excellence, a society of pure persons, our language is irremediably deficient. Let us keep in mind this essential point, which is the proper difficulty of and the key to the precisions to follow, namely that, if the person of itself requires "to be part of" society, or "to be a member of society," this in no wise means that it must be in society in the way in which a part is in a whole and treated in society as a part in a whole. On the contrary, the person, as person, requires to be treated as a whole in society.

To get the right idea of human society, we must consider it as located in the analogical scale between the uncreated exemplar, the superanalogue of the concept of society, namely, the divine society, and something which is not even an analogue of the concept of society, except in an improper and metaphorical sense, namely, animal society. Infinitely above the city of men, there is a society of pure Persons, who are at the summit of individuality, but without the shadow of individuation by matter (or even by a form, distinct from the act of existence). Each one is in the other through an infinite communion,[31] the common good of which is strictly and absolutely the proper good of each, since it is that which each person is and their very act of existing. Far below the society of men, below even the level of all society properly so-called, there is a "society" of material individuals which are not persons, which are so isolated each within itself that they do not tend toward any communion and have no common good,[32] but each is totally subservient to the proper good of the whole. Human society is located between these two; a society of persons who are material individuals, hence isolated each within itself but nonetheless requiring communion with one another as far as possible here below in anticipation of that perfect communion with one another and God in life eternal. The terrestrial common good of such a society is, on the one hand, superior to the proper good of each member but flows back upon each. On the other hand, it sustains in each that movement by which it strives toward its own eternal good and the transcendent Whole. This is the same movement by which each goes beyond the order in which the common good of the terrestrial city is constituted.

The person as such is a whole, an open and generous whole. In truth, if human society were a society of *pure persons,* the good of society and the good of each person would be one and the same good. But man is very far from being a pure person; the human person is the person of a poor material individual, of an animal born more helpless than any other animal. Though the person as such is an independent whole and that which is noblest in all of nature, nonetheless the human person is at the lowest degree of personality, naked and miserable, indigent and full of wants. When it enters into society with its kind, therefore, it happens that, by reason of its deficiencies—evidences of its condition as an individual in the species—the human person is present *as part* of a whole which is greater and better than its parts, and of which the common good is worth more than the good of each part. Yet, because of personality as such and the perfections which it implies as an independent and open whole, the human person requires membership in society. Whence, as previously noted, it is essential to the good of the social whole to flow back in some fashion upon the person of each member. It is the human *person* who enters into society. As an individual, it enters society as a part whose proper good is inferior to the good of the whole, of the whole constituted of persons. But the good of the whole is what it is, and so superior to the private good, only if it benefits the individual persons, is redistributed to them and respects their dignity.

On the other hand, because it is ordained to the absolute and is summoned to a destiny beyond time, or, in other words, because of the highest requirements of personality as such, the human person, as a spiritual totality referred to the transcendent whole, *surpasses* and is superior to all temporal societies. From this point of view, or if you will, in respect to things *which are not Caesar's* both society itself and its common good are indirectly subordinated to the perfect accomplishment of the person and its supratemporal aspirations as to an end of another order, an end which transcends them. A single human soul is worth more than the whole universe of material goods. There is nothing higher than the immortal soul, save God. With respect to the eternal destiny of the soul, society exists for each person and is subordinated to it.

We have just stated that the common good is what it is only if it is redistributed to persons. Let us now add a consideration which is derived from the same principle but goes farther, namely, that the common good of the city or of civilization— an essentially human common good in which the whole of man is engaged—does not preserve its true nature unless it respects that which surpasses it, unless it is subordinated, not as a pure means, but as an infravalent end, to the order of eternal goods and the supratemporal values from which human life is suspended.

This intrinsic subordination refers above all to the supernatural beatitude to which the human person is directly ordained. It is also and already related, a fact which a philosopher cannot ignore, to everything which of itself transcends political society, because all such things belong to the order of the absolute.[33] We have in mind the natural law, the rule of justice and the requirements of fraternal love; the life of the spirit and all that which, in us, is a natural beginning of contemplation; the immaterial dignity of the truth, in all domains and all degrees however humble they may be, of theoretical knowledge, and the immaterial dignity of beauty, both of which are nobler than the things of common life and which, if curbed by it, never fail to avenge themselves. In the measure that human society attempts to free itself from this subordination and proclaim itself the supreme good, in the very same measure it perverts its own nature and that of the common good, in the same measure it destroys the common good. The common good of political society is a *bonum honestum*. But it is a practical good, and not the absolute good which, as we noted in the beginning, is the supreme object of the theoretical intellect. The common good of the *vita civilis* is an ultimate end, but an ultimate end *secundum quid* and in a certain order. It is lost if it is closed within itself, for, of its very nature, it is intended to favor the higher ends of the human person.

The human person's vocation to goods which transcend it is embodied in the essence of the common good. To ignore these truths is to sin at the same time and by the same token against both the human person and the common good.

When, against social pressures, the human person upholds right, justice, fraternal charity, when it raises itself above social life to enter into the solitary life of the spirit, when it deserts the banquets of common life, to feed upon the transcendentals, when, seeming to forget the city, it fastens to the adamantine objectivity of beauty and truth, when it pays obeisance to God rather than to men. In these very acts it still serves the common good of the city and in an eminent fashion.

And when the person sacrifices to the common good of the city that which is dearest to it, suffers torture and gives its life for the city, in these very acts because it wills what is good and acts in accordance with justice, it still loves its own soul, in accordance with the order of charity, more than the city and the common good of the city.

We see, then, that the true conception of political life is neither exclusively personalist nor exclusively communal. As we wrote many years ago, it is both personalist and communal in such a way that these two terms call for and imply one another. Hence, there is nothing more illusory than to pose the problem of the person and the common good in terms of opposition. In reality, it is posed in terms of reciprocal subordination and mutual implication.

Thus it is in the nature of things that man, as part of society, should be ordained to the common good and the common work for which the members of the city are assembled.[34] It is in the nature of things that he should, as the need arises, renounce activities which are nobler in themselves than those of the body politic for the salvation of the community. It is also in the nature of things that social life should impose numerous restraints and sacrifices upon his life as a person, considered as a part of the whole. But in the measure that these sacrifices and restraints are required and accepted in the name of justice and amity, they raise higher the spiritual level of the person. "Man finds himself by subordinating himself to the group, and the group attains its goal only by serving man and by realizing that man has secrets which escape the group and a vocation which the group does not encompass."[35]

And when, as we just noted, man freely accepts death, not as an enslaved fanatic or blind victim, but as a man and a citizen, for the sake of his people and his country, in that very act of extraordinary virtue, he affirms at the same time the supreme independence of the person in relation to the things of this world. In losing itself, in a temporal sense, for the sake of the city, the person sacrifices itself in the most real and complete fashion. Yet the person is not defeated. The city still serves it because the soul of man is immortal and because the sacrifice gives grace one more chance.

We might observe in passing, that the sheer fact of existing is neither the supreme good nor any one of the absolute goods to which the person as such is ordained. It is, however, the first prerequisite condition of the person's ordination to these goods.[36] A human life is less precious than the moral good and the duty of assuring the salvation of the community is less precious than the human and moral patrimony of which the community is the repository, and is less precious also than the human and moral work which the community carries on from one century to the next. It is, nonetheless, as the life of a person, superior to every value of mere social utility. For it is the life of a substance endowed with a spiritual soul and possessing a right to its own existence. Not the least paradox of our condition is the fact that this good, which is metaphysically so precious, is by nature exposed, and even squandered, in all manner of adventures frequently for very slight reasons. In the name of goods and interests, which are only remotely connected with the common good, society itself does not hesitate to abuse it for any ends, even to waste it. The history of mankind is proof enough that human life, as the life of an individual in the group, is indeed cheap. Only yesterday, across the Rhine, we saw to what atrocities a purely biological conception of society can lead. The destruction of human lives, which were believed to have become a burden on the community, was not only permitted, but even extolled.

In reality, the privilege connected with the dignity of the person is inalienable, and human life involves a sacred right. Whether to rid society of a useless member or for *raison d'état*, it is a crime to kill an innocent man. It is a crime to doom a prisoner to death in order to test some drugs which may save thousands of the sick. The social body does have the right, in a just war, to oblige its citizens to expose their lives in combat. It does not have the right to demand more than this risk, or to decree the death of a man for the salvation of the city. When it is a question of special missions in which men go to certain or almost certain death, volunteers are called for. This fact is itself an additional testimony to the right of the human person to life. Even in these extreme cases, something still bears witness to the transcendent value of human life insofar as it is the life of a person. The person can be obligated in conscience and, if necessary even constrained, to expose its life, but never can it be branded like an animal for the slaughterhouse. It is still as master of itself and by an act of virtue that it faces death. Apart from these ultimate demands of its dignity, it remains true that the person is duty-bound, in justice, to risk its own existence for the salvation of the whole when the whole is imperiled. It is so bound precisely because, as an individual, the person is in its entirety a part of the community from which, in a certain fashion, it has received all that it is. But it is thus obliged only because the terrestrial common good itself includes suprahuman values and is indirectly related to the absolutely ultimate end of man. "If the common good of human society were uniquely and exclusively a sum of temporal advantages and achievements, like the common good—not really common but totalitarian—of an apiary or anthill, it would surely be nonsensical to sacrifice the life of a human person for it. Thus war, which pushes to the extreme limit the subordination of the individual person to the temporal community, at the same time attests the supratemporal implications and suprasocial finalities that this subordination presupposes. It can be seen, on the other hand, that, by reason of their very nature, the totalitarian states—the very states that devour human lives in the name of the nation—lose, as such, the right to ask of a man that he sacrifice his life for them."[37]

In short, though the person as such is a totality, the material individual, or the person as a material individual, is a part. Whereas the person, as person or totality, requires that the common good of the temporal society flow back over it, and even transcends the temporal society by its ordination to the transcendent whole, yet the person still remains, as an individual or part, inferior and subordinated to the whole and must, as an organ of the whole, serve the common work.

Two texts of St. Thomas, which supplement and balance one another, can guide us to a deeper penetration of these ideas. "Each individual person," St. Thomas writes, "is related to the entire community as the part to the whole."[38] From this point of view and in this respect, that is because it is by reason of certain of its proper conditions a part of society, the person is in its entirety engaged in and ordained to the common good of society.

But let us add at once that, although man in his entirety is engaged as a part of political society (since he may have to give his life for it), he is not a part of political society *by reason of his entire self* and all that is in him . On the contrary, by reason of certain things in him, man in his entirety is elevated above political society. St. Thomas' second text that completes and balances the first is pertinent here; "Man is not ordained to the body politic according to all that he is and has."[39]

There is an enormous difference between this statement: "Man, by reason of certain things which are in him, is *in his entirety* engaged as a part of political society" and this other statement: "Man is part of political society *by reason of himself as a whole and by reason of all that is in him.*" The first one is true, and the second one is false. Here lie both the difficulty and the solution of the problem. Anarchical individualism denies that man, by reason of certain things which are in him, is engaged in his entirety as a part of political society. Totalitarianism asserts that man is a part of political society by reason of himself as a whole and by reason of all that is in him ("all in the state, nothing against the state, nothing outside of the state"). The truth is that man is engaged in his entirety, but not by reason of his whole self, as a part of political society, a part ordained to the good of the society. In the same way, a good philosopher is engaged in his entirety in philosophy, but not by reason of all the functions and all the finalities of his being. He is engaged in his entirety in philosophy by reason of the special function and special finality of the intellect in him. A good runner engages the whole of himself in the race but not by reason of all the functions or all the finalities of his being. He engages the whole of himself in the race, but by reason of the neuromuscular machinery in him, not by reason of his knowledge of the Bible, for example, or of astronomy. The human person is engaged in its entirety as a part of political society, but not by reason of everything that is in it and everything that belongs to it. By reason of other things which are in the person, it is also in its entirety above political society. For in the person there are some things, and they are the most important and sacred ones, which transcend political society and draw man in his entirety above political society—the very same whole man who, by reason of another category of things, is a part of political society. By reason of certain relations to the common life which concern our whole being, we are a part of the state; but by reason of other relations (likewise of interest to our whole being) to things more important than the common life, there are goods and values in us which are neither by nor for the state, which are outside of the state.

Man is a part of and inferior to the political community by reason of the things in and of him which, due as they are to the deficiencies of material individuality, depend in their very essence upon political society and which in turn may be used as means to promote the temporal good of the society. In this sense, a mathematician has learned mathematics by reason of the educational institutions that social life alone makes possible. This progressive formation, which is received from others and is a proof of the limitations of the individual, depends upon the community. Consequently, the community can in given circumstances, require the mathematician to serve the social group by *teaching* mathematics.

On the other hand, by reason of the things in and of man, which are derived from the ordination of personality as such to the absolute and which thus depend in their essence on something higher than the political community and so concern properly the supratemporal accomplishment of the person as person, man excels the political community. Thus mathematical truths do not depend upon the social community, but concern the order of the absolute goods of the person as such. The community will never have the right to require the mathematician *to hold as true* some one mathematical system rather than any other, or to teach such mathematics as is deemed to be more in conformity with the law of the social group (e.g., "Aryan" mathematics or "Marxist-Leninist" mathematics).[40]

Man is constituted a person, made for God and life eternal, before he is constituted a part of the city; and he is constituted a part of the family society before he is constituted a part of the political society. This is the origin of those primordial rights which political society must respect and which it may not injure when it requires the services of its members.

We have stated that, on the one hand, it is the person itself which enters into society and, on the other, that it is ultimately by reason of its material individuality that it is in society as a part whose good is inferior to the good of the whole. If that is the case, it is understandable that society cannot live without the perpetual gifts which come from persons, each one of whom is *irreplaceable* and incommunicable; and that, nevertheless, the very thing of persons which in social usage is retained is transmuted into something communicable and *replaceable*, always individualized but depersonalized.

We might add also that society, its life, and its peace, cannot subsist without that amity, namely, civil amity, which is the animating form of society and essentially personal.[41] However, the relations which make up the structure of society concern, as such, only *justice*, which is essentially impersonal because it is measured on things, and does not make acceptance of persons.

From the above considerations we can draw two conclusions. The first concerns the mutual relations of the person and society. To characterize these relations we might make use of the following formulae: just as the person requires society both *per abundantiam* or as a person, and *per indigentiam* or as an individual, so the common good, by its very essence, directs itself to the persons as persons and directs the persons as individuals to itself. It directs itself to persons in a twofold way. First, insofar as the persons are engaged in the social order, the common good by its essence must flow back over or redistribute itself to them. Second, in so far as the persons transcend the social order and are directly ordained to the transcendent Whole, the common good by its essence must favor their progress toward the absolute goods which transcend political society. From the first point of view, we have the law of redistribution of the common good to the parts of society because these parts are persons. From the second point of view, we have the law of transcendence by which the transcendence of the person over society is manifested.

The second conclusion concerns the state of tension and conflict which is inherent in human society. Social life is naturally ordained—in the way in which we have tried to describe—to the good and the freedom of the person. And yet there is in this very same social life a natural tendency to enslave and diminish the person in the measure that society considers the person as a part and as a mere material individual. "When ever I have been among men," Seneca wrote, "I have come back less a man."

The person as person insists on serving the community and the common good freely. It insists on this while tending toward its own fullness, while transcending itself and the community in its movement toward the transcendent Whole. The person as an individual is necessarily bound, by constraint if need be, to serve the community and the common good since it is excelled by them as the part by the whole.

This paradox, this tension, and this conflict are something natural and inevitable. Their solution is not static but dynamic, *in motu*. For, in this way, a double movement is generated, a movement far more profound than the dialectical movement to which the Marxists appeal. The first of these movements is a dearly bought and, ceaselessly hampered movement of the societies themselves as they develop in time. It is like a thrust, due above all to the energies of the spirit and of freedom, across an ebb-tide in which the corruption, which belabors us, ceaselessly appears. For insofar as it advances, this movement tends to realize gradually in social life itself man's aspiration to be treated as a person in the whole, or, if you will, as a whole and not as a part. To us this is a very abstract but exact expression of the ideal to which, from their inception, modern democracies have been aspiring, but which their philosophy of life has vitiated. This ideal, the complete realization of which cannot be expected here below, is an upper limit drawing to itself the ascending part of history. It calls for an heroic philosophy of life fastened to absolute and spiritual values. It can be gradually realized only by the development of law, of a kind of sacred sense of justice and honor, and by the development of civic amity. For justice and right, by imposing their law upon man as upon a moral agent and by appealing to reason and free will, concern, as such, personality. They transform into a relation between two wholes, the whole of the individual person and the social whole, that which otherwise would be no more than the pure subordination of the part to the whole. And love, by assuming voluntarily that which would otherwise be servitude, transfigures it into liberty and a free gift.[42]

The second movement is, so to speak, a vertical movement of the life of the persons themselves in the midst of social life. It arises out of the difference in altitude between the level where the person has the center of its life as a person and the level where it is constituted as a part of a social community. Because of this difference in level, the person demands society and always tends to go beyond it, "until, at last, it enters into a society of pure persons, that is, into the society of Divine Persons, which overwhelms it with the gift of infinitely more than that to which it could of its own nature properly aspire." From the family group (which is more fundamental than the State because it touches upon the generic difference of the human being, man passes into civil society (which touches upon the specific difference) where he feels the need of clubs and fellowships that will interest his intellectual and moral life. These he enters of his own free choice; they assist the soul in its efforts to ascend to a higher level. In the end these also fail to satisfy; the soul is cramped and forced to go beyond them. Above the level of civil society, man crosses the threshold of supernatural reality and enters into a society that is the mystical body of an incarnate God, a society the proper office of which is to lead him to his spiritual perfection and his full liberty of autonomy, to his eternal welfare. The Church is at once Desert and City.[43] Within her precincts, she nourishes human personality on a divine food and leads it away from the crowds at the circumference, where the soul finds contentment in life *inter homines,* towards the deeper solitude at the center, where it finds its highest contentment in life *inter divinas personas.* At last, in the vision in which the intellect apprehends the Divine Essence, the person is more than ever lost in the life of the Church. But the common good of the Church is now unveiled and the human being, exalted by supernatural power to share as a pure personality in the Uncreated Society of the Divine Persons, enters into the Kingdom of God and the Light of Glory. "Strive not, ye men, to socialize the life of the spirit. It tends of its own nature to live in society and finds its fulfillment only there."[44]

It will be noted that these considerations enable us to understand in its true sense the statement of Aristotle, so often repeated by St. Thomas and already alluded to at the beginning of this essay; the good of the city is more noble, *more divine* than that of the individual. Here, as on so many other points, Aristotle has expressed a remarkably pure principle whose significance could be penetrated only by eyes more illuminated than those of the pagan wisdom. This principle must be understood in a very precisely formal way; in the very same line of values in which the person is *a part* in relation to the social whole. Then it is clear, as explained above, that the good of the community (the authentic and true common good) is superior to the good of the individual person *in the order of terrestrial values* according to which the person is a part of the community. But these values are not equal to the dignity and destiny of the person. By reason of the law of transcendence or transgression, which we have described, the person is raised to a higher level than the level at which it is but a part; at this level, the good of the person is the more elevated. However, at this higher level, it is still a part, but of a higher community, so that the *dictum authenticum* of Aristotle is verified anew, under altogether different conditions, and on an altogether different plane.

Thus in the natural order there is a community of minds inasmuch as minds communicate in the love of truth and beauty, in the life and work of knowledge, art and poetry, and in the highest values of culture. However, this community does not succeed in constituting itself as a society in the proper sense of the word, the kingdom of minds, as Leibniz put it. We could speak of its common good only in an analogical sense. In fact, the common good of the intellects can be understood in two ways. In the first way, it is truth and beauty themselves, through the enjoyment of which minds receive a certain natural irradiation or participation of the Uncreated Truth and Beauty or of the separated common good. This common good of the intellects is obviously superior to the personal act by which each intellect conquers a fragment of it; but it is not a social good, a common good in the strict sense. This common good of the intellects is the immensity of the supratemporal object, to some aspect of which, each adheres in solitude.

In the second way, the common good of the intellects is the intelligible treasure of culture in which minds communicate with one another. This treasure of culture, in relation to which minds accomplish a common work, more or less perfectly flows back over each of them. In this sense, it is undoubtedly a schema of social or common good in the strict sense without an organized social body and in a certain way, *extensive et diffusive*, it is something better than the proper good of each. From the point of view of extension, or from the point of view of the multiplicity by which the diverse aspects of the search for truth are manifested, it is better to have Plato, Aristotle, Kant and St. Thomas, than to have St. Thomas alone, even though, personally, we would be willing to dispense with all the others for St. Thomas. It is better to have Ruysbroeck and the pseudo-Dionysius, Gertrude and Catherine of Sienna, St. Theresa and St. John of the Cross than to have St. John of the Cross alone. But, absolutely speaking, the communion in which each mind enters, in a personal and solitary fashion, with truth through theoretical knowledge, and with God through contemplation, is better than the treasures of communicable culture which minds receive from one another. Thus the law of transcendence still holds with regard to the community of minds, as it does with regard to every human community. The person will still emerge above the community of minds and demand more, at least so long as the community in which it is engaged is not the supernatural society whose life is the communicated life of God—the Church herself, whose good is the same as the person's. There, in the community of the saints, the person no longer tends to emerge above the community and pass into a better society, for it is in the Church herself that its participation in the divine life is accomplished. Here, it is more than ever true that in different respects the person is for the community and the community is for the person. For there is for the Church a common work, which is continued redemption, to which each is ordained as the part to the work of the whole. But this common work is itself ordained to the personal good of each, to the union of each with God Himself, and to the application of the redeeming blood to each as a single person.

On the one hand, the proper good of the person as a person is achieved in the union of grace and charity with God, with the Uncreated Good, which is the Common Good of the Church—a transcendent common good which no longer is a practical good to be realized, but the subsisting good to which to adhere—above all human good and all communications of created goods found in the Church. In this sense, Francis de Vitoria wrote: "In the corporeal organism, the natural part exists directly for the whole. But in the Church, each man exists only for God and himself, at least directly and principally, because neither grace nor faith, nor hope, nor any other supernatural formality resides immediately in the entire community as in its subject."[45]

On the other hand, the proper good of the person, as an individual, that is, as a part of the created whole of which the head is the Incarnate Word, is not only inferior to the divine common Good of this whole. It is also inferior to the collection of human goods and of the communications of created goods which derive in this whole from its union of grace with the uncreated Good.

Thus, if we consider this grand City as living in its entirety upon a common good which is the very life of God, communicated to the multitude of the just and seeking out the errant sheep, then each stone is for the city. But if we consider each stone as living itself, in its personal participation in this common good, upon the very life of God that is communicated, or as sought after personally by God, who wills to communicate His own life to it, then it is toward each one that all the goods of the city converge to flow back in the measure of his capacity to receive of their plenitude. In this sense, the city is for each stone. It is for each of God's saints, St. Thomas writes, that it is spoken in Matthew: *Super omnia bona sua constituet eum.*[46] And of each, St. John of the Cross writes: "Mine are the heavens and mine the earth, mine are all men, the just and the wicked; the angels are mine and the Mother of God, all things are mine; God Himself is mine and for me. What then dost thou demand and after what dost thou seek, oh my soul? For thine is all of this, and all of this is for thee."[47]

Finally, in the beatific vision, through the intuition of the divine essence, each blessed soul becomes God, in an intentional way, as Cajetan says, and thus enters into the uncreated society of the Divine Persons. The proper eternal good of each, in the degree that its vision grasps it, is the common Good itself of the Divine Persons. Each beholds but does not "comprehend" it, for it still exceeds infinitely the capacity of each. And each one loves it more than itself. Further, because there is a multitude of blessed souls which partake of the same uncreated Good, this Good actually becomes the common Good of both the Divine Persons and the Church of Heaven. Being God Himself, it is of course *more divine* than the act, entitively considered, by which each created member of the heavenly community, according to the degree of its vision, takes possession of its personal good. This, be it noted, is more truly the good of the created person since it excels it infinitely. But in what sense might the personal good, of which each soul thus takes possession, be inferior to this common good? They are identical. The personal good is also God Himself. In relation to the divine service and the divine praise, each soul is a part of the community of the blessed. In relation to the object of the vision, there is no longer a question of being a part but of being identified with the Whole in this society of the blessed, the common object of which is better only because it is, for the multitude of the members, the same object in which each one shares, though in different degrees, as a whole identified with the Whole. Here, in the intentional identification of each soul with the divine essence, the law of the primacy of the common good over the personal

good comes to an end in a certain sense.[48] It is accomplished here precisely because the personal good is at that moment the common good. "The personal
good of each of the blessed is as divine as the separated common Good of the
entire universe: it is identically this very same Good, spiritually possessed."[49]

Translated by John J. FitzGerald, University of Notre Dame

Notes

Reprinted from *The Review of Politics* 8, no. 4 (October 1946): 419–55.

1. R. P. Schwalm, O.P., *Leçons de Philosophic Sociale,* reedited in part under the title,
La Societé et l'État (Paris: Flammarion, 1937).

2. R. P. Garrigou-Lagrange, O.P., *La Philosophie de l' tre et le Sens Commun* (Paris:
Beauchesne, 1904).

3. Eberhard Welty, O.P., *Gemeinschaft und Einzelmensch* (Salzburg-Leipzig: Pustet,
1935).

4. Maritain, *Three Reformers* (New York: Scribner's, 1932); *True Humanism* (New
York: Scribner's, 1938); *Scholasticism and Politics* (New York: Macmillan, 1939); *The Rights
of Man and Natural Law* (New York: Scribner's, 1943).

5. M. Rohner, O.P., "Kommentar des hl. Albertus Magnus zur Einführung in die
Politik des Aristoteles," *Divus Thomas* (Friburg, Switzerland, 1932), 95 ff.

6. I. Th. Eschmann, O.P., "In Defense of Jacques Maritain," *The Modern Schoolman*
22, no. 4 (May 1945): 192.

7. Each intellectual substance is made, first, for God, the separated common good of
the universe, second, for the perfection of the order of the universe (not only as the universe of bodies but also as the universe of spirits), and third, for itself, that is, for the
action (immanent and spiritual) by which it perfects itself and accomplishes its destiny.
(Cf. *Sum. Theol.,* I, 65, and Cajetan's commentary [New York: George Olms Verlag, 2000].)
Using a distinction established further on, we may say that as individual or part, the intellectual substance is first willed and loved for the order of the universe and the perfection
of the created whole; as person, it is first willed and loved for itself. Yet, like every creature,
it differs from God, or Personality in pure act, more than it resembles Him. Hence, absolutely speaking, it is part or "individual" more than "person" and before it as a "person."
It is this that Kant failed to see. It follows from this that, absolutely speaking, the intellectual substance is loved and willed for the order of the universe of creation before being
loved and willed for itself. This in no wise hinders it, in contrast to irrational beings, from
being really for itself and referred directly to God.

Let us add that if we pass to the supernatural order, the order of formal participation
in the deity, this priority of the universe of created nature over the person is reversed.

Each person is here willed and loved for its own sake, *puta ut fruatur Deo* (He truly died for each of them) before being willed and loved for the order and perfection of *this world* or of the universe of nature and creation (Ephes. 1:4) (Whereas "respectu vitae naturalis non est electio, neque liber vitae," *Sum. Theol.*, I, 24, 2 ad 2). In the words of St. Augustine, the justification of the impious is a work greater than the creation of heaven and earth. In his teaching that the justification of the impious is *maximum opus Dei*, St. Thomas proposes the following objection: "Justificatio impii ordinatur ad bonum particulare unius hominis, sed *bonum universi est majus quam bonum unius hominis*, ut patet in I Ethic. Ergo majus opus est creatio coeli et terrae, quam justificatio impii." To it, he answers: "*Bonum universi est majus quam bonum particulare unius, si acciapiatur utrumque in eodem genera. Sed bonum gratiae unius majus est, quam bonum naturae totius universi*, the good of grace of one alone is greater than the good of nature, of the whole universe," including the angelic natures (*Sum. Theol.*, I-II, 113, 9, ad 2).

On the other hand, in this same supernatural order, each person, willed and loved for itself and for the communication of the divine goodness which is made to it, is also and *first of all*, willed and loved (by the same act of transcendent love which grasps all at once the whole and the part) for the communication of the divine goodness which is made to the whole city of the blessed in the sense that each of its members beholds the untreated essence according to the multiple degrees of their participation in the light of glory.

Finally if in the order of grace, the person itself desires God as its good, it does so in loving God for Himself, more than itself, and in willing the good of God more than its own proper good. Indeed, if it wills God for *itself* ("*sibi*"), it is not for the sake of itself as final reason (non "*propter se,*" at least "*simpliciter*") but rather for the sake of God purely and simply as final reason. (Cf. the invaluable commentary of Cajetan on the relations between Hope and Charity, II-II, 17, 5).

8. [See *Sum. Contra Gentiles* III, 112 and III, 113 for the entire Latin text. Ed.]

9. That the extrinsic or separated common good of a multitude, to which it is ordained, is greater than the immanent common good of the multitude is a universal principle. [See *Sum. Theol.*, II-II, 39, 2, ad 2 for the entire Latin text. Ed.]

10. *Sum. Theol.*, I, 93, 2.

11. 1 Cor. 13:12.

12. *Sum. Theol.*, I-II, 4, 8, ad 3.

13. St. Thomas, 2 *Sent.*, d. 26, 1, 1 ad 2.

14. *De Civ. Dei*, XIX, 13.

15. *Sum. Theol.*, I-II, 4, 8 ad 3.

16. *Sum. Theol.*, I-II, 3, 5 ad 1.

17. *Sum. Theol.*, II-II, 47, 2 and 11.

18. 3 *Sent.*, 35, I, 4 sol. lc et ad 2 et 3, 4 *Sent.*, 49, I, 1, sot. 3 ad 1.

19. *Sum. Theol.*, II-II, 188, 8.

20. *Sum Theol.*, I-II, 113, 9, ad 2.

21. St. Thomas, in *Eth.*, I, 2.

22. As expressed by Pope Pius XII in His Christmas Message of 1942, "The origin and the primary scope of social life is the conservation, development and perfection of the

human person, helping him to realize accurately the demands and values of religion and culture set by the creator for every man and for all mankind, both as a whole and in its natural ramifications." (Translation published by *The Catholic Mind*, Jan. 1943.)

From the Encyclical *Mystici Corporis*: "In a natural body the principle of unity so unites the parts that each lacks its own individual subsistence; on the contrary in the Mystical Body that mutual union, though intrinsic, links the members by a bond which leaves to each intact his own personality. Besides, if we examine the relation existing between the several members and the head, in every physical, living body, all the different members are ultimately destined to the good of the whole alone; while every moral association of men, if we look to its ultimate usefulness, is in the end directed to the advancement of all and of every single member. For they are persons, *utpote personae sunt.*" (Prepared by Joseph J. Bluett, S.J., The America Press, New York.) This passage is truly the charter of the Christian doctrine on the person.

23. Giorgio La Pira, "Problemi della persona umana," *Acta Pont. Academiae Romanae Sancti Thomas Aq.*, vol. 8 (Rome-Torino: Marietti, 1945).

24. *Sum. Theol.*, I, 29, 3.

25. And also collective realities constituted of individuals, such as society (*unum per accidens*).

26. Cf. my work *The Degrees of Knowledge* (New York: Scribner's, 1938), Appendix IV.

27. Cf. R. Garrigou-Lagrange, *Le Sens Commun, la philosophie de l' tre et les Formules Dogmatiques*, 3e et 4e editions, 3e Partie, Chap. II.

28. In an animal society, the *individual* is not a person; hence, has not the value of a moral "whole" and is not a subject of right. If the good of the whole profits the parts, as the good of the body profits its members, it does not in the sense that it is turned back or *redistributed* to them. It is merely in order that the whole itself might subsist and be better served that its parts are kept alive or maintained in good condition. Thus, they partake of the good of the whole but only as parts of the whole. Indeed, how could it be the good of the whole without thereby profiting the parts which compose the whole (except when it requires the sacrifice of this or that part which then spontaneously exposes itself to peril, as the hand to save the body, because by nature it loves the whole more than itself, cf. Cajetan, in I, 60, 5)? Such a good is a common good in a general and improperly social sense. It is not the *formally social* common good with which we are concerned in this paper. It is common to the whole and to the parts only in an improper sense, for it does not profit the parts *for themselves* (*finis cui*) at the same time as *for the whole* according to the characteristic exigencies of a whole constituted of persons. It is rather the proper good of the whole, not foreign to the parts, to be sure, but benefiting them only for its own sake and the sake of the whole.

This kind of common good of an animal society is analogically a "bonum honestum" (reached *materialiter et executive, sub directione Dei auctoris naturae*), but in its proper order, where the whole is composed of individuals who are not persons. The common good, formally social, of human society, in order to be truly common good and to attain, as common good, the character of "bonum honestum," implies redistribution to the persons as persons.

29. In 3 *Sent.* d. 5, 3, 2, St. Thomas, in this text, refers to the human composite (*unum per se*) and shows that, because it is only a part of the human being, the separated soul cannot be a person. To anyone whose knowledge of Thomism is sufficiently deep it is clear that the principle, the *ratio* of part is repugnant to that of personality, is an entirely general principle and is applied analogically depending on the case. Thus, John of St. Thomas shows, in speaking of the hypostatic union, which takes place in *persona* (*Sum. Theol.*, III, 2, 2) that God can be united to human nature only as person just as He can be united to human intelligence only as *species intelligibilis* because in both cases He is united to them as term and as whole, not as part (*Cursus Theol.*, "De Incarnatione Disput." IV, a. 1). The same principle must evidently come into play also, though under completely different conditions and following another line of application, when the notion of person is considered with respect to wholes. They are no longer, like the human composite, substantial but have only an accidental unity, and are themselves composed of persons like the social whole.

30. *Sum. Theol.*, I, 30, ad 4.

31. *Sum. Theol.*, I, 42, 5.

32. In the formally social sense specified above, note 28.

33. In this sense, because there do exist supratemporal goods of the natural order (e.g., the contemplative life as conceived by Aristotle), it is perfectly true to say with Mortimer Adler and the Rev. Walter Farrell that the natural happiness of the human being transcends in certain essential elements the political common good (cf. Walter Farrell, O.P., "Person and the Common Good in a Democracy," *Proceedings of the American Catholic Philosophical Association*, vol. 20, Dec. 27 and 28, 1945). The supratemporal natural goods, by reason of which, even in the natural order, the human person transcends the State, are refracted imperfectly and diminishingly, in accordance with a certain social-temporal participation, in the political common good itself. It is much the same with the supernatural virtues of the saints insofar as they add to the moral patrimony and glory of their temporal fatherland. But of themselves, they are related to the order of civilization, and even more to the order of what, farther on, we call the community of minds. They are integrated in the common good of civilization (and this is "temporal" in contrast to the "spiritual" or supernatural order of the kingdom of God, but its highest natural values are "supratemporal" or of the absolute order) and they arise directly out of the common good of the community of minds. Yet both the common good of civilization and that of the community of minds are themselves subordinated to the supernatural common good.

34. Maritain, *The Rights of Man and Natural Law*, 39–43.

35. Ibid., 32.

36. For this reason, Christ could say of Judas: "*Bonum erat ei, si natus non fuisset homo ille.*" (Matt. 26:24). Of course the act of existing never ceases to be *per se* good and desirable; but *per accidens* it ceases to be so when it fails completely and lacks everything to which it is ordained (*Sum. Theol.*, I, 5, 2, ad 3).

37. Jacques Maritain, *De Bergson à Thomas D'Aquin* (New York: Éditions de la Maison française, 1944), 148–49.

38. [For Maritain's Latin citations, see *Sum. Theol.*, II-II, 64, 2. See also: I-II, 96, 4; II, 61, 1; II, 65, 1; II, 65, 5. Ed.]

39. *Sum. Theol.*, I-II, 21, 4, ad 3.

40. See Maritain, *The Rights of Man and Natural Law*, 17.

41. Cf. Gerald B. Phelan, "Justice and Friendship" in *The Maritain Volume* of The Thomist (New York: Sheed and Ward, 1943), 153–70.

42. Let us note here that just as the "extrinsic common good" of an army (victory) is superior to its "immanent common good," so the "extrinsic common good" of the social life of men in the course of terrestrial history (victory over servitude and the antagonisms that divide humanity) is superior to its "immanent common good" and completes its evolution. Out of this fact arises the historical dynamism which, through trials and disasters in the direction of an end, which perhaps will never be attained in the conditions of life here below, carries along with it the social forms of peoples and civilizations.

43. Cf. H. Clérissac, *Le Mystère de l'Eglise*, Chap. VI.

44. Cf. Jacques Maritain, *Freedom in the Modern World* (New York: Charles Scribner's Sons, 1936), 51–52.

45. Francisco de Vitoria, *De potestate Ecclesiae*, II, 5. Cf. Genito, *Relécciones del Maestro Fray Francisco de Vitoria* (Madrid 1934), t. II, 117.

46. St. Thomas, *Expos. in Ep. ad Rom.* c. 8, lect. 6.

47. St. John of the Cross, *Avisos y Sentencias* (ms. d'Andujar), *Silv.* IV, 235.

48. In another sense, this law always holds; in the sense that the infinite communicability of the incomprehensible Essence forever transcends the communication which, through its vision, the creature receives of it.

49. Charles Journet, "La cause materiélle de l'Église glorieuse," *Nova et Vetera* 1 (January–March, 1945): 86.

Fig. 1. Waldemar Gurian. Photo courtesy of Notre Dame Archives.

Fig. 2. Notre Dame in 1938. Photo courtesy of Notre Dame Archives.

Fig. 3. Frank O'Malley, Waldemar Gurian, and Rev. Thomas T. McAvoy, C.S.C. Photo courtesy of Notre Dame Archives.

Fig. 4. Jacques Maritain standing in front of Alumni Hall at Notre Dame, 1955. Photo taken by Yves R. Simon. Courtesy of Anthony O. Simon.

Fig. 5. Desmond Fitzgerald. Photo courtesy of Notre Dame Archives.

Fig. 6. C. J. Friedrich circa 1943, Harvard University, when Friedrich was running the School for Overseas Administration. Photo courtesy of Paul Friedrich.

Fig. 7. John U. Nef circa 1950s. Photo courtesy of Mrs. John U. Nef.

Fig. 8. Aron Gurwitsch. Photo courtesy of Lester Embree,
Center for Advanced Research in Phenomenology.

Fig. 9. Josef Pieper. Photo courtesy of the University of Münster Library.

Fig. 10. Leo Strauss. Courtesy of the University of Chicago Library.

Fig. 11. Eric Voegelin. Courtesy of Ellis Sandoz, Eric Voegelin Institute.

Fig. 12. Hannah Arendt. Courtesy of Hannah Arendt Bluecher Literary Trust.

Fig. 13. Russell Kirk. Photo courtesy of Annette Kirk.

Fig. 14. Glenn Tinder.
Photo courtesy of Glenn Tinder.

Fig. 15. Yves R. Simon.
Photo courtesy of Anthony O. Simon.

CHAPTER 10

Architecture and Western Civilization

JOHN U. NEF

I

All aspects of the life of an age are interrelated, even when the interrelations express themselves in cross purposes and intellectual dissolution. Whether or not they embody forms and ideas worthy to be dignified by the name of architecture, the buildings of any period are an expression of it. They reflect, in varying degrees, its economic and social development, the enactments of its legislative bodies, the acts of its administrative officials, the decisions of its law courts, the character and course of its wars. They also express, again in varying degrees, its methods of education, its religious life, its natural science, its thought and its art. They are, to some extent, the expression of past traditions and works of the mind which have retained a hold on the life of the period or have been revived by its thinkers and artists, as classical antiquity has been revived again and again in Western European history since the eleventh century.

At the same time, the buildings have important influences of their own upon the individuals who see them, live in them or pass through them. They have important influences upon the collective political, economic, intellectual and religious activities of the age in which they are built. So long as the buildings endure or leave their trace, such influences are prolonged into distant ages. The character and the extent of the impression the buildings make depends partly upon the condition of the minds and hearts of men and the nature of the society in which they live. Men's sensitiveness to the art of architecture fluctuates within wide limits. But as long as buildings stand and are used, the ways they are constructed and embellished, the ways they are related or unrelated to each other in neighborhoods and cities, will leave marks on the human side of our species, unless and until men and women have all humanity mechanized out of them.

These reflections are obvious. Is that a reason for failing to consider their significance for the United States, the most highly industrialized and mechanized of all countries since the late nineteenth century, and of all Western countries the one whose future is confided to an admixture of all national and racial strains, including besides the Latin and the Nordic elements of Europe, Africans and Orientals? In so vastly complicated and bewildered a society as that of the United States, may it not be the historian's duty to emphasize the common sense observations, to illuminate with simple concrete illustrations what any sensible person vaguely knows (but has generally forgotten) rather than to devote himself to the obscure, the esoteric, the particular? During the last half century or so, scholars generally have acted on a different assumption. They have left the important matters for the charlatan to exploit or, as the condition of considering problems that are of universal recurring interest, have turned into charlatans themselves. Thus they have denied the important matters their importance. One may almost say of scholars what Paul Valéry has said of the bourgeoisie. They have invested their capital in phantoms, in the fabulous, in the objectivity of controlled experiments interpreted by a tiny number of specialists. By their natures, men and women are obliged in the fundamental questions of life and death, which cannot be settled finally in this world, to wager on something. They cannot escape this necessity simply by ceasing to wager on eternal truth. So they have put their stakes on the ruin of common sense, they have refused to give substantial weight to generally accepted propositions which once carried irresistible force into the speculative realm.[1]

Perhaps we may be allowed in this essay to revert to an earlier world more familiar to the modern Latin than to the modern Anglo-Saxon; perhaps we may be permitted in what is now unscholarly fashion to assume that there are obvious commonsense reflections upon which general agreement is possible; perhaps we may be permitted to employ such reflections as a kind of framework for this sketch of the relation of architecture to Western civilization. Then let us make two further assumptions, in addition to those we have made already concerning the bearing of architecture upon the history of an age. Let us assume that it matters what kind of influences upon man buildings have, both of themselves and through their relations to other buildings, to groups of buildings, as in a city and the surrounding suburbs. Let us assume, finally, that human beings have a measure of free choice in the construction, embellishment and position of buildings. If these assumptions are granted, at least for the sake of argument, then human beings evidently have responsibilities for the kind of influence, good or bad, that architecture imprints upon the citizens of our time and of the future. Those concerned in one way or another with building and city planning, from the highest to the humblest, have duties independent of the tasks of adding to comforts, promoting full employment in the building trades, increasing wages, salaries, fees and commissions. The responsibilities we refer to are responsibilities in the speculative realm. Architecture is one of the arts. So the responsibilities of society that call for emphasis are the responsibilities to art. It is our purpose to try, in the light of history, to define tentatively the nature of the artistic responsibilities in connection with architecture and city planning, as they confront the world today. From what we have said concerning the interrelations between building and general history, it should be apparent that these responsibilities cannot be divorced from further responsibilities—moral, intellectual and religious—of Western civilization in an age of world wars.

II

In the history of building among the Western peoples, it is possible to distinguish three main periods. Each has a certain unity. Perhaps in connection with the third, we should say a certain lack of unity. There is, first, the age of Gothic architecture. It began with the marvelous Romanesque transition to Gothic early in the twelfth century. This was the time of the first two crusades. A strong sense of the solidarity of Christendom, in an era of increased travel, exchange of goods, of knowledge and ideas, helped to bind the peoples of Europe to each other. It was the time of Abélard, the Abbé Suger and Saint Bernard, all of whom were born between 1079 and 1091. Their creative lives expressed, each in a different way, the interdependence of faith, politics, learning, joy and art, an interdependence which strengthened the bonds of a common belief. Their creative lives expressed, each in a different way, as did also the lives of some thirteenth-century scholastics, masons and saints, an attempt to bring in words, stone or other materials all the essential aspects of an immensely complicated and rapidly changing civilization, whose inhabitants were multiplying, into an intelligible unified relation, which embodied a common purpose for man in eternal life. As a very great age of building, the Gothic lasted at least well into the last half of the thirteenth century. In the sense that no fundamentally different conception of building presented itself, the Gothic lasted longer. It lasted about four hundred years until the early fifteenth century.

At that time there appeared what may be called, following Geoffrey Scott, the architecture of humanism.[2] The development and elaboration of the new styles, like the development and elaboration of the Gothic styles, spread over many generations, in forms known familiarly as Renaissance, Baroque and Rococo. Just when the architecture of humanism began to deteriorate is a matter of much dispute, like the question of its aesthetic value. The classical conception of architecture may be even represented as prolonged in the Empire style. But by the juncture of the eighteenth and nineteenth centuries, the architecture of humanism was certainly losing its integrity, although the great classical musical forms, which had come down from Monteverdi through Rameau and Bach, were still enriched by the masterpieces of Haydn, Mozart, Beethoven and Schubert. With the death of the Empire style in the early nineteenth century, humanism as a coherent artistic conception for architecture was dead.

It is the death of a unified artistic tradition, rather than a new life, which has thus far characterized the third period in the history of Western architecture. No living conception has yet put its stamp upon the modern world as earlier conceptions put their stamps upon the medieval and the early modern world of Western civilization.

Could a new conception grow out of the United States and perhaps out of the Middle West, which have been spared the material destruction of the Second World War? If such a conception were to grow, America might embody in a contribution to beauty the sense of gratitude it could feel for the sheltered position it has occupied thus far during the destructive twentieth century. That would be a contribution to a world culture upon the appearance of which the future of Western civilization in large measure depends. The Chicago school of architecture goes back to Sullivan and Wright. Into it has now been infused the blood of an important European school, which Mies van der Rohe represents in its most substantial and least pretentious form. The former president of the Chicago Chapter of the Institute of Architects, Alfred Shaw, is doing much to call attention to the opportunities that these great architects have given our country at a time when a large part of the most civilized cities and towns all over the world have been blown into rubble. He and Mies van der Rohe recently paid a compliment to the more youthful Chicago school of learning brought into being by Robert Hutchins (which owes in its turn a profound debt to Jacques Maritain, who emerges from the war a great French citizen of the world). They invited us to offer a series of lectures upon the role of order and delight in architecture and city planning. We are in the fullest sense allies. Like ourselves, these architects seek in respect to different but related materials a conception of man as a whole in relation to a common purpose. That the work of the Chicago school of architects may help to create a unified conception in architecture and that this may lead towards a reawakening in mankind of the sense of beauty and true delight, which has been generally lost, is our hope. But nothing would be gained by minimizing the formidable obstacles which have risen and which continue to rise in the way of its fulfillment.

III

The great majority of men and women who reflect at all upon the characteristics of our times, see them in statistical terms. In connection with building, their memories may go back as far as the fabulous 1920s, when bank presidents in all the large cities of a country of large cities considered tearing down their buildings mainly for the sake of putting up new ones to attract the attention of wealthy depositors, to whom in those days, as perhaps also in days to come, a hundred million dollars was little more than pocket change. Even persons whose memories are shorter are aware of the tremendous constructive efforts made during the past six years to produce the mammoth flow of tanks, airplanes, and warships from assembly lines, onto the earth, up in the air and into the water. Men and women not unnaturally see ours as an age of building which dwarfs all past ages.

There is a sense in which their view is perfectly correct. Never before have so many material conveniences and comforts for bathing, sanitation, heating, cooling, lighting, and entertaining been provided. Never before has anything remotely approaching the quantity of industrial materials now harnessed been driven into construction work. The output per capita of such materials is possibly a hundredfold what it was in the middle ages, and the population of France alone is now perhaps almost as large as that of Europe west of the Oder when the greater part of Chartres Cathedral was built. But there is also a statistical sense in which this view is seriously warped. If we consider the *proportion* of the Western peoples who have earned their living directly and indirectly from the building industries and the industries of decoration which embellish and furnish buildings, it is by no means certain that it is now larger even in the United States than it was in twelfth and thirteenth-century France. The proportion of the capital, the income and the time of the Western peoples devoted directly and indirectly to building was possibly even greater then than in the nineteenth and early twentieth centuries.

During six or seven generations of Gothic architecture, a large part of all the industrial workpeople of Europe participated in a fascinating variety of ways in building enterprises. Overwhelmingly the most important calls made upon them came in the construction, the embellishment, the decoration, the amplification, the remodeling and the restoration of cathedrals, smaller churches and monasteries. The mere magnitude of the efforts in relation to the size of the population, the economic resources and conditions of the Gothic age can be compared only to the efforts put forth by the chief nations of the earth in the world wars of the twentieth century. Indeed, in that sense, the Gothic builders certainly operated on a greater scale than the modern destroyers, because the intense effort went on from year to year with few interruptions at all comparable to those which modern mankind has been allowed hitherto in the intervals between wars. The purpose given to daily life by war, even during the past three decades of unprecedented military preparations and operations, has been fitful compared with the continuity of developing purpose embodied in two centuries of Gothic architecture.

It might be supposed that the magnitude of the efforts involved in Gothic building can be explained by the lack of machinery, particularly of any machinery driven by steam or hydroelectric power. It is true that the growing use of power and machinery in modern times has reduced overwhelmingly the manual labor required to transport, manufacture and place a given quantity of materials. The use of power and machinery has also reduced (though less extensively) the manual labor required to extract from the earth ores, minerals and other raw materials needed directly or indirectly in building. But there is another side to this balance sheet, which the modern statistical view of life, so inappropriate to the Gothic age, is forcing us to make. As we have just remarked, the *quantity* of materials per capita used in building was exceedingly small then compared with now. And it was usual to build mainly out of stone and earth found close at hand. So heavy materials had to be moved in very much smaller doses and for very much shorter distances. It is by no means certain that the proportion of the time spent by building workers in the actual extraction, movement and placing of materials was larger during the Gothic Age than now.

The main differences between the labor of medieval and twentieth-century builders were not in the use of muscle, in the brute force expended. The main differences were in calls made upon the mind and spirit, in the opportunities afforded for constructive artistry, thought and contemplation. We have today architects, some decorators and a few engineers who devote themselves to problems of construction and embellishment with an intelligence (and more rarely with an imaginative insight) comparable to that of the greatest medieval architects and planners. But the participation of workmen generally in sustained efforts of the mind is slight compared with that of the hosts of craftsmen engaged in building and decoration during the twelfth and thirteenth centuries. The artistic decisions that workers have to make are negligible now in comparison with the Gothic Age.

That was an age when the arts and crafts were one. Artistic and technical problems had not begun to be divorced. It is true that specifications laid down by churchmen or by communal authorities for windows, statues and other objects of art, which formed an integral part of buildings, were exceedingly rigorous and minute. Men of great learning and of practical political experience sometimes composed what were virtually handbooks of instructions for the guidance of the artistic craftsmen who participated in the building of a monastery or a church.[3] Yet the people of Europe were united in the Christian faith and by a belief in an Eternity transcending time, space and matter, an Eternity which Christ had revealed as man's last end. The principal buildings and each small part of them were intended to express or to celebrate, in a great variety of ways, this common purpose of the human spirit into which men sought to distill the individual demands of each particular body of bones and flesh. As men and women generally shared the intention behind specifications for building, or at least the knowledge and beliefs on which they were based, the specifications seldom appeared to craftsmen as fetters. They provided the kind of framework that contributes to the genuine intellectual and spiritual freedom of the ordinary human being, likely to be bewildered and even overwhelmed when the choices confronting him are very numerous. There was room within the specifications for the development of artistic ideas. There was scope for human initiative that is denied when movements are dictated by machines and the workman takes no direct part in the manipulation of materials. Taste in workmanship was widely diffused; it had not become the specialty of the few.

Emile Mâle has said that the cathedral deserved to be called "The Bible of the Poor."[4] From it the citizens and the peasants who came into the towns got much of their knowledge, their moral and religious education, their sense of beauty. The lessons were written into stone and glass for all to see and to feel, not only those who participated in the actual labor, but the rest who came daily to the services and who saw the spires whenever they left their homes. The great buildings of the Gothic age gathered European life into their fold. They helped everyone from the most powerful to the humblest to an education, a sense of humanity, and a hope in eternal life. The time now given to flashes of motion pictures, to the din of the radio, to travel in street cars, subways, automobiles and express trains was all compressed into quiet rest, accompanied by the plain chant, the voices of the priests softened against deep stone walls, by prayers and the tolling of bells.

Cathedral, town walls and many-gabled houses, all were interrelated. All were parts of one, just as a statue on the central portal of the cathedral, a pillar inside, a window in colored glass, and a spire belonged together. The cluster of beauty formed by the whole town was the central jewel in a harmonious countryside closely set over by abbeys and villages, built firmly into the landscape through three centuries of expanding economic life and growing material prosperity.[5]

The rise of Gothic architecture reflected a growing sense of the solidarity and common purpose of the Western peoples that involved the whole of their lives and not merely the parts which we call religious. Relentless wars became less frequent. European men and women lost some of their appetite for settling scores by killing each other. With the erection of tremendously thick and ingeniously contrived fortresses, like the one at Carcassonne, the advantages in warfare tended to shift from the attackers to the defenders.[6]

Part of the tragedy and the hope of human nature, as borne by individuals, by social groups, or by nations, consists in its susceptibility to the most extravagant contradictions. Expressed in social and political life, these contradictions seem to have made it impossible for states or civilizations to pursue to a logical conclusion, any process of development, whether it is essentially good or essentially bad. Gothic society was groping toward a universal harmony. Yet, in spite of so much that favored success, it failed to achieve this harmony. The age of greatest Gothic architecture ended in dissension, bitterness and confusion of purpose. Reflections of the disillusionment appear all through the finest long poem in the Western languages, Dante's *Divine Comedy*, written at the beginning of the fourteenth century. The dissolution of harmony and common purpose can be observed by the historian in the claims and counter-claims of rival popes and the degradation of a part of the clergy. It can be observed by the statistically-minded economic historian in the slowing down or ending of industrial progress as measured by the volume of production, though it should not be assumed that the reduction in the rate of material progress was itself a disruptive force. The dissolution is reflected also in the deterioration during more than two centuries of Gothic architecture.

By the middle of the sixteenth century that style of building was dead, together with much of the craftsmanship that had been a part of it. The Western peoples had only to await the Gothic revival, late examples of which can be seen in American cities, sticking up out of a checkerboard of streets, in the midst of houses built in every style and mixture of styles known to the Western past and imported from foreign civilizations such as the Persian, the Indian, the Aztec, or the Chinese. Examples of the Gothic revival can be seen in the very area now appropriated by what is regarded vaguely, but hardly correctly, as the modern haunt of Thomas Aquinas—the University of Chicago. There is even a pale reflection at one street intersection of the marvelous twelfth-century spire of Chartres Cathedral.

That old spire at Chartres itself is still intact, rising out of the hill into which the town is built. It has caught the eyes of thirty generations of peasants, travelers and warriors for distances of some thirty miles in every direction, through the flat and treeless grain land of Beauce. What does it matter to the present age that a modern replica of the most beautiful and most perfectly placed spire in the world can be seen mainly when one looks down from the higher buildings in the neighborhood—and then hardly as part of a church, still less of a neighborhood, not at all of a city? Orderliness and appropriate placing are now considered almost exclusively in relation to efficiency, to the saving of motions and computations; they are reserved for the somewhat inhuman filing cabinets of libraries, business offices and university departments, or for the scarcely more human distribution of objects in factories, warehouses, filling stations and stores.

Among the conditions essential to the creation of any great work of art is some promise of permanence. Unless men wish and are permitted to strive toward a result independent of their time and place, independent of particular material, social and political circumstances, ways of making money, ways of having fun, ways of getting around the world in a hurry, they cannot possess the seriousness of purpose without which anything worthy of the name of art is impossible. They cannot detach from the commonplace, particular every day occurrence, the unique abstract human meaning—the love, the suffering, the joy—which are forever fresh because they belong not to one race, one country, one group or one generation but to all. What Gothic architecture embodies is this faith in permanence. To an even greater degree than the Greeks who built the Parthenon, or the Romans who built at Orange the theater with its great wall which Louis XIV fifteen centuries afterwards called the finest in France, the builders of Gothic Europe aimed at Eternity.

IV

In spite of the remarkable growth in the European population and the remarkable increase in material prosperity, the twelfth century and even the thirteenth preserved and cultivated the sense of human permanence, inherited in such different ways from Greek and Hebrew cultural origins. The humble and the powerful alike had faith that something human endured in the same form for all men always. As it is always difficult to maintain plausibly that anything material, anything that man can actually observe with his senses, will remain what it is, the faith focused upon the immortality of the mind and soul.

When the physical conditions of life change very rapidly among such extraordinarily active-minded peoples as the Western Europeans proved to be, the notion of permanence can only be maintained at all generally with the help of symbols which have a widely understood common meaning in liturgical habits, in customs and in laws. Whatever shakes these habits, customs and laws puts a heavy strain on faith. The conception of permanence itself is menaced. At the end of the Middle Ages this conception, which was the basis of such European unity as existed and of the hope in a more general human unity, was threatened from several directions. Gunpowder was a discovery of the late thirteenth century, at least in so far as Europe was concerned. Eventually it made possible terrific destruction, without much close fighting of the kind for which Western man felt a growing distaste. At the turn of the fifteenth and sixteenth centuries new weapons, based on gunpowder, transferred decisively but temporarily the advantages in warfare from the defenders to the attackers. Though on a much smaller scale, the change in the character of military operations was hardly less striking than that which has accompanied the shift in recent decades from trench to mechanized warfare. During the later Middle Ages and at the beginning of modern times, the Empire and the Papacy, the chief unifying institutions and symbols in Gothic Europe, lost much of their effective hold over the peoples of Western Christendom. Their stabilizing and harmonizing influences were undermined. The anchorage provided by a single Christian worship in a world of economic change was loosened by the Reformation. The notion of Eternity transcending matter, time and space, in which human beings participated by virtue of their mind and spirit, was gradually blotted from the human intellect as the physical universe took on new aspects and new subtleties, as men saw new tangible treasure troves to penetrate, explore, contrast and explain.

In the beginning these manifestations of human curiosity begot a reaction hardly less damaging to Western unity than the new tendencies towards individualism themselves. In the heads of the later scholastics, the scholastic doctrines of learning hardened into an uncompromising dogmatism, fatal to art and thought as well as to the advances in natural science that a few men were beginning to make. This invited the modern attack on the whole scholastic system of knowledge, an attack which was eventually to deprive men largely of the speculative nourishment which the faith, thought and art of the twelfth and thirteenth centuries had helped to supply.

For a time the disintegrating forces in Gothic society and culture were not abetted by any great economic development in the direction of the kinds of mechanized and standardized labor which tend to dull the intellect and the imagination of participant and spectator alike. During the fourteenth and early fifteenth centuries, industrial and commercial progress was far less conspicuous than during the twelfth and thirteenth. The population stopped increasing; the volume of output ceased to grow. But latent forces of economic expansion and economic individualism came into their own for a short period soon after the birth of Leonardo Da Vinci, in 1452, and the end of the Hundred Years' War in 1453. First in Italy, then in central Europe, southern Spain and France, then in the Spanish Netherlands, and finally during the late sixteenth and early seventeenth centuries in England, Holland, Scotland and Sweden industrial progress and the growth of trade again became striking. Industry spilled over the boundaries of Gothic towns, whose ancient limits were marked by old twelfth or thirteenth-century walls. New industrial agglomerations also grew on a center provided by some old village, hitherto the preserve of farmers. Along irregular trails and cowpaths, workmen's cottages and warehouses were built, along rivers and streams fulling, tanning and paper mills appeared, until the irregular lines of fresh industrial activity seemed to be shooting out in all directions from the middle of the village "like the rays from a great star."[7] The framework of cities and towns, derived from the Gothic period, had no validity for the new economic world. The new warehouses, bridges and water-driven wheels, the merchants' palaces, even the town halls and the halls of justice, were irrelevant to the design which had guided the Gothic builders.

It was in Great Britain during the long reigns of Elizabeth and James I, which stretched from 1558 to 1625, and again during the decade, 1630–39, preceding the civil war, that the new European movement of economic expansion was carried farthest. Between 1540 and 1640 the population of London grew about sixfold from 60,000 or so to more than 300,000. Londoners who sauntered out for an afternoon stroll in the days of Shakespeare and during Milton's early life were accustomed to the continual noise of saws and hammers, to the sight of scores of new dwellings, of large workshops and warehouses, in various stages of construction, with carpenters, masons, plasterers and bricklayers busy at their trades. As in the growing American cities of the late nineteenth and early twentieth centuries, houses were put up helter-skelter, often with a complete disregard of the building rules promulgated by the English Crown for the capital city.[8] Early in 1637, no less than two hundred new buildings, erected during the previous summer in what was then the suburb of Wapping, were ordered torn down because they failed to conform to regulations concerning height and position.[9] London expanded in every direction, into areas once meadow and woodland. It absorbed many old villages. Brickmakers were accused of spoiling the neighboring fields in their search for earth.[10]

The economic expansion which accompanied the change from the medieval to the modern world carried Europeans all over the globe. They settled in North and South America to form the nuclei of vast and populous nations. Until the nineteenth century the fronts presented by the settlements of the Western peoples were still thinly held. But the clearings and cultivated fields about the multiplying villages and the slowly growing towns were portents of the modern industrialized world with its enormous congested cities and suburbs.

It seems a far cry from the harmony and repose of the Gothic cathedral even to the London of the early Stuarts, where one prominent Scottish courtier, the Earl of Carlisle, consumed in little more then twenty years a fortune equivalent in modern money to over ten million dollars.[11] Why was it that the great expansion of early modern times brought no such confusion in building styles, no such fundamental disagreement concerning the principles of architecture, as has accompanied the industrial revolution of the nineteenth and early twentieth centuries? In the teeth of disruptive forces like the Discoveries, the Reformation, the Thirty Years' War, and the rise of the pushing, profit-seeking mercantile elements in society at the expense of the ancient nobility, how was it possible for Europe to create and accept the architecture of humanism, and to make it the basis for building not only in old towns but in the rising industrial villages? Renaissance and even baroque are, above all, styles of moderation and suitable proportions, styles with the most delicate taste, styles in their spirit antithetical to expansion, haste and material success for its own sake. The disposition, common in Victorian times, to dismiss baroque and even renaissance styles as decadent, has been shown to rest on a series of fallacies concerning the nature of the art of architecture. While these styles can be represented properly as less religious than the Gothic, they made equal, if not stronger, calls on the artistic intelligence, on taste and at least through most of the sixteenth century on aesthetic imagination. In their development, the mind was making good its claims to an independence of circumstances—physical, economic, social and political.

If we are to understand the power of the humanistic styles in architecture in an age when the European nations were staking out claims to the whole habitable earth, we must take account of at least two important conditions which were part and parcel of every aspect of European civilization in early modern times. One was material scarcity. The other was cultivated taste.

After the Reformation a rapid growth in the population of Europe, a rapid increase in the volume of commodities produced for comfort, and equally a multiplication in destructive weapons based on gunpowder and other explosives, depended on new economic developments. They depended upon the discovery and extensive exploitation of new seams of ore and other earthly substances, upon new technical inventions capable of reducing greatly the costs of production and transportation and of increasing greatly the power behind machinery. The element needed above all to light the fires of industrial progress and military destruction was cheap fuel.

But during early modern times the fuel upon which Western civilization had chiefly depended became more and more expensive. Beginning in Great Britain in Elizabeth's reign, inroads made upon the forests for lumber, firewood and charcoal produced a timber crisis in one European country after another.[12] The scarcity of wood placed limits upon the production of all kinds of construction materials, especially in the north of Europe, where the manufacture of such commodities as bricks in the heat of the sun was impracticable. Nothing was accomplished to relieve the shortage by substituting stone, brick, metal or glass for wood as structural materials unless coal replaced charcoal and firewood in their manufacture. At the beginning of the eighteenth century, Great Britain was the only country in Europe where any extensive use was made of coal in manufacturing. Even there iron, the metal most spendthrift of fuel, was still generally extracted from its ore in a charcoal fire. As long as the European peoples remained dependent upon forests for fuel, iron, steel and glass construction lay beyond the range of architectural possibilities.

Shortages of fuel and other substances limited the quantities of materials which the builders in early modern times could draw upon. Supplies were insufficient for a general and sustained expansion of building, such as modern builders have indulged in to meet and also to create economic demands. If carefully husbanded and selected, the supplies were adequate to the restricted needs of peoples whose ancestors, except for a few rich and privileged, had known no way of earning a livelihood except by heavy toil and sweat. It should be recognized that the European peoples of early modern times, like their Gothic ancestors, could command by their technical skill and labor much more than enough material goods to satisfy the basic needs of societies with high death rates and not yet trained to waste. If labor had been employed in Europe on the same principles as in *Utopia,* Thomas More's six-hour day might have proved enough to provide a rude abundance almost everywhere. Though modern prosperity was lacking, the Europeans had time on their hands beyond that required to meet the material standards of living which then prevailed.

In *The Republic,* Socrates explains to Adeimantus the two causes for a deterioration in the arts. They are, he says, "wealth and poverty."[13] Like the Greeks in the fifth century, B.C., the Europeans in early modern times, when not engaged in wars to the death, had commodity without profusion. "In der Beschränkung zeigt sich der Meister," Goethe once remarked. Circumstances were favorable in early modern times to the rigid selection of the artistically valuable, to the use by the artist of those limited means without which, paradoxically, the human mind cannot achieve in art anything approaching the unlimited artistic objectives which it seeks. The hasty and reckless expansion of building that went on for a time in London and some other places could not be repeated everywhere.

Let us not suggest that economic conditions were doing for the artist what the artist can do only for himself. Material scarcity of the kind which prevailed during the age of humanistic architecture, may be represented as having helped to provide the kind of soil in which, if history is a guide, the arts can flourish. But neither by what they give nor by what they deny do economic conditions of themselves generate works of beauty. In relation to the environment out of which it is thrust, a masterpiece of building cannot be compared to a flower or even to a mountain. A work of art is always a creation of the specifically human powers. It rests its claim to exist and endure largely upon the delight which it infuses into the human mind and spirit. Delight is to a considerable extent dependent upon the release from physical sense and material concern given man in the reflective contemplation which is even more essential to the success of the creator than to the enjoyment of the participating spectator. What Geoffrey Scott has written about the relations between architecture and mechanical science, is equally true of the relations between architecture and all economic conditions. "The art of architecture," Scott says, "studies not structure in itself, but the effect of structure on the human spirit. . . . It creates, by degrees, a humanized dynamics. For that task, constructive science is a useful slave, and perhaps a natural ally, but certainly a blind master."[14] Of all architectural styles in the Classical and the Christian traditions, renaissance and baroque are those which take the greatest liberties with constructive science. Judged by twentieth-century American standards of material convenience, which were largely alien to the seventeenth century, they take equally great liberties with utility. Of all architectural styles, renaissance and baroque are those which proceed most freely in accordance with the claims of intelligent taste, with which seventeenth-century standards of material comfort, especially in France, were more in harmony than twentieth-century standards.

The architecture of humanism was in part the expression of a new kind of European unity. It was less religious and more intellectual than medieval unity. It was therefore less universal because it made demands upon the minds of men far more exacting than the faith which had helped Europe unite in the eleventh, twelfth and thirteenth centuries. With the distribution of human endowments that have prevailed even in the most intelligent ages, the new demands were such as only the few could supply. Subjects, for example, became increasingly erudite. Jupiter, Hercules, Mars and other pagan gods, Alexander, Caesar, Nero and other pagan emperors were figures much less warm and meaningful to the unlettered than subjects from Scripture had been in an age of a single universal faith.[15]

The decorative arts and crafts, which employed considerable numbers of workpeople, retained much importance in the world of renaissance and baroque architecture. In France and most continental states seventeenth-century princes gave the crafts a new lease on life, both by maintaining and extending old gild forms under the tutelage of the Crown, and by helping financially in the establishment of artistic workshops, operated or supervised by royal officials. But there was an increasing standardization of the materials supplied. Building tended to become more stereotyped and routine. Considerably more machinery was used in extracting, preparing and placing materials than in the thirteenth century. As art grew more self-conscious, as the artist came to be distinguished more and more sharply from the craftsman, the quest for beauty tended to become more specialized than it had been in the Gothic age.

The price of the loss of religious meaning in architecture and of the divorce between such arts as painting or sculpture and manual work was a reduction in the spiritual and intellectual participation of the common man in building.[16] This was parcel of a general reduction in the share of the humble in the life of the mind and in history. Not only were the great majority of the population more excluded from artistic appreciation and delight by the changes in the subjects of architecture and other arts and in the nature of workmanship, the proportion capable through education and experience of appreciating learned allusions, wit, and the charm of color and constructive form seems to have diminished. With the weakening of belief in the value of the sacraments and church services, and, during the late seventeenth and eighteenth centuries, in the truth of Christianity itself, the proportion capable of being deeply moved by religious art diminished. At that time, after religious, civil and national strife had torn Europe apart in early modern times, a renewed horizontal unification of European society was taking place among the rising political, economic and cultural elite. Among them interest and participation in architecture and art and enthusiasm for both were hardly less intense, however different they may have been in character, than among sensitive and religious medieval people. But the new unification was accompanied by a vertical split. In certain occupations, especially heavy industries like mining and metallurgy, and in the growing standing armies, a sort of social scum was thrown up, and out. These pariahs, the new wage slaves and conscripts, were excluded from the European community to a greater extent than in the thirteenth century any groups had been, even the serfs, who, at that time, were in process of being emancipated.[17]

At the beginning of the eighteenth century the new outcasts still formed only a minority among the wage-earning population in most European countries. But the appearance of this minority was portentous for the future of the intelligence and for the future of taste. It was portentous for the future of architecture.

V

During the era of the French Revolution, the elements of expansion, active in European civilization at least as early as the eleventh century, began to get out of control of the intelligent taste which had established the claims of art in early modern times. After the 1730s and 1740s the rate of increase in the population of Western Europe became more striking than at any period since the time of Dante (1265–1321). At the turn of the eighteenth and nineteenth centuries the rate of increase shot up still further, first in Great Britain and then on the Continent. During the nineteenth century the European inhabitants multiplied as never before in civilized history. They swarmed all over the globe in the wake of the explorers and early colonizers. In two hundred years the world population has doubled, the people of European extraction have become more than five times as numerous as they were in 1740, when Frederick the Great began the fierce campaigns of Prussia against the neighboring states of central Europe. Hundreds of cities have grown in area and population much faster than London grew during the reigns of Elizabeth and James I. The volume of industrial output per capita has increased at a more rapid rate than the population. For the first time in history a considerable proportion of the human race—particularly the Anglo-Saxon part of it and above all the people of the United States—have been ushered from an economy of scarcity into one of abundance.

For city planning, architecture and the building trades the revolution in economic conditions produced by the triumph of industrialism has had momentous consequences. Industrialism has obviously complicated enormously the problem of creating a beautiful and enduring civilization and an architecture such as might express it.

The nature of art cannot be adequately understood in terms of rigid rules or formulae, any more than it can be adequately explained in terms of its environment. Yet a few broad principles concerning the problems of the builder seem to have a validity independent of time. A repetition of these principles, repeatedly set forth by the greatest students of architecture, will help in showing why industrialism has increased the difficulty of achieving an art of architecture.

The builder needs to serve three distinct objectives. One is firm structure; his building cannot disregard the requirements of structural science, if for no other reason because it will fall apart if it does. Another is utility; the building has to serve the economic or social or political or religious purposes for which it is built. If it is a dwelling or an apartment house full of dwellings, it has to meet the requirements of comfort which prevail among the people who are expected to inhabit it. The third objective may be called "delight," following Sir Henry Wotton, who in turn followed Vitruvius.[18] This means that the building, both within and without and also in its position with respect to other buildings and to the city as a whole, should satisfy the requirements of beauty. It is these last requirements that are least recognized today and about which the public generally, and scholars as well, are most confused.

Building can hardly be satisfactory unless it reconciles these three objectives. If we are to have an *art* of architecture there would seem to be only one valid general principle concerning this reconciliation. It should be based on the requirements of beauty. Structure and utility, as Geoffrey Scott suggests, have their place as servants of delight; it is to be hoped that they may have their place as allies.

By virtue of the fresh problems of engineering which have emerged in our age of steel, concrete and glass construction, structure has assumed a greater importance than in early modern times, and the problems with which the architect has to deal have been changed accordingly, just as the problems of the wood carver differ from those of the painter in oils commissioned to decorate the ceilings and walls of a large church. By virtue of the remarkable developments in plumbing, heating, ventilating, cooling, lighting, and communication, by virtue of the changes in the methods and the scale of manufacturing, storing, financing, selling and transporting every sort of commodity, utility has to take account of new conditions which have altered enormously the purposes for which buildings are used. It remains true nevertheless that if either structure or utility master delight, we cannot have art. We cannot hope for enduring architecture.

The need for art in architecture and city planning has become more not less compelling with the triumph of modern industrial civilization, because the problems of the architect who seeks an artistic total solution are much more complicated and because he meets with much more opposition and much less understanding among his associates, his clients and his workmen than his predecessors in the era of Gothic or of humanistic building. During the very age when there has been a great diminution in the opportunities for the artistic craftsmanship and the contemplation needed to arouse the creative thought and imagination inherent in the human race, these qualities (adjusted to different materials, greater dimensions and to new kinds of domestic, social and political relations) have become more necessary than ever to the future of Western civilization.

Industrialism has brought with it an unprecedented insistence upon the claims of structural science and comfort. This has made it increasingly difficult in architecture to subordinate science and comfort to delight. This insistence, together with the further difficulties put by industrialism in the way of cultivating art, actually threaten to extinguish altogether the claims of beauty. The increasing importance of the technological achievements which have their origins in the discoveries of the natural sciences have naturally focused the attention of engineers and architects upon the new kinds of materials now available for building and upon the structural problems which emerge from their use on a tremendous scale.

Let us not permit ourselves to be misunderstood. There is nothing wrong in itself with an interest in concrete, iron, steel and glass, or with the erection of skyscrapers, warehouses and airplane terminals. We are not suggesting that salvation for the art of architecture lies in a return to classical architecture, medieval architecture or the architecture of humanism. We are simply suggesting that in so far as architects become primarily engineers they cease to be architects. The pressure of modern engineering and modern technology is in the direction of a preoccupation of builders generally (whatever a few individuals are doing to withstand the pressure) with problems of engineering to the exclusion of problems of art. Modern technology and mechanization have thrown a further and more serious obstacle in the way of the art of architecture. They have reduced to exceedingly small numbers the workers engaged directly and indirectly in building whose labor calls for artistic decisions. Therefore the modern architect has not the opportunity offered to the Gothic builder, and even to the architect in the period of renaissance, baroque and empire architecture, to call on craftsmen whose training and experience have made them sensitive to the claims of delight, in and of itself, and have made them capable of carrying through an artistic intention in the spirit in which it was conceived. Such a premium has been put on doing work in a hurry that the modern architect cannot even find workmen capable of carrying out adequately his intentions to provide the firm structure which is indispensable, especially with modern materials, to give his work artistic body.

Industrialism has operated with even greater insistence to swell to disproportionate size the claims of utility or comfort in connection with architecture and city planning. At the same time the nature of these claims has become increasingly capricious and changing. It is now becoming indispensable to add air-conditioning to central heating; oil burning supersede coal burning furnaces. The installation of power-driven machinery, of barrack-like space for storing tremendous quantities of materials and commodities *en route* to the consumers, or for accommodating small armies of clerks, salesmen and saleswomen, has conditioned the builders of large structures to meet the demands of an economic world whose all-consuming interest is the sale at a profit of goods in larger and larger quantities. The installation of elevators, of plumbing, of bathing quarters, of refrigeration, of radio-receiving sets has led increasingly to the building of homes and apartments suited or supposed to be suited to the desires of modern householders. These persons and still more the middleman, whose main job has become that of deciding what the consumers can be induced to want, have tended more and more to confuse cleanliness with charm and convenience with taste.

Let us again take care not to be misunderstood. Cleanliness can contribute to charm and convenience to taste. But the relation of each side of these pairs to the other resembles the relation of structure to delight and of utility to beauty. Charm and taste are enhanced by cleanliness and convenience only when the more subtle and lasting qualities are put first, only when cleanliness, such as continuous washing and dusting alone can maintain, and convenience, the notions of which are continually undergoing rapid changes, are made to serve beauty rather than to obscure its true meaning.

Experience in the highly industrialized countries, and particularly in the United States, suggests that in matters of taste the population is at least as corruptible as it is instructible. Corruption has been made easy by abundance, by lessons provided in methods of salesmanship, and by the advertising, installment selling and other kinds of pressure resulting from a notion (which has been abhorrent to many serious economic thinkers) that the only test of value is the capacity of a product or a service to command in the open market a higher price than it costs. More and more during the past seventy-five years or so the object of all business, including the real estate, the furniture and the building supply businesses, has been to sell in vast quantities and in a hurry. Salesmen have been schooled to aim at a lower and lower common denominator, if not of superficial utility, certainly of taste. One effect has been to reduce the public taste below its natural level. Since buildings, like other commodities, have been subjected to what came to be regarded as a natural law of salability, the efforts of the few architects and city planners, with a sense of beauty, who try to keep even a modest place for delight in the appearances of the modern city and countryside are defeated. The frustrations of the true architect arising, not as our modern psychoanalysts lead some to suppose from his family troubles, his love life or his digestion, but from his profession, incline him towards bitterness or compromise. Both prevent him from making the full gift to mankind of which he is capable.

The difficulties do not end with the disproportionate emphasis accorded to structural science and utility. The claims of art have been directly undermined also in their own citadel, in the fortress of delight itself. Success in erecting a building, like success in any other considerable enterprise, depends upon the organization of all the work connected with it. During the Middle Ages and even in early modern times organization in building was generally inefficient where speed, quantity and sanitation were concerned. But organization in building (or to some extent what would now be called lack of organization) was then at the service of artistic excellence, which consists in giving all the parts body, charm and perfection in relation to a unified whole. Insofar as architects and designers had a notion of beauty and a knowledge of the procedure necessary to realize it, conditions did not interfere with the formulation of an artistic purpose. Such a purpose, even when conceived in many different minds, was bound to have common characteristics when there was a single main tradition in art such as existed in the Gothic age and in a different form in the seventeenth and eighteenth centuries.

Modern business administration has helped make it possible to carry out effectively operations in the construction industries directed towards speed, quantity and sanitation. But the very success achieved in these respects has made it increasingly difficult for architects and designers to formulate an artistic purpose. That requires time for reflection and for new beginnings. It involves waste on a small scale. And while waste on the grand collective scale is applauded in modern American society because of the orders that it brings to business, the waste on a small individual scale indispensable for the achievement of artistic ends is confused with idleness. It is generally condemned. Rich Americans put millions into business or into endowment funds for colleges without hesitation, although they refuse to spend a few extra thousand dollars to permit a son who wants to be a poet or a painter to devote himself to such work after he has completed his education or even to allow him to drop his education for such dilettante and unremunerative pursuits. Efficiency is now confused with excellence, when the two are distinct, and when disproportionate importance can be given to the one only at the expense of the other. As A. C. Bossom, a British town planning expert is reported to have explained during the war, it is efficient to design new buildings "to last no longer than twenty-five or fifty years." They should then be scrapped to make room for others provided with the new conveniences devised in the interval. Is such an efficient purpose likely to contribute to their excellence?

The sense of delight has been eclipsed by the worship of material utility and activity. The difficulties the individual artist has to face are multiplied in the case of the architect, for to serve delight in architecture requires more human cooperation and collective planning than the service of delight in other arts. Planning has meaning for modern Americans almost exclusively as an economic or political device. Business and political planning have certainly a great importance for economic and political ends. For artistic ends, as such, they have none. An editorial writer of the *New York Times* recently explained that, with technology "standardizing the world, . . . it is harder than ever to be different." Art depends upon the cultivation and the use of creative differences; to be successful, economic and political planning, as they are practiced in our time, level human differences after the manner of a steamroller preparing a newly laid roadbed for heavy traffic. So planning is now less an ally than an enemy of architectural delight.

It is necessary for a great age of architecture that the claims of structure, utility and delight should be reconciled. That reconciliation is not only impeded by the disposition to exaggerate the value of utility and even structure. It is impeded even more by the multiplication of obstacles that block a clear view of the nature in art of body, charm and perfection, when such a view is the only possible starting point for a satisfactory reconciliation in artistic terms.

VI

Conditions in the higher learning are partly responsible for the growth of such obstacles. The tendency has been for the natural sciences to become more and more practical in their objectives. This has found a reflection in the kind of instruction in science given in the colleges and high schools, and has helped to confuse the public about the nature of science and technology, and the reciprocal relations between them which make for human happiness. At the same time, the prestige attached to the natural sciences has led the methods of observation and of the collection of data to assume in the humanities and social sciences a disproportionate place, sometimes to the exclusion of other rational processes necessary in the creation of art. Theology and even speculative philosophy have lost their positions as integral and guiding elements in humanistic and social studies.

The artist can and often should make use of scientific knowledge and scientific methods. Here again science is an excellent slave, a useful ally, but not a good master. A subtle and decisive use of the imaginative qualities of the intellect is essential to great art. It is necessary to deal with material in human terms by analogy and metaphor rather than by methods derived from chemical analysis or the study of logic. The artist sees the world not as it is but as humanity at its best would like to have it. His art is closely akin also to the experiences inherent in the profound religious faith of the saint. So it has followed that the tendency in recent times in learning and education to reduce to small dimensions the place of humanity and faith, and of the imagination necessary to both, the tendency to deny any rational validity to results which are not susceptible to positive material proof, have increased the difficulties in the way of architectural art. This tendency has not made impossible the emergence of occasional artists in architecture. But it has left them with little influence upon manufacturers, bankers, householders, real estate agents, building contractors, political authorities concerned with housing and even upon interior decorators and fellow architects. The result is that the good work of the few is drowned in the mediocrity and want of artistic craftsmanship of the many.

Among the conditions essential to the creation of beauty is the power of selection, of simplification. *Choice* is of the essence of art. It involves of course continual uncompromising rejections, completely irrelevant to a political and economic world of compromisers and chiselers and also irrelevant to the rational and meritorious business principle of operating at a profit. Compromise is inevitable and even desirable in practical life; in the speculative realm it can produce only disaster. If we may paraphrase some words attributed to Paul Valéry, one of the most important ways in which the artist reveals himself is by the character of his refusals. It is unnecessary to labor the point that the overwhelming increase in the quantity of almost all materials and commodities during the past two hundred, and especially the past hundred years, has made it indispensable for the artist to reject far more ruthlessly than in the past, has added enormously to the problems of choice and simplification.

It is not only that quantity has increased overwhelmingly. In many lines there has been a tendency for quality to deteriorate. One of the obstacles in early modern times to the use of coal as fuel, in place of charcoal and wood, was the aesthetic damage done by the new fires to products such as glass and iron. The aesthetic difficulties created by the scarcity of timber, which forced manufacturers to abandon eventually the use of firewood and charcoal, have not yet been solved. Nor have the aesthetic difficulties created by the introduction and spread of methods of manufacturing cheap paper. Both are symptoms of a growing pressure in the direction of shoddy workmanship, fatal to the sense of permanence which is an essential ingredient in the work of an artist. When one looks at certain modern groups of buildings, for example in the region of Hollywood and Los Angeles, one has some-times a not altogether deceptive impression that they resemble *papier-mâché*. Indeed one sometimes wonders whether the whole modern machine-made world may not crumble away. A piece of a modern building, unlike a piece of a renaissance building, has no longer the substance necessary to keep it intact if the building tumbles down. When the parts are rotten what can be expected of the whole? The factories thrown up at the turn of the eighteenth and nineteenth centuries in north Wales, where industrial civilization has already petered out, have disappeared without trace, leaving mediaeval churches and monasteries in command of the scene. Can we be sure that the same process will not be repeated in country after country? And what then of countries which have no medieval churches and monasteries, which have not even renaissance town halls and law courts?

It should be obvious even in the United States to anyone who reads the newspapers that modern warfare also constitutes a terrible menace to the hope of relative permanence—a prospect which encourages the artist to husband and practice his aesthetic talents to the full. One result of the increasing abundance of materials and of the decline in the sense of humanity and taste, which bound the Western peoples together after the religious wars of early modern times, has been the advent of total war.[19] Indiscriminate shelling and bombing from flocks of heavy airships and the ruthless use of atomic bombs threaten to wipe out the last vestiges of Western architecture, which has been a part of the tradition of thirty generations of Europeans, Latins and Nordics alike.

We cling to these old buildings as records of the past, partly alas because the modern trade of scholarship, which occupies many hands, is threatened with unemployment when they disappear. The work of the modern artist has not even this limited protection. Is it likely that the air forces of the future will spare the masterpieces of Sullivan or Wright, Mies van der Rohe or Le Corbusier, or their most illustrious contemporaries and followers? Their buildings have never achieved anything like the general recognition accorded Notre-Dame de Chartres, Saint Peter's or even the churches of Wren, most of which have already gone. It did not require bombing planes to get rid of Wright's Midway Gardens, which could once be seen from the rooms in the University where "the Chicago school" does its teaching. After hardly a decade of life for that striking building, it was torn down to make room for a modern garage. Anyone who visits Chicago can have his car washed there, but the mechanic who serves him will never have heard of the Midway Gardens or of Wright.

What war means and is likely to mean to the future of architecture can be gleaned from the following Associated Press dispatch of August 16, 1944, from Domfront in Normandy, described by the newspaper correspondent as "a turreted medieval place." "There is heavy damage in the middle of the town," we read. "About mid-day a single blast broke the stillness. It was a platoon of United States army engineers destroying the town's old Louis XIV arched bridge, deemed unsafe for military travel. . . . The officer in charge said it would take two hours to put another bridge in its place, 'after we get this stuff out.'"

VII

In the shadow of the most comprehensive and materially destructive war in history, which appears as a continuation of an earlier long world war no less deadly, in the face of historical evidence that wars are inclined to beget wars, it would be somewhat overoptimistic to suggest that architects can now build confidently in the hope that their work will endure, will leave its trace long after they are dead. With conditions what they are, with the general loss of faith in the value of the independent and imaginative mind, dedicated to truth and to beauty in and of themselves, the chances are slight for the few who have genius, force and integrity to influence a world disposed to settle all questions on the basis of profits made, votes recorded or dicta issued by some political leader. But it would be inhuman to abandon all hope for art. As we remarked at the beginning of this essay, the human species is full of strange contradictions. Among these is its incapacity to carry any movement, even a destructive one, to its logical conclusion. As we consider the Western peoples today, we are bound to ask what are the elements of hope? On what does their cultivation depend?

It is more than a decade since Valéry, with his genius for rolling the essential into a phrase, remarked in 1931, "le temps du monde fini commence." More than a decade before that, in 1919, he had written a sentence which is much more famous, "Nous autres, civilizations, nous savons maintenant que nous sommes mortels."[20] Let us consider the significance of the two statements, and particularly of the one made later in time, for the problem we have set ourselves in this essay. In six words Valéry says what the lamented Wendell Wilkie was destined twelve years later to try, less successfully, to put in a substantial pamphlet that sold by the hundred thousand in the United States. What did Valéry mean? Among many important things, he meant that the possibilities for territorial expansion, characteristic of Western civilization since its beginnings in the eleventh century, were at an end. The human race has no longer any place to go, unless it be to the north or south pole or to the moon. Everywhere on this globe—in trains, in offices, in elevators, on sidewalks, in subways, in battle, in the rubble of what were once towns and industrial suburbs, in the remnants of concentration camps and cantonments— man stands face to face with his brother. It is open to him to kill his brother. The events of the past thirty years would make it somewhat overoptimistic to exclude the general collapse of civilization as a possibility. Are we Westerners any less mortal in 1945 and 1946 than we appeared in 1918 and 1919? Have we really understood the lessons of the uneasy peace that intervened between two world wars?

Man has the alternative of learning to live with these brothers, whatever be their color, their class, their race or their nationality. The alternative to pushing out, as our ancestors have done, at the expense of others is for each of us to settle down where he is. Now that there is little open territory left on the globe to colonize, now that the phenomenal growth in population shows signs of ending, the conditions may possibly again be at hand where it will be feasible to assert the claims of the permanent in human nature. But this will only be possible if nations and groups learn to live together.

Man cannot live with his brother unless he recognizes their common human nature, which is partly an imaginative and spiritual nature, with rational burdens, hopes, joys and tragedies. Machinery and rapid communications have made it more difficult in many ways for men to recognize their brothers. In many ways they have made it more difficult to meet the overwhelming problem which has always beset mankind of living at peace. But by bringing all men everywhere face to face, they have helped to clarify what the technical revolution of recent times has made it impossible to escape.

In spite of the popular inanities of education and the pedantry of most of what passes for scholarship, learning in its higher reaches has done much during the past fifty years to reveal the nature of the fundamental issues which confront modern man and consequently the modern architect and city planner. As an outsider and historian, I write with diffidence concerning recent basic discoveries in the natural sciences. But do not the results obtained in astronomy suggest that the physical universe itself, like the terrestrial globe, is finite, and not infinite? Does not Professor Whittaker's article on "Newton, Einstein, Aristotle," published on this side of the water in *Science* in September, 1943,[21] suggest that the new physics, which has emerged from the quantum theory and the theory of relativity is less in accord with the modern philosophical systems that have been based on Newton's view of the physical universe, than it is with the Aristotelian metaphysics which preceded them? Does not Professor Sherrington's *Man On His Nature*[22] suggest that the great scientific advances of our time in physiology, and in a knowledge of the structure of the brain, have left men no better off, when it comes to understanding the actual workings of the mind and the imagination, so essential to art, than was Aristotle?

The Aristotelian metaphysics and the Aristotelian ethics and politics, are among the conceptions which laid the foundations for the humanist view of the world. These were later made part of the Christian view of the world. If conclusions such as those of the great modern scientists indicate the new directions in which speculative scientific thought is moving, science may be clearing the way, by defining its own limitations, for an artistic view of man and the world and even for an art of architecture. The sphere of natural science, like the material world and the physical universe accessible to man, is finite not infinite. The artist, like the saint, has access to deeper and more universal sources. He has therefore the opportunity and the duty to lead.

To clarify problems is not to solve them, especially when the clarifying voices are drowned in a sea of noise and headlines or blurred beyond recognition in the process of transmission. The scientific clarification, together with the study of history, ought to help nevertheless to make plain the nature of the responsibilities of architects, city planners, scholars, writers and teachers. If their object were a future art of architecture, they should throw all the free choice they possess in the direction of reestablishing man's claim to be a rational creature, with an imagination and a soul as well as a body. They should work to restore art to its rightful place as the directing principle in architecture and city planning. This can be done only by subordinating the values in sales promotion, advertising and publicity, as well as the values (if any exist) in totalitarian leadership, to other more human and less transient values, that we have now largely lost sight of.

If they feel called, a few historians can help the architect by ceasing to be mere specialists, by selecting their materials in the light of philosophical and artistic objectives. A historian of that kind would recognize his responsibilities as a judge, with recurring human values as his measure. He would recognize his responsibilities as an artist to breathe the spirit of art into the composition that embodies the materials which he selects. In spite of the great differences between the particular problems of the various arts, the serious and successful cultivation of one is of benefit to the others. Works of art are not competing products. There will never be enough of them to produce an economy of abundance. The danger is that they will be lost altogether in the craze for pseudo-artistic products which multitudes can be seduced or forced to accept.

If he feels called, the teacher in colleges, high schools and elementary schools has a duty to concentrate in his teaching upon the same human values that should guide a few historians. Another kind of teacher concerned with the making of material things, if he feels called, can emphasize the possibilities for artistic craftsmanship. He can help to train labor capable of executing effectively and in the spirit of delight the artistic conceptions of responsible architects.

Such new directions for manual labor will involve great new expenses. But technological advances have provided us with opportunities for leisure, without endangering the abundance which industrialism has provided. The people of the United States, on a continent spared the destruction which has shattered Europe, have managed to live an existence which our ancestors could have regarded as highly comfortable, while much more than half our productive efforts have been directed to waging war. There has been no rise in the death rate among the noncombatant population such as would suggest that the restricted supplies constitute a danger to physical well-being. But war only complicates the problem which leisure now presents. A sense of common purpose in constructive building offers one way of approaching its solution. We have the means to create an art of architecture; what we lack is the imagination and the will. What the public and its leaders lack is the desire and the courage to make the right refusals.

Neither faith nor art is of any "use" in the ordinary sense of utility, as the word appears on the lips of the technician, the business man, the wage earner, the social welfare worker, the military general or the ordinary pacifist. Yet it is through faith and art that mankind might move toward salvation. Without a redemption Western civilization may disappear leaving less trace than earlier great civilizations—the Greek, the Hebrew, the Roman. The contributions of these civilizations to the last millennium of European life are evident not only in every work of Western genius, but in the customs and traditions of over thirty generations of men and women, unlettered as well as lettered, poor as well as rich, humble as well as proud. Are the contributions of that millennium to be lost or preserved? As architecture is both a reflection of civilization and an influence upon it, the answer to this question will appear in the future of architecture.

NOTES

Reprinted from *The Review of Politics* 8, no. 2 (April 1946): 192–222.

1. Paul Valéry, *Regards sur le monde actuel* (Paris: Stock, Delamain et Boutelleau, 1931), 181–82; Pascal, *Pensées*, "Necessité de la recherche de la verité, le pari."

2. Geoffrey Scott, *The Architecture of Humanism: A Study in the History of Taste*, 2nd ed. (New York: Charles Scribner's Sons, 1924).

3. Emile Mâle, *L'Art religieux du XIIIe siècle en France*, 4th ed. (Paris: A. Colin, 1919), 458–59. He deals with the book left by the Abbé Suger, who built the abbey church at Saint-Denis.

4. The interpretation of the Gothic Age in this article is based largely on Emile Mâle's work; on Henry Adams' *Mont-Saint Michel and Chartres*; Lethaby's *Medieval Art*; Pirenne's *Medieval Cities, Economic and Social History of Medieval Europe*; books and articles

by Gilson, Maritain, and Kantorowicz, and my own research into the history of medieval mining and metallurgy. [For the later publication of the research to which Nef is referring, see *Cambridge Economic History of Europe*, 2nd ed. (Cambridge: Cambridge University Press, 1966). Ed.]

5. Cf. Lethaby, *Medieval Art*, 144.

6. Cf. Sidney Toy, *Castles: A Short History of Fortifications* (London: W. Heinemann, 1939), esp. pp. 139–40.

7. H. Pirenne, *Histoire de Belgique*, vol. 3, 3rd ed. (Brussels: H. Lamertin, 1923), 236.

8. W. Cunningham, *The Growth of English Industry and Commerce: Modern Times*, 6th ed. (Cambridge: Cambridge University Press, 1919), 315–17.

9. *Calendar of State Papers Domestic, 1636–37*, 542.

10. *Calendar of State Papers Domestic, 1637–38*, 107.

11. Earl of Clarendon, *The History of the Rebellion and Civil Wars in England* (Oxford: Oxford University Press, 1843), 25.

12. J. U. Nef, *The Rise of the British Coal Industry*, vol. 1 (London: George Routledge & Sons, 1932), 156–64.

13. *The Republic*, IV, 421.

14. Scott, *The Architecture of Humanism*, 120.

15. Mâle, *L'Art religieux du XIIIe siècle en France*, 464.

16. For his share in the artistic life of the Italian communes on the eve of the Renaissance, see Helene Wieruszowski, "Art and the Commune in the Time of Dante," *Speculum* (January 1944): 31–32 and passim.

17. See J. U. Nef, "La vie de l'ésprit et la grande paix, 1815–1914," in *La République Française* 1, nos. 11–12 (December 1944): 11–12.

18. Scott, *The Architecture of Humanism*, p. 1 and passim.

19. Nef, "La vie de l'ésprit et la grande paix," 15–16; and *La République Françoise* (January 1945): 14–16.

20. Valéry, *Regards sur le monde actuel*, 35; Valéry, "La Crise de l'ésprit," in *Variété* (Paris: Gallimard, 1924), 11.

21. E. T. Whittaker, "Aristotle, Newton, Einstein," *Science* 98 (September 1943): 267–88.

22. [Charles Scott Sherrington, *Man on His Nature* (Cambridge: Cambridge University Press, 1951), 2nd rev. ed. Ed.]

CHAPTER 11

On the Christian Idea of Man

JOSEF PIEPER

Josef Pieper (1904–1997) was born in Elte, Germany. Pieper was deeply influenced by the works of Thomas Aquinas. After earning his doctorate in philosophy from the University of Berlin, he attempted in his first book to demonstrate the identity of the good and reality. Before the onset of World War II, he also developed an interest in the investigation of concrete social problems. But due to restrictions imposed on Christian social scientists by National Socialism, he confined his professional life to the study of philosophy. After the war Pieper became a lecturer and then professor at the Pedagogical Institute of Essen (Ruhr) and the University of Münster. His philosophical interests evolved beyond Aquinas and scholasticism to include Plato and the philosophy of history. But the central theme of Pieper's thought was what he believed to be the necessary relation between moral and intellectual virtue. Human beings can only come to know the truth, he argued, if their souls are ordered to correspond to that truth. Such ordering is achieved by acting upon the divine virtues, such as faith, hope, and love, which are completed through God's grace. Pieper considered his most important scholarship to be his book On Love.

I

The second part of the *Summa Theologica* of the "Universal Doctor," Thomas Aquinas, begins with the following sentence: *Because man has been created in God's image, now after having spoken of God, the archetype, we must still deal with His image which is man* (*Sum. Theol.*, I, II, *Prologus*). There is something peculiar about this sentence; its meaning must not be misunderstood. It is stated as a matter of fact but its meaning is not to be taken for granted. This first sentence of Moral Theology expresses a fact which has almost entirely disappeared from the knowledge of Christians of today; namely, the fact that moral doctrine is primarily and above all a doctrine about man; that moral doctrine must plainly reveal the conception of man, and that, therefore, the doctrine of Christian morals must concern the Christian model of man. This fact was a matter of course in the Christianity of the high Middle Ages. This fundamental conception which, to be sure, was not definitely taken for granted as the polemical wording shows, compelled Meister Eckhart to say two generations after St. Thomas that people should not think about what they ought to do, they should rather think about what they ought to be. But later on Moral Theology and above all Moral preaching and exposition have more or less lost this awareness. This is so true that textbooks of Moral Theology, which explicitly professed to be written "in the spirit of St. Thomas" differed with him on this main point. Here lies the root of the fact that the average Christian of today does not expect to find in moral doctrine anything about the true being of man or anything about the idea of man at all. On the contrary, the average Christian is wont to associate with the conception "moral doctrine" the idea of a doctrine about the deed and especially about the omission, about the permissible and especially about the impermissible, about what is bidden and especially about what is forbidden. But the first moral thesis of the "Universal Doctor" remains: moral doctrine must deal with the true conception of man. Naturally it must also treat of actions, of duties, of commandments and of sins. But its primary subject is the right being of man, the idea of the good man.

The resolution of this problem of the Christian idea of man can be given in one sentence, even in one word: *Christ.* The Christian ought to be another Christ; he ought to be perfect like the Father of Jesus Christ. But this idea of the perfection of the Christian, all-comprehensive and, therefore, inexhaustible, needs to be analyzed, applied and interpreted. Without such interpretation proceeding from the empirical nature of man and reality, this idea would always be exposed to the danger of abuse and misunderstanding, caused by short-circuiting. It is impossible to derive directly the concrete action in the concrete situation from the highest and ultimate idea of perfection. "Be perfect as your Father in heaven." It is precisely this formulation of the ultimate idea of a Christian to which the fourth Council referred in its famous sentence of the *analogia entis: Inter Creatorem et creaturam non potest tanta similitudo notari, quin inter eos maior sit dissimilitudo notanda.* Such a great similarity between creator and creature cannot be mentioned without at the same time mentioning a still greater dissimilarity. This sentence is directed against the possibility of a direct deification of man. Man, the Christian, albeit the perfect Christian, remains a creature, a finite being, even in eternal life. Now there certainly is more than one way of interpreting this ultimate Christian idea, not only "theoretically" but also historically. There are, for instance, an Eastern-Christian and a Western-Christian form of interpretation.

Thomas Aquinas, the great teacher of Western Christianity, decided to express the Christian idea of man in seven theses which may be summarized as follows:

The Christian is a man who, in faith, becomes aware of the Triune God.

The Christian in hope waits for the final fulfillment of his nature in the Eternal Life.

The Christian, in the divine virtue of charity, inclines towards God and his fellowmen with an affirmation exceeding all natural power of love.

The Christian is prudent, that is, he does not permit the Yes and No of the will to disturb his view of reality; on the contrary, he makes the Yes or No of the will depend on the truth of actual things.

The Christian is just, that is, he is able to live in truth "with the other"; he is conscious of being a member with others in the Church, in the nation, and in every community.

The Christian is brave, that is, he is ready to suffer wounds and, if need be, death for the sake of truth and the realization of justice.

The Christian is moderate, that is, he does not allow his will to have and his will to enjoy to destroy himself.

These seven theses suggest that the ethics of classical theology, as an explanation of the idea of man, is essentially a doctrine of virtues. More exactly they interpret the Biblical description of the perfection of the Christian by means of the sevenfold image of the three theological and the four cardinal virtues. It is, I think, most important to reveal once more to the general consciousness of our time this grand fresco of the idea of man as originally expressed in classical theology, a fresco which has faded to some extent and, even worse, which has been painted over many a time. This idea of man is significant not merely as a matter of "historical" interest, as a matter of showing "how it actually was." This interpretation of the ultimate human ideal is one that continues to hold good and it is, I think, truly essential for us to see clearly and to accept this idea of man. I shall now try to mark the contours of this image, above all in the realm of the four cardinal virtues, particularly at those points where the image has faded or has been painted over.

At the outset something must be said about the conception of virtue in itself. A few years ago, in a speech before the Academie Française on virtue, Paul Valéry[1] said: "Virtue, gentlemen, the word virtue is dead, or at least it is dying. It no longer presents itself as a direct expression of a conceivable reality of our time. Rather, I have heard it mentioned in social conversation only rarely and then in an ironical sense. This could mean that I mix with bad company only, unless I add that I don't remember ever having found virtue in today's books, in those most often read and most highly esteemed. Furthermore I do not know of any paper which prints it, nor, I am afraid, would risk printing this word without a humorous intention. So it has come about that the words 'virtue' and 'virtuous' can be found only in the catechism, in the Academy and in comic operas." This diagnosis by Paul Valéry is undoubtedly correct. But there is no reason to be too much surprised by it. On the one hand, it certainly indicates an entirely natural phenomenon, the natural fate of great words. On the other hand, it is quite possible that in a de-Christianized era, demoniacal rules of language will effectively prevail. Accordingly, the good will appear as ridiculous in the "usage" of a language. Apart from this possibility we must not forget that Christian moral literature and moral preaching have not always made it very easy for the average man to perceive the true sense of the conception and the reality of virtue.

Virtue does not signify the mere correctness of an isolated action or omission. Rather virtue signifies that man *is* right in the supernatural and natural sense. Virtue means the enhancing of the being of man. Virtue is, as St. Thomas says, the *ultimum potentiae* (*Quaest. disp. de virtutibus in communi* 17), the ultimate of what man is able to be. The virtuous man "is" the man who develops goodness through his deeds out of his innermost inclination and substance. No less important than the correct and true notion of virtue is a true insight into the hierarchy of the virtues. Today there is much talk about the "heroic" character of Christianity or about the "heroic" conception of life as the distinguishing characteristic of Christian life. Such expressions are only half true and therefore half false. The first and distinguishing virtue of the Christian is the supernatural love of God and neighbor. And all the divine virtues are superior to the cardinal virtues. And under the cardinal virtues bravery is not the first, but the third.

II

Among the cardinal virtues prudence ranks first. Prudence is not only the first among otherwise equivalent virtues; but it "gives birth" to all moral virtue. This thesis about the priority of prudence, the true meaning of which we are scarcely able to conceive, expresses more than a mere accidental sequence of the cardinal virtues. As it is, it expresses the fundamental constitution of reality in relation to the realm of ethics. Good presupposes truth and truth presupposes reality. For what does the priority of prudence mean? It means nothing but the realization of good presupposing the awareness of reality. The first thing that is demanded of an active man is that he should be knowing, as St. Thomas says (*Quaest. disp. de virtutibus card.* 17). Whoever does not know the true condition of real things cannot do good; for good is that which complies with reality. Naturally, here "knowledge" does not mean knowledge in the sense of the exact notions of modern science. What it does mean is real contact with objective reality. This contact, for instance, may be reached by a mode of revelation superior to the "scientific" mode. To prudence belongs also the quality of docility, which means an attentive submission to the genuine knowledge of a superior mind. In prudence the unbiased perception of reality is decisive for our actions. So the prudent person, on the one hand, looks at the objective reality of things, and on the other hand, concerns himself with the willing and doing. But it is the reality at which he looks in the first place. And then, in virtue of the knowledge of reality he decides what is to be done and what not, and how it should be done and how not. So, really, all virtue depends upon prudence. And somehow all sin contradicts prudence, *omne peccatum opponitur prudentiae* (*Sum. Theol.,* II, II, 119, 37). Our habit of language, which is also our habit of thinking, has rather considerably deviated from this statement. According to our usage, prudence seems to be an evasion rather than a presupposition of good. It is hard for us to believe that it should always and necessarily be prudent to be just and true. And prudence and bravery above all seem to be most incompatible: to be brave is mostly imprudent.

But we have to remember that the true sense of this connection is as follows. The just and the brave acting, all good acting, is not just and brave and good unless corresponding to the truth of real things; it is the virtue of prudence in which this truth of real things becomes effective, fertile and decisive. This doctrine of the priority of prudence has an immense "practical" importance. It includes, for instance, the educational principle that education and self-education aiming at moral development must be rooted in the virtue of prudence, that is to say, the ability to see objectively the realities surrounding our acts, and to make them decide our course of action. Furthermore, the classical doctrine of the virtue of prudence offers the only chance to overcome radically the phenomenon of "moralism." The substance of moralism, which most people regard as a thing peculiarly Christian, is that it severs what we are from what we ought to do, that it proclaims a duty without perceiving and without showing that duty is rooted in what we are. On the contrary, the nucleus as well as the proper concern of the doctrine of prudence is as follows: to prove as necessary the coherence of what we ought to do with what we are; in the act of prudence what we ought to do is decided by what we are. Moralism says: good is what should be, because it should be. The doctrine of prudence says: good is what agrees with reality; it should be because it corresponds with reality. (It is perhaps important to perceive here the distinctly inner connection of "Christian" moralism with modern voluntarism.) And a third "practical" and "actual" point must be intimated. The fundamental attitude of justness (in the sense of agreement with reality), of objectivity, as expressed in the classical doctrine of prudence, was summarized in the Middle Ages in the following sentence, a sentence both grand and simple: Wise is man if all things taste to him as they really are. Now it is an important experience of modern psychology or, more exactly, of modern psychotherapy that a man to whom things do *not* taste as they are, who instead tastes in all things nothing but himself because he looks only at himself, that this man has lost not only the real capacity for justice (and for all moral virtue) but also his psychical sanity. Thus a whole group of psychical diseases is substantially due to such egotistic lack of objectivity. Such experience sanctions and illumines the ethical realism of the doctrine of the priority of prudence. Prudence is one of the spiritual regions where the mysterious connection between sanity and sanctity, between illness and sin becomes visible. A psychological theory which does not willfully overlook them is likely to see very deep connections here. The ethical doctrine of prudence should be able to illumine in an amazing way the central notion of self-deception (which is nothing but a lack of objectivity in perceiving reality, and which is rooted in the will).

III

Prudence and justice are more closely connected than appears at first sight. Justice, we have said, is the ability to live truly "with others." Now it is easy to see that this ability to live in community (which nearly signifies the ability to live at all) depends upon the objective perception and acknowledgment of reality. This means that this ability depends upon prudence. Only an objective man is just; and lack of objectivity and injustice mean, even in the very usage of language, almost the same thing.

It is prudence in which the real capacity for being good is rooted; only the prudent man has, in presupposition, the capacity for being good. This is why prudence ranks so high. But the rank of justice is based on the fact that justice is the highest and truest mode of this goodness itself. Such a statement must be emphasized since "Christian" middle-class people have for some generations proclaimed altogether different things as the primary and true criterion of a good man, specifically, "morality" so-called. A good man is primarily just. Man as a member of the community has the task of realizing justice. One can almost say that it is not so much the individual who represents justice (although, naturally, and strictly speaking the person alone can be "virtuous"), but instead We, the social entity, the people. This means that justice is the perfection of the We.

Now, the structure of each commonwealth is based on three fundamental relations; and if these three relations are right we can say that justice rules in it. First, there are the mutual relations of the members; the justness of these relations corresponds to the exchange of justice (*justitia commutativa*). Second, there are the relations of the whole to the members; the justness of these relations corresponds to distributive justice (*justitia distributiva*). Third, there are the relations of the individual members to the whole We; the justness of these relations corresponds to "legal" justice (*justitia legalis*). These things may sound very natural, as if they were a matter of course. But they are not a matter of course. The social doctrine of individualism, for example, sees only one of these three relations, namely, the mutual relations of the individual members. Individualism does not acknowledge the true independence of the social whole, and therefore it knows of no actual connection of the individuals to the whole, nor of the whole to the individuals. And accordingly the *justitia commutativa* is the unique form of justice which individualism knows of, if it is consistent. On the other hand, anti-individualism has created a "universalistic" social doctrine which frankly denies any existence of relations among individuals as individuals, and which, in consequence, declares the *justitia commutativa* to be an "individualistic misconception." The reality of the "totalitarian state" shows that such an "academic theory" is not inclined to remain on the level of mere "theory"; its coercive power hardly admits "private" relations among individuals who merely come together as functionaries to serve the ends of the state.

St. Thomas Aquinas also says that the whole moral life of man is closely bound to the *bonum commune;* the *justitia legalis,* therefore, really has a very particular rank and place. But we must not overlook the ambiguity of this statement of St. Thomas. One of its senses is this: there is a true obligation of the individual with respect to the common weal, and this obligation comprises the whole man. The other sense is this: all individual virtue has an importance for the common weal. This means that the common weal needs the virtue of all individuals, that it cannot be realized unless the individual members of the community are good, not only just, but good, virtuous in the most individual and secret and, so to speak, "private" way.

IV

Another error about justice (at bottom quite liberalist but not at all limited to the era of liberalism) declares: it is possible to be just without having to be brave. This is not so much an error about the nature of justice as an error about the real structure of "this" world, in which justice is to be realized. For "this" world is constructed in such a manner that justice, and good generally, could not be successful of its own accord without the fighting man, ready to die for it. Evil is mighty in "this" world. This fact becomes manifest in the necessity for fortitude which means readiness to endure injuries for the sake of the realization of good. So, St. Augustine says, fortitude itself is an irrefutable witness of the existence of evil in the world. Now, it is a bad and false answer to the liberalist error to believe that it is possible to be brave without being just. Fortitude as a virtue is present only where justice is intended. Who is not just cannot be brave in the strict sense. Thomas Aquinas says: "The praise of fortitude depends upon justice" (*Sum. Theol.,* II, II, 123, 12). This means that simultaneously I may praise anyone for his fortitude only if I can praise him for his justice. True fortitude, therefore, is essentially connected with the will of justice.

It is no less important to perceive that the idea of fortitude is not identical with the idea of an aggressive fearlessness at all costs. There even is a sort of fearlessness which is opposed to the virtue of fortitude. Here we must consider the place occupied by fear in the structure of human existence. The common and mitigating foreground-talk of everyday life is based on the denial of the existence of anything terrible. The terrible is pushed back into the realm of mere appearances. This mitigation, effective (or not effective) at all times today finds a remarkable counterpart in the fact that in the philosophical, psychological and poetical literature of our time no conception plays such a large part as the conception of fear. Another counterpart of that everyday attempt at making human existence harmless and "fearless" is a new stoicism which has found an imposing human representation and a fascinating formulation in literature. This new stoicism is "proclaimed" above all by a group of men who consider the events of the last wars as a destruction which includes the promise and the threat of new, still greater and apocalyptic catastrophes. And the thesis is: life is always terrible, but there is nothing so terrible that a strong man could not endure it with greatness. But if you read the books, for example, of Ernst Jünger,[2] who is one of the most remarkable heads of this new "Stoa," you have to agree that nearly all dreams of these "adventurous hearts" are dreams of anxiety.

To this question the ultimate and most profound Christian answer is: the notion of the fear of the Lord. But this conception runs the risk of being depleted, deprived of its reality, and concealed by the Christian common-consciousness. The fear of the Lord is not the same as "respect" for the absolute God, but real fear in the strict sense of the word. The common signification of fear, anxiety, fright, horror and terror is that they are all different answers to the different manners of the diminution of being, the ultimate one of which is annihilation. It is not at all the way of Christian theology to deny the existence of the fearsome in human life; furthermore, the Christian doctrine of life does not say that man should not or must not fear the fearsome. But the Christian asks for the *ordo timoris;* he asks for what is really and ultimately fearsome; and he is afraid of fearing perhaps that which is not at all really and definitely fearsome, and afraid of considering perhaps as harmless that which is definitely fearsome. That which is properly fearsome comes to this: the possibility of man's voluntarily separating himself from his ultimate origin of being. This is the ultimate peril of his existence. And it is man's fear of this possible separation from the Ultimate Origin of being, to which the fear of the Lord is the adequate answer. This fear which accompanies all human life, even that of the saint, as a real possibility, is a fear that cannot be overcome by any manner of "heroism." On the contrary, this fear is the presupposition of all genuine heroism. The fear of the Lord as a fear is to be endured and suffered right up to the definite security of the Eternal Life. When fortitude saves us from loving our life in such manner that we lose it, then this implies that the fear of the Lord, as a fear of losing Eternal Life, is the basis of all Christian fortitude. It should be considered, however, that the fear of the Lord is the negative counterpart of the hopeful love of God. St. Augustine says that all fear is the feeling of love.

The fear of the Lord is the "fulfillment" of the natural anxiety of man with respect to the diminution of being and of annihilation. All moral goodness is likewise a sort of extension of natural inclinations. And man fears the *nihil* by nature. And as the natural desire for life in community is accomplished in the virtue of justice, and as the natural desire for self-dependence is perfected in the virtue of magnanimity, and as the natural impulse for enjoyment is perfected in the virtue of temperance—so the natural anxiety of annihilation becomes also destructive, unless perfected in the fear of the Lord. The fact that the fear of the Lord in its proper form as *"timor filialis"* is a gift of the Holy Ghost and not, as for example, with the cardinal virtues, the natural fulfillment of a natural human faculty; this fact implies that only realized supernatural perfection is able to free man from the tyranny of unsatisfied anxiety. As it is, the destructive effect of this unsatisfied anxiety and its tyranny are proved not only in ethical spheres but also in the sphere of the natural psychical life, as psychiatry may confirm. Here is once more a point clearly revealing the coherence of sanity and sanctity. The distinctness, however, is limited to the fact of this coherence: in what precise manner sanity and sanctity and above all guilt and illness are interwoven and on which terms this connection becomes effective—a statement about this is hardly possible. In any case the "sanity" of justice, of magnanimity, of temperance, of fear of the Lord and of all virtue consists in their conforming to the objective reality, both natural and supernatural. Compliance with reality is the principle of both sanity and goodness.

V

Earlier we noted that the natural desire for enjoyment can become destructive. This fact is concealed by the liberalist thesis: man is good. Enlightened liberalism, by virtue of its most fundamental presuppositions could not acknowledge the possible existence in man of a revolt of inferior spiritual forces against the government of mind; it denies that man has lost the spontaneous inner order of his nature through original sin. And so, judged from this aspect, the virtue of temperance necessarily passes for something nonsensical and objectless. For the virtue of temperance presupposes that the above-mentioned destructive revolt of the senses against the mind is possible and is perceived as possible. This depletion of the virtue of temperance by enlightened liberalism the common doctrine of many Christians (I will not say the doctrine of the Church, nor even theology) has countered by an overaccentuation of this very virtue. So for the Christian common consciousness the virtue of temperance, in its typical forms of chastity and abstinence, has become the conspicuous and all-dominating trait of the Christian idea of man. Now this answer of Christianity has, nevertheless, remained a child of its adversary, that is, of liberalism. This dependence upon the liberalistic-individualistic adversary becomes manifest insofar as the virtue of temperance is the most "private" among the four cardinal virtues; temperance refers to the individual as an individual. So the most "private" virtue passes for the most Christian virtue. In classical theology, however, this "private" character of temperance was the very reason for declaring this virtue to be the last instead of the first of the four cardinal virtues.

The overvaluation of temperance has had very considerable effects and extensions. The fact, for example, that in our everyday usage of language the words "sensuality," "passion," "desire," and "inclination" have received a very negative meaning although they are ethically neutral conceptions, is partly due to this overvaluation of temperance. But if by the word "sensuality" is exclusively meant sensuality as revolting against the spirit, and by "passion" exclusively bad passion, and by "desire" exclusively mutinous desire—then of course, there are no names left for the non-mutinous sensuality, which St. Thomas says, belongs to virtue. And this defect of the usage of language strongly inclines toward a dangerous confusion of notions, even of life itself. On the other hand, this defect of the usage of language has arisen from a confusion of notions and of life.

Perhaps it may be good to cite here an example from the *Summa Theologica* which shows what the "Universal Doctor" thinks of this matter. It is an example, not a principle, but an example which illustrates a principle. In the *Summa Theologica* (*Sum. Theol.*, I, II, 22–48) there is a chapter about the *passiones animae,* the passions of the soul. The expression involves all motions of the sensuous faculty, such as love, hate, desire, delight, sadness, fear and anger. One of the approximately twenty-five questions of this chapter deals with the "remedies against grief and sadness" (*Sum. Theol.*, I, II, 38). In five special articles St. Thomas enumerates five such remedies. Before mentioning them we should like to pose the question: What information could be given today by the moral common consciousness of Christianity concerning the "remedies against the sadness of soul"? Everyone may answer the question himself. The first general remedy mentioned by St. Thomas is that any sort of delight, for sadness is like a weariness of the soul, but delight is like a rest. The second remedy is tears! The third remedy is the compassion of friends. The fourth is the contemplation of truth, which is more able to alleviate grief the more a man loves wisdom. As to the fifth remedy mentioned by St. Thomas, we should bear in mind that we have a textbook of theology before us, and certainly not an ordinary one. The fifth remedy against sadness of soul is sleeping and bathing, for a sleep and a bath cause a feeling of well-being in the body which in return reacts upon the soul. Naturally, St. Thomas is well acquainted with the possibilities and necessities of a supernatural overcoming of human sorrow; he is even of the opinion that there are forms and degrees of human sorrow which can only be overcome by supernatural energies. But St. Thomas, on the other hand, does not think of putting aside natural possibilities (e.g., sleeping and bathing). And he does not at all feel embarrassed to speak about them in the midst of a theological discourse.

VI

All four of the cardinal virtues—prudence, justice, fortitude, temperance—are principally connected with the natural sphere of human reality. But as Christian virtues they grow out of the fertile ground of faith, hope and charity. Faith, hope and charity are the answer to the reality of the Triune God, which is supernaturally revealed to the Christian by the revelation of Jesus Christ. And the three theological virtues are not only the answer to that reality, but they are at the same time the faculty and the source of this answer; they are not the answer itself but they are, so to speak, also the mouth which alone is able to give this answer. All three theological virtues are closely connected with each other; "they are," as St. Thomas says in his tract about hope, "flowing back into themselves in a holy ring; who by hope has been led to charity has also a more perfect hope, just as his faith is stronger than before" (*Quaest. disp. de spe,* 3 ad 1).

As the cardinal virtues are rooted in the theological virtues the supernatural ethos of the Christian differs from the natural ethos of the gentleman, that is, the naturally noble man. This origin itself, the manner and means of the coherence of natural and supernatural virtue, is expressed in the well-known sentence that grace does not destroy nature but presupposes and perfects it. This sentence seems to be very clear and really is so. But its clearness cannot affect the impossibility of making a mystery comprehensible by a simple statement. And there is nothing more mysterious than the manner in which God acts in man, and man in God.

Nevertheless, the difference between a Christian and a gentleman becomes clearly manifest and in many ways. The Christian can, for example, appear to act contrary to natural prudence because in his acting he must conform to realities which only faith perceives. Incidentally, about this supernatural prudence St. Thomas has written a sentence which, I think, is particularly important for the Christian of today. "Obviously," St. Thomas says, "the natural virtue of prudence presupposes quite a degree of acquired knowledge." Now, when the theological virtues augment in a supernatural manner the cardinal virtues, what about prudence? Does grace replace the natural knowledge of natural things? Does faith supersede the objective estimate of the concrete situation or the concrete deed, or does it replace it? In this case, how can grace and faith be useful to the "plain man," who does not possess this knowledge which is sometimes rather difficult? To these questions St. Thomas gives, I think a quite grand, and also most consoling, answer: "The men who require the advice and counsel of others can, providing they are in a state of grace, advise themselves in so far as they ask for the advice of other people and that they (this is most important) are able to distinguish a good counsel from a bad one" (*Sum. Theol.*, II, II, 47, 3). If they are in the state of *grace!* It goes without saying why this answer is consoling in the present situation of the plain Christian.

The difference between a Christian and a gentleman is especially evident in the gap dividing Christian fortitude from the natural bravery of the gentleman. This point really closes the consideration of the Christian idea of man. The difference between a Christian fortitude and a merely natural fortitude lies eventually in the theological virtue of hope. All hope says that it will turn out well, it will end well. Supernatural hope says: for the man who stays in the reality of grace it will turn out well in a manner which infinitely exceeds all expectation; for this man it will end with nothing less than Eternal Life.

Now it may come to pass that in an era of temptation to despair, all imminent and secular prospects for a "happy end" become gloomy. So it can come to pass that there is nothing left to the natural man limited to nature than the desperate fortitude of an "heroic end." And particularly the true gentleman will consider this way as the only possibility; for he of all persons will be able to renounce the "way out of happiness" (as Ernst Jünger says). In short, sometimes it may happen that supernatural hope remains the unique possibility of hope at all. This is not to be understood in any sense of "eudaemonism," it is not a question of anxiety about a last possibility of subjective happiness. The Biblical sentence "May He kill me, nevertheless I shall hope in Him" (Job 13:15) is far from a "eudaemonic" anxiety about happiness. No, the Christian hope is first and above all the existential adjustment of man to fulfillment, to the ultimate realization, to the fullness of being (to which, of course, the fullness of happiness or rather of beatitude corresponds). If then all natural hopes sometimes become senseless, it means that supernatural hope for man remains truly the unique possibility of adjusting his being. The desperate fortitude of the "heroic end" is at bottom "nihilistic," since it believes that it can suffer the unknown. Christian fortitude, however, is fed by hope for the abundant reality of Life, for the Eternal Life, for a new heaven and for a new earth.

NOTES

Reprinted from *The Review of Politics* 11, no. 1 (January 1949): 3–16.

1. [Paul Valéry (1871–1945), the poet and essayist, gained fame as a leader of France's Symbolist school of poetry, although his interests extended to many other fields, including history, music, and the natural sciences. Valéry was generally noncommittal about his political views, but unlike some of his contemporaries, he clearly distanced himself from extremist movements of all kinds. Ed.]

2. [The novelist, Ernst Jünger (1895–1998), is widely regarded as one of twentieth-century Germany's greatest writers. At the same time, he has been the subject of great controversy, regarded by some as a defender of German nationalist traditions and by others as complicit in the rise of National Socialism. Ed.]

CHAPTER 12

Natural Right and
the Historical Approach

LEO STRAUSS

Leo Strauss (1899–1973) was born in Kirchhain, in the state of Hessen, Germany. He served in the German army during World War I, and subsequently studied at the University of Hamburg, where he received a doctoral degree in philosophy. After the rise of National Socialism in Germany, he moved first to England and then to the United States, where he taught political philosophy at the New School for Social Research and the University of Chicago. Raised as an orthodox Jew and educated in Jewish and Islamic philosophy, Strauss spent much of his career attempting to recover an understanding of the tension between reason and revelation, and the importance of this understanding for political life. He also believed that classical political philosophy was a much needed alternative to modern political thought, in part because it could demonstrate the weaknesses of a value-free conception of politics. By addressing permanent and universal questions, it would serve to return the field to its original focus on discovering the best political order. As a result of this way of thinking, Strauss became a noteworthy critic of contemporary liberal democratic politics.

The attack on natural right in the name of history takes in most cases the following form: natural right claims to be a right that is discernible by human reason and is universally acknowledged; but history (including anthropology) teaches us that no such right exists; instead of the supposed uniformity we find an indefinite variety of notions of right or justice. Or, in other words, there cannot be natural right if there are no immutable principles of justice, but history shows us that all principles of justice are mutable. One cannot understand the meaning of the attack on natural right in the name of history, before one has realized the utter irrelevance of this argument. In the first place, "consent of all mankind" is by no means a necessary condition of the existence of natural right. Some of the greatest natural right teachers have argued that, precisely if natural right is rational, its discovery presupposes the cultivation of reason, and therefore natural right will not be known universally: one ought not even to expect any real knowledge of natural right among savages.[1] In other words by proving that there is no principle of justice that has not been denied somewhere or at some time, one has not yet proven that any given denial was justified or reasonable. Furthermore, it has always been known that different notions of justice obtain at different times and in different nations. It is absurd to claim that the discovery of a still greater number of such notions by modern students has in any way affected the fundamental issue. Above all, knowledge of the indefinitely large variety of notions of right and wrong is so far from being incompatible with the idea of natural right, that it is the essential condition for the emergence of that idea: realization of the variety of notions of right is *the* incentive for the quest for natural right. If the rejection of natural right in the name of history is to have any significance, it must have a basis other than historical evidence. Its basis must be a philosophic critique of the possibility, or of the knowability, of natural right—a critique somehow connected with "history."

The conclusion from the variety of notions of right to the nonexistence of natural right is as old as political philosophy itself. Political philosophy seems to begin with the contention that the variety of notions of right proves the non-existence of natural right or the conventional character of all right.[2] We shall call this view conventionalism. To clarify the meaning of the present-day rejection of natural right in the name of history, we must first grasp the specific difference between conventionalism on the one hand, and "the historical sense" or "the historical consciousness" characteristic of nineteenth and twentieth century thought on the other.[3]

Conventionalism presupposed that the distinction between nature and convention is the most fundamental of all distinctions. It implied that nature is of incomparably higher dignity than convention or the fiat of society, or that nature is the norm. The thesis that right and justice are conventional meant that right and justice have no basis in nature, that they are ultimately against nature, and that they have their ground in arbitrary decisions, explicit or implicit, of communities: they have no basis but some kind of agreement, and agreement may produce peace but it cannot produce truth. The adherents of the modern historical view on the other hand reject as mythical the premise that nature is the norm; they reject the premise that nature is of higher dignity than any works of man. On the contrary, either they conceive of man and his works, his varying notions of justice included, as equally natural as all other real things, or else they assert a basic dualism between the realm of nature and the realm of freedom or history. In the latter case they imply that the world of man, of human creativity, is exalted far above nature. Accordingly, they do not conceive of the notions of right and wrong as fundamentally arbitrary. They try to discover their causes; they try to make intelligible their variety and sequence; in tracing them to acts of freedom, they insist on the fundamental difference between freedom and arbitrariness.

What is the significance of the difference between the old and the modern view? Conventionalism is a particular form of classical philosophy. There are obviously profound differences between conventionalism and the position taken by Plato, for example. But the classical opponents agree in regard to the most fundamental point: both admit that the distinction between nature and convention is fundamental. For this distinction is implied in the idea of philosophy. Philosophizing means to ascend from the cave to the light of the sun, that is, to the truth. The cave is the world of opinion as opposed to knowledge. Opinion is essentially variable. Men cannot live, that is they cannot live together if opinions are not stabilized by social fiat. Opinion thus becomes authoritative opinion or public dogma or *Weltanschauung.* Philosophizing means then to ascend from public dogma to essentially private knowledge. The public dogma is originally an inadequate attempt to answer the question of the all-comprehensive truth or of the eternal order.[4] Any inadequate view of the eternal order is, from the point of view of the eternal order, accidental or arbitrary; it owes its validity not to its intrinsic truth but to social fiat or convention. The fundamental premise of conventionalism is, then, nothing other than the idea of philosophy as the attempt to grasp the eternal. The modern opponents of natural right reject precisely this idea. According to them all human thought is historical and hence unable ever to grasp anything eternal. Whereas, according to the ancients philosophizing means to leave the cave, according to our contemporaries all philosophizing essentially belongs to a "historical world," "culture," "civilization," "*Weltanschauung,*" that is, to what Plato had called the cave. We shall call this view historicism.

We have noted before that the contemporary rejection of natural right in the name of history is based, not on historical evidence, but on a philosophic critique of the possibility or knowability of natural right. We note now that the philosophic critique in question is not particularly a critique of natural right or of moral principles in general. It is a critique of human thought as such. Nevertheless, the critique of natural right played an important role in the formation of historicism.

Historicism emerged in the nineteenth century under the protection of the belief that knowledge or at least divination of the eternal is possible. But it gradually undermined the belief which had sheltered it in its infancy. It suddenly appeared within our lifetime in its mature form. The genesis of historicism is inadequately understood. In the present state of our knowledge, it is difficult to say at what point in the modern development the decisive break occurred with the "unhistorical" approach that prevailed in all earlier philosophy. For the purpose of a summary orientation it is convenient to start with the moment when the previously subterranean movement came to the surface and began to dominate the social sciences in broad daylight. That moment was the emergence of the historical school.

The thoughts that guided the historical school were very far from being of a purely theoretical character. The historical school emerged in reaction to the French Revolution, and to the natural right doctrines that had prepared that cataclysm. In opposing the violent break with the past, the historical school insisted on the wisdom and on the need of preserving or continuing the traditional order. This could have been done without a critique of natural right as such. Certainly pre-modern natural right did not sanction reckless appeal from the established order, or from what was actual here and now, to the natural or rational order. Yet the founders of the historical school seemed to have realized somehow that the acceptance of any universal or abstract principles has necessarily a revolutionary, disturbing, unsettling effect as far as thought is concerned, and that this effect is wholly independent of whether the principles in question sanction, generally speaking, a conservative or a revolutionary course of action. For the recognition of universal principles forces man to judge the established order, or what is actual here and now, in the light of the natural or rational order, and what is actual here and now is more likely than not to fall short of the universal and unchangeable norm.[5] The recognition of universal principles thus tends to prevent men from wholeheartedly identifying themselves with, or accepting, the social order that fate has allotted to them. It tends to alienate them from their place on the earth. It tends to make them strangers, and even strangers on the earth.

By denying the significance, if not the existence, of universal norms, the eminent conservatives who founded the historical school were in fact continuing and even sharpening the revolutionary effort of their adversaries. That effort was inspired by a specific notion of the natural. It was directed against both the un-natural or conventional, and the supranatural or other-worldly. The revolution-ists assumed, we may say, that the natural is always individual, and that therefore the uniform is unnatural or conventional. The human individual was to be liber-ated or to liberate himself so that he could pursue not just his happiness, but his own version of happiness. This meant however that one universal and uniform goal was set up for all men: the natural right of each individual was a right uni-formly belonging to every man as man. But uniformity was said to be unnatural and hence bad. It was evidently impossible to individualize rights in full accor-dance with the natural diversity of individuals. The only kind of rights that was neither incompatible with social life nor uniform were "historical" rights: rights of Englishmen, for example, in contradistinction to the rights of man. Local and temporal variety seemed to supply a safe and solid middle ground between anti-social individualism and unnatural universality. The historical school did not dis-cover the local and temporal variety of notions of justice: the obvious does not have to be discovered. The utmost one could say is that it discovered the value, the charm, the inwardness of the local and temporal, or that it discovered the supe-riority of the local and temporal to the universal. It would be more cautious to say that, radicalizing the tendency of men like Rousseau, the historical school as-serted that the local and the temporal have a higher value than the universal. As a consequence, what claimed to be universal, appeared eventually as derivative from something locally and temporally confined, as the local and temporal *in statu evanescendi*. The natural law teaching of the Stoics for example, was likely to appear as a mere reflex of a particular temporal state of a particular local society: of the dissolution of the Greek city.

The effort of the revolutionists was directed against all otherworldliness or transcendence.[6] Transcendence is not a preserve of revealed religion. In a very important sense it was implied in the original meaning of political philosophy as the quest for the natural or best political order. The best regime, as Plato and Aristotle understood it, is, and is meant to be, for the most part, different from what is actual here and now, or beyond all actual orders. This view of the tran-scendence of the best political order was profoundly modified by the way in which "progress" was understood in the eighteenth century, but it was still pre-served in that eighteenth century notion. Otherwise the theorists of the French Revolution could not have condemned all or almost all social orders which had ever been actual. By denying the significance, if not the existence, of universal norms the historical school destroyed the only solid basis of all efforts to transcend the actual. Historicism can therefore be described as a much more extreme form of modern this-worldliness than the French radicalism of the eighteenth century had been. It certainly acted as if it intended to make men absolutely at home in "this world." Since any universal principles make at least most men potentially homeless it depreciated universal principles in favor of historical principles. It believed that by understanding their past, their heritage, their historical situation, men could arrive at principles that would be as objective as those of the older, pre-historicist political philosophy had claimed to be, and, in addition, would not be abstract or universal and hence harmful to wise action or to a truly human life but concrete or particular: principles fitting the particular age or particular nation, principles relative to the particular age or particular nation.

In trying to discover standards which, while being objective, were relative to particular historical situations, the historical school assigned to historical studies a much greater importance than they had ever possessed. Its notion of what one could expect from historical studies was, however, not the outcome of historical studies, but of assumptions that stemmed directly or indirectly from the natural right doctrine of the eighteenth century. The historical school assumed the existence of folk-minds, that is, it assumed that nations or ethnic groups are natural units, or it assumed the existence of general laws of historical evolution, or it combined both assumptions. It soon appeared that there was a conflict between the assumptions that had given the decisive impetus to historical studies, and the results as well as the requirements of genuine historical understanding. In the moment these assumptions were abandoned the infancy of historicism came to its end.

Historicism now appeared as a particular farm of positivism, that is, of the school which held that theology and metaphysics had been superseded once and for all by positive science or which identified genuine knowledge of reality with the knowledge supplied by the empirical sciences. Positivism proper had defined "empirical" in terms of the procedures of the natural sciences. But there was a glaring contrast between the manner in which historical subjects were treated by positivism proper and the manner in which they were treated by the historians who really proceeded empirically. Precisely in the interests of empirical knowledge it became necessary to insist that the methods of natural science be not considered authoritative for historical studies. In addition, what "scientific" psychology and sociology had to say about man, proved to be trivial and poor if compared with what could be learned from the great historians. Thus history was thought to supply the only empirical, and hence the only solid knowledge of what is truly human, of man as man, of his greatness and misery. Since all human pursuits start from and return to man, the empirical study of humanity could seem to be justified in claiming a higher dignity than all other studies of reality. History, history divorced from all dubious or metaphysical assumptions, became the highest authority.

But history proved utterly unable to keep the promise that had been held out by the historical school. The historical school had succeeded in discrediting universal or abstract principles; it had thought that historical studies would reveal particular or concrete standards. Yet the unbiased historian had to confess his inability to derive any norms from history: no objective norms remained. The historical school had obscured the fact that particular or historical standards can become authoritative only on the basis of a universal principle which imposes an obligation on the individual to accept, or to bow to, the standards suggested by the tradition or the situation which has molded him. Yet no universal principle will ever sanction the acceptance of every historical standard or of every victorious cause; to conform with tradition or to jump on "the wave of the future" is not obviously better, and it is certainly not always better than to burn what one has worshipped, or to resist the "trend of history." Thus all standards suggested by history as such proved to be fundamentally ambiguous and therefore unfit to be considered standards. To the unbiased historian, "the historical process" revealed itself as the meaningless web spun by what men did, produced, and thought, no more than by unmitigated chance: a tale told by an idiot. The historical standards, the standards thrown up by this meaningless process, could no longer claim to be hallowed by sacred powers behind that process. The only standards that remained were of a purely subjective character, standards that had no other support than the free choice of the individual. No objective criterion allowed henceforth the distinction between good and bad choices. Historicism culminated in nihilism. The attempt to make man absolutely at home in this world ended in man's becoming absolutely homeless.

The view that "the historical process" is a meaningless web or that there is no such thing as the "historical process" was not novel. It was fundamentally the classical view. In spite of considerable opposition from different quarters, it was still powerful in the eighteenth century. The nihilistic consequence of historicism could have suggested a return to the older, pre-historicist view. But the manifest failure of the practical claim of historicism, that it could supply life with a better, a more solid guidance than the pre-historicist thought of the past had done, did not destroy the prestige of the alleged theoretical insight due to historicism. The mood created by historicism and its practical failure was interpreted as the unheard of experience of the true situation of man as man—of a situation which earlier man had concealed from himself by believing in universal and unchangeable principles. In opposition to the earlier view, the historicists continued to ascribe decisive importance to that view of man that arises out of historical studies, which as such are particularly and primarily concerned, not with the permanent and universal, but with the variable and unique. History as history seems to present to us the depressing spectacle of a disgraceful variety of thoughts and beliefs and, above all, of the passing away of every thought and belief ever held by men. It seems to show that all human thought is dependent on unique historical contexts that are preceded by more or less different contexts, and that emerge out of their antecedents in a fundamentally unpredictable way: the foundations of human thought are laid by unpredictable experiences or decisions. Since all human thought belongs to specific historical situations, all human thought is bound to perish with the situation to which it belongs, and to be superseded by new, unpredictable thoughts.

The historicist contention presents itself today as amply supported by historical evidence, or even as expressing an obvious fact. But if the fact is so obvious, it is hard to see how it could have escaped the notice of the most thoughtful men of the past. As regards the historical evidence, it is clearly insufficient to support the historicist contention. History teaches us that a given view has been abandoned in favor of another view by all men, or by all competent men, or perhaps only by the most vocal men; it does not teach us whether the change was sound, or whether the rejected view deserved to be rejected. Only an impartial analysis of the view in question—an analysis that is not dazzled by the victory or stunned by the defeat of the adherents of the view concerned—could teach us anything regarding the worth of the view and hence regarding the meaning of the historical change. If the historicist contention is to have any solidity, it must be based not on history but on philosophy: on a philosophic analysis proving that all human thought depends ultimately on fickle and dark fate, and not on evident principles accessible to man as man. The basic stratum of that philosophic analysis is a "critique of reason" that allegedly proves the impossibility of theoretical metaphysics, and of philosophic ethics or natural right. Once all metaphysical and ethical views can be assumed to be strictly speaking untenable, that is, untenable as regards their claim to be simply true, their historical fate necessarily appears to be deserved. It then becomes a plausible, although not very important task to trace the prevalence, at different times, of different metaphysical and ethical views, to the times at which they prevailed. But this leaves still intact the authority of the positive sciences.

The second stratum of the philosophical analysis underlying historicism is the proof that the positive sciences rest on metaphysical foundations. Taken by itself, this philosophic critique of philosophic and scientific thought—a continuation of the efforts of Hume and of Kant—would lead to skepticism. But skepticism and historicism are two entirely different things. Skepticism regards itself as in principle coeval with human thought; historicism regards itself as belonging to a specific historical situation. For the skeptic, all assertions are uncertain and therefore essentially arbitrary; for the historicist, the assertions that prevail at different times and in different civilizations are very far from being arbitrary. Historicism stems from a nonskeptical tradition: from that modern tradition which tried to define the limits of human knowledge and which therefore admitted that within certain limits genuine knowledge is possible. In contradistinction to all skepticism, historicism rests at least partly on such a critique of human thought as claims to articulate what is called "the experience of history."

No competent man of our age would regard as simply true the complete teaching of any thinker of the past. In every case experience has shown that the originator of the teaching took things for granted which must not be taken for granted, or that he did not know certain facts or possibilities which were discovered in a later age. Up to now all thought has proved to be in need of radical revisions, or to be incomplete or limited in decisive respects. Furthermore, looking back at the past, we seem to observe that every progress of thought in one direction was bought at the price of a retrogression of thought in another respect: when a given limitation was overcome by a progress of thought, earlier important insights were invariably forgotten as a consequence of that progress. On the whole, there was then no progress, but merely a change from one type of limitation to another type. Finally, we seem to observe that the most important limitations of earlier thought were of such a nature that they could not possibly have been overcome by any effort of the earlier thinkers; to say nothing of other considerations, any effort of thought which led to the overcoming of specific limitations, led to blindness in other respects. It is reasonable to assume that what has invariably happened up to now will happen again and again in the future. Human thought is essentially limited in such a way that its limitations differ from historical situation to historical situation, and that the limitation characteristic of the thought of a given epoch cannot be overcome by any human effort. There always have been and there always will be surprising, wholly unexpected changes of outlook which radically modify the meaning of all previously acquired knowledge. No merely human view of the whole, and in particular no merely human view of the whole of human life, can claim to be final or universally valid. Every human doctrine, however seemingly final, will be superseded sooner or later by another doctrine. There is no reason to doubt that earlier thinkers had insights which are wholly inaccessible to us and which cannot become accessible to use however carefully we might study their works, because our limitations prevent us from even suspecting the possibility of the insights in question. Since the limitations of human thought are essentially unknowable, it makes no sense to conceive of them in terms of social, economic and other conditions, that is, in terms of knowable or analyzable phenomena: the limitations of human thought are set by fate.

The historicist argument has a certain plausibility which can easily be accounted for by the preponderance of dogmatism in the past. We are not permitted to forget Voltaire's complaint: "nous avons des bacheliers qui savent tout ce que ces grands hommes ignoraient."[7] Apart from this, many thinkers of the first rank have propounded all-comprehensive doctrines which they regarded as final in all important respects—doctrines which invariably have proved to be in need of radical revision. We ought therefore to welcome historicism as an ally in our fight against dogmatism. But dogmatism—or the inclination "to identify the goal of our thinking with the point at which we have become tired of thinking"[8]—is so natural to man that it is not likely to be a preserve of the past. We are forced to suspect that historicism is the guise in which dogmatism likes to appear in our age. It seems to us that what is called the experience of history is a bird's eye view of the history of thought, as that history came to be seen under the combined influence of the belief in necessary progress (or in the impossibility of returning to the thought of the past) and of the belief in the supreme value of diversity or uniqueness (or of the equal right of all epochs or civilizations). Radical historicism does not seem to be in need of those beliefs any more. But it has never examined whether the "experience" to which it refers is not an outcome of these questionable beliefs.

When speaking of the "experience" of history, people imply that this "experience" is a comprehensive insight which arises out of historical knowledge, but which cannot be reduced to historical knowledge. For historical knowledge is always extremely fragmentary and frequently very uncertain, whereas the alleged experience is supposedly global and certain. Yet it can hardly be doubted that the alleged experience ultimately rests on a number of historical observations. The question then is whether these observations entitle one to assert that the acquisition of new important insights necessarily leads to the forgetting of earlier important insights, and that the earlier thinkers could not possibly have thought of fundamental possibilities which came to the center of attention in later ages. It is obviously untrue to say, for instance, that Aristotle could not have conceived of the injustice of slavery, for he did conceive of it. One may say, however, that he could not have conceived of a world state. But why? The world state presupposes such a development of technology as Aristotle could never have dreamed of. That technological development, in its turn, required that science be regarded as essentially in the service of the "conquest of nature," and that technology be emancipated from any moral and political supervision. Aristotle did not conceive of a world state because he was absolutely certain that science is essentially theoretical and that the liberation of technology from moral and political control would lead to disastrous consequences: the fusion of science and the arts together with the unlimited or uncontrolled progress of technology has made universal and perpetual tyranny a serious possibility. Only a rash man would say that Aristotle's view, that is, his answers to the questions of whether or not science is essentially theoretical and whether or not technological progress is in need of strict moral or political control, has been refuted. But whatever one might think of his answers, certainly the fundamental questions to which they are the answers, are identical with the fundamental questions that are of immediate concern to us today. Realizing this, we realize at the same time that the epoch which regarded Aristotle's fundamental questions as obsolete, completely lacked clarity about what the fundamental issues are.

Far from legitimizing the historicist inference, history seems rather to prove that all human thought and certainly all philosophic thought, is concerned with the same fundamental themes or the same fundamental problems, and therefore that there exists an unchanging framework which persists in all changes of human knowledge of both facts and principles. This inference is obviously compatible with the fact that clarity about these problems, the approach to them, and the suggested solutions to them differ more or less from thinker to thinker or from age to age. If the fundamental problems persist in all historical change, human thought is capable of transcending its historical limitation, or of grasping something transhistorical. This would be the case even if it were true that all attempts to solve these problems are doomed to fail, and that they are doomed to fail on account of the "historicity" of "all" human thought.

To leave it at this, would amount to regarding the cause of natural right as hopeless. There cannot be natural right if all that man could know about right were the problem of right, or if the question of the principles of justice would admit of a variety of mutually exclusive answers, none of which could be proved to be superior to the others. There cannot be natural right if human thought, in spite of its essential incompleteness, is not capable of solving the problem of the principles of justice in a genuine and hence universally valid manner. More generally expressed, there cannot be natural right if human thought is not capable of acquiring genuine, universally valid, final knowledge within a limited sphere or genuine knowledge of specific subjects. Historicism cannot deny this possibility. For its own contention implies the admission of this possibility. By asserting that all human thought or at least all relevant human thought is historical, historicism admits that human thought is capable of acquiring a most important insight that is universally valid, and that will in no way be affected by any future surprises. The historicist thesis is not an isolated assertion: it is inseparable from a view of the essential structure of human life. This view has the same transhistorical character or pretension as any natural right doctrine.

The historicist thesis is then exposed to a very obvious difficulty which cannot be solved but only evaded or obscured by considerations of a more subtle character. Historicism asserts that all human thoughts or beliefs are historical, and hence deservedly destined to perish; but historicism itself is a human thought; hence historicism can only be of temporary validity, or it cannot be simply true. To assert the historicist thesis means to doubt it and thus to transcend it. As a matter of fact, historicism claims to have brought to light a truth which has come to stay, a truth valid for all thought, for all time: however much thought has changed and will change, it will always remain historical. As regards the decisive insight into the essential character of all human thought and therewith into the essential character or limitations of humanity, history has reached its end. The historicist is not impressed by the prospect that historicism may be superseded in due time by the denial of historicism. He is certain that such a change would amount to a relapse of human thought into its most powerful delusion. Historicism thrives on the fact that it inconsistently exempts itself from its own verdict about all human thought. The historicist thesis is self-contradictory or absurd. We cannot see the historical character of "all" thought—that is, of all thought with the exception of the historicist insight and its implications—without transcending history, without grasping something transhistorical.

If we call all thought that is radically historical a comprehensive worldview or a part of such a view, we must say: historicism is not itself a comprehensive worldview but an analysis of all comprehensive worldviews, an exposition of the essential character of all such views. Thought that recognizes the relativity of all comprehensive views has a different character from thought which is under the spell of, or which adopts, a comprehensive view. The former is absolute and neutral; the latter is relative and committed. The former is a theoretical insight that transcends history; the latter is the outcome of a fateful dispensation.

The radical historicist refuses to admit the transhistorical character of the historicist thesis. At the same time he recognizes the absurdity of unqualified historicism as a theoretical thesis. He denies therefore the possibility of a theoretical or objective analysis, which as such would be transhistorical, of the various comprehensive views or "historical worlds" or "cultures." This denial was decisively prepared by Nietzsche's attack on nineteenth century historicism, which claimed to be a theoretical view. According to Nietzsche, the theoretical analysis of human life that realizes the relativity of all comprehensive views and thus depreciates them would make impossible human life itself, for it would destroy the protecting atmosphere within which life or culture or action is alone possible. Moreover, since the theoretical analysis has its basis outside of life, it will never be able to understand life. The theoretical analysis of life is noncommittal and fatal to commitment, but life means commitment. To avert the danger to life, Nietzsche could choose one of two ways: he could insist on the strictly esoteric character of the theoretical analysis of life, that is restore the Platonic notion of the noble delusion, or else he could deny the possibility of theory proper and so conceive of thought as essentially subservient to, or dependent on, life or fate. If not adopted by Nietzsche himself, at any rate his successors adopted the second alternative.[9]

The thesis of radical historicism can be stated as follows. All understanding, all knowledge, however limited and "scientific," presupposes a frame of reference; it presupposes a horizon, a comprehensive view within which understanding and knowing take place. Only such a comprehensive vision makes possible any seeing, any observation, any orientation. The comprehensive view of the whole cannot be validated by reasoning since it is the basis of all reasoning. Accordingly, there is a variety of such comprehensive views, each as legitimate as any other: we have to choose such a view without any rational guidance. It is absolutely necessary to choose one; neutrality or suspension of judgment is impossible. Our choice has no support but itself; it is not supported by any objective or theoretical certainty; it is separated from nothingness, the complete absence of meaning, by nothing but our choice of it. Strictly speaking we cannot choose among different views. A single comprehensive view is imposed on us by fate: the horizon within which all our understanding and orientation takes place is produced by the fate of the individual, or of his society. All human thought depends on fate, on something that thought cannot master and whose workings it cannot anticipate. Yet the support of the horizon produced by fate is ultimately the choice of the individual, since that fate has to be accepted by the individual. We are free in the sense that we are free either to choose in anguish the worldview and the standards imposed on us by fate, or else to lose ourselves in illusory security or in despair.

The radical historicist asserts then that only to thought that is itself committed or "historical" does other committed or "historical" thought disclose itself, and above all, that only to thought that is itself committed or "historical" does the true meaning of the "historicity" of all genuine thought disclose itself. The historicist thesis expresses a fundamental experience which by its nature is incapable of adequate expression on the level of noncommitted or detached thought. The evidence of that experience may indeed be blurred but it cannot be destroyed by the inevitable logical difficulties from which all expressions of such experiences suffer. With a view to his fundamental experience the radical historicist denies that the final and in this sense transhistorical character of the historicist thesis makes doubtful the content of that thesis. The final and irrevocable insight into the historical character of all thought would transcend history only if that insight were accessible to man as man and hence in principle at all times; but it does not transcend history if it essentially belongs to a specific historic situation. It belongs to a specific historic situation: that situation is not merely the condition of the historicist insight, but its source.[10]

All natural right doctrines claim that the fundamentals of justice are in principle accessible to man as man. They presuppose therefore that a most important truth can be in principle accessible to man as man. Denying this presupposition, radical historicism asserts that the basic insight into the essential limitation of all human thought is not accessible to man as man, or that it is not the result of the progress or the labor of human thought, but it is an unforeseeable gift of unfathomable fate. It is due to fate that the essential dependence of thought on fate is realized now, and was not realized in earlier times. Historicism has this in common with all other thought that it depends on fate. It differs from all other thought in this, that, thanks to fate, it has been given to realize the radical dependence of thought on fate. We are absolutely ignorant of the surprises which fate may have in store for later generations, and fate may in the future again conceal what it has revealed to us; but this does not impair the truth of that revelation. One does not have to transcend history in order to see the historical character of all thought: there is a privileged moment, an absolute moment in the historical process, a moment in which the essential character of all thought becomes transparent. In exempting itself from its own verdict, historicism claims merely to mirror the character of historical reality or to be true to the facts: the self-contradictory character of the historicist thesis should be charged, not to historicism, but to reality.

The assumption of an absolute moment in history is essential to historicism. In this, historicism surreptitiously follows the precedent set in a classic manner by Hegel. Hegel had taught that every philosophy is the conceptual expression of the spirit of its time, and yet maintained the absolute truth of his own system of philosophy by ascribing absolute character to his own time; he assumed that his own time was the end of history and hence the absolute moment. Historicism explicitly denies that the end of history has come, but it implicitly asserts the opposite: no possible future change of orientation can legitimately make doubtful the decisive insight into the inescapable dependence of thought on fate, and therewith into the essential character of human life; in the decisive respect the end of history, that is, of the history of thought, has come. But one cannot simply assume that one lives or thinks in the absolute moment; one must show, somehow, how the absolute moment can be recognized as such. According to Hegel the absolute moment is the one in which philosophy, or quest for wisdom, has been transformed into wisdom, that is, the moment in which the fundamental riddles have been fully solved. Historicism, however, stands or falls by the denial of the possibility of theoretical metaphysics, and of philosophic ethics or natural right; it stands or falls by the denial of the solubility of the fundamental riddles. According to historicism, therefore, the absolute moment must be the moment in which the insoluble character of the fundamental riddles has become fully manifest, or in which the fundamental delusion of the human mind has been dispelled.

But one might realize the insoluble character of the fundamental riddles and still continue to see in the understanding of these riddles the task of philosophy; one would thus merely replace a non-historicist and dogmatic philosophy by a non-historicist and skeptical philosophy. Historicism goes beyond skepticism. It assumes that philosophy in the full and original sense of the term, namely the attempt to replace opinions about the whole by knowledge of the whole, is not only incapable of reaching its goal, but absurd, because the very idea of philosophy rests on dogmatic, that is, arbitrary premises or, more specifically, on premises that are only "historical and relative." For clearly, if philosophy, or the attempt to replace opinions by knowledge, itself rests on mere opinions, philosophy is absurd.

The most influential attempts to establish the dogmatic and hence arbitrary or historically relative character of philosophy proper proceed along the following lines. Philosophy or the attempt to replace opinions about the whole by knowledge of the whole, presupposes that the whole is knowable, that is, intelligible. This presupposition leads to the consequence that the whole as it is in itself is identified with the whole insofar as it is intelligible or insofar as it can become an object; it leads to the identification of "being" with "intelligible" or "object"; it leads to the dogmatic disregard of everything that cannot become an object, that is, an object for the knowing subject, or the dogmatic disregard of everything that cannot be mastered by the subject. Furthermore, to say that the whole is knowable or intelligible, is tantamount to saying that the whole has a permanent structure, or that the whole as such is unchangeable or always the same. If this is the case, it is in principle possible to predict how the whole will be at any future time: the future of the whole can be anticipated by thought. The presupposition mentioned is said to have its root in the dogmatic identification of "to be" in the highest sense with "to be always," or in the fact that philosophy understands "to be" in such a sense that "to be" in the highest sense must mean "to be always." The dogmatic character of the basic premise of philosophy is said to have been revealed by the discovery of history or of the "historicity" of human life. The meaning of that discovery can be expressed in theses like these: what is called the whole, is actually always incomplete and therefore not truly a whole; the whole is essentially changing in such a manner that its future cannot be predicted; the whole as it is in itself can never be grasped, or it is not intelligible; human thought essentially depends on something that cannot be anticipated or that can never be an object, or that can never be mastered by the subject; "to be" in the highest sense cannot mean, or at any rate it does not necessarily mean, "to be always."

We cannot even attempt to discuss these theses. We must leave them with the following observation. Radical historicism compels us to realize the bearing of the fact that the very idea of natural right presupposes the possibility of philosophy in the full and original meaning of the term. It compels us at the same time to realize the need for unbiased reconsideration of the most elementary premises whose validity is presupposed by philosophy. The question of the validity of these premises cannot be disposed of by adopting, or clinging to a more or less persistent tradition of philosophy, for it is of the essence of traditions that they cover or conceal their humble foundations by erecting impressive edifices on them. Nothing ought to be said or done which could create the impression that unbiased reconsideration of the most elementary premises of philosophy is a merely academic or historical affair. Prior to such reconsideration, however, the issue of natural right can only remain an open question.

For we cannot assume that the issue has been finally settled by historicism. The "experience of history" and the less ambiguous experience of the complexity of human affairs may blur, but they cannot extinguish the evidence of those simple experiences regarding right and wrong which are at the bottom of the philosophic contention that there is a natural right. Historicism either ignores or else distorts these experiences. Furthermore, the most thoroughgoing attempt to establish historicism culminated in the assertion that if and when there are no human beings, there may be *entia*, but there cannot be *esse*, that is, that there can be *entia* while there is no *esse*. There is an obvious connection between this assertion and the rejection of the view that "to be" in the highest sense means "to be always." Besides, there has always been a glaring contrast between the way in which historicism understands the thought of the past and genuine understanding of the thought of the past; the undeniable possibility of historical objectivity is explicitly or implicitly denied by historicism in all its forms. Above all, in the transition from early (theoretical) to radical ("existentialist") historicism, the "experience of history" was never submitted to critical analysis. It was taken for granted that it is a genuine experience and not a questionable interpretation of experience. The question was not raised whether what is really experienced does not allow of an entirely different and possibly more adequate interpretation. In particular, the "experience of history" does not make doubtful the view that the fundamental problems, such as the problems of justice, persist or retain their identity in all historical change, however much they may be obscured by the temporary denial of their relevance, and however variable or provisional all human solutions to these problems may be. In grasping these problems as problems the human mind liberates itself from its historical limitations. No more is needed to legitimize philosophy in its original, Socratic sense: philosophy is knowledge that one does not know; that is to say, it is knowledge of what one does not know, or awareness of the fundamental problems and, therewith, of the fundamental alternatives regarding their solution that are coeval with human thought.

If the existence and even the possibility of natural right must remain an open question as long as the issue between historicism and non-historicist philosophy is not settled, our most urgent need is to understand that issue. The issue is not understood if it is seen merely in the way in which it presents itself from the point of view of historicism; it must also be seen in the way in which it presents itself from the point of view of non-historicist philosophy. This means, for all practical purposes, that the problem of historicism must first be considered from the point of view of classical philosophy—which is non-historicist thought in its pure form. Our most urgent need can then be satisfied only by means of historical studies which would enable us to understand classical philosophy exactly as it understood itself, and not in the way in which it presents itself on the basis of historicism. We need in the first place a non-historicist understanding of non-historicist philosophy. But we need no less urgently a non-historicist understanding of historicism, that is, an understanding of the genesis of historicism that does not take for granted the soundness of historicism.

Historicism assumes that modern man's turn towards history implied the divination and eventually the discovery of a dimension of reality that had escaped classical thought, namely, of the historical dimension. If this is granted one will be forced in the end into extreme historicism. But if historicism cannot be taken for granted, the question becomes inevitable whether what was hailed in the nineteenth century as a discovery, was not in fact an invention, that is, an arbitrary interpretation of phenomena which were always known and which were interpreted much more adequately prior to the emergence of "the historical consciousness" than afterwards. We have to raise the question whether what is called the discovery of history is not in fact an artificial and makeshift solution to a problem that could arise only on the basis of very questionable premises.

I suggest this line of approach. History meant throughout the ages primarily political history. Accordingly, what is called the discovery of history is the work, not of philosophy in general, but of political philosophy. It was a predicament peculiar to eighteenth century political philosophy that led to the emergence of the historical school. The political philosophy of the eighteenth century was a doctrine of natural right. It consisted in a peculiar interpretation of natural right, namely, the specifically modern interpretation. Historicism is the ultimate outcome of the crisis of modern natural right. The crisis of modern natural right or of modern political philosophy could become a crisis of philosophy as such, only because in the modern centuries philosophy as such had become thoroughly politicized. Originally, philosophy had been the humanizing quest for the eternal order, and hence it had been a pure source of humane inspiration and aspirations. Since the seventeenth century philosophy has become a weapon, and hence an instrument. It was this politicization of philosophy that was discerned as the root of our troubles by an intellectual who denounced the treason of the intellectuals.[11] He committed the fatal mistake however of ignoring the essential difference between intellectuals and philosophers. In this he remained the dupe of the delusion which he denounced. For the politicization of philosophy consists precisely in this, that the difference between intellectuals and philosophers—a difference formerly known as the difference between gentlemen and philosophers on the one hand, and the difference between sophists or rhetoricians and philosophers on the other—becomes blurred and finally disappears.

Notes

Reprinted from *The Review of Politics* 12, no. 4 (October 1950): 422–42.

[Strauss based this essay on his Walgreen lectures on Natural Right and History delivered at the University of Chicago, in October 1949. The article later provided the foundation for his influential study, *Natural Right and History* (Chicago: University of Chicago Press, 1953). Ed.]

1. Consider Plato, *Republic*, 456b12–c2, 452a7–8 and c6–dl, Laches, 184d1–185a3; Hobbes, *De Cive*, II, 1; Locke, *Of Civil Government*, Book II § 12 in conjunction with *An Essay on the Human Understanding*, Book I, ch. 3. Compare Rousseau, *Discours sur l'origina de l'inégalité*, preface; Montesquieu, *De l'ésprit des lois*, I, 1–2; also *Marsilius, Defensor Pacis*, II, 12 sect. 8.

2. Aristotle, *Eth. Nic.*, 1134b24–27.

3. The legal positivism of the nineteenth and twentieth centuries cannot be simply identified with either conventionalism or historicism. It seems, however, that it derives its strength ultimately from the generally accepted historicist premise. See particularly Karl Bergbohm, *Jurisprudenz und Rechtsphilosophie*, vol. 1 (Leipzig: Duncker & Humblot, 1892), 409 ff. Bergbohm's strict argument against the possibility of natural right (as distinguished from the argument that is merely meant to show the disastrous consequences of natural right for the positive legal order) is based on "the undeniable truth that nothing eternal and absolute exists except the One Whom man cannot comprehend, but only divine in a spirit of faith" (p. 416 n), that is, on the assumption "that the standards with reference to which we pass judgment on the historical, positive law . . . are themselves absolutely the progeny of their time and are always historical and relative" (p. 450 n).

4. Plato, *Minos*, 314610–31562.

5. ". . . (les imperfections des États), s'ils en ont, comme la seule diversité, qui est entre eux suffit pour assurer que plusieurs en ont. . . . ," Descartes, *Discours de la méthode*, Second part.

6. As regards the tension between the concern with the history of the human race and the concern with life after death, see Kant's "Idea for a universal history with cosmo-

politan intent," propos. 9. See *The Philosophy of Kant*, ed. C. J. Friedrich (New York: The Modern Library, 1949), 130. Consider also the thesis of Herder, whose influence on the historical thought of the nineteenth century is well known, that "the five acts are in this life." See M. Mendelssohn, *Gesammelte Schriften*, Jubiläums-Ausgabe, III, 1, xxx–xxxii.

7. *Dictionnaire Philosophique*, ed. J. Benda, I, 19.

8. See Lessing's letter to Mendelssohn of January 9, 1771.

9. For the understanding of this choice, one has to consider its connection with Nietzsche's sympathy with "Callicles" on the one hand, and his preferring the "tragic life" to the theoretical life on the other. See Plato, *Gorgias* 481d and 502 ff., and *Laws*, 658d2–5. Compare Nietzsche's *Vom Nutzen und Nachteil der Historie für das Leben* (Leipzig: Insel Verlag), 73. This passage reveals clearly the fact that Nietzsche adopted what one may call the fundamental premise of the historical school.

10. The distinction between "condition" and "source" corresponds to the difference between Aristotle's "history" of philosophy in the first book of the *Metaphysics* and historicist history.

11. [Strauss is probably referring to Julien Benda's, *La trahison des clercs* (Paris: Grasset, 1927). Ed.]

CHAPTER 13

The Origins of Totalitarianism

ERIC VOEGELIN

Eric Voegelin (1901–1985) was born in Cologne, Germany. He earned his doctorate in political science from the University of Vienna and left Europe before the onset of World War II. Voegelin became a professor of political philosophy in the United States, holding positions at such institutions as Louisiana State University and the University of Notre Dame. Drawing upon his mastery of multiple fields of knowledge, Voegelin sought to formulate a comprehensive social and historical account of the human condition. He wrote about a wide range of topics, including politics, religion, classical philosophy, and the rise of totalitarian ideologies. He was especially interested in the relation between Christian spiritual life and political experience. Political life, he believed, could be understood in two different ways. It could either point beyond itself to the mystery of humanity's origins or it could be used as a tool to manipulate people's spiritual needs in order to serve unsavory ambitions. On these grounds, Voegelin opposed all forms of ideological thought, including totalitarianism and modern Gnosticism.

The vast majority of all human beings alive on earth is affected in some measure by the totalitarian mass movements of our time. Whether men are members, supporters, fellow-travelers, naïve connivers, actual or potential victims, whether they are under the domination of a totalitarian government, or whether they are still free to organize their defenses against the disaster, the relation to the movements has become an intimate part of their spiritual, intellectual, economic, and physical existence. The putrefaction of Western civilization, as it were, has released a cadaveric poison spreading its infection through the body of humanity. What no religious founder, no philosopher, no imperial conqueror of the past has achieved—to create a community of mankind by creating a common concern for all men—has now been realized through the community of suffering under the earthwide expansion of Western foulness.

Even under favorable circumstances, a communal process of such magnitude and complexity will not lend itself easily to exploration and theorization by the political scientist. In space the knowledge of facts must extend to a plurality of civilizations. By subject matter the inquiry will have to range from religious experiences and their symbolization, through governmental institutions and the organization of terrorism, to the transformations of personality under the pressure of fear and habituation to atrocities; in time the inquiry will have to trace the genesis of the movements through the course of a civilization that has lasted for a millennium. Regrettably, though, the circumstances are not favorable. The positivistic destruction of political science is not yet overcome, and the great obstacle to an adequate treatment of totalitarianism is still the insufficiency of theoretical instruments. It is difficult to categorize political phenomena properly without a well developed philosophical anthropology, or phenomena of spiritual disintegration without a theory of the spirit. For the morally abhorrent and the emotionally existing will overshadow the essential. Moreover, the revolutionary outburst of totalitarianism in our time is the climax of a secular evolution. And again, because of the unsatisfactory state of critical theory, the essence that grew to actuality in a long historical process will defy identification. The catastrophic manifestations of the revolution, the massacre and misery of millions of human beings, impress the spectator so strongly as unprecedented in comparison with the immediately preceding more peaceful age that the phenomenal difference will obscure the essential sameness.

In view of these difficulties the work by Hannah Arendt on *The Origins of Totalitarianism* deserves careful attention.[1] It is an attempt to make contemporary phenomena intelligible by tracing their origin back to the eighteenth century, thus establishing a time unit in which the essence of totalitarianism unfolded to its fullness. And as far as the nature of totalitarianism is concerned, it penetrates to the theoretically relevant issues. This book on the troubles of the age, however, is also marked by these troubles, for it bears the scars of the unsatisfactory state of theory to which we have alluded. It abounds with brilliant formulations and profound insights, as one would expect only from an author who has mastered her problems as a philosopher, but surprisingly, when the author pursues these insights into their consequences, the elaboration veers toward regrettable flatness. Such derailments, while embarrassing, are nevertheless instructive— sometimes more instructive than the insights themselves—because they reveal the intellectual confusion of the age, and show more convincingly than any argument why totalitarian ideas find mass acceptance and will find it for a long time to come.

The book is organized in three parts: Antisemitism, Imperialism, and Totalitarianism. The sequence of the three topics is roughly chronological, though the phenomena under the three titles do overlap in time. Antisemitism begins to rear its head in the Age of Enlightenment; the imperialist expansion and the pan-movements reach from the middle of the nineteenth century to the present; and the totalitarian movements belong to the twentieth century. The sequence is, furthermore, an order of increasing intensity and ferocity in the growth of totalitarian features toward the climax in the atrocities of the concentration camps. And it is, finally, a gradual revelation of the essence of totalitarianism from its inchoate forms in the eighteenth century to the fully developed, nihilistic crushing of human beings.

This organization of the materials, however, cannot be completely understood without its emotional motivation. There is more than one way to deal with the problems of totalitarianism; and it is not certain, as we shall see, that Dr. Arendt's is the best. Anyway, there can be no doubt that the fate of the Jews, the mass slaughter and the homelessness of displaced persons, is for the author a center of emotional shock, the center from which radiates her desire to inquire into the causes of the horror, to understand political phenomena in Western civilization that belong to the same class, and to consider means that will stem the evil. This emotionally determined method of proceeding from a concrete center of shock toward generalizations leads to a delimitation of subject matter. The shock is caused by the fate of human beings, of the leaders, followers, and victims of totalitarian movements. Hence, the crumbling of old and the formation of new institutions, the life-courses of individuals in an age of institutional change, the dissolution and formation of types of conduct, as well as of the ideas of right conduct, will become topical. Totalitarianism will have to be understood by its manifestations in the medium of conduct and institutions just adumbrated. And indeed there runs through the book as the governing theme the obsolescence of the national state as the sheltering organization of Western political societies, owing to technological, economic, and the consequent changes of political power. With every change sections of society become "superfluous," in the sense that they lose their function and therefore are threatened in their social status and economic existence. The centralization of the national state and the rise of bureaucracies in

France makes the nobility superfluous; the growth of industrial societies and new sources of revenue in the late nineteenth century make the Jews as state bankers superfluous; every industrial crisis creates superfluity of human beings through unemployment; taxation and the inflations of the twentieth century dissolve the middle classes into social rubble; the wars and the totalitarian regimes produce the millions of refugees, slave-laborers, and inmates of concentration camps, and push the membership of whole societies into the position of expendable human material. As far as the institutional aspect of the process is concerned, totalitarianism, thus, is the disintegration of national societies and their transformation into aggregates of superfluous human beings.

The delimitation of subject matter through the emotions aroused by the fate of human beings is the strength of Arendt's book. The concern about man and the causes of his fate in social upheavals is the source of historiography. The manner in which the author spans her arc from the presently moving events to their origins in the concentration of the national state evolves distant memories of the grand manner in which Thucydides spanned his arc from the catastrophic movement of his time, from the great *kinesis,* to its origins in the emergence of the Athenian polls after the Persian Wars. The emotion in its purity makes the intellect a sensitive instrument for recognizing and selecting the relevant facts. And if the purity of the human interest remains untainted by partisanship, the result will be a historical study of respectable rank—as in the case of the present work, which in its substantive parts is remarkably free of ideological nonsense. With admirable detachment from the partisan strife of the day, the author has succeeded in writing the history of the circumstances that occasioned the movements, of the totalitarian movements themselves, and above all of the dissolution of human personality, from the early anti-bourgeois and anti-semitic resentment to the contemporary horrors of the "man who does his duty" and of his victims.

This is not the occasion to go into details. Nevertheless, a few of the topics must be mentioned in order to convey an idea of the richness of the work. The first part is perhaps the best short history of the antisemitic problem in existence. Special attention should be singled out for the sections on the court-jews and their decline, on the Jewish problem in enlightened and romantic Berlin, the sketch of Disraeli, and the concise account of the Dreyfus Affair. The second part—on Imperialism—is theoretically the most penetrating, for it creates the type-concepts for the relations between phenomena which are rarely placed in their proper, wider context. It contains the studies on the fateful emancipation of the bourgeoisie that wants to be an upper class without assuming the responsibilities of rulership, on the disintegration of Western national societies and the formation of elites and mobs, on the genesis of race-thinking in the eighteenth century, on the imperialist expansion of the Western national states and the race problem in the empires, on the corresponding continental pan-movements and the genesis of racial nationalism. Within these larger studies are embedded previous miniatures of special situations and personalities, such as the splendid studies of Rhodes and Barnato, of the character traits of the Boers and their race policy, of the British colonial bureaucracy, of the inability of Western national states to create an imperial culture in the Roman sense and the subsequent failure of British and French imperialism, of the element of infantilism in Kipling and Lawrence of Arabia, and of the Central European minority question. The third part—on Totalitarianism—contains studies on the classless society that results from general superfluity of the members of a society, on the difference between mob and mass, on totalitarian propaganda, on totalitarian police, and the concentration camps.

The digest of this enormous material, well documented with footnotes and bibliographies, is sometimes broad, betraying the joy of skilful narration by the true historian, but still held together by the conceptual discipline of the general thesis. Nevertheless, at this point a note of criticism will have to be allowed. The organization of the book is somewhat less strict than it could be, if the author had availed herself more readily of the theoretical instruments which the present state of science puts at her disposition. Her principle of relevance that orders the variegated materials into a story of totalitarianism is the disintegration of a civilization into masses of human beings without secure economic and social status; and her materials are relevant in so far as they demonstrate the process of disintegration. Obviously this process is the same that has been categorized by Toynbee as the growth of the internal and external proletariat. It is surprising that the author has not used Toynbee's highly differentiated concepts; and that even his name appears neither in the footnotes, nor in the bibliography, nor in the index. The use of Toynbee's work would have substantially added to the weight of Arendt's analysis.

This excellent book, as we have indicated, is unfortunately marred, however, by certain theoretical defects. The treatment of movements of the totalitarian type on the level of social situations and change, as well as of types of conduct determined by them, is apt to endow historical causality with an aura of fatality. Situations and changes, to be sure, require, but they do not determine a response. The character of a man, the range and intensity of his passions, the controls exerted by his virtues, and his spiritual freedom, enter as further determinants. If conduct is not understood as the response of a man to a situation, and the varieties of response as rooted in the potentialities of human nature rather than in the situation itself, the process of history will become a closed stream, of which every cross-cut at a given point of time is the exhaustive determinant of the future course. Arendt is aware of this problem. She knows that changes in the economic and social situations do not simply make people superfluous, and that superfluous people do not respond by necessity with resentment, cruelty, and violence. She knows that a ruthlessly competitive society owes its character to an absence of restraint and of a sense of responsibility for consequences. And she is even uneasily aware that not all the misery of National Socialist concentration camps was caused by the oppressors, but that a part of it stemmed from the spiritual lostness that so many of the victims brought with them. Her understanding of such questions is revealed beyond doubt in the following passage: "Nothing perhaps distinguishes modern masses as radically from those of previous centuries as the loss of faith in a Last Judgment: the worst have lost their fear and the best have lost their hope. Unable as yet to live without fear and hope, these masses are attracted by every effort which seems to promise a man-made fabrication of the paradise they longed for and of the hell they had feared. Just as the popularized feature of Marx's classless society have a queer resemblance to the Messianic Age, so the reality of the concentration camps resembles nothing so much as medieval pictures of hell" (p. 419). The spiritual disease of agnosticism is the peculiar problem of the modern masses, and the man-made paradises and man-made hells are its symptoms; and the masses have the disease whether they are in their paradise or in their hell. The author, thus, is aware of the problem. But, oddly enough, the knowledge does not affect her treatment of the materials. If the spiritual disease is the decisive feature that distinguishes modern masses from those of earlier centuries, then one would expect the study of totalitarianism not to be delimited by the institutional breakdown of national societies and the growth of socially superfluous masses, but rather by the genesis of the spiritual disease, especially since the response to the institutional breakdown clearly bears the marks of the disease. Then the origins of totalitarianism would not have to be sought primarily in the fate of the national state and attendant social

and economic changes since the eighteenth century, but rather in the rise of immanentist sectarianism since the high Middle Ages. And the totalitarian movements would not be simply revolutionary movements of functionally dislocated
people, but immanentist creed movements in which medieval heresies have
come to their fruition. Arendt, as we have said, does not draw the theoretical conclusions from her own insights.

Such inconclusiveness has a cause. It comes to light in another one of the profound formulations which the author deflects in a surprising direction: "What
totalitarian ideologies therefore aim at is not the transformation of the outside world or the revolutionizing transmutation of society, but the transformation of human nature itself" (p. 432). This is, indeed, the essence of totalitarianism as an immanentist creed movement. Totalitarian movements do not
intend to remedy social evils by industrial changes, but want to create a millennium in the eschatological sense through transformation of human nature.
The Christian faith in transcendental perfection through the grace of God has
been converted—and perverted—into the idea of immanent perfection through
an act of man. And this understanding of the spiritual and intellectual breakdown is followed in Arendt's text by the sentence: "Human nature as such is at
stake, and even though it seems that these experiments succeed not in changing
man but only in destroying him . . . one should bear in mind the necessary limitations to an experiment which requires global control in order to show conclu-
sive results" (p. 433). When I read this sentence, I could hardly believe my eyes.
"Nature" is a philosophical concept; it denotes that which identifies a thing as a
thing of this kind and not of another one. A "nature" cannot be changed or transformed; a "change of nature" is a contradiction of terms; tampering with the "nature" of a thing means destroying the thing. To conceive the idea of "changing
the nature" of man (or of anything) is a symptom of the intellectual breakdown
of Western civilization. The author, in fact, adopts the immanentist ideology;
she keeps an "open mind" with regard to the totalitarian atrocities; she considers the question of a "change of nature" a matter that will have to be settled by
"trial and error"; and since the "trial" could not yet avail itself of the opportunities
afforded by a global laboratory, the question must remain in suspense for the
time being.

These sentences of Dr. Arendt, of course, must not be construed as a concession to totalitarianism in the more restricted sense, that is, as a concession
to National Socialist and Communist atrocities. On the contrary, they reflect

a typically liberal, progressive, pragmatist attitude toward philosophical problems. We suggested previously that the author's theoretical derailments are sometimes more interesting than her insights. And this attitude is, indeed, of general importance because it reveals how much ground liberals and totalitarians have in common. The essential immanentism which unites them overrides the differences of ethos which separate them. The true dividing line in the contemporary crisis does not run between liberals and totalitarians, but between the religious and philosophical transcendentalists on the one side, and the liberal and totalitarian immanentist sectarians on the other side. It is sad, but it must be reported, that the author herself draws this line. The argument starts from her confusion about the "nature of man": "Only the criminal attempt to change the nature of man is adequate to our trembling insight that no nature, not even the nature of man, can any longer be considered to be the measure of all things." This sentence, if it has any sense at all, can only mean that the nature of man ceases to be the measure, when some imbecile conceives the notion of changing it. The author seems to be impressed by the imbecile and is ready to forget about the nature of man, as well as about all human civilization that has been built on its understanding. The "mob," she concedes, has correctly seen "that the whole of nearly three thousand years of Western civilization . . . has broken down." Out go the philosophers of Greece, the prophets of Israel, Christ, not to mention the Patres and Scholastics; for man has "come of age," and that means "that from now on man is the only possible creator of his own laws and the only possible maker of his own history." This coming-of-age has to be accepted; man is the new lawmaker; and on the tablets wiped clean of the past he will inscribe the "new discoveries in morality" which Burke had still considered impossible.

It sounds like a nihilistic nightmare. And a nightmare it is rather than a well considered theory. It would be unfair to hold the author responsible on the level of critical thought for what obviously is a traumatic shuddering under the impact of experiences that were stronger than the forces of spiritual and intellectual resistance. The book as a whole must not be judged by the theoretical derailments which occur mostly in its concluding part. The treatment of the subject matter itself is animated, if not always penetrated, by the age-old knowledge about human nature and the life of the spirit which, in the conclusions, the author wishes to discard and to replace by "new discoveries." Let us rather take comfort in the unconscious irony of the closing sentence of the work where the author appeals, for the "new" spirit of human solidarity, to Acts 16:28: "Do thyself no harm; for we are all here." Perhaps, when the author progresses from quoting to hearing these words, her nightmarish fright will end like that of the jailer to whom they were addressed.

NOTES

Reprinted from *The Review of Politics* 15, no. 1 (January 1953): 68–76.

  1. Hannah Arendt, *The Origins of Totalitarianism* (New York: Harcourt, Brace and Company, 1951).

A Reply

HANNAH ARENDT

Much as I appreciate the unusual kindness of the editors of *The Review of Politics* who asked me to answer Prof. Eric Voegelin's criticism of my book, I am not quite sure that I decided wisely when I accepted their offer. I certainly would not, and should not, have accepted if his review were of the usual friendly or unfriendly kind. Such replies, by their very nature, all too easily tempt the author either to review his own book or to write a review of the review. In order to avoid such temptations, I have refrained as much as I could, even on the level of personal conversation, to take issue with any reviewer of my book, no matter how much I agreed or disagreed with him.

  Professor Voegelin's criticism, however, is of a kind that can be answered in all propriety. He raises certain very general questions of method, on one side, and of general philosophical implications on the other. Both of course belong together. But while I feel that within the necessary limitations of a historical study and political analysis I made myself sufficiently clear on certain general perplexities which have come to light through the full development of totalitarianism, I also know that I failed to explain the particular method which I came to use, and to account for a rather unusual approach—not to the different historical and political issues where account or justification would only distract—to the whole field of political and historical sciences as such. One of the difficulties of the book is that it does not belong to any school and hardly uses any of the officially recognized or officially controversial instruments.

The problem originally confronting me was simple and baffling at the same time: all historiography is necessarily salvation and frequently justification; it is due to man's fear that he may forget and to his striving for something which is even more than remembrance. These impulses are already implicit in the mere observation of chronological order and they are not likely to be overcome through the interference of value-judgments which usually interrupt the narrative and make the account appear biased and "unscientific." I think the history of antisemitism is a good example of this kind of history-writing. The reason why this whole literature is so extraordinarily poor in terms of scholarship is that the historians—if they were not conscious antisemites, which of course they never were—had to write the history of a subject which they did not want to conserve; they had to write in a destructive way and to write history for purposes of destruction is somehow a contradiction in terms. The way out has been to hold on, so to speak, to the Jews, to make them the subject of conservation. But this was no solution, for to look at the events only from the side of the victim resulted in apologetics, which of course is no history at all.

Thus my first problem was how to write historically about something, totalitarianism, which I did not want to conserve but on the contrary felt engaged to destroy. My way of solving this problem has given rise to the reproach that the book was lacking in unity. What I did—and what I might have done anyway because of my previous training and the way of my thinking—was to discover the chief elements of totalitarianism and to analyze them in historical terms, tracing these elements back in history as far as I deemed proper and necessary. That is, I did not write a history of totalitarianism but an analysis in terms of history; I did not write a history of antisemitism or of imperialism, but analyzed the element of Jew-hatred and the element of expansion insofar as these elements were still clearly visible and played a decisive role in the totalitarian phenomenon itself. The book, therefore, does not really deal with the "origins" of totalitarianism, as its title unfortunately claims, but gives a historical account of the elements which crystallized into totalitarianism. This account is followed by an analysis of the elemental structure of totalitarian movements and domination itself. The elementary structure of totalitarianism is the hidden structure of the book while its more apparent unity is provided by certain fundamental concepts which run like red threads through the whole.

The same problem of method can be approached from another side and then presents itself as a problem of "style." This has been praised as passionate and criticized as sentimental. Both judgments seem to me a little beside the point. I parted quite consciously with the tradition of *sine ira et studio* of whose greatness I was fully aware, and to me this was a methodological necessity closely connected with my particular subject matter.

Let us suppose, to take one among many possible examples, that the historian is confronted with excessive poverty in a society of great wealth, such as the poverty of the British working classes during the early stages of the industrial revolution. The natural human reaction to such conditions is one of anger and indignation because these conditions are against the dignity of man. If I describe these conditions without permitting my indignation to interfere, I have lifted this particular phenomenon out of its context in human society and have thereby robbed it of part of its nature, deprived it of one of its important inherent qualities. For to arouse indignation is one of the qualities of excessive poverty insofar as poverty occurs among human beings. I therefore can not agree with Professor Voegelin that the "morally abhorrent and the emotionally existing will overshadow the essential," because I believe them to form an integral part of it. This has nothing to do with sentimentality or moralizing, although, of course, either can become a pitfall for the author. If I moralized or became sentimental, I simply did not do well what I was supposed to do, namely to describe the totalitarian phenomenon as occurring, not on the moon, but in the midst of human society. To describe the concentration camps *sine ira* is not to be "objective," but to condone them; and such condoning cannot be changed by a condemnation which the author may feel duty bound to add but which remains unrelated to the description itself. When I used the image of Hell, I did not mean this allegorically but literally. It seems rather obvious that men who have lost their faith in Paradise, will not be able to establish it on earth; but it is not so certain that those who have lost their belief in Hell as a place of the hereafter may not be willing and able to establish on earth exact imitations of what people used to believe about Hell. In this sense I think that a description of the camps as hell on earth is more "objective," that is, more adequate to their essence than statements of a purely sociological or psychological nature.

The problem of style is a problem of adequacy and of response. If I write in the same "objective" manner about the Elizabethan age and the twentieth century, it may well be that my dealing with both periods is inadequate because I have renounced the human faculty to respond to either. Thus the question of style is bound up with the problem of understanding which has plagued the historical sciences almost from their beginnings. I do not wish to go into this matter here, but I may add that I am convinced that understanding is closely related to that faculty of imagination which Kant called *Einbildungskraft* and which has nothing in common with fictional ability. The *Spiritual Exercises* are exercises of imagination and they may be more relevant to method in the historical sciences than academic training realizes.

Reflections of this kind, originally caused by the special nature of my subject, and the personal experience which is necessarily involved in an historical investigation that employs imagination consciously as an important tool of cognition, resulted in a critical approach toward almost all interpretation of contemporary history. I hinted at this in two short paragraphs of the Preface where I warned the reader against the concepts of Progress and of Doom as "two sides of the same medal" as well as against any attempt at "deducing the unprecedented from precedents." These two approaches are closely interconnected. The reason why Professor Voegelin can speak of "the putrefaction of Western civilization" and the "earthwide expansion of Western foulness" is that he treats "phenomenal differences," which to me as differences of factuality are all-important, as minor outgrowths of some "essential sameness" of a doctrinal nature. Numerous affinities between totalitarianism and some other trends in Occidental political or intellectual history have been described with this result, in my opinion. They all failed to point out the distinct quality of what was actually happening. The "phenomenal differences," far from "obscuring" some essential sameness, are those phenomena which make totalitarianism "totalitarian," which distinguish this one form of government and movement from all others and therefore can alone help us in finding its essence. What is unprecedented in totalitarianism is not primarily its ideological content, but the *event* of totalitarian domination itself. This can be seen clearly if we have to admit that the deeds of its considered policies have exploded our traditional categories of political thought (totalitarian domination is unlike all forms of tyranny and despotism we know of) and the standards of our moral judgment (totalitarian crimes are very inadequately described as "murder" and totalitarian criminals can hardly be punished as "murderers").

Voegelin seems to think that totalitarianism is only the other side of liberalism, positivism and pragmatism. But whether one agrees with liberalism or not (and I may say here that I am rather certain that I am neither a liberal nor a positivist nor a pragmatist), the point is that liberals are clearly not totalitarians. This, of course, does not exclude the fact that liberal or positivistic elements also lend themselves to totalitarian thinking; but such affinities would only mean that one has to draw even sharper distinctions because of the *fact* that liberals are not totalitarians.

I hope that I do not belabor this point unduly. It is important to me because I think that what separates my approach from Professor Voegelin's is that I proceed from facts and events instead of intellectual affinities and influences. This is perhaps a bit difficult to perceive because I am of course much concerned with philosophical implications and changes in spiritual self-interpretation. But this certainly does not mean that I described "a gradual revelation of the essence of totalitarianism from its inchoate forms in the eighteenth century to the fully developed," because this essence, in my opinion, did not exist before it had not come into being. *[sic]*[1] I therefore talk only of "elements," which eventually crystallize into totalitarianism, some of which are traceable to the eighteenth century, some perhaps even farther back, (although I would doubt Voegelin's own theory that the "rise of immanentist sectarianism" since the late Middle Ages eventually ended in totalitarianism). Under no circumstances would I call any of them totalitarian.

For similar reasons and for the sake of distinguishing between ideas and actual events in history, I cannot agree with Voegelin's remark that "the spiritual disease is the decisive feature that distinguishes modern masses from those of earlier centuries." To me, modern masses are disintegrated by the fact that they are "masses" in a strict sense of the word. They are distinguished from the multitudes of former centuries in that they do not have common interests to bind them together nor any kind of common "consent" which, according to Cicero, constitutes *inter-est*, that which is between men, ranging all the way from material to spiritual and other matters. This "between" can be a common ground and it can be a common purpose; it always fulfills the double function of binding men together *and* separating them in an articulate way. The lack of common interest so characteristic of modern masses is therefore only another sign of their homelessness and rootlessness. But it alone accounts for the curious fact that these modern masses are formed by the atomization of society, that the mass-men who lack all communal relationships nevertheless offer the best possible "material" for movements in which peoples are so closely pressed together that they seem to have become One. The loss of interests is identical with the loss of "self," and modern masses are distinguished in my view by their self-lessness, that is their lack of "selfish interests."

I know that problems of this sort can be avoided if one interprets totalitarian movements as a new—and perverted—religion, a substitute for the lost creed of traditional beliefs. From this, it would follow that some "need for religion" is a cause of the rise of totalitarianism. I feel unable to follow even the very qualified form in which Professor Voegelin uses the concept of a secular religion. There is no substitute for God in the totalitarian ideologies. Hitler's use of the "Almighty" was a concession to what he himself believed to be a superstition. More than that, the metaphysical place for God has remained empty. The introduction of these semi-theological arguments in the discussion of totalitarianism, on the other side, is only too likely to further the widespread and strictly blasphemous modern "ideas" about a God who is "good for you"—for your mental or other health, for the integration of your personality and God knows what—that is "ideas" which make of God a function of man or society. This functionalization seems to me in many respects the last and perhaps the most dangerous stage of atheism.

By this, I do not mean to say that Professor Voegelin could ever become guilty of such functionalization. Nor do I deny that there is some connection between atheism and totalitarianism. But this connection seems to me purely negative and not at all peculiar to the rise of totalitarianism. It is true that a Christian cannot become a follower of either Hitler or Stalin; and it is true that morality as such is in jeopardy whenever the faith in God who gave the Ten Commandments is no longer secure. But this is at most a condition *sine qua non,* nothing which could positively explain whatever happened afterward. Those who conclude from the frightening events of our times that we have got to go back to religion and faith for political reasons seem to me to show just as much lack of faith in God as their opponents.

Voegelin deplores, as I do, the "insufficiency of theoretical instruments" in the political sciences (and with what to me appeared as inconsistency accuses me a few pages later of not having availed myself more readily of them). Apart from the present trends of psychologism and sociologism about which I think Voegelin and I are in agreement, my chief quarrel with the present state of the historical and political sciences is their growing incapacity for making distinctions. Terms like nationalism, imperialism, totalitarianism, etc. are used indiscriminately for all kinds of political phenomena (usually just as "high-brow" words for aggression) and none of them is any longer understood with its particular historical background. The result is a generalization in which the words themselves lose all meaning. Imperialism does not mean a thing if it is used indiscriminately for Assyrian and Roman and British and Bolshevik history; nationalism is discussed in times and countries which never experienced the nation state; totalitarianism is discovered in all kinds of tyrannies or forms of collective communities, etc. This kind of confusion—where everything distinct disappears and everything that is new and shocking is (not explained but) explained away either through drawing some analogies or reducing it to a previously known chain of causes and influences—seems to me to be the hallmark of the modern historical and political sciences.

In conclusion, I may be permitted to clarify my statement that in our modern predicament "human nature as such is at stake," a statement which provoked Voegelin's sharpest criticism because he sees in the very idea of "changing the nature of man or of anything" and in the very fact that I took this claim of totalitarianism at all seriously a "symptom of the intellectual breakdown of Western civilization." The problem of the relationship between essence and existence in Occidental thought seems to me to be a bit more complicated and controversial than Voegelin's statement on "nature," (identifying "a thing as a thing" and therefore incapable of change by definition) implies, but this I can hardly discuss here. It may be enough to say that, terminological differences apart, I hardly proposed more change of nature than Voegelin himself in his book on *The New Science of Politics*. Discussing the Platonic-Aristotelian theory of soul, he states: "one might almost say that before the discovery of psyche man had no soul."[2] In Voegelin's terms, I could have said that after the discoveries of totalitarian domination and its experiments we have reason to fear that man may lose his soul.

In other words, the success of totalitarianism is identical with a much more radical liquidation of freedom as a political and as a human reality than anything we have ever witnessed before. Under these conditions, it will be hardly consoling to cling to an unchangeable nature of man and conclude that either man himself is being destroyed or that freedom does not belong to man's essential capabilities. Historically we know of man's nature only insofar as it has existence, and no realm of eternal essences will ever console us if man loses his essential capabilities.

My fear, when I wrote the concluding chapter of my book, was not unlike the fear which Montesquieu already expressed when he saw that Western civilization was no longer guaranteed by laws although its peoples were still ruled by customs which he did not deem sufficient to resist an onslaught of despotism. He says in the Preface to *L'Esprit des Lois,* "L'homme, cet être des autres, est également capable de connaître sa propre nature flexible, se pliant dans la societe aux pensées et aux impressions lorsqu'on la lui montre, et d'en perdre jusqu'au sentiment lorsqu'on la lui derobe." (Man, this flexible being, who submits himself in society to the thoughts and impressions of his fellowmen, is equally capable of knowing his own nature when it is shown to him as it is and of losing it to the point where he has no realization that he is robbed of it.)

NOTES

Reprinted from *The Review of Politics* 15, no. 1 (January 1953): 76–84.

    1. [Arendt may mean: "did not exist before it had come into being." Ed.]
    2. Eric Voegelin, *The New Science of Politics* (Chicago: University of Chicago Press, 1952), 67.

Concluding Remark

ERIC VOEGELIN

It does not happen often these days that a work in political science has sufficient theoretical texture to warrant an examination of principles. Since Dr. Arendt's book was distinguished by a high degree of theoretical consciousness, I felt obliged to acknowledge this quality and to pay it a sincere compliment by criticizing some of the formulations. The criticisms had the further pleasant consequence of stimulating the preceding, more elaborate explanation of the author's views concerning method. But this should be enough as an aid to the reader of the book. My word in conclusion, requested by the Editors of the *Review,* will therefore be of the briefest—a ceremony rather than an argument.

I shall do no more than draw attention to what we agree is the question at stake, though Arendt's answer differs from mine. It is the question of essence in history, the question of how to delimit and define phenomena of the class of political movements. Arendt draws her lines of demarcation on what she considers the factual level of history; arrives at well-distinguished complexes of phenomena of the type of "totalitarianism"; and is willing to accept such complexes as ultimate, essential units. I take exception to this method because it disregards the fact that the self-formation of movements in history, institutionally and ideologically, is not theoretical formation. The investigation inevitably will start from the phenomena, but the question of theoretically justifiable units in political science cannot be solved by accepting the units thrown up in the stream of history at their face-value. What a unit is will emerge when the principles furnished by philosophical anthropology are applied to historical materials. It then may happen that political movements, which on the scene of history are bitterly opposed to one another, will prove to be closely related on the level of essence.

NOTE

Reprinted from *The Review of Politics* 15, no. 1 (January 1953): 86–87.

CHAPTER 14

Social Justice and Mass Culture

RUSSELL KIRK

Russell Kirk (1918–1994) was born in Plymouth, Michigan, and received his doctorate from St. Andrew's University in Scotland. He taught at Michigan State University, where he specialized in the Anglo-American conservative intellectual tradition. Kirk left university life in 1959 with the goal of becoming an independent scholar. He was soon recognized as one of America's leading conservative writers. As an ardent Roman Catholic, Kirk understood conservatism to be primarily a moral cause, and believed that prioritizing economics over morality and religion would result in the loss of that which is valuable in the tradition of Western civilization. In his seminal work, The Conservative Mind, *Kirk argued for the necessity of understanding political problems in moral and religious terms. He emphasized the importance of recognizing the complexity of the human experience and thus, he opposed all forms of reductionism, such as Marxism and utilitarianism. Kirk also favored the application of traditional methods to the study of humanity over the application of abstract social theories.*

A friend of mine has the misfortune of owning a number of stone cottages. I say "misfortune" because the cottages are in Scotland, and their rents are fixed at the level of 1914. The cottages were built long before 1914—some of them are eighteenth-century work, with their pan-tiled roofs and trick rubble walls and irregular little windows; but they are good to look upon still, with their white door-sills and their little gardens along the path to the road. The law compels my friend to keep them in tolerable repair, if they are tenanted, and to pay most of what rent he receives either to local authorities or to the Exchequer, in the form of rates and income taxes. But the rent of each cottage amounts to a mere five shillings a week—seventy cents, at the present rate of exchange. This is not particularly depressing to my friend, for the rents of his farms are fixed at levels no higher than they were during the Napoleonic wars, let alone the First World War. The cottages are a cause of expense to him, of course, rather than a source of income; but persons of his station are now resigned to being ruined, and for some of his cottages he asks no rent at all, letting them to old people who can afford to pay next to nothing. Some of his tenants, however, are better off, according to their lights, than my friend himself. They have risen in the economic scale while he has descended. His income is still much greater than theirs, but his expenses are much greater, and his responsibilities. These tenants now have better wages and shorter hours than they ever did before; they can afford their little luxuries, extending sometimes to television sets. Some of them have come to look upon rent as a luxury—for, after all, many of their neighbors are the recipients of my friend's charity, paying nothing for their cottages. Accordingly, my friend's agent occasionally has his difficulties when he goes from door to door, on Mondays, collecting five shillings here and five shillings there. One morning the agent knocked at the door of a tenant who was in good health and employed at good wages. The tenant came to the door and announced that he had decided to pay no more rent; he could not afford it; prices were high, and he could use that five shillings himself.

"Will you be honest with me?" the agent asked.

The tenant said he would.

"Well, then," said the agent, "how much do you spend a month on cigarettes?"

"Thirty shillin's," replied the tenant, in righteous defiance, "and not a penny more."

When a man feels that he is entitled to withhold his rent, though he spends on tobacco fifty percent more per month than he does for his cottage, his notion of justice seems to be confused. This is not so serious a confusion, however, as the revolution of belief in nearly the whole of eastern Europe, where the possessor of property has come to be looked upon as an enemy of society, and is lucky if he escapes being driven out into the woods to die of pneumonia, or herded off to a labor camp. My friend is in no immediate danger of such a fate, though, as things are going, the old farms that have been in his family for two hundred years will have to be sold at auction when he dies, and perhaps the roof will be taken off the big handsome house that his fathers knew before him. In Scotland, fortunately for my friend, the destruction of old institutions is gradual, not violent. But at bottom the same force which has effaced traditional life in eastern

Europe is ruining my Scottish friend: a confusion about first principles. Among these principles which have sustained our civilization and our very existence ever since man rose above the brutes, the principle of justice has been the great support of an orderly and law-abiding society.

From the time when men first began to reflect upon such matters, the nobler and more serious minds have been convinced that justice has some source and sanction more than human and more than natural. Either justice is ordained by some Power above us, or it is mere expediency, the power of the strong over the weak,

> the simple plan,
> That they shall take, who have the power,
> And they shall keep who can.[1]

A great part of mankind, nowadays, has succumbed to this latter concept of justice; and the consequence of that belief is plain to be seen in the violence and ruin that have overtaken most nations in this century.

Now our traditional idea of justice comes to us from two sources: the Judaic and Christian faith in a just God whom we fear and love, and whose commandments are expressed in unmistakable language; and the teachings of classical philosophy, in particular the principles expressed in Plato's *Republic* and incorporated into Roman jurisprudence by Cicero and his successors. The concept of justice upon earth which both these traditions inculcate is, in substance, this: the idea of justice is implanted in our minds by a Power that is more than human; and our mundane justice is our attempt to copy a perfect justice that abides in a realm beyond time and space; and the general rule by which we endeavor to determine just conduct and just reward may be expressed as "To each man, the things that are his own."

Plato perceived that there are two aspects of this justice: justice in private character, and justice in society. Personal or private justice is attained by that balance and harmony in character which shines out from those persons we call "just men," men who cannot be swayed from the path of rectitude by private interest, and who are masters of their own passions, and who deal impartially and honestly with everyone they meet. The other aspect of justice, *social* justice, is similarly marked by harmony and balance; it is the communal equivalent of that right proportion and government of reason, will, and appetite which the just man displays in his private character. Socrates says to Glaucon, "And is not the creation of justice the institution of a natural order and government of one faculty by another in the parts of the soul? And is not the creation of injustice the production of a state of things at variance with the natural order?" The happy man, Socrates maintains, is the just man; and the happy society is the just society. It is the society in which every man minds his own business, and receives always the rewards which are his due. The division of labor is a part of this social justice; for true justice requires that "the carpenter and the shoemaker and the rest of the citizens to do each his own business, and not another's." Injustice in society comes when men try to undertake roles for which they are not fitted, and claim rewards to which they are not entitled, and deny other men what really belongs to them. Quite as an unjust man is a being whose reason, will, and appetite are at war with one another, so an unjust society is a state characterized by "meddlesomeness, and interference, and the rising up of a part of the soul against the whole, an assertion of unlawful authority, which is made by a rebellious subject against a true prince, of whom he is the natural vassal—what is all this confusion and delusion but injustice, and intemperance and cowardice and ignorance, and every form of vice?"

It is perfectly true, then, both in the eyes of the religious man and the eyes of the philosopher, that there is a real meaning to the term "social justice." The Christian concepts of charity and obedience are bound up with the Christian idea of a just society; while for the Platonic and Ciceronian philosopher, no government is righteous unless it conforms to the same standards of conduct as those which the just man respects. We all have real obligations toward our fellow men, for it was ordained by Omniscience that men should live together in charity and brotherhood. A just society, guided by the lights, will endeavor to provide that every man be free to do the work for which he is best suited, and that he receive the rewards which that work deserves, and that no one meddle with him. Thus cooperation, not strife, will be the governing influence in the state; class will not turn against class, but all men will realize, instead, that a variety of occupations, duties, and rewards is necessary to civilization and the rule of law.

As classical philosophy merged with Christian faith to form modern civilization, scholars came to distinguish between two types or applications of justice— not divine and human justice, not private and social justice, precisely, but what we call "commutative" justice and "distributive" justice. "Commutative" justice, in the words of old Jeremy Taylor, three centuries ago, is "that justice which supposes exchange of things profitable for things profitable." It is that righteous relationship by which one man gives his goods or services to another man and re-

ceives an equivalent benefit, to the betterment of both. Now "distributive" justice, again in Jeremy Taylor's words, "is commanded in this rule, 'Render to all
their dues.'" Distributive justice, in short, is that arrangement in society by which
each man obtains what his nature and his labor entitle him to, without oppression or evasion. Commutative justice is righteous dealing between particular individuals; distributive justice is the general system of rewarding each man according to his deserts. Both concepts of justice have been badly misunderstood
in our time, but distributive justice has fared the worse.

Edmund Burke, a hundred and sixty-five years ago, perceived that radical reformers suffered from a disastrous misconception of the idea of justice. The followers of Rousseau, asserting that society is simply a compact for mutual benefit
among the men and women who make up a nation, declared that therefore no
man has any greater rights than his fellows, and that property is the source of all
evil. Burke turned all the power of his rhetoric against this delusion. Men do indeed have natural rights, he answered; but those rights are not what Rousseau's
disciples think they are. The foremost of our *true* natural rights is the right to
justice and order, which the radical fancies of the French revolutionaries would
abolish:

> Men have a right to the fruits of their industry, and to the means of making
> their industry fruitful. They have a right to the acquisitions of their parents;
> to the nourishment and improvement of their offspring; to instruction in
> life, and to consolation in death. Whatever each man can separately do, with-
> out trespassing upon others, he has a right to do for himself; and he has a
> right to all which society, with all its combinations of skill and force, can do
> in his favour. In this partnership all men have equal rights; but not to equal
> things. He that has but five shillings in the partnership, has as good a right to
> it, as he that has five hundred pounds has to his larger proportion. But he has
> not a right to an equal dividend in the product of the joint stock; and as to
> the share of power, authority, and direction which each individual ought to
> have in the management of the state, that I deny to be amongst the direct
> original rights of man in civil society; for I have in my contemplation the civil
> social man, and no other. It is a thing to be settled by convention.[2]

This is the Christian and classical idea of distributive justice. Men have a right
to the product of their labors, and to the benefits of good government and of the
progress of civilization. But they have no right to the property and the labor of

others. The sincere Christian will do everything in his power to relieve the distresses of men and women who suffer privation or injury; but the virtue of charity is a world away from the abstract *right* of equality which the French radicals claimed. The merit of charity is that it is voluntary, a gift from the man who has to the man who has not; while the radicals' claim of a *right* to appropriate the goods of their more prosperous neighbors is a vice—the vice of covetousness. True justice secures every man in the possession of what is his own, and provides that he will receive the reward of his talents. But true justice also ensures that no man shall seize the property and the rights that belong to other classes and persons, on the pretext of an abstract equality. The just man knows that men differ in strength, in intelligence, in energy, in beauty, in dexterity, in discipline, in inheritance, in particular talents; and he sets his face, therefore, against any scheme of pretended "social justice" which would treat all men alike. There could be no greater injustice to society than to give the good, the industrious, and the frugal the same rewards as the vicious, the indolent, and the spendthrift. Besides, different types of character deserve different types of reward. The best reward of the scholar is contemplative leisure; the best reward of the soldier is public honor; the best reward of the quiet man is the secure routine of domestic existence; the best reward of the statesman is just influence; the best reward of the skilled craftsman is the opportunity to make fine things; the best reward of the farmer is a decent rural competence; the best reward of the industrialist is the sight of what his own industry has built; the best reward of the good wife is the goodness of her children. To reduce all these varieties of talent and aspiration, with many more, to the dull nexus of cash payment, is the act of a dull and envious mind; and then to make that cash payment the same for every individual is an act calculated to make society one everlasting frustration for the best men and women.

How was it that this traditional concept of social justice, which took into account the diversity of human needs and wishes, came to be supplanted, in the minds of many people, by the delusion that social justice consists in treating every man as if he were an identical cog in a social machine, with precisely the same qualities and hopes as his neighbor? One can trace the fallacy that justice is identical with equality of condition far back into antiquity, for human folly is as old as human wisdom. But the modern form of this notion arose late in the eighteenth century, and Burke and John Adams and other conservative thinkers foresaw that it was destined to do immense mischief in our world. Condorcet, for example, eminent among the philosophers who ushered in the French Revolution, proclaimed that "Not only equality of right, but equality of fact, is the goal of the socialist art"; he declared that the whole aim of all social institutions should be to benefit physically, intellectually, and morally the poorest classes. Now the Christian concept of charity enjoins constant endeavor to improve the lot of the poor; but the Christian faith, which Burke and Adams held in their different ways, does not command the sacrifice of the welfare of one class to that of another class; instead, Christian teaching looks upon the rich and powerful as the elder brothers of the poor and weak, given their privileges that they may help to improve the character and the condition of all humanity. Instead of abolishing class and private rights in the name of an abstract equality, Christian thinkers hope to employ commutative and distributive justice for the realization of the peculiar talents and hopes of each individual, not the confounding of all personality in one collective monotony.

Karl Marx, casting off the whole moral legacy of Christian and classical thought, carried the notion of "social justice" as pure equality further yet. Adapting Ricardo's labor theory of value to his own purposes, Marx insisted that since all value comes from "labor," all value must return to labor; and therefore all men must receive the same rewards, and live the same life. Justice, according to this view, is uniformity of existence. "In order to create equality," Marx wrote, "we must first create inequality." By this he meant that because men are *not* equal in strength, energy, intelligence, or any other natural endowment, we must take away from the superior and give to the inferior; we must depress the better to help the worse; and thus we will deliberately treat the strong, the energetic, and the intelligent unfairly, that we may make their natural inferiors their equals in condition. Now this doctrine is the callous repudiation of the classical and Christian idea of justice. "To each his own." Such was the definition of justice in which Plato and Cicero and the fathers of the Church and the Schoolmen agreed. Each man should have the right to the fruit of his own labors, and the right to freedom from being meddled with; and each man should do that work for which his nature and his inheritance best qualified him. But Marx was resolved to turn the world inside out, and a necessary preparation for this was the inversion of the idea of justice. Marx refused to recognize that there are various kinds and degrees of labor, each deserving its peculiar reward; and he ignored the fact that there is such a thing as the postponed reward of labor, in the form of bequest and inheritance. It is not simply the manual laborer who works: the statesman works, and so does the soldier, and so does the scholar, and so does the priest, and so does the banker, and so does the landed proprietor, and so does the inventor, and so does the manufacturer, and so does the clerk. The highest and most productive forms of labor, most beneficial to humanity both in spirit and in matter, commonly are those kinds of work least menial. Only in this sense is it true that all value comes from labor.

In the history of political and economic fanaticism, there are few fallacies more nearly transparent than the central principles of Marxism. But the publication of Marx's *Capital* coincided with the decay of established opinions in the modern world, and with all the confusion which the culmination of the Industrial Revolution and the expansion of European influence had brought in their train. Thus men who had repudiated both the old liberal educational disciplines and the bulk of Christian teaching embraced Marx's theories without reflection; for men long to believe in *something,* and the declaration that everyone is entitled by the laws of social justice to the possessions of his more prosperous neighbor was calculated to excite all the power of envy. The doctrinaire socialists and communists began to preach this new theory of justice—the dogma that everything belongs of right to everyone. That idea has been one of the chief causes of our modern upheaval and despair, throughout most of the world. In its milder aspect, it has led to the difficulties of my Scottish friend in collecting his rents; in its fiercer aspect, to the dehumanization of whole peoples and the wreck of ancient civilizations.

True distributive justice, which prescribes the rights and duties that connect the state, or community, and the citizen or private person, does not mean "distribution" in the sense of employing the power of the state to redistribute property among men. Pope Pius XI, in 1931, made it clear that this was not the Christian significance of the phrase. "Of its very nature the true aim of all social activity," the Pope wrote, "should be to help individual members of the social body, but never to destroy or absorb them. The aim of social legislation must therefore be the reestablishment of vocational groups." This encyclical, in general, urges the restoration of *order,* through the encouragement or resurrection of all those voluntary associations which once interposed a barrier between the Leviathan state and the puny individual. The state ought to be an arbiter, intent upon justice, and not the servant of a particular class or interest. The late William A. Orton, in his last book, *The Economic Role of the State,* discussing commutative and distributive justice in the light of Papal encyclicals, reminds us of how sorely the concept of distributive justice has been corrupted:

> Distributive justice does not primarily refer, as does the economic theory of distribution, to the sharing-out of a given supply of goods and services, because the state has no such supply. Yet that is the conception which tends

to develop in the late stages of all highly centralized societies, including our own: the notion that the masses can and ought to receive from the state goods and services beyond what they could otherwise earn for themselves. The popularity of this notion has obvious causes, ranging from genuine al- truism through political expediency to undisguised class interest. It is note- worthy that, as organized labor becomes a major political force, it is no longer content—as Gompers might have been—to rely on the economic power of the trade-unions but goes on, while resisting all limits on that, to make de- mands for state action in the interests of wage-earners as a class. And the point is not whether those demands are justifiable as desiderata; quite possibly they are, since, like the king in wonder-working days of old, we would all like every- body to have everything. The point is that this whole notion of the providen- tial state invokes and rests upon the coercive power, regarded solely from the standpoint of the beneficiaries. Furthermore, there are practical limits to this sort of procedure; and it is less painful to recognize them in advance than to run into them head on.[3]

And Orton proceeds to examine the necessity of reasserting moral principles in the complex economic negotiations of our time. It is impossible to determine a "fair wage," or the proper relationship between employer and union, or the aims of social security, or the boundary between a just claim and extortion, or the proper regulation of prices, or the degree of freedom of competition, without ref- erence to certain definitions that depend upon moral sanctions. Of those defini- tions, "justice" is the cardinal term. The Benthamite delusion that politics and economics could be managed on considerations purely material has exposed us to a desolate individualism in which every man and every class looks upon all other men and classes as dangerous competitors, when in reality no man and no class can continue long in safety and prosperity without the bond of sympa- thy and the reign of justice. It is necessary to any high civilization that there be a great variety of human types and a variety of classes and functions.

A true understanding of what "social justice" means would do more than any- thing else to guard against that bitter resentment of superiority or differenti- ation which menaces the foundations of culture. We hear a good deal of talk, some of it sensible, some of it silly, about the "anti-intellectualism" of our time. But it is undeniably true that there exists among us a vague but ominous detesta- tion of the life of the mind—apparently on the assumption that what one man has, all men must have; and if they are denied it, then they will deny it to the

privileged man. The late C. E. M. Joad, a writer scarcely given to reactionary
or anti-democratic opinions, noted with alarm this resentment of the masses
against anything that they cannot share; and they now have it in their power, he
suggested, to topple anything of which they disapprove. It is not even necessary
for the masses to employ direct political action; the contagion of manners works
for them: formerly a class of thinkers and artists could flourish in the midst of
general ignorance, but now the mass-mind, juke-box culture, penetrates to every
corner of the Western world, and the man of superior natural endowments is
ashamed of being different; he feels, perhaps, that it is "unjust" to indulge tastes
which the majority cannot appreciate. Tocqueville, more than a century ago,
remarked that this silent tyranny of the masses, enforced only by the glower-
ing disapproval of public opinion, tended even then to suppress high attainment
of mind in democracies. Joad summarizes the problem thus:

> In all previous ages the masses were indeed uneducated and the influence of
> their tastes and desires was, therefore, negligible. There was no question of
> *their* concepts of the pleasant, the good, the beautiful and the true being im-
> posed upon any but themselves. In our own day for the first time in history
> most human beings in Europe and the U.S.A. can read; they also have some
> money to spend and leisure in which to spend it. As a result there has sprung
> up for the first time in human history a vast industry devoted to stimulating
> and satisfying the untrained tastes of the masses. The mass products of this
> industry are novels of the two-penny library class, the cinema and "light
> music" in all its forms, the first substituting for literature, the second for
> painting and poetry, the third for music. When people urge that public taste
> is lower today than it was in the eighteenth century, what they mean is not so
> much that the taste of the class which in our age is analogous to the class of
> the eighteenth-century scholars, critics and creative authors of Dr. Johnson's
> circle is lower; what they mean is that in our own time this class is set in the
> midst of an environment of bad literature, bad art and bad music which did
> not in the eighteenth century exist and which through the influence of the
> environment it sets up lowers the standard of the whole. . . . Pitch, we say,
> defiles what it touches; but it defiles in the aesthetic no less than in the moral
> sphere, and it may well be that it is impossible for men to live continually
> in an environment of cinema and radio and "light music," cheap magazines
> and sensational Sunday papers without being to some extent affected by that
> environment.[4]

One could elaborate upon Joad's suggestion almost interminably. The gradual reduction of public libraries, intended for the elevation of the popular mind, to mere instruments for idle amusement at public expense; the cacophony of noise which fills almost all public places, converting even the unwilling into a part of the captive audience, so that only by spending a good deal of money and traveling some distance can one eat and drink without being oppressed by blatant vulgarity; the conversion of nominal institutions of learning to the popular ends of sociability and utilitarian training—all these things, and many others, are so many indications of the advance of the masses into the realm of culture. The nineteenth-century optimists believed that the masses would indeed make culture their own, by assimilating themselves to it; it scarcely occurred to the enthusiasts for popular schooling that the masses might assimilate culture to themselves. The magazine-rack of any drugstore in America would suffice to drive Robert Lowe or Horace Mann to distraction. Now we cannot undo the consequences of mass-schooling, even if we would; but what we can contend against is the spirit of vulgar intolerance which proclaims that if the masses cannot share in a taste, that taste shall not be suffered to exist. And this is closely bound up with the idea of social justice. If justice means uniformity, then the higher life of the mind which is confined to a few has no right to survival; but if justice means that each man has a right to his own, we ought to try to convince modern society that there is no injustice or deprivation in the fact that one man is skilled with his hands, and another with his head, or that one man enjoys baseball and another chamber music. We must go beyond the differences of taste, indeed, and remind modern society that differences of function are as necessary and beneficial as differences of opinion. That some men are richer than others, and that some have more leisure than others, and that some travel more than others, and that some inherit more than others, and that some are educated more than others, is no more unjust, in the great scheme of things, than that some undeniably are handsomer or stronger or quicker or healthier than others. This complex variety is the breath of life to society, not the triumph of injustice. Poverty, even absolute poverty, is not an evil; it is not evil to be a beggar; it is not evil to be ignorant; it is not evil to be stupid. All these things are either indifferent, or else are positive virtues, if accepted with a contrite heart. What really matters is that we should accept the station to which "a divine tactic" has appointed us with humility and a sense of consecration. Without inequality, there is no opportunity for charity, or for gratitude; without differences of mind and talent, the world would be one changeless expanse of uniformity.

I am inclined to believe, then, that the need of our time is not for greater progress toward equality of condition and distribution of wealth, but rather for the clear understanding of what commutative and distributive justice truly mean: "to each his own." It is very easy to run with the pack and howl for the attainment of absolute equality. But that equality would be the death of human liveliness, and probably the death of our economy. I know, of course, that we have all about us examples of wealth misspent and opportunities abused. In our fallen state, we cannot hope that all the members of any class will behave with perfect rectitude. But it would be no wiser to abolish classes, for that reason, than to abolish humanity. We do indeed have the duty of exhorting those who have been placed by a divine tactic in positions of responsibility to do their part with charity and humility; and, before that, we have the more pressing duty of so exhorting ourselves. There are signs, in most of the countries of the Western world, that what remains of the old leading classes are learning to conduct themselves with courage and fortitude. If they are effaced utterly, we shall not be emancipated totally from leadership, but shall find ourselves, instead, at the mercy of the commissar. The delusion that justice consists in absolute equality ends in an absolute equality beneath the weight of a man or a party to whom justice is no more than a word.

At the back of the mind of the man who declined to pay his rent, I think, was the notion that under a just domination, all things would be supplied to him out of a common fund, without the necessity of any endeavor on his part. It is easy enough to describe the genesis of such concepts; it is much more difficult to remedy them. The real victim of injustice, in this particular case, was my friend the landed proprietor—though he never thought of complaining. No one subsidizes him; his garden lies choked with weeds; he has sold his Raeburns and Constables and his ancestors' furniture to keep up his farms and pay for his children's education; he continues to serve in local office at his own expense; he labors far longer hours than his own tenants; he can indulge, nowadays, very few of his tastes for books and music, though the cottagers can gratify theirs, in comparable matters, beyond anything they dreamed of in former days. My friend endures these things—and the prospect that when he is gone, everything that his family loved will pass away with him—because of the ascendancy of the idea that justice consists in leveling, that inherited wealth and superior station are reprehensible, and that society and culture can subsist and flourish without being rooted in the past. He himself, to some extent, is influenced by this body of opinion.

Thus the unbought grace of life may be extinguished by the power of positive law within a single generation.

Probably the traditional leading classes of Europe were at their worst in the Russia of the czars. But what humane and rational man can maintain that the leading classes of Soviet Russia constitute an improvement upon their predecessors? Man was created not for equality, but for the struggle upward from brute nature toward the world that is more than terrestrial. The principle of justice, in consequence, is not enslavement to a uniform condition, but liberation from arbitrary restraints upon a man's right to fulfill his moral nature.

NOTES

Reprinted from *The Review of Politics* 16, no. 4 (October 1954): 438–51.

1. [William Wordsworth, "Rob Roy's Grave." Ed.]

2. [Kirk is likely quoting from Burke's masterpiece, *Reflections on the Revolution in France*, first published in 1790. Ed.]

3. William A. Orton, *The Economic Role of the State* (Chicago: University of Chicago Press, 1950), n.p.

4. [C. E. M. Joad was a popular English philosopher. Because he wrote over seventy five books, it is difficult to identify the source of this quotation. Ed.]

CHAPTER 15

On War and Peace

ROBERT STRAUSZ-HUPÉ

Robert Strausz-Hupé (1903–2002) was born in Vienna, where he received a classical education that included French and English. He left Austria for the United States in search of employment, first working in the bond business but then returning to Europe where, in Paris, he caught the attention of the American foreign policy community with his analyses of the rise of Nazi Germany. This success earned him an invitation to the University of Pennsylvania where he received a PhD and subsequently a teaching position. An originator of the interdisciplinary approach to the study of world politics, Strausz-Hupé became well known as a Cold War strategist. He was an avowed critic of all forms of Marxist thought and an ardent campaigner for a firm stance against the Soviet Union. He also believed that Europe's adoption of American-style democratic federalism was the only way to create a bulwark against communism. Strausz-Hupé's conviction that the American people needed to become better educated about the leading role of the United States in the world led him to found the Foreign Policy Research Institute. His career took a new turn during the Kennedy years and the Vietnam War when US President Richard Nixon appointed him to the diplomatic corps. He served as ambassador to numerous countries and to NATO.

Millions of men stand under arms to defend democracy Their weapons are fashioned by scientific technology which, now as always before, has placed its highest ingenuity at the service of its most important client: the military establishment. The state, the schools and the mass media do not shirk the task of indoctrination: they have employed every available technical device in order to spread awareness of the dangers which threaten democracy as well as national survival. Yet the flame of the martial spirit flickers but feebly in the heart of Western man, more feebly indeed than in any epoch of the West's dangerous history. Citizens respond dutifully to the call to arms. They cannot do otherwise in the face of the comprehensive controls and sanctions available to the state. Individual men among them are still capable of high feats of heroism at war, as high as those performed by warriors in ages past. Yet no one can deny that the democracies are loath to fight and that abiding popular aversion to war has forced democratic statesmen into a long series of diplomatic retreats. Science that has done so much to defend the democracies against aggression has also taught them that there is no defense against aggression and that its latest tools might prove as deleterious to the victor as to the defeated. More important still, science has taught men to value life as their highest possession and to abhor death, to abhor death not so much as the ineluctable fate of all living things but as the break in a process of expanding knowledge and possession of the physical environment.

There is little in the history of our times to show that modern man is more averse to violence than were his forebears. There is some evidence showing that he views and handles violence with an impersonal detachment that would have shocked his ancestors inured to the precariousness and brutality of a pre-scientific civilization. Modern man, like all men before him, eschews violence that begets retribution, seeks to avoid pain and cherishes the good things upon earth. What sets him apart from preceding generations is his belief in his perfectibility upon earth and the dreadful and absurd finality of death.

It is impossible to explore the meaning of life without encountering the enigma of death. Since the meaning of death is sealed to the human mind, man can know about life only by pinning his faith on a hypothesis. He defies the uncertainty of his condition by an act of faith. The fables of the Golden Age and the groves of Arcadia are woven from man's yearning for surcease from the struggle with his divided self. Each great religion has owed its sway to the power it gave men to defy and to bear the burden of the unknowable. If men nowadays profess themselves capable only of devotion to scientific method, it is because they have endowed the object of their devotion with the power of salvation. That power is as much derived from an act of faith as is religious certainty. The model of a universe in which all processes conform to a "unified" theory is a close kin of the classic fable, the tale of Arcadia, and of doubt defied, told in the language of modern science.

In all epochs, men have been assailed by doubts about the natural order of things and the institutions of society. Doubt beat as heavily upon medieval man as upon the ages of reason and science. Then, however, doubt was contained by religion and by a philosophy that reconciled nature with religious faith. Popular opinions and dogmas of the doctors did not conflict. Society was whole. Its wholeness was reflected by its optimism, an optimism all the more sturdy because it was not based upon the notion of social progress. The individual's lot was harsh; there had been a marked regression from the material ease of Roman and Hellenic civilization. The scourge of Asian invasions threatened to overwhelm the lands of Christendom torn by feudal strife. Whatever expectations medieval man may have entertained, security of life and property was not among them. Yet his optimism was impervious to the grim historic climate because it rested upon a simple notion, namely, the unequivocal distinction between absolute goodness and absolute evil. Because man, through divine grace, had the power to choose goodness, he was granted the certainty of ultimate reward.

Upon the closing of the Middle Ages, intellectual and moral tensions sought release in a vast effort of domination. As man became estranged from the eternal verities, he sought all the more intently power over things. Nowadays, science mounts the defense of mind and society against the anguish of the spirit and the afflictions of the body. Science has devised methods for solving all conceivable problems—except one. The one that it has not solved is how to supply mind and society with a unifying inner vision. Like the universe of the galaxies, the universe of knowledge appears to be flying apart. The sciences are moving away from each other; specializations are inaccessible to each other. The natural scientist, only yesterday a "natural philosopher," is now a superbly trained, narrow-minded mechanic, ignorant of the arts, of politics and even of the history of his own profession. The professions trained in the older branches of learning, the law and the humanities, are ignorant of the methods of the natural sciences. The disintegration of the body of knowledge which, only a century ago, was potentially the common property of all minds, is but the intellectual aspect of the disintegration of body politic and social. The paradox of a society that clutches the notion of material progress and acclaims pessimistic philosophies, that believes man's lot on earth is susceptible to improvement and behaves as if death were final, signifies the modern impasse from which there is no exit.

Modern morality has cultivated a sentimental standard by which evil has ceased to be an absolute. Evil is not a terrible corruption of the spirit but a state of things that can be improved progressively. Modern morality, incapable as it is of encompassing the complex reality of life and the awful truth of death, must take its stand upon man's capacity for improving himself, or rather, of improving his environment. Modern morality cannot concede that the absolute good *was* before time and *is* beyond time and that man may attain it through divine grace and not through his ingenuity.

Faith in progress was nourished by the scientific and economic achievements of the nineteenth century. It was put to the test by the cataclysms of the twentieth century. If statistics are enough to sustain faith, faith in progress should be stronger now than at any time since it first challenged traditional religion: the world population has absorbed the losses of two world wars and has increased, since 1914, by several hundred million. Even the belligerent nations have grown in numbers. International industrial productivity has risen substantially in the face of tremendous physical destruction.

Everywhere, people now live longer lives and almost everywhere, more comfortable ones. Yet hardly anywhere does faith in progress still induce that happy mood and placid confidence which, despite a few regrettable regressions such as the troubles of the 1840s, fortified nineteenth-century society in western Europe and America against the less pleasant consequences of the scientific and industrial revolution. To be sure, it is still a widely held axiom that rising standards of living will cure almost every political and social ill. But a rising standard of living is conceived nowadays not as a simple progression from want to plentitude, from squalor to health. It is also conceived as a race against time and against hostile, regressive forces threatening the destruction of all that man has wrought not only after he perceived that he was progressing but long before he thought he did. To help country X to raise economic productivity is no longer a means to insure the welfare of X's population, but to save it from Communism and to shore up the defense of democratic institutions the world over, that of the donating nations included. Growth of population and increasing expectancy of life are fraught, especially in backward nations, with ominous political and ideological implications. Life—long life and healthy life—has become a menace. Yet all the while industrial and scientific development improves the chances of survival and stimulates new wants. More people are taught to live longer and better furnished lives. They also are taught to produce more things and thus to stimulate production. This is the industrial and scientific spirit.

In the Middle Ages, morality assigned the highest place to the ascetic and the warrior, the former because he chose the life of the spirit and the latter because he chose the risk of death. Neither satisfies the norms of the modern standard which requires men to be both producers and consumers. Modern morality assigns the highest place to the scientist-technologist and the "common man," the former because he is the *deus ex machina* of the production of things, the latter because his unlimited capacity for wants is the *raison d'être* of production. Modern morality, therefore, assigns the lowest place in its hierarchy of values to the ascetic and the warrior, the former because he wants nothing and the latter because he produces nothing. The ascetic holds life and things cheap because they deny the spirit. The warrior holds life and things cheaper than the issue of the battle.

The Middle Ages are said to have been dark and bloody. Yet they were the age when optimistic philosophies arose. They were one of the greatest epochs of lyrical effervescence. They were also the epoch of short lives intensively lived. The ascetic and the warrior joined in brotherly communion: they came to terms with the transitoriness of life and thus won freedom. Anguish and sorrow have been man's companions in all ages. Medieval man knew both. But medieval society accepted unflinchingly the dangers of sorrow and anguish whereas modern society seeks to avoid them. Because medieval society accepted these dangers, it knew joy. Where in modern creative writing do we meet that joyous rapture which burst into the song of the mystic and the knight, of Francis of Assisi and Walter von der Vogelweide? Modern literature strikes many chords: nostalgia, anxiety, despair, frustration, brutality and absurdity. The modern poet sings of all of these; he does not sing of joy. Never before has civilization made man's lot so safe and so grim.

In modern society, the watchwords of proper conduct are cooperation and adjustment, not honor and valor. Modern morality enjoins the individual from courting risk and the challenge of life-consuming passions. These norms of individual conduct determine national attitudes toward peace and war.

Pacifism, the manifestation of modern morality in international politics, enjoins nations from the use of force, opposes all war and calls for the settlement of all issues between nations by cooperation and adjustment. Although pacifism can invoke the sanction of the scriptures, it is not its religious ethos that accounts for its popular attractiveness. The political doctrine of pacifism accords perfectly with modern morality with its emphatically this-worldly conception of relative good and relative evil, of salvation through material progress and of life as the highest good.

Pacifism has become a secular political movement. Its religious element is residual. It draws its force from the powerful materialist tendencies that dominate modern civilization. If pacifism were purely inspired by religious conviction, its following would be confined to a few small religious sects and a few solitary thinkers. Then the peace propaganda of the Soviets and of sympathetic pressure groups operating outside the Soviet orbit would not elicit that mass response which has forced the hands of Western policy makers. If mass attitudes toward sports, crime and vehicular traffic express modern man's regard for the lives of his fellow men then his moral stature has not grown perceptibly since the Middle Ages. As ages go, ours is remarkably tolerant about killing. Thus popular aversion to war does not spring from deep religious convictions but from abiding attachment to life and its material furnishings. It would be merely to compound the materialist fallacy were one to deny that many adherents of pacifism are motivated by religious scruples. Some of pacifism's most persuasive spokesmen undoubtedly have been sustained by selfless devotion to humanity and have been willing to pay with their lives for their cause. Yet they have reached the point where they meet with the bulk of their followers from the opposite direction. The moral ambiguity of pacifism is at the root of much confusion. It makes the critical approach to the political problems which pacifism creates, so difficult and so delicate an undertaking. Pacifism accommodates both the pure faith of the Catacombs and the gross denial of the spirit.

The Middle Ages knew the dilemma of faith and power, the cross and the sword. Medieval history abounds in moving records of proud men wrestling with their consciences, of violence and penance, of the monk's garb beneath the shirt of mail. There is hardly a solution applied by this generation to the problems of prevention of war which had not been worked out by medieval thinkers. Arbitration and mediation of conflict and the enforcement of the peace, these and other concepts were exhaustively argued and vigorously advocated seven centuries before the Covenant of the League of Nations was signed. The medieval quest for peace was triggered by the desire to bend the will of princes to the will of God. The bloody contests among Christians for domination over each other was to be halted by the Truce of God. But that truce was conceived as an act of Christian self-restraint and thus as man's victory over his own nature, and not as a surrender to fear and to love of self. No true Christian could mistake the Truce of God for the truce with evil. The conscience of the Middle Ages did not object to militant service in the cause of God. Medieval man may have taken all too parochial a view of God's writ upon earth, of believer and infidel. But his distinction between inflicting death and suffering death and the rightness of either act was clear and free of moral hypocrisy. He did not hold, among other things, that he should not suffer what he could inflict upon others. If he can be said to have been a pacifist, he was not a unilateral one.

Pacifism as a secular political movement must be subjected not only to moral scrutiny but also to the test of rationality. The fact that the political philosophy which informs one of the two principal world powers does not include pacifism, should be sufficient reason to render pacifism an academic subject and to reject it as a practical formula of foreign policy. The Communists have been emphatic in their condemnation of pacifism as a typical excrescence of decadent capitalism. Their peace propaganda distinguishes explicitly between peace-loving peoples and war-mongering capitalists. The latter are thus excluded from the dispensation of the Communists' love of peace. Their annihilation by any means—war or revolution—is still the principal aim of all good Communists inside and outside the Soviet Union. No one has yet been able to show that class warfare and peace are synonyms. Moreover, the temper of the Russian people, proud of their army and delighted by its braided splendors, is far from anti-militarist. More important still, the domestic politics and institutions of the Soviet Union offer about the worst schooling imaginable for the theory and practice of arbitration and mediation which is at the core of pacifist ideology. Since the Soviet government does not tolerate or even recognize conflict on vital issues between labor and management, it has never developed a system of arbitration and mediation of labor disputes.

The Soviet Union knows no legitimate system of change in government: succession to office has, for the last thirty years, been assured by cooption or murder, usually by both. The Soviet government is not a legitimate government; there is no separation of powers; there is no protection of minorities. Arbitration and mediation of international conflict implies respect for judicial authority and a becoming sense of self-restraint. The ruling classes of the Soviet Union have shown themselves singularly uninhibited by legal and moral scruples. The Charter of the United Nations is a characteristically Western document: it takes a nice minimum of such scruples for granted. This is perhaps the simplest explanation why the United Nations failed to command the loyalty of the Soviet Union. The realization of pacifist expectations must wait upon a profound change of heart on the part of the Soviet Union—which probably cannot be brought about except by defeat in war.

The destructiveness of nuclear weapons is nowadays adduced as the most massive argument of pacifist logic. It is said that a future war will destroy civilization and that therefore war has become absurd as a social institution. War has always been an absurd institution. Most social institutions are found to be absurd when they are subjected to scientific analysis. War is absurd because violence negates the purpose of the human community. But a war that kills only a few is no better than one that kills many. The evil of war is not proportionate to its statistical consequences.

Let us follow the pacifist argument to its *reductio ad absurdum!* To avoid nuclear war it may become necessary to accept the Soviet writ for the whole world. Would the liquidation by the approved methods of Soviet legality of many millions of assorted capitalists, kulaks and enemies of the working class represent a moral improvement over the possible annihilation of millions of men by atomic blast? It is doubtful that the final statistical returns would show even a gain in biological lives saved. It is certain that a civilization that is prepared to pay such a price for its physical survival is not worth saving.

The propaganda efforts of the democratic nations at war have led to a dangerous inflation of moral values. It was thought necessary to rouse the masses from their inertia by appeals which exaggerated the iniquity of the opponent. The masses were promised opulence with security as a reward for their exertions. The road to peace was littered by broken pledges and bitter disappointments. The confidence in the democratic cause was shaken. Pacifism derived much of its strength from the skepticism of the masses. If the Germans and the Japanese were in fact not as beastly as they were said to have been when they were fighting Americans and Englishmen and were hailed, only a few years after their unconditional surrender, as conditional allies of democracy, is then the monstrousness of the Soviet system not perhaps another clever hoax concocted by publicists, professors and politicians? The violent gyrations of public sentiment between complacency and uneasiness, self-absorbed indifference and angry suspicion not only impede consistent foreign policies, but also invite the demagogue to exploit the tensions flowing from the instability of popular mood. This unhealthy state of affairs cannot be remedied by the application of clever propaganda techniques. For its underlying causes are the moral ambiguity and the creeping cynicism engendered by the contradiction between the professed ideals and the everyday mores of materialist society. Social devices must meet a double test: efficiency and morality. The divorce of efficiency from morality threatens to sever the link between man and society. Men cannot communicate with one another but for the mental images of reality they share. The more efficient have become the means for handling men and things the more blurred have become the images of reality which guide individual and collective action.

The overarching fact of our times is the struggle between freedom and tyranny. To be sure, it is also the struggle between rival world powers and groups of nation states. But if the moral order under which mankind shall live were not the supreme stake, then the contest would be a frivolous diversion of mankind's best energies. Then the contest would be over "national interest" and "national survival," terms that in an epoch of moral crisis, encompassing all peoples and shaking the entire structure of human society, have lost their meaning. No nation can "survive" the strains of ceaseless political warfare, not to speak of the test of total war, that does not identify its cause with that of mankind. Viewed from the great divide of mankind's destiny, even the greatest nation's interests appear petty. The wars of national liberation of the first half of the 19th century kindled a patriotism in which love of country and love of mankind were blended: to be a citizen of a free nation was to be a citizen of the community of all free peoples. The *esprit de corps* of freedom, although it sparked the national risings against foreign oppressors, transcended *Lokalpatriotismus*—as the Germans call particularist nationalism. *Lokalpatriotismus* is not enough for rousing the democratic peoples to fight and vanquish an international conspiracy against freedom. In the Middle Ages, the defense of the faith was the common concern of Christendom: international armies defended the Marches. Pacifism is abetted by the manifest absurdity, if not the dishonesty, of a nationalism that conceives of freedom as if it were an industry in need of protection against foreign competition.

A materialist philosophy can teach men how to live with others: it cannot teach them how to die for others. The self-sacrificing devotion of the convinced Communist is nourished by man's need for purpose beyond his earthly self, not by the conceptual elegance of the "surplus value" and "dialectic." The democratic call to arms will not arouse the masses if it merely bids them to mount the defense of the national standard of living or participate vicariously in the purging of governmental and academic bureaucracies. The alliance of tyranny and scientific technology poses the greatest treat to human dignity and freedom which history has ever known. Throughout centuries of painful struggle, the western mind has wrested that dignity and freedom from unreason and cruelty. They are the sacred trophies of its war upon evil. Defeat would now be final: there will be no sanctuaries, no catacombs. Modern tyranny, armed by science, need not fear the rising of the serfs. Democracy now plays for keeps. It cannot win if free men are not prepared to match with their sacrificial ardor the fanaticism of their foes. If the attack can be met by the reasoned arguments and grave deliberations of diplomacy, free men of the world over will give thanks to God. If that attack must be met in war, free men under God must face the unspeakable disaster of war. The price of spiritual and political freedom has not dropped since the days of Salamis and the Catalaunian plains and of Liegnitz when Christian knights, fighting against hopeless odds, went down before the warriors of Genghis Khan.

Whosoever does not stake his life shall not win it. This holds for individual men, for nations and for civilizations.

NOTE

Reprinted from *The Review of Politics* 16, no. 4 (October 1954): 485–94.

CHAPTER 16

The Catholic Publicist

WALDEMAR GURIAN

Waldemar Gurian (1902–1954) was born in St. Petersburg, Russia. He was educated in Berlin by two of the foremost thinkers of his day, Max Scheler and Carl Schmitt. As a political historian and theorist, he made his major scholarly contributions to the study of politics in the 1930s, writing about such diverse topics as Bolshevism, Catholicism, and French nationalism. He was also an unremitting opponent of National Socialism, which led him to flee first to Switzerland and then the United States where he assumed a professorship at the University of Notre Dame. In his new position, Gurian had his greatest intellectual impact when he founded The Review of Politics. *Because of his ability to address the concerns of multiple academic disciplines as well as his commitment to linking fundamental theoretical issues with concrete problems before humanity, such as war and dictatorship, he was able to persuade scores of prominent political theorists, philosophers, theologians, and historians to write for the journal.*

In the progressive alienation of the modern world from Christianity and the Church, in what is described as intellectual secularization, the publicist plays a decisive role.[1] The mere mention of the name of Voltaire suggests what the significance of anti-Church publicist work may be. In the name of reason it appeals against the superstition of religion, in the name of justice it covers with contempt and ridicule the claims of tradition, it directs its attacks against existing institutions, and it contrasts the light of secular philosophy to the darkness of Church dogma. All that is done in a facile, universally understandable way. The enlightened publicist does not seek to make an impression on the learned. He does not try to astonish by the fullness of his knowledge. He tries to draw the public opinion of good society to his side and to gain it for his cause. With such assurance does he proceed that he seems to achieve his goal. An educated man who has been shaped by eighteenth century France cares to hear nothing more about the Church as a divine institution. Enlightenment and public opinion became the same thing. Public opinion simply coincided with what the Enlightened publicist prescribed for it. Indeed, it was already apparent in the eighteenth century that it is not a simple thing to decide what corresponds to reason, justice, and untutored human nature. In the name of a sentimental inner religion Rousseau fought against the negative Enlightenment of the Encyclopedists, the circle of Voltaire and Diderot. But this struggle changed nothing in the general situation. Public opinion remained decisive. It was self-evidently opposed to tradition generally and, thus, also to the Church. If the reader of Voltaire jeered and ridiculed religion, the reader of Rousseau shed tears over the Savoyard Vicar, who, in metamorphosing Church dogma into a religion of feeling and humanity, thus deprived religion of its substance. Both would hear nothing of that fosterer of superstition and that oppressor of knowledge, that Church against which they had set themselves up as priests of public opinion, as publicists.

The experiences of the Revolution did not make for any loosening of the tie between the activity of the publicist and those efforts to insulate social life against all transcendence or to contrast religion as an inner affair to the non-human juristic institution of the Church. There had developed, however, a counter-revolutionary publicist activity, which exalted tradition. Against Voltaire there appeared de Maistre,[2] and against Rousseau Chateaubriand whose *Génie du Christianisme*[3] argued that the Catholic religion was able to satisfy all the demands of a religion of beauty and of feeling. And in Germany Görres used the slogans of justice and national self-determination to deliver mighty blows against the foreign domination of Napoleon.[4] But in spite of traditionalism and Romanticism the tie between bourgeois Enlightenment and publicist work persisted. Enlightened publicism simply appeared to be the necessary response to the uninterrupted development of the modern state, which rested upon the rights of man or, at the very least, since the bourgeois constitutional state (*Rechtsstaat*) was decisively shaped by them. The publicist work, which opposed this outlook with its negation of the past and tradition, was simply unable to succeed with public opinion, even though in spiritual content it was often greatly superior.

Liberalism is the name which describes this relationship between the rising bourgeois community and Enlightened publicism of all kinds. Its attack on reaction was made in the name of public opinion, which was more or less defined as synonymous with reason, progress and justice.

But gradually there began to appear a phenomenon which is decisive for the development of modern journalism. The latter became dependent upon the various currents of public opinion. It had to establish a connection with them. It became an escort, rather than a leader as in the eighteenth century. A tragic fate! The journalist had turned against the powers of tradition in order to be free, to be able to express his opinion without restraint—and he became a servant, a functionary, a slave of the power which he himself had at first promoted. The bourgeois society had found him necessary for its rise to dominance—but upon reaching its goal had pushed him aside. Now he is its agent, the representative of its interests, he still fights against the threatening gestures of reaction, he may amuse the citizens and entertain them with the latest reports from the marketplace of the spirit. But he has not acquired the position for which he had contested with the representatives of the old Church. He does not have a place in society, but only with its servants. He is its intellectual lackey and errand boy.

This decline of the publicist in the modern world proceeds apace with the rise of the bourgeois world of business and unlimited discussion. Ultimately, the publicist is not distinguishable from any other commercial employee. His job is simply that of acting as mouthpiece for the groups which shape public opinion. He must write what they dictate to him. He may have no opinion of his own—he may not earnestly express views that are unacceptable to his paymasters. The eighteenth century has taught the lesson that a revolutionary literary world, if it is not bridled, can actually lead to a revolution.

But the influencing of public opinion is prized as a very important line of business. For this, specialists are needed, although they cannot have the right to decide on what shall be given to the public and which views shall be presented to it. The publicist becomes a purely technical journalist who in an effective way expounds the views of his employers. This degradation of the publicists to the level of literary hacks makes the situation in Soviet Russia, which permits only communist publicist work, appear to be almost a better condition. There, at any rate, the technical exploitation of the work of the publicist is in the service of a definite, though false, idea. There the publicist does take a stand for a belief.

A consideration of the history of the publicist in modern times would suggest that the question about the possibility of Catholic publicist work as an independent thing is meaningless. Indeed, the statement that there can be no Catholic publicist work, that true publicist work must serve the cause of the Enlightenment and progress, is false, and appears so even at a first glance. The long list of Catholic publicists, among whom Görres in Germany and Louis Veuillot[5] in France figure most prominently, supports this first impression. But then the objection is raised that such publicist work is nothing more than a manipulation of public opinion in the service of the Church involving a defense against anti-Church movements and an explanation of the true teaching of the Church in the face of popular misinterpretations. Görres defended the Church against the encroachments of a State-Church Establishment policy. He showed that her cause is the cause of freedom against a rigid, bureaucratic outlook. Veuillot was the dauntless fighter against the absurdities of liberalism, which sought to supplant Divine Authority by the ever changing currents of public opinion. But is there a unique and proper mission for Catholic publicist work that rises above the more negative, defensive service? Is Catholic publicist work only a concession to the modern world, where public opinion has become so important? Is the Catholic publicist limited only to being a technical specialist in controlling and influencing public opinion? Or does his activity have a special function beyond the tasks of repelling attacks and providing information? This question arises with all the greater urgency in view of the present dubious estate of the publicist as heir of the Enlightenment, when he was considered as a priest of Reason.

For the liberal and socialist publicists these questions are answered. In their case the aspiration to a dictatorship of the spirit has led only to a transformation of the spirit into a political and social affair. Instead of the spirit as absolute ruler it became the slave of the very force, society, for whose liberation it had contended. When society grows weary of dallying with the spirit, when it begins to look for solid codes and norms which may invest its activity with limits and meaning, it falls under a despot in the form of the powerful state, the avowed despiser of the spirit. Thereafter, the spirit is confined to rigid and narrow limits, such as the Soviet experience reveals. Thus, the claim of the publicist to autonomy, to shape public opinion as he, the spokesman of reason, sees fit, must lead to self-destruction. The alliance with the rising bourgeois society in its fight against tradition, against all limitations imposed on its activity by the authorities of past ages, including the Church, proves to be a negation of the basis of the publicist's own work. He wishes to be honest, he wishes to serve justice, he wishes to be a timely writer, to grasp and to penetrate his own time—and what becomes of him? He has to serve as a source of intellectual entertainment, an advertising manager and superintendent of the intellectual department. He sought to educate and enlighten the public—and what does he have to do today? He presents whatever the prevailing fashion calls for; and his approval or rejection of it does not matter. He had hoped to be able to shape his own time and, instead, he finds that his work is determined for him by his time, whether he submits to it or in impotent hatred resists it. Even his resistance becomes a vendible article, if it interests or entertains the public.

In this situation, is the publicist to give in to despair? Shall he close his eyes and simply continue working without thinking about the fundamentals of his work? But is that possible for the publicist, who in a very personal way must always be conscious of the question of the meaning of his work, the effectiveness of his writings? Or shall he become consciously cynical and explain: "Business is business"—I write to live and to earn money and because I must kill time somehow? Shall he become a publicist in the style of Voltaire without having Voltaire's ready belief in reason and the intellect? This would be to become a publicist who rages over everything, but only as a nihilist, for he would recognize: nothing can be done about it. Or shall he, as an heir of Heinrich Heine, treat everything simply as a pretext for mockery and irony, being incapable of even taking himself seriously and using his very despair as an occasion for play?

In this situation the Catholic publicist must also examine the fundamentals of his position. The necessity for this reflection did not arise so pressingly in the nineteenth century. Then the liberal, enlightened publicists of all sorts still believed in the mind. Even so disintegrated a spirit as Heine could regard himself as a functionary of an imminent Third Reich. Then society, which had already turned away from the transcendental and valued it at best as a luxury item, had not attained to full self-knowledge. It was still growing and still had enemies who seemed to be dangerous. The liberal publicist did not as yet know about his own nothingness. Nor had the time turned finally away from him. He could still appear as its spokesman and prophet. As for the Catholic publicist, he was then simply the representative of truth against the presumptions of public opinion. His task was to show that the Church still lived and that the Church stood for true freedom and learning against their liberal, nineteenth century distortions. Louis Veuillot was able to make merry over the presumptions of liberalism and to reveal its rationalism as more foolish than the ignorance of a believer. Above all the defense of the public existence of the Church against a State-Church establishment and pseudo-scientific *hybris* was so important that there was no time to consider fundamental questions about the relationship of the publicist to public opinion. Public opinion itself had not become a problem—and to stand for the Church against it was an obvious necessity.

Today, of course, it is also the task of the Catholic publicist to stand publicly for the Church, for there still survives that anti-spirit which slanders, defames the

Church as the haven of the superstitious, as a political institution, as the shepherd of old-fashioned viewpoints and as an organization to advance clerical power. The Church in its true light is still not sufficiently known. Today the Catholic publicist may also be considered as the communicator of the pronouncements of ecclesiastical authorities, which without his work would not be heard or would be subject to distortions. But along with the activity of the Catholic publicist on public opinion there appears in a wholly new guise the question about his position, for public opinion has become a problem. Earlier it was taken for granted that science as well as the intellectuals appealed to public opinion. Today, those circles, which formerly stood forth as champions of public opinion, realize how inconsequential that appeal is. Relativism and historicism have not stopped before the fundamentals of liberalism. Thus, the contemporary world—that is, its intellectual and social elite—is more inclined than formerly to show an understanding of the Catholic Church. But this understanding is not wholly a matter for rejoicing, in spite of its being a sign that the old anti-clerical attacks, still conducted by some of the mass parties, have lost their real effectiveness in the contemporary world. This understanding is but an expression of the fact that an effort is being made to manipulate the Church. Just as there were counter-revolutionaries after the French Revolution, who publicly acted as pious sons of the Church while continuing to venerate Voltaire privately, and, in effect, sought to use the Church for political and social ends, so there are today many circles, which venerate the Church as the defender of the spirit and of political order, although they do not admit its divine foundation and, indeed, do not even give it a thought. Of course, only a few intellectuals publicly subscribe to that secularized Catholicism, which venerates the Church without Christ, which inclines to agreement with the leaders of *Action Française* that the greatness of the Church consists in its taming of Christianity by Roman order and discipline.[6] Nevertheless, there is a widespread, contemporary state of mind, which considers politics and society as the only realities and the Church as a kind of efficient and useful background for the socio-political world. Can the Catholic publicist cooperate with that anti-liberalism? He cannot, even though he may welcome certain practical effects of the reversion from liberalism. In fact, one of his most urgent tasks must be to see to it that the picture of the Church in the contemporary world is not falsified by its worldly friends.

Today, Catholic publicist work must be done on quite different fronts from those of an earlier day. It can no longer, as in the nineteenth century, be satisfied with a defensive position or content itself with the defense of natural communities and their bases. The collapse of liberalism poses questions which demand lively examination of the bases of the very existence of Catholic publicist work. It has to prove that it is capable of undertaking and discharging the functions to which liberal publicist work did not measure up. Liberal publicist work broke down in this fundamental respect: it presented a norm to its age or revealed and claimed the norm as the true tendency of the present age and, then, proved all too transient itself. A particular historical task was discharged, and, thereafter, the liberal publicist could not maintain himself. Its basis in principle merely co-incided with the rise of the bourgeois society. When that society has won its po-sition, the publicist becomes simply a servant of society and is strictly forbidden to face further questions about the meaning and direction of his existence.

Catholic publicist activity possesses an entirely different basis. It rests upon the membership of the publicists in Christ's Church. This is to say that it cannot become a temporal-social matter. It is, indeed, publicist work, for which the ac-tions of the moment, the knowledge of what is timely, the concrete and actual practice are, as distinguished from scholarship, central. But the work is not lim-ited to time. It not only defends the Church against external attacks—it seeks to make manifest the enduring actuality of the Church for all times. The Catholic publicist has the task of showing that all times may be embraced by the Church, that Church life and Church teaching, as the timeless objectification of the ab-solute, cannot be separated from and contrasted to the flux and changes of time. The Catholic publicist must be concerned with the actual moment of existence, or fail to be a publicist; he must see in Christ and His Church the fullness of life and truth, or fail to be a Catholic. He may never forget that he, even as a child of his time, must explain its meaning *sub specie aeternitatis*. But for him eternity may never be a mask to veil contemporary concerns in timeless formulas, which can only acquire a concrete meaning by interpretation of the actual situation.

Today it is necessary to stress this special function of the publicist—the per-sistent search to comprehend eternity in his age. The more negative and defen-sive work of the Catholic publicist is not sufficient. In our time of crisis, when everything has become doubtful, it is not enough simply to defend the Church against attacks. The failure of the liberal outlook, the loss of the absolute belief in human reason and progress and the reaction against "the stupid" nineteenth century, which is rather undervalued than overprized, threaten the Church in a more dangerous way than did the avowed anti-clericalism of earlier days. The Church is looked upon merely as one of many powers, as a form of tradition, as the pragmatic satisfier of religious needs, which are unalterably planted in human nature. But the uniqueness of the Church is not seen, for these views exclude the belief that Christ is the savior of the world.

Thus, mere defensive activity, confined to protecting the Church by influencing public opinion, proves ineffective, however necessary it may be. Above all, it must be recognized that the contemporary situation is not met by simply expounding the cultural, political, social and economic significance of the Church but requires the confrontation of the contemporary crisis of the European mind and an alert understanding of its travail. Today the Catholic publicist must act as a missionary in the modern world, and not primarily as a soldier fighting it. He can do his work only if his spirit is capable of making distinctions. And only as a son of the Church does he possess this mind and spirit. He has it only if in his own life, he follows Him, who is the Savior of the world and the Lord of all ages. Only then is he able to go beyond the bounds of his own subjectivity and to fashion his own subjectivity into a medium of eternity. Only then may he overcome that spirit of satiety, which tempts even the publicist to content himself with his work as a means of getting the necessities of life, as a job without raising any issues about its meaning. Only then is he possessed by that unrest, stemming in the Christian from the contrast of his own life to that life, which, as a son of the Church, as another Christ, he should lead. This unrest is decisive for the continuous urge to gain knowledge and wisdom, for the task of working from the experiences of this world to ultimate clarity. Only then, too, may he protect himself against the dangers of using himself as the source of norms and standards of conduct, for the fact that the Church, as the living Christ, as the mystical body of Christ is a visible authority, steadily drives him to self-scrutiny and engenders in him an alert skepticism about his own wishes and prejudices. Only the Catholic publicist, who recognizes himself as a son of the Church, may sustain his lot as a man in ceaseless search for the real meaning of his age without surrendering to relativism and despair or growing torpid and stiff in an objectivism that only appears to transcend the temporal flux.

The Catholic publicist may never rest satisfied with the knowledge of his superiority to the liberal publicist. He may never despise the world in which he must be a missionary. He must share its needs and regard as his own its anxieties, which should appear as questions directed at him. Nor may he be satisfied with answers which this world cannot understand. It is his constant task to show that answers to the questions of his age may be found in Church teaching, for he finds no chasm between reason and reality, the tides of time and unchangeable eternity. The

Church presupposes the concrete reality and resists all attempts to embezzle this reality, whether they derive from false theories or from a pragmatic activism to which all theories are indifferent. This very affirmation of time and its requirements, this stand for the real and concrete, this direct participation in the contemporary situation, makes the Catholic publicist a critic of his age.

Such a function does not mean an openness to the world that expresses itself in a genteel discussion of errors and a refusal to use sharp language. Gentility and mildness of that sort are often the mark of a diplomatic mind, a mind which considers Catholicism as a world closed on itself and has no desire to fight for the Church. This has been expressed in the judgment that "there is no point in fighting modern errors, if they have not appeared among Catholics." But here is a failure to observe how even the Catholic mind is gradually and unobtrusively disintegrated and endangered by the currents of the contemporary world. The genteel treatment of errors is but a mark of a lack of understanding of one's age, an incomprehension which welcomes a superficially favorable attitude to the Church as evidence of Catholicity. This fatal state of mind is content with an appearance of correctness and is unconcerned about what may well be hidden behind correctness. Openness to the world can never be maintained at the cost of the capacity to make distinctions. That requires as much emphasis as the necessity never to regard Catholicism as a certain social condition, existing along with "the rest of the world," about which the Catholic need not trouble himself, for its exists and apparently always will exist.

Especially in our time is it urgently important for Catholic publicists to combine an openness to the world and a capacity to make distinctions. It is necessary because the rupture with the nineteenth century has seen the return to elements of tradition, which, so it seemed in the nineteenth century, were maintained almost exclusively by Catholics. Authority and order, discipline and obedience are now highly valued. This is a matter for rejoicing—but it should not be forgotten that the contemporary world did not reject the liberal spirit because it perceived the errors of liberalism. It turned from liberalism in despair. Experience has revealed where it leads: Soviet Russia stands ready as the executor of bourgeois society; there is a general weariness with seeking and constant discussion; there is a desire for decision, for strong measures simply to preserve existence from foundering in the midst of necessity and the dominance of power. The belief that politics and economics are the major forces in life relegates all intellectual and spiritual things to secondary matters. To justify, to support, to preserve, only such activities are useful—and this is not a mere accusation—it is generally acknowledged. This condemnation of the mind, the sentence which unmasks the intellect as a fabricator of ideologies, is characterized by others as an insubstantial nihilism.

We are threatened with the dominance of mentality which may be described as social activism. All theories and philosophies are despised, for they are the merest preliminaries of the all-powerful fact. This social activism does not involve any denial of metaphysics and all transcendence. If it did, it would not be a pure activism. Usually it takes the form of regarding the mind and spirit as a fixed and given thing. Solutions are ready and all that is needed is to organize and use them. The masses have to be won over to these solutions and organizations have to be created. On this basis all spiritual and intellectual independence can be suppressed, for it simply appears as a disquieting source of problems. That is the state of mind which the liberal claim to establish a purely human truth and secularize the mind and religion has created as an end effect. But it should, also, be said that this state of mind afflicts groups which do not even want to know anything about liberalism.

This is the state of mind which makes the work of the Catholic publicist so difficult today. The position of the scholar is still understood and appreciated, for he can occupy a university chair and so add to the social prestige of Catholics. At any rate he has an influence on practical life as the educator of the bureaucracy and of the academic and liberal professions. And it goes without saying that the successful politician, the influential lawyer or doctor, and other officials are valued. But what about the publicist? Really, what is he? How can he have a real influence, since he, unlike the practical and effective journalist, does not deal only with day to day matters. Newspapers are necessary and it follows that so are journalists. But publicists? Of course, their articles now and then are interesting. Do they not then fall under the heading of entertainment? After all, scholars are ill-regarded, if they write as publicists.

Of course, the Church as the protector of the mind—Jacques Maritain did not casually call Thomas Aquinas the apostle of the modern intellect—can have nothing to do with this social activism. Is it even necessary to say that anymore? But social activism openly believes that it can make use of the Church. It does not note that in hoping to do so it confuses its own rejection of intellectual problems with the claim of the Church to the supratemporal character of its dogma. More or less impressively it attempts to act against the publicist, who tries to serve not just as a technical, day-to-day journalist, but as one who comprehends, clarifies and influences his time. The attack is not frontally made but is directed to excluding him from his public sphere of activity. This line of attack suggests that he is a kind of scholar, who studies the present.

This social activism may be called the major obstacle to the work of today's Catholic publicist. I am not thinking of the present economic crisis, I am thinking above all of the atmosphere, the climate which surrounds him. He is not understood and he is suspect. It is doubtful that his work is thereby advanced, even if one disagrees with the opinion that publicist work can be organized with the aid of economic and social measures. This social activism, which misunderstands the decisive missionary work of the Catholic publicist, constantly recognized by the Church, and does not even know the names of Theodor Häcker[7] and Hugo Ball[8] must be reminded of the words recently published in the *New Reich*: "The unspiritual Catholic is the worst of all evils." Activity is good and necessary. Organizations are important and indispensable. But there must also be room for the free life of the spirit. Otherwise, Catholicism is threatened with a transformation into but one social viewpoint among others; otherwise, the life strength of the Church, which is for all time, will, as in the eighteenth century, cease to throb vibrantly in the world. The unspiritual Catholic endangers the effectiveness of the Church by his un-Catholic passivity in spiritual matters, by his false belief that organizations and the influencing of the masses are more important than spiritual work. These practical activities are truly important, but without the sustained and sustaining bases they will inevitably be torpid and incapable of the performance expected of them.

Although the Catholic publicist has a right to raise his voice against the overestimation of practical activity in contemporary life, however, he may under no circumstances forget that he has a definite work to do and that his calling does not involve an intellectual dictatorship. The liberal publicist raised this demand, and we have seen where it has led him. He can maintain it only if he, like the revolutionary Marxist, becomes a servant of a movement with a particular world outlook. But even such a movement does not give him a leading position, when its power is consolidated. In Soviet Russia Stalin triumphed over the Marxist publicist, Trotsky. Such an exaggerated estimate of a mind wholly concerned with timely problems cannot develop among Catholic publicists. It is their characteristic that they are formed by the Church, that, instead of their own spirituality shaping the Church, the Church shapes their spirituality. But it may happen that publicists will exaggerate their own importance and believe their own spiritual and intellectual forms of expression to be the only permissible ones.

Therefore, the Catholic publicist must constantly bear in mind that in the long run his activity can only flourish if it is related to Catholic theology and philosophy. No publicist work is possible at all without association with science and learning. Just as the work of the liberal publicist dealt with the needs and questions of the hour by drawing on its own philosophy and history, so must the work of Catholic publicists maintain a close relation, above all, with theology, philosophy and church history. Of course, the publicist is not a scholar, who is engaged in research, although the scholar, also, may deal with the questions agitating his own world and time. The publicist's special function is to be timely and the very canon of timeliness permits him to understand and to influence his age. Without knowledge, however, and without familiarity with the world of learning and the experiences of tradition, he can do nothing constructive. He is not a poet, who creates works of pure, timeless meaning, even though he may draw on materials from tradition and his own age. But just because the publicist is steeped in his own time he may never be purely impressionistic or individualistic about it.

His membership in the Church of itself determines his outlook. But any serious reflection will convince him that he may not leave the question at that. He must ponder and meditate on its teachings, and cannot content himself with supporting and protecting the Church by universal considerations alone. The very fact that he approaches the questions of the age and the hour in the light of Church teaching, that according to his own conviction these questions can be answered in the light of the Church, compels him to a zealous study of the learning of the Church, to a careful examination of the always pressing questions about the relationship of faith and knowledge to philosophy and theology. This study educates him in discretion and modesty. He is compelled to perceive that he is not the solver of the world's problems or the discoverer of theories which make the world's ills curable or, at any rate, open the way to a cure. He recognizes that each moment of actuality is but one of many actualities and does not take refuge in the flux of any time or time itself. In the pathos of life's present struggle he senses the peace of eternity, knowing that he is not the savior of the world. His claim derives not from his own strength; his own life is always insufficient, his will to help and understand always exceeds his own power. He knows that the human spirit is not an end in itself; that there is no more an absolute literary profession and publicist work than there is an absolute philosophy.

In this humility is his pride. In this knowledge of his unalienable insufficiency is his mission. He is never authority, but he points the way to the authority, himself always fearful and concerned lest he make his own subjectivism figure too prominently, lest he proclaim the truth in so interesting a manner that it will not be taken seriously. The insecurity of his existence inheres in the publicist as a constant warning never to be satisfied with himself, never to lose that unrest, without which all publicist work is only an idle pastime. This unrest, moreover, may not become an occasion for trifling—it must really be the unrest of which St. Augustine spoke: "Our heart is restless, until it rests in Thee."

NOTES

Reprinted from *The Review of Politics* 17, no. 1, The Gurian Memorial Issue (January 1955): 5–18.

1. [In the original version of the article, Gurian writes, "This apologia, delivered as a lecture in 1931, has been translated by M. A. Fitzsimons." Ed.]

2. [Joseph-Marie de Maistre (1753–1821) was an unremitting critic of the French Revolution who saw France's only hope for recovery in the restoration of the Monarchy. Ed.]

3. [The French writer and novelist, François-René de Chateaubriand (1768–1848), first published *Génie du christianisme* in 1802. He saw the book as a defense of Christianity against the anti-religious elements in Enlightenment thought and culture. Ed.]

4. [Johann Joseph von Görres (1776–1848) was a liberal nationalist and Catholic essayist, who founded the newspaper, *Rheinische Merkur*, a path-breaking publication in modern journalism. Ed.]

5. [Louis Veuillot (1813–1883) was a French writer and publicist who wrote articles defending Catholicism for the journal *Univers*. Ed.]

6. [The Action Française was a French Monarchist counter-revolutionary movement and periodical. The movement became a symbol of Right-wing nationalism in France until its dissolution after World War II. Ed.]

7. [Theodor Häcker (1879–1945) was a German writer, translator, and Catholic convert who opposed the Nazi regime and took part in the German resistance. Ed.]

8. [Hugo Ball (1886–1927) was a writer, artist, and key participant in Zürich's DaDa movement. He founded the "Cabaret Voltaire" in 1916, which championed independent thinking in the face of war and nationalism. Ed.]

CHAPTER 17

Authority in the Twentieth Century

HANNAH ARENDT

Hannah Arendt (1906–1975) was born in Hanover, Germany. She studied philosophy with Martin Heidegger at Marburg University, and earned her doctoral degree at the University of Heidelberg under the supervision of Karl Jaspers. During World War II, she escaped to New York City where she first worked in the field of publishing and then went on to teach political philosophy at Princeton, the University of Chicago, and the New School for Social Research. In her first major political work, The Origins of Totalitarianism, *Arendt claimed that the regimes of Nazi Germany and Stalinist Russia constituted a new form of dictatorship—totalitarianism. In writing this study and subsequent works, Arendt distanced herself from past conceptual and empirical approaches to political philosophy. Her goal was to reconstruct political theorizing in terms of a phenomenological examination of the human experience. Following Heidegger, she considered the autonomy of the political realm to be threatened by the social and historical forces of the twentieth century. Thus, Arendt spent much of her career seeking to uncover and preserve the distinctive structures and characteristics of authentic political activity.*

I

The rise of fascist, communist and totalitarian movements and the development of the two totalitarian regimes, Stalin's after 1929 and Hitler's after 1938, took place against a background of a more or less general, more or less dramatic breakdown of all traditional authorities. Nowhere was this breakdown the direct result of the regimes or movements themselves, but it seemed as though totalitarianism, in the form of regimes as well as of movements, was best fitted to take advantage of a general political and social atmosphere in which the validity of authority itself was radically doubted.

The most extreme manifestation of this climate which, with minor geographical and chronological exceptions, has been the atmosphere of our century since its inception, is the gradual breakdown of the one form of authority which exists in all historically known societies, the authority of parents over children, of teachers over pupils and, generally of the elders over the young. Even the least "authoritarian" forms of government have always accepted this kind of "authority" as a matter of course. It has always seemed to be required as much by natural needs, the helplessness of the child, as by political necessity, the continuity of an established civilization which can be assured only if those who are newcomers by birth are guided through a preestablished world into which they are born as strangers. Because of its simple and elementary character, this form of a strictly limited authority has, throughout the history of political thought, been used and abused as a model for very different and much less limited authoritarian systems.[1]

It seems that ours is the first century in which this argument no longer carries an overwhelming weight of plausibility and it announced its anti-authoritarian spirit nowhere more radically than when it promised the emancipation of youth as an oppressed class and called itself the "century of the child." I cannot here follow the implications of this early self-interpretation which are manifold, nor am I now interested in the various schools of "progressive education" where this principle found its realization. But it may be worth noting that the anti-authoritarian position has been driven to the extreme of education without authority only in the United States, the most egalitarian and the least tradition-bound country of the West, where precisely the results of this radical experiment are now, more than any other single political or social factor, leading to a reevaluation of the very concept of authority. Neo-Conservatism, which has won a surprisingly large following in recent years, is primarily cultural and educational, and not political or social, in outlook; it appeals to a mood and concern which are direct results of the elimination of authority from the relationship between young and old, teacher and pupil, parents and children.

I mentioned this strangest, but in other respects least interesting, aspect of the problem of authority in our world only because it shows to what extremes the general decline of authority could go, even to the neglect of obvious natural necessities. For this indicates how very unlikely it is that we shall find in our century the rise of authentic authoritarian forms of government and, hence, how careful we must be lest we mistake tyrannical forms of government, which rule by order and decree, for authoritarian structures. Our century, it is true, has seen quite a number of new variations of tyranny and dictatorship, among which we must count the fascist and early communist types of one-party systems. But these differ as much in institutional structure, type of organization and political content from authoritarian bodies as they differ from totalitarian domination. Unless we define authority without regard to its historical and verbal content, and identify it with arbitrary orders and total abolition of freedom, that is, with political realities always thought to be its very opposite, we shall find it hard indeed to understand why not only journalists but even political scientists can speak of a "rise of authoritarian forms of government in the twentieth century." The most one can say is that up to now one authentically authoritarian institution has managed to survive the onslaught of the modern age, the Catholic Church, which of course has long ceased to be a body politic, properly speaking.

Tyrannies and authoritarian forms of government are very old, the first going back to Greek antiquity and the other having its origin in the spirit of the Roman Republic. Only totalitarian domination is new, as new as the word itself and the claim to *total*, and not only political, domination. Our knowledge of it is still very limited, the only variety open to our inquiries being the Hitler regime, for which documentary material has become available in recent years. No doubt this limitation tempts us to examine the newest body politic in our history with conceptual tools which apply to or are derived from more familiar experiences, but by such identification—with tyranny on one hand and with authoritarianism on the other—we lose sight of precisely those characteristics and institutions which belong to this and no other phenomenon.

The identification of totalitarianism with authoritarianism occurs most frequently among liberal writers. They start from the assumption that "the constancy of progress . . . in the direction of organized and assured freedom is the characteristic fact of modern history"[2] and look upon each deviation from this course as a reactionary process leading in the opposite direction. This makes them overlook the differences in principle between the restriction of freedom in authoritarian regimes, the abolition of political freedom in tyrannies and dictatorships, and the total elimination of spontaneity itself, that is, of the most general and most elementary manifestation of human freedom, at which only totalitarian regimes aim by means of their various methods of conditioning; for terror and concentration-camps are meant not so much to frighten as to condition people. The liberal writer, concerned with history and the progress of freedom rather than with forms of government, sees only differences in degree here, and ignores that authoritarian government committed to the restriction of liberty remains tied to the freedom it limits to the extent that it would lose its very substance if it abolished it altogether, that is, would change into tyranny. The same is true for the distinction between legitimate and illegitimate power on which all authoritarian government hinges. The liberal writer is apt to pay little attention to it because of his conviction that all power corrupts and that the constancy of progress requires constant loss of power, no matter what its origin may be.

Behind the liberal identification of totalitarianism with authoritarianism, and the concomitant inclination to see "totalitarian" trends in every authoritarian limitation of freedom, lies an older confusion of authority with tyranny, and of legitimate power with violence. The difference between tyranny and authoritarian government has always been that the tyrant rules in accordance with his own will and interest, and even the most draconic authoritarian government is bound by laws. Its acts are tested by a code which either was not made by man at all, as in the case of the law of nature or God's Commandments or the Platonic ideas, or at least not by those actually in power. The source of authority in authoritarian government is always a force external and superior to its own power; it is always this source, this external force which transcends the political realm, from which the authorities derive their "authority," that is, their legitimacy, and against which their power can be checked.

Modern spokesmen of authority, who, even in the short intervals when public opinion provides a favorable climate for neo-Conservatism, remain well aware that theirs is an almost lost cause, are of course eager to point to this distinction between tyranny and authority. Where the liberal writer sees an essentially assured progress in the direction of freedom, which is only temporarily interrupted by some dark forces of the past, the Conservative sees a process of doom which started with the dwindling of authority, so that freedom, after it lost the restricting limitations which protected its boundaries, became helpless, defenseless and bound to be destroyed. It is hardly fair to say that only liberal political thought is primarily interested in freedom; there is hardly a school of political thought in our history which is not centered around the idea of freedom, much as the concept of liberty may vary with different writers and in different political circumstances. The only exception of any consequence to this statement seems to me to be the political philosophy of Thomas Hobbes, who, of course, is anything but a Conservative. Tyranny and totalitarianism are again identified, except that now totalitarian government, if it is not directly identified with democracy, is seen as its almost inevitable result, that is, the result of the disappearance of all traditionally recognized authorities. Yet the differences between tyranny and dictatorship on one side, and totalitarian domination on the other, are no less distinct than those between authoritarianism and totalitarianism. The proverbial quiet of the cemetery with which tyrants, from the rulers of ancient city-states to modern dictators, have covered their countries once they have suppressed all organized opposition and destroyed all actual enemies, has never yet been enjoyed by people living under a totalitarian regime.

Modern one-party dictatorships resemble tyrannies to the extent that their rule rests on parties, and not movements. It is true, though, that already in the case of most fascist dictatorships, it was a movement which brought the dictator into power; but the point is that the movement was frozen into a party after the seizure of power. The very articulate and often repeated criticism the Nazis voiced against Mussolini and Italian fascism, as well as their no less articulate admiration for Stalin and the Bolshevism of the Stalinist era, center around this vital difference between a party dictatorship and a totalitarian movement, or, to use their own language, between the dictatorial head of a normal state and a "world revolutionary." The totalitarian form of domination depends entirely upon the fact that a movement, and not a party, has taken power, that the rulers are chiefly concerned with keeping the movement moving, and preventing its "degeneration" into a party, so that instead of the tyrant's brutal determination and the dictator's demagogic ability to keep himself in power at all costs, we find the totalitarian leader's single-minded attention directed to the acceleration of the movement itself. This is the significance of the purges of the Stalin regime, as it is of Hitler's "selection process which should never be permitted to come to an end." Its outstanding characteristic was that it could function only as an extermination process.[3] (*Auslese-* and *Ausmerzungsprozess* in Nazi parlance meant the same thing.)

Closely connected with this characteristic is the apparently senseless use of terror in totalitarian regimes, which distinguishes them most conspicuously from modern as well as past dictatorships and tyrannies. Terror is no longer a means to frighten and suppress opponents, but, on the contrary, increases with the decrease of opposition, reaches its climax when opposition no longer exists and directs its full fury not so much against the enemies of the regime as against people who are innocent even from the viewpoint of the persecutor. Only the category of "objective or potential enemies," that is, people who have committed no crimes but share certain objective characteristics which at any moment can be decided to be "criminal," is capable of providing enough human material for "purges" or "exterminations" to keep the movement in constant acceleration.

In contradistinction to dictatorships, whose notions of freedom are much less sophisticated, the totalitarian leader justifies all his measures with the argument that they are necessary for freedom. He is not against freedom, not even for a limitation of it. The trouble is only that his concept of freedom is radically different from that of the non-totalitarian world. It is the historical process of world revolution, or the natural process of race selection that has to be "liberated" through purges and extermination. As in certain seventeenth century philosophers, freedom is here understood to be a movement unrestrained by external force or impediment, something like the free flow of water in a river. The unpredictable initiative of men, even if they should decide to support this movement, is as great an impediment to the free-flowing process as laws, traditions or stable institutions of any sort, even the most tyrannical. A whole school of legal theorists in Nazi Germany tried their best to prove that the very concept of law was so directly in conflict with the political content of a movement as such that even the most revolutionary new legislation would eventually prove to be a hindrance to the movement.[4] And one need only read carefully certain speeches of Stalin to realize that he had arrived at very similar conclusions.[5]

All the dialectical niceties in discussions of the concept of freedom between the dialectical materialists who are prepared to defend the horrors of the Bolshevik system for the sake of history, and their anti-totalitarian opponents, rest ultimately on a simple and non-dialectical misunderstanding: what they have in mind when they talk about freedom is the freedom of a process, which apparently needs to be liberated from the meddlesome interfering activities of men, and what we have in mind is freedom of people, whose movements need protection by fixed and stable boundaries of laws, constitutions and institutions.

The task of the totalitarian ruler—to clear the way for the processes of History or Nature and to sweep from the path of his movement the unpredictable spontaneity of human beings—demands much more radical measures than the mere transformation of laws into decrees, which is characteristic of all bureaucratic forms of tyranny, where government and due process of law are replaced by administration and anonymous decision. By the same token, it is only superficially correct to see in the movement's blind devotion to the leader a kind of order-obedience relationship as in an army, a relationship which is occasionally carried into political-civil affairs, as in the case of a military dictatorship. The Nazis, who especially in later years developed a surprisingly precise terminology, proclaimed that the highest law in Germany is the *will,* not the order, of the Führer.[6]

What swings the movement into motion and keeps it that way is this ever-changing "will," whose outward manifestations—orders, decrees, ordinances—are so unstable that they are not even officially published and brought to the notice of those whose very life depends upon obeying them.[7] The motivation for this extraordinary behavior, which indeed far outstrips the most arbitrary whims of tyrants, who at least knew they had to express and make public their "will" in order to be obeyed, is not so much fear of opposition or concern for conspiratorial secrecy as it is a well-calculated, conscious misgiving that even such a draconic and "revolutionary" decree as the one with which Hitler started the second World War—namely, to kill all incurably ill people—could by its very publication become a stabilizing factor and hinder the further development and radicalization of the movement: for example, in this instance the introduction of a national Health Bill by which in his plans for the postwar period Hitler intended to remove even those in whose family one member with an incurable lung or heart disease could be found.[8]

Differences of so decisive a nature must manifest themselves in the whole apparatus of rule and the very structure of the body politic. Such distinctions can be valid only if they can be carried down to the level of technical forms of administration and organization. For brevity's sake, it may be permitted to sum up the technical-structural differences between authoritarian, tyrannical and totalitarian government in the image of three different representative models. As an image for authoritarian government, I propose the shape of the pyramid, which is well known in traditional political thought. The pyramid is indeed a particularly fitting image for a governmental structure whose source of authority lies outside itself, but whose center of power is located at the top, from which authority and power is filtered down to the base in such a way that each successive layer possesses some, but less authority than the one above it, and where precisely because of this careful filtering process all layers from top to bottom are not only firmly integrated into the whole, but are interrelated like converging rays whose common focal point is the top of the pyramid as well as the transcending source of authority above it. This image, it is true, can be used only for the Christian type of authoritarian rule as it developed through and under the constant influence of the Church during the Middle Ages. This was when the focal point above and beyond the earthly pyramid provided the necessary point of reference for the Christian type of equality, the strictly hierarchical structure of life on earth notwithstanding. The Roman understanding of political authority, where the source of authority lay exclusively in the past, in the foundation of Rome and the greatness of ancestors, leads into institutional structures whose shape would require a different kind of image; but that is of no great importance in our context. In any event, an authoritarian form of government with its hierarchical structure is the least egalitarian of all forms; it incorporates inequality and distinction as its all-permeating principles.

All political theories concerning tyranny agree that it belongs strictly among the egalitarian forms of government; the tyrant is the ruler who rules as one against all, and the "all" he oppresses are all equal, namely equally powerless. If we stick to the image of the pyramid, it is as though all intervening layers between top and bottom were destroyed, so that the top remains suspended, supported only by the proverbial bayonets, over a mass of carefully isolated, disintegrated and completely equal individuals. Classical political theory used to rule the tyrant out of mankind altogether, to call him a "wolf in human shape" (Plato), because of this position of One against all, in which he had put himself and which sharply distinguished his rule, the rule of One, which Plato still calls indiscriminately *mon-archy* or tyranny, from various forms of kingship or *basileia*.

In contradistinction to both tyrannical and authoritarian regimes, the proper image of totalitarian rule and organization seems to me to be the structure of the onion, in whose center, in a kind of empty space, the leader is located. Whatever he does, whether he integrates the body politic as in an authoritarian hierarchy, or oppresses his subjects like a tyrant, he does it from within, and not from without or above. All the extraordinarily manifold parts of the movement—the front organizations, the various professional societies, the party-membership, the party hierarchy, the elite formations and police groups—are related in such a way that each forms the facade in one direction and the center in the other, that is, plays the role of normal outside world for one layer and the role of radical extremism for another. The civilian members of Himmler's General SS, for example, represented a rather philistine facade of normality to the SS Leader Corps, and at the same time could be trusted to be ideologically more trustworthy and extreme than the ordinary member of the NSDAP.

The same is true for the relationship between sympathizer and party member, between party member and party officer or SA-man, between the Gauleiter and a member of the secret police, etc.[9] The great advantage of this system is that the movement provides for each of its layers, even under conditions of totalitarian rule, the fiction of a normal world along with a consciousness of being different from and more radical than it. Thus, the sympathizers of the front organizations, whose convictions differ only in intensity from those of the party membership, surround the whole movement and provide a deceptive facade of normality to the outside world because of their lack of fanaticism and extremism while, at the same time, they represent the normal world to the totalitarian movement whose members come to believe that their convictions differ only in degree from those of other people, so that they need never be aware of the abyss which separates their own world from that which actually surrounds it. The onion structure makes the system organizationally shock-proof against the factuality of the real world.

The second advantage of this type of organization is that it permits a kind of doubletalk of great importance to the relationship between totalitarian regimes and the outside, non-totalitarian world. In close correspondence with the dual role of each layer—to act as facade in one direction and as interior center in the other—stands the curious fact that the same official pronouncements frequently can be understood either as mere propaganda or as serious indoctrination. Hitler's violently nationalistic speeches, for instance, which he used to address to his officer corps, were meant as indoctrination for the officers of the *Wehrmacht*. Within the higher Nazi hierarchy, however, where the slogan of "Right is what is good for the German people" had even officially been replaced by "Right is what is good for the Movement,"[10] they were nothing but propaganda for an outside world not yet "mature" enough to understand the true aims of the movement.

It would lead us too far afield to show how this particular structure is connected with these facts: totalitarian rule is based on a movement in the word's most literal significance; the movement is international in scope; the rise to power in one country does not mean that the totalitarian ruler cuts himself loose from the interest or goal of the movement as a whole; and consequently, the country in which he happens to seize power is much less the seat and source of his personal power than the headquarters for the movement itself.

II

It is obvious that these reflections and descriptions are based on the conviction of the importance of making distinctions. To stress such a conviction seems to be a gratuitous truism in view of the fact that, at least as far as I know, nobody has yet openly stated that distinctions are nonsense. There exists, however, a silent agreement in most discussions among political and social scientists that we can ignore distinctions and proceed on the assumption that everything can eventually be called anything else, and that distinctions are meaningful only to the extent that each of us has the right "to define his terms." Yet does not this curious right, which we have come to grant as soon as we deal with matters of importance— as though it were actually the same as the right to one's own opinion—already indicate that such terms as tyranny, authority, totalitarianism have simply lost their common meaning, or that we have ceased to live in a common world where the words we have in common possess an unquestionable meaningfulness, so that short of being condemned to live verbally in an altogether meaningless world we grant each other the right to retreat into our own worlds of meaning and demand only that each of us remain consistent within his own, private terminology? If, under these circumstances, we assure ourselves that we still understand each other, we do not mean that together we understand a world common to us all, but that we understand the consistency of arguing and reasoning, of the process of argumentation in its sheer formality.

However that may be, to proceed under the implicit assumption that distinctions are not important or, better, that in the social-political-historical realm, that is, in the sphere of human affairs, things do not possess that distinctness which traditional metaphysics used to call their "otherness" (their *alteritas*) has become the hallmark of a great many theories in the social, political and historical sciences. Among these, two seem to me to deserve special mention because they touch the subject under discussion in an especially significant manner.

I mentioned the first when I described the liberal and the conservative theories. Liberalism, we saw, measures a process of receding freedom, and conservatism measures a process of receding authority; both call the expected end-result totalitarianism and see totalitarian trends wherever either one or the other is present. No doubt, both can produce excellent documentation for their findings. Who would deny the serious threats to freedom from all sides since the beginning of the century, and the rise of all kinds of tyranny at least since the end of the first World War? Who can deny, on the other side, that disappearance of practically all traditionally established authorities has been one of the most spectacular characteristics of the modern world? It seems as though one has only to fix his glance on either of these two phenomena to justify a theory of progress or a theory of doom according to his own taste or, as the phrase goes, according to his own "scale of values." If we look upon the conflicting statements of conservatives and liberals with impartial eyes, we can easily see that the truth is equally distributed between them and that we are in fact confronted with a simultaneous recession of both freedom and authority in the modern world. As far as these processes are concerned, one can even say that the numerous oscillations in public opinion, which for more than a hundred and fifty years has swung at regular intervals from one extreme to the other, from a liberal mood to a conservative one and back to a more liberal again, at times attempting to reassert authority and at others to reassert freedom, have resulted only in further undermining both, confusing the issues, blurring the distinctive lines between authority and freedom, and eventually destroying the political meaning of both.

Both liberalism and conservatism were born in this climate of violently oscillating public opinion and they are tied together, not only because each would lose its very substance without the presence of its opponent in the field of theory and ideology, but because both are primarily concerned with restoration, with restoring either freedom or authority or the relationship between both to its traditional position. It is in this sense that they form the two sides of the same coin, just as their progress-or-doom ideologies are but the two sides where the historical process, as process, can be understood, if one assumes, as both do, that historical processes have definable directions and a predictable end.

It is, moreover, in the nature of the very image in which History is usually conceived, as process or stream or development, that everything can change into everything else, that distinctions become meaningless because they are obsolete, submerged, as it were, by the historical stream, the moment they are pronounced. From this viewpoint, liberalism and conservatism present themselves as the political philosophies which correspond to the much more general and comprehensive philosophy of history of the nineteenth century. In form and content, they are the political expression of the history-consciousness of the last stage of the modern age. Their inability to distinguish, theoretically justified by the concepts of history and process, progress or doom, testifies to an age in which certain notions, clear in their distinctness to all previous centuries, have begun to lose their clarity and plausibility because they have lost their meaning in the public-political reality— without altogether losing their significance.

The second and more recent theory implicitly challenging the importance of making distinctions is, especially in the social sciences, the almost universal functionalization of all concepts and ideas. Here, as in the example quoted above, liberalism and conservatism differ not in method, viewpoint and approach, but only in emphasis and evaluation. A convenient instance may be provided by the widespread conviction in the free world today that Communism is a new "religion," notwithstanding its avowed atheism, because it fulfills socially, psychologically and "emotionally" the same function traditional religion fulfilled and still fulfills in the free world. The concern of the social sciences does not lie in what Bolshevism as ideology or as form of government is, nor in what its spokesmen have to say for themselves; that is not the interest of the social sciences, and many social scientists believe they can do without the study of what the historical sciences call the sources themselves. Their concern is only with functions, and whatever fulfills the same function can, according to this view, be called the same. It is as though I had the right to call the heel of my shoe a hammer because I, like most women, use it to drive nails into the wall.

Obviously one can draw quite different conclusions from such equations. Thus, it would be characteristic of conservatism to insist that after all a heel is not a hammer, but that the use of the heel as a substitute for the hammer proves that hammers are indispensable. In other words, they will find in the fact that atheism can fulfill the same function as religion the best proof that religion is necessary, and recommend the return to true religion as the only way to counter a "heresy." The argument is weak of course; if it is only a question of function and how a thing works, the adherents of "false religion" can make as good a case for using theirs as I can for using my heel, which does not work so badly either. The liberals, on the contrary, view the same phenomena as a bad case of treason to the cause of secularism and believe that only "true secularism" can cure us of the pernicious influence of both false and true religion on politics. But these conflicting recommendations at the address of free society to return to true religion and become more religious, or to rid ourselves of institutional religion (especially of Catholicism with its constant challenge to secularism) hardly conceal the opponents' agreement on one point: that whatever fulfills the function of a religion, is a religion.

The same argument is frequently used with respect to authority: if violence fulfills the same function as authority, namely makes people obey, then violence is authority. Here again we find those who counsel a return to authority because they think only a reintroduction of the order-obedience relationship can master the problems of a mass society, and those who believe that a mass society can rule itself like any other social body. Again both parties agree on the one essential point: authority is whatever makes people obey. All those who call modern dictatorships "authoritarian" or mistake totalitarianism for an authoritarian structure, implicitly have equated violence with authority, and this includes those conservatives who explain the rise of dictatorships in our century by the need to find a surrogate for authority. The crux of the argument is always the same: everything is related to a functional context, and the use of violence is taken to demonstrate that no society can exist except in an authoritarian framework.

The dangers of these equations, as I see them, lie not only in the confusion of political issues and in the blurring of the distinctive lines which separate totalitarianism from all other forms of government. I do not believe that atheism is a substitute for or can fulfill the same function as a religion any more than I believe that violence can become a substitute for authority. But if we follow the recommendations of the conservatives who at this particular moment have a rather good chance of being heard, I am quite convinced that we shall not find it hard to produce such substitutes, that we shall use violence and pretend to have restored authority or that our rediscovery of the functional usefulness of religion will produce a substitute-religion—as though our civilization were not already sufficiently cluttered up with all sorts of pseudo-things and nonsense.

Compared with these theories, the distinctions between tyrannical, authoritarian and totalitarian systems which we proposed are unhistorical, if one understands by history not the historical space in which certain forms of government appeared as recognizable entities, but the historical process in which everything can always change into something else. And they are antifunctional insofar as the content of the phenomenon is taken to determine both the nature of the political body and its function in society, and not vice-versa. Politically speaking, they have a tendency to assume that in the modern world authority has disappeared almost to the vanishing point, and this in the so-called authoritarian systems no less than in the free world, and that freedom, that is, the freedom of movement of human beings, is threatened everywhere, even in free societies, but abolished radically only in totalitarian systems, and not even in tyrannies and dictatorships.

NOTES

Reprinted from *The Review of Politics* 18, no. 4 (October 1956): 403–17.

1. The first to use this argument seems to be Aristotle, when in his *Politics* he wished to demonstrate that "every political community is composed of those who rule and those who are ruled" (1332b12). There he said: "Nature herself has provided the distinction . . . (between) the younger and the older ones, of whom she fitted the ones to be ruled and the others to rule" (1332b36).

2. The formulation is Lord Acton's in his "Inaugural Lecture on the 'Study of History'" reprinted in *Essays on Freedom and Power* (New York: World Publishing Co., 1955), 35.

3. This formulation occurs frequently in Nazi literature. We quote here from Heinrich Himmler, "Die Schutzstaffel als antibolschewistische Kampforganisation." *Schriften aus dem Schwarzen Korps*, no. 3, 1936.

4. The most interesting item in this literature is Theodor Maunz, *Gestalt und Recht der Polizei* (Hamburg: Hanseatische Verlag, 1943). Maunz is one of the very small number of legal experts in the Third Reich who had fully succeeded in cleansing himself of the "prejudice" that the notion of Law has a certain connection with the concept of justice. His is the best conceptualization of Nazi "legal" practice.

5. Quite characteristic is the speech of Stalin on the occasion of the publication of the Soviet Constitution of 1936.

6. Otto Gauweiler, *Rechtseinrichtungen und Rechtsaufgaben der Bewegung* (Munich, 1939), 10. Also, Werner Best, *Die Deutsche Polizei* (Darmstadt: L. C. Wittich, 1941), 21: "Der Wille der Führung, gleich in welcher Form er zum Ausdruck gelangt ... schafft Recht und ändert bisher geltendes Recht ab." There exist numerous documents which show clearly that there could be a great difference between an order and the will of the Führer. See for instance "PS 3063 of the Nuremberg Documents" which reports on the pogroms of November 1938: The order to the SA-men in charge of the pogroms demanded that they carry their pistols, but the implication was that "every SA-man should know now what he must do ... that Jewish blood should flow, that according to the *will* of the leadership the life of a Jew did not matter" (my italics). A reliable Nazi was not the one who obeyed unquestioningly the orders of Hitler, but who was able to discern Hitler's "will" behind these orders. Needless to say that this "will" was always more radical than the orders. In the formulation of Hans Frank, *Technik des Staates* (Munich, 1940): "Der kategorische Imperativ des Handelns im Dritten Reich lautet: Handle so, daß der Führer, wenn er von Deinem Handeln Kenntnis haette, dieses Handeln billigen wuerde."

7. The most famous of these decrees is of course the ordinance with which Hitler started the second World War and which, on September 1, 1939, ordered "allen unheilbar Kranken den Gnadentod zu gewähren." But there exist a great many similar decrees, from 1933 onwards, which were valid law in the Third Reich and yet were never published. They were collected by

Martin Bormann during the war into five large volumes under the title *Verfügungen, Anordnungen, Bekanntgaben,* indicating in the Preface: "Nur für interne Parteiarbeit bestimmt und als geheim zu behandeln." A set of the first four volumes is in the Archives of the Hoover Library at Stanford, CA.

8. For this plan of Hitler for the post-war period, see Nuremberg documents published in Vol. 8 of *Nazi Conspiracy and Aggression* (Washington: GPO, 1946), 175 ff.

9. Only a detailed description and analysis of the very original organizational structure of totalitarian movements could justify the use of the onion-image. I must refer to the chapter on "Totalitarian Organization" in my book *The Origins of Totalitarianism* (New York: Harcourt, Brace, 1951).

10. The formulation: "Recht ist was der Bewegung nützt" appears very early, see for instance *Dienstvorschrift für die P.O. des NSDAP*, 1932, p. 38, which preceded the later *Organisationsbuch der NSDAP* that carries the same sentence among the "duties of party-members" in all its editions.

CHAPTER 18

What St. Thomas Means Today

LOUIS DE RAEYMAEKER

Msgr. Louis de Raeymaeker (1895–1970) was born in Saint-Peters Rode, Belgium. After attending the Seminary of Pope Leo XIII and serving in World War I, he received a doctorate from the Institute of Philosophy at the University of Louvain. He then spent three years at the Grand Seminaire de Maline, were he was ordained a priest. De Raeymaeker taught philosophy, psychology, and metaphysics in the scholastic tradition at the Seminary of Maline for eight years, until he was asked to return to the Institute of Philosophy. In the spirit of the Louvain School's founders, Leo XIII and Cardinal Désiré Joseph Mercier, he sought to apply the wisdom of Aquinas to contemporary philosophy by approaching it in a personal way and applying it to Christian intellectual life in its modern social context. In the process, de Raeymaeker made an important contribution to neo-Thomistic thinking by emphasizing the Platonic aspects of Aquinas's metaphysics. Following the Institute's phenomenological focus in the post-war years, he argued in his book, Philosophy of Being, *that Thomistic doctrine could be used to find coherent solutions to metaphysical problems but that philosophers still needed to seek the foundations of this doctrine in individual experience.*

I

There are schools of philosophy whose task it is to guard and transmit a definite doctrine, which generally gets its designation from the name of the thinker who was the first to elaborate it. It is in this sense that one speaks, say, of the Thomist, Scotist, Averroist schools. Certain schools receive their inspiration from the conceptions of a master but endeavor to renovate these conceptions; so we can speak of neo-Kantian schools, neo-Hegelian currents, and neo-Thomist ideas.

It seems, then, that there is more than one way of adhering to St. Thomas, for neo-Thomists have to be distinguished from other Thomists. How do the latter differ from the former? In general, what is the role of the school in the matter of philosophy? What is the meaning of the renewal of traditional doctrine? These are important questions to which the answers are not simple.

In comparing the Thomist school to others, we must recognize its unusual homogeneity. Although seven centuries old and of worldwide influence, Thomist doctrine constitutes a complete and coherent system whose primary theses scarcely permit any divergencies within the school itself.

Nevertheless, there is Thomism and Thomism, since there are Thomists who call themselves neo-Thomists. What is the difference?

It is a fact that the followers of the school do not all take the same attitude toward the writings of St. Thomas. Thus, we need only mention those who confine themselves to the reading of the printed text, unconcerned about the critical value of the edition employed, unsuspecting of any evolution in the vocabulary or ideas of the Angelic Doctor himself. Nor need we delay over those who imagine that an attentive and repeated reading of the text, critically exact, suffices to rediscover its authentic and adequate sense and who are inclined to regard as futile, if not even dangerous from the doctrinal viewpoint, the historical study of questions. Such thinkers ought to realize that it is no easy matter to comprehend perfectly the writings of a great philosopher. The multiple interpretations of the works of Plato, Aristole, Kant, and Hegel readily support this statement. Surely it can hardly be pretended that geniuses of this rare kind could have been inept in their thinking and/or incapable of handling their mother-tongue. But it appears that the more brilliant the philosopher, the more difficult it is to discern his thought. Brilliant conceptions are, in one way or another, inexhaustible and can give rise to innumerable studies. This does not apply to third-rate philosophers. But St. Thomas is a genius. All scientific, critical, and historical resources at one's disposal must be put into operation, so as to do justice to him and to establish his doctrine with greater and greater precision and reality.

Still, is it sufficient for the Thomist to reproduce, if possible with perfect and integral exactitude, the doctrinal conceptions of St. Thomas? Some have thought that for the Thomist school to be worthy of its name it must perform the task of the neo-Thomist.

But if one is convinced of the truth of a doctrine, why renovate it, why rejuvenate it? Does truth grow old? Is it not immutable? Would anyone dream of rejuvenating arithmetic? It is a question worth examining. What are we to understand exactly by neo-Thomism? To find an answer, let us consider the approach of Cardinal Mercier, the most eminent and lucid representative of the neo-Thomist movement launched towards the close of the last century.

Philosophy is a matter of personal research and understanding. Mercier had no place for a philosophy *per decretum*. His adherence to Thomist philosophy is based upon his grasp of its intrinsic truth. Incapable of lying to his own conscience, he could not refuse Thomism his adherence. He was convinced that the conceptions of St. Thomas represent "the most potent effort of thought, the closest solution of the primordial problems of the spirit. . . . It is a duty to subscribe thereto, under pain of betraying the truth."[1]

This nowise implies that one must turn to the past to be locked up in its vaults. There is no question here of returning to the thirteenth century. Mercier said so directly: "There simply can be no question of returning."[2] How then can one be a Thomist?

The question raises a more general problem, that of every "doctrinal renaissance." Is there any way of reviving ideas pertaining to the "past," ideas that are "dead"? Yes and no. An idea is a manifestation of life, the immanent product of a spiritual and personal activity. As with all life, the human spirit develops, flows in time and forms a current of thought which follows its course, or else halts and dies. We must also note that by means of his thought flowing in time man transcends the course of time and reaches definitive truth and its value. But that immutable content of thought can be transmitted, can actually traverse the centuries.

The intellectual life is not inert. It develops in continuity. That is why Mercier declared that Thomism is not "a sort of mummy shrouded in a tomb around which we have merely to mount guard, but an organism that is always young, always in activity, and which personal effort ought to cherish, to sustain, so as to assure its perpetual growth."[3] He did not hesitate to proclaim for the same reason: "Philosophic thought is not a completed work; it is living like the spirit that conceives it."[4] What precisely is the import of these declarations?

Mercier had in mind the conception of science coming more and more to the fore in his own time—science as something which makes itself without ceasing, develops itself indefinitely, and hence is never a completed thing. The spirit then can never refrain from the ceaseless pursuit of its own researches. One can distinguish between "achieved science" that is the *ensemble* of results from completed research already consigned to the manuals of professional teaching and the "science being made"—that effort of research with a view to arriving at new conquests. It goes without saying that it is "science being made," the science of the vanguard, which eminently embodies the scientific spirit and is the warrant of the intellectual and indeed the human future.

But in Mercier's eyes, this was true of philosophy and, consequently, also of Thomism, which to him represented the true philosophy. Thomism had not arrived at the end of its course. It remained and would ever remain alive. But it could not remain alive unless it moved—for to halt life is to die, unless it progressed, unless it was animated with a spirit of research and of conquest. Thomist thought, then, had to grow unceasingly. Yet there is the crucial question. Is it proper to view philosophy in the same way as the sciences? Cardinal Mercier seems to have done just that. In the sciences, discoveries are made and new facts continuously brought forward. Nobody expects to see the end of the era of discoveries from lack of matter to be discovered! So science progresses: new facts do not suppress the old ones; the growth is quantitative. Besides, new facts sometimes throw new light on the old and provide a significance hitherto unsuspected. But in philosophy one gets the impression that the situation is different, for there it is much less a question of discovering new facts. The facts which constitute the object of reflections for the modern philosopher seem hardly to differ from those which form the object of reflections for the philosophers of antiquity. It is therefore necessary to clarify what is "proper" in the course of philosophic thought and to indicate more precisely the nature of the perpetual growth Mercier had in mind.

Undoubtedly, fifty years ago it would have been difficult to give a precise answer to our problem, since the "critique of the sciences" was then only in its infancy and had not sufficiently clarified the nature of modern sciences and philosophy's difference from them. Furthermore, the positivist and scientific spirit saturating the atmosphere of that epoch was too much inclined to lead the philosopher into adopting scientific knowledge as the ideal and model of all forms of cognition and to neglect those distinguishable specific traits of forms of knowledge in the sciences of nature. The situation, however, has changed; and it has now become easier to define and estimate the character of philosophy.

II

For many people, the history of philosophy is an object of scandal. They notice that from the beginning, basically irreconcilable systems have confronted one another. They see how, in the course of centuries, the number of systems has not ceased to grow and that conflict among philosophers has increased. The fact is blatant. But how should we explain it? Because each philosopher pretends he is in possession of philosophic truth, and since there is no common agreement, one might be tempted to conclude that without exception they were all wrong, excepting one perhaps. At least one might be tempted to conclude that philosophic truth ought to be regarded as multiple and variable. This is a conclusion which the categorical tone of each thinker appears decidedly to exclude.

In contrast to philosophy, the sciences achieve an accord of minds without much difficulty, at least regarding conclusions acquired. In the sciences this result followed their establishment on new bases, independent of philosophy. Of course, the result was not obtained with the wave of a magic wand. It took time and considerable effort but it was obtained. On considering the path traversed it is to be remarked that the progress realized was always a function of purifying the scientific notions at work; that is to say, of an effort destined to remove from these notions all purely philosophic content, and to give them a sense either purely mathematical or purely empirical as the case demanded.

Ever since the appearance of scientific thought there has been a great temptation to see in philosophic thought only a provisional, precritical stage destined to make room for scientific thought. Indeed that has been the thesis of the "scientism" which arose in the last century. But the fact is that the prodigious development of the sciences, far from damaging philosophic activity, has stimulated it. The development of the sciences has permitted effective reflection upon the nature of scientific methods as well as upon the import of the result obtained. But this "critique of the sciences" has caused the proper character and limits of the different sciences to become apparent. Thus, one might attempt the identification of philosophy's sphere, situated as it is outside that of the sciences, and avoid confusing ideas, methods, and philosophic results with the notions, techniques, and results relevant to the sciences. Nonetheless, the progress of philosophy has not diminished the number of systems or their fundamental oppositions. Rather, philosophic doctrines breed fast and *inter se* appear more irreducible than ever. The problem must be considered frankly—it may not be ignored. Neither should we halt at the simplest or ridiculous solutions, such as to suppose that all thinkers whose opinions differ from ours lack either intelligence or sincerity. The problem is to find out the source of the multitude of divergent doctrines in philosophy and what is the meaning of the divergence. Is it inevitable or is it not? Is it good or bad?

Instead of applying ourselves to a direct examination of philosophy and the sciences in order to reveal their nature and properties, we shall first and foremost consider the behavior of the philosopher and of the man of science. We shall limit ourselves to pointing out some essential traits which might help in measuring the vast distance separating philosophy from the scientific disciplines.

Take a primary fact. In works of philosophy one normally finds quotations from various writings together with references to other works sometimes going back to remote antiquity. Is that not an indication that philosophic thought is earmarked in some way by and for history? This is hardly the case with the sciences. No one would expect a mathematical treatise to be crammed with quotations. In his laboratory work, the physicist is not much preoccupied about what the Greeks of antiquity or the Arabs of the middle ages thought. This is not to say that the history of the sciences is devoid of interest. Far from it. But if it is true that such history presents an incontestable *historical* interest and even a *philosophical* interest (notably in epistemology), it is not indispensable to the *actual development* of the sciences. Moreover, scientists having precise knowledge of the history of their special disciplines are relatively rare.

Take a second fact. The philosopher of today moves with ease among the philosophic texts of the past. It is no more difficult for him to study a passage from Plato than a page from Heidegger; it demands no greater effort on his part to understand Plotinus than to know the writings of Hegel. He is as much at home interpreting St. Thomas as Edmund Husserl. The situation is quite different in the sciences. Our contemporaries experience a feeling of strangeness reading a scientific treatise of antiquity or of the middle ages. They feel they are moving in another world. If, by study they get to know perfectly the sense of such a treatise, scientists cannot help thinking there is an abyss between the science of old and the science of today.

Take a third fact of decisive importance: that of the persistent actuality of all philosophic thought, whatever the epoch or whatever the human group to which it may belong. From that viewpoint above all, the comparison of philosophy and sciences becomes worthwhile. With each act of scientific progress, the existing situation slides into the past, becomes ensconced there and is bypassed. In science what pertains to the past is deprived of efficacy. It is no longer productive, no longer "actual": its importance is solely of the "historical" order. To be abreast of developments in current science, it is necessary and sufficient to refer to recent writings. The memory of men of science belonging to past centuries may be preserved in scientific laws, institutes, or even streets and places which bear their name—but only the name, not the work. Writings of men of science of the past are but rarely consulted, no matter what their former importance may have been. Their "actual" scientific influence tends towards zero; they belong only to history. Scientifically speaking, they are dead.

How different is the fate of the philosopher! No matter what the value of his successors, his own writings will continue to be read with profit. How much has been published since the Greeks! Yet what philosopher would dispense himself from reading Plotinus, the Stoics, Aristotle, Plato, even the Pre-Socratics? Contrariwise, no man of science would bother himself much with the scientific writings of antiquity. That is why people have come to speak of a *perennial philosophy*, though no one would dream of proposing a perennial physics. And people believe that philosophers of past centuries have not only enriched their own time but also, and above all, have not ceased to contribute to the development of philosophy, thanks to the constantly renewed efficacy of their influence on the minds of men.

We do not for a moment pretend that it is a question of constructing one and the same system according to some plan preestablished from the dawn of our civilization, towards the realization of which all the thinkers of all times have successively labored. Much less do we pretend that philosophy has developed in the course of time just as an organism grows and dies in conformity with a determined law. Such a conception is simplistic. It would not correspond to the reality; nor could it account for, notably, the persistent efficacy of thinkers whose conceptions are antipodal. How could such thinkers collaborate in the construction of such a perennial philosophy?

What then exactly is in question? Let us make a preliminary remark. A great many stars scintillate in the philosophic heaven, some of the first magnitude. But a great many draw their light from these. We will take into consideration only the suns, leaving the others aside for the moment. The situation is thus simplified, for all in all, true creators are relatively rare, in philosophy as in everything else, amounting to some few dozens from Greek antiquity to our own day, including the Arab and mediaeval Christian.

Philosophic reality presents itself to us as follows: Some twenty-six centuries back, there was constituted a "symposium," so to speak, which has continued even to our own day, and in which great thinkers of all times have participated and still continue actively to participate. There is a certain undeniable continuity in the activity of this symposium. In proportion to the passing of the centuries, new thinkers have regularly arisen, who have taken their place in the philosophic symposium. But they did so taking into account the presence of the ancients whose opinions they have noted and discussed, accepting them or rejecting them.

The intervention of these new forces generated philosophic interest, permitted the revival of problems, allowed more light to be cast upon the elements of solution. But all this did not culminate in ousting the ancients. Far from being reduced to silence, they have continued to make their voices heard as of old. The exchange of views in philosophy is made not only among contemporaries but among philosophers of all times, among all members of the philosophic symposium. Young and old form a concert of voices and each performs his part in the philosophic polyphony.

How should we explain these facts? How should we justify them? Let us try to account for a situation that seems paradoxical.

For centuries it has been commonplace to pretend that philosophers have agreed on nothing, neither on the proposed solution, nor even on the terms in which problems are to be posed. In a sense this is true. At the same time philosophic dissensions must not be exaggerated. We must not forget what has been said: philosophers are engaged in a dialogue, discussing among themselves farther than the eye can reach. They have always retained contact and they meet on common ground. It is not exact to hold that they agree on absolutely nothing, despite appearances.

What then are we to admit: that they agree or that they do not? There seems to be no middle ground. However, one must not draw conclusions too hastily, for in a sense there is a mean. In the present case affirmations that are too peremptory, like negations that are too brutal, are out of order. One must be respectful of nuances.

The solution we seek is based on the *personal* mark which characterizes all philosophy. Recall that every *person* possesses an "incommunicable" sense and value proper to himself. This holds unquestionably for the thinker, for the artist, and for the man in the street. There can be but one Demosthenes and one Alexander, one Dante and one Rubens, one Johann Sebastian Bach and one Mozart. To pretend that any other man could be identical with any one of these is senseless. A person is unique in himself.

But if the concrete orientation of a man's life, his "initial project," has impressed upon it the *seal* of the person from whom it proceeds, as has every work of art, so has every philosophic work. We hasten to add that implied here is no purely subjective conception of philosophy. But if this is true, then we will no longer be perplexed by the sight of different philosophic conceptions; and we will understand that the systems, each of which corresponds to a personal inspiration, cannot discard or supplant one another decisively.

We here touch on a fundamental difference between philosophy and the sciences. Unless we take notice of it, we cannot have an adequate idea of philosophy. The sciences, as they have developed, study reality from a strictly abstract point of view, "from the point of view of Sirius," that is to say, from a neutral, impersonal viewpoint, which is not merely universal but univocal, exactly adapted to each and everyone. In the domain of the sciences, needless to remark, it is this viewpoint that imposes itself. At least the results obtained afford sufficient proof of its efficacy.

But philosophy differs from the sciences. By definition it has its own viewpoint. It seeks to explain reality in its entirety. It cannot be content, therefore, with a strictly abstract viewpoint, since it is reality as such—things taken in their sense and value—that it has to consider. For this reason, right from the start, philosophy must uphold a knowledge that is concrete, enveloping in a certain way integral reality, a knowledge covering all without exception, a knowledge that is "transcendental" in the scholastic sense of the word. Such knowledge cannot be reduced to a univocal concept, for it does not occur as the term of a process of abstraction, of abstraction properly speaking (under pain of ceasing to be transcendental, universally enveloping). So philosophy develops on the basis of a fundamental experience which nourishes it, inspires and orientates it, and from which it could not be separated without being deprived of its sap, without becoming withered. But this fundamental experience inevitably carries the mark of the concrete personality who is its subject, so that the philosophic activity itself remains impregnated therewith. This is more so as the experience is richer, denser, more profound, and as the personality is more eminent and powerful.

In a general way, we may limit ourselves to observing that if the same events are not known in the same way by different persons and if, notably, the profound meaning and fundamental value of these events happen to appear to the one and not to the other, the main reason is, that the power of penetration and apocalyptic capacity are far from equal among all men. On final reckoning, it is the finesse and power of the personality that are the cause.

In any system of philosophy two elements are to be accounted for. First, there is the richness and variety of the fundamental significations which personal experience has brought to the surface; second, there is the putting into operation of various means, such as logical reduction and the reduction of concepts and abstract principles, with a view to elaborating a doctrinal *ensemble* solidly framed. Each of these elements is imperatively required in a fully developed system of philosophy. But it seems that the definitive value and import of a philosophic system attach more to the first than to the second of these elements. We all know certain orators, writers, and professors who have important things to communicate and who do so without much order or care. At the same time others show an impeccable order in the exposition of a clear and precise doctrine, a doctrine which, unfortunately, appears to be too clear because it is too empty, too fruitless. To cap everything, it may testify to a personality without depth or density.

The human person is a complicated reality. It envelops man—who is at the same time material and spiritual—in his entirety, but it guards no less his substantial unity. The spiritual and material factors, far from finding themselves there juxtaposed, mutually compenetrate. Together, they form a dynamic structure each of whose constitutive principles operates as a function of the others. The human act, which proceeds from this ordered *ensemble*, reveals to us the principles of the structure and the sense of their correlation. That is why man's "behavior" incorporates and always manifests a human "sense," which as such, is of a spiritual order. But, *vice versa*, by its very definition, the human spirit implies *rapport* with the matter in which it is substantially incarnated. As such, its activity, entirely immanent though it be, is naturally a function of the spatial and temporal order.

St. Thomas does not hesitate to say that the *primal matter* is the principle of individuation of the entire man, and that implies the human *spirit;* and that this *spirit* is identical with the human soul, with the unique principle of life, which is also the unique substantial form of the human soul, with the unique principle of life, which is also the unique substantial form of the human individual, and which therefore is equally a principle of life and a principle of *corporeity.* It would be difficult to conceive a closer union of spirit and matter than that proposed by St. Thomas. This extremely daring theory the Angelic Doctor has not constructed *a priori.* He formulated it in transposing to the plane of substance the correlation which he observed between the material properties and the spiritual properties on the plane of certain data, particularly those alluding to the human activity of knowing. For St. Thomas, man, a conscious personal being endowed with a spiritual life, adheres to the world by all that constitutes him. The essential dependence of intellectual activity in relation to sensible experience is ample testimony of that. The attachment of man to the world is so fundamental, according to the Angelic Doctor, that it persists after death. In the beyond, the human spirit, separated from matter, does not cease to be a soul, a principle of animation. It remains thus "unifiable" to matter, and even now, it is by this relation substantially orientating it toward the cosmic order, that it is individuated.

If human activity is conditioned to this extent by temporal and spatial factors, it goes without saying that Kant's *Critique of Pure Reason* could not have been conceived at Athens in the century of Pericles, just as it would have been impossible for Christian thinkers living in Europe in the thirteenth century to construct the philosophic system of Ramanudja. On the other hand, since human activity is of itself conditioned by the spiritual factors relevant to the intelligence and the will, it is, naturally, endowed with liberty. Within certain limits, those of his auto-determination, human activity is self-constructive and controls its own development. The result is that, within these limits, the interior richness and the force of penetration proper to the person are in proportion to the autonomous development of that person and depend equally on his free choice.

But if it is established that of itself an autonomous factor intervenes—at the same time as other factors and in correlation with them—in the elaboration of personality, if it is established that it is from the thinker's personality that a philosophic system draws its abundance and depth, its proper color, its "timbre," one must conclude that the historical evolution of philosophic thought is not determined solely by factors of the purely logical order. In fact, philosophy does not develop outside and beyond men in some ideal stratosphere. For example, it is undoubtedly possible to connect logically the conceptions of Malebranche with those of Descartes. Nevertheless, as Gouhier emphasizes, if Malebranche's system of ideas did appear, it is because of its conception by none other than Malebranche.

The essential part which liberty assumes in the real development of all human activity leads us to the thought that it is impossible to foresee the future direction of philosophic thought. For the same reason, however, no one can foresee the form that social questions will take in fifty years, or the values that will then prevail.

It is equally understandable why a philosophic genius does not replace another to the point of eliminating him entirely. The diversity of philosophic systems, so far as it corresponds to the variety of temperaments and characters, cannot be considered solely as a deficiency. One could be in perfect disagreement with the conceptions of Plato and admit that if the text of the *Dialogues* had been lost, the intellectual patrimony of humanity would have been seriously diminished. And surely this remark holds for all the great names in the history of philosophy.

It is incontestable that philosophic geniuses are guardians of a value which assures them a real efficacy at all times. They are also the bearers of a personal message which must always be taken into account. But this does not mean that all are of equal value or that everything they have written is of value.

The preceding observations do not lead to relativism, above all if one adds another which is obvious. We have to take into account a certain relativity in our knowledge, and that we also transcend that relativity. It is certain I am always "situated," but it is no less true that I know that, for I proclaim it. My thought always has a personal accent, but that does not hinder me from noticing it myself and comparing my theories to those of others. This implies a point of view which transcends at the same time my person and that of others, since it allows me to turn my attention to myself and to others and to devote myself to a work of comparison. If, however, I do not raise myself to this transcendental plane and if the others are not established there, neither I nor they will be able to meet. We will not be in accord on the content of any idea or on the sense of any word; and *all* dialogue will have to be abandoned. But it is a fact that there is an intersubjective activity and that philosophers have never ceased discussing among themselves. We can take it as established, on the one hand, that our activity of knowing bears a mark of subjectivity, of relativity. On the other hand, we can assume that we transcend it to the point of defining its reasons and tracing its limits. Consequently, since we are in a position to throw an attentive glance upon the history of philosophy, to assist in the role of spectators at the great philosophic symposium, at this universal "round-table conference," we cannot withhold passing a judgment of value. All thinkers do not appear to us as being of equal stature. Indeed among them, there are some who, while offering reflections not devoid of interest, deviate from the truth on important points. But if we are right in not putting them all in one line, why may we not prefer a particular philosopher to all the others, on the supposition that our choice is founded on reason?

To return to the two conclusions already formulated: all human knowledge—and that comprises philosophic knowledge—is marked with relativity since it is the achievement of a person who is finite and situated in space and time. This relativity is ineluctable, for no man alive can free himself from his human limits or escape the spatial and temporal conditions of his existence. Nonetheless, all human knowledge is marked by absoluteness, that is to say that it is established on the plane of truth, for it is accompanied by the consciousness of our relativity, bypasses it, and can bear judgment thereon. And this absoluteness is also ineluctable, since it pertains to an essential element of the person, namely the spirit, the source of an activity (intellectual and voluntary) whose formal object is transcendental, a formal object implying in an indeterminate way all without exception, and that embraces the Absolute.

Is it not contradictory to attribute to knowledge a value that is at the same time absolute and relative? The contradiction cannot fail to appear since the two qualifications, absolute and relative, are imposed on us by the facts. Hence there is not a contradiction but instead a *problem*. How do we reconcile these two properties of knowledge?

This problem, which we cannot scrutinize here, can ultimately be solved only on the metaphysical plane, for the formal object of intellectual cognition is the same as that of metaphysics: being as being. So also, the basic metaphysical problem is that of multiplicity, and therefore of relativity, on the plane of being. How should we explain that there can be beings, multiple, finite, relative one to the other, briefly an order of beings, though the value of being is absolute, excluding whatever is opposed to it? But it is only in solving these problems that we can understand how different beings can attain the same truth, absolute, immutable, unique, while each knows only in his own way, within the limits traced by his finite nature. It is a question of the problem of the participation of being, *perfectio perfectionum*, the solution to which must be sought on the level of a metaphysical structure constitutive of finite being. It must also be sought on that of a relation of total dependence of all finite being with regard to the infinite Being, an absolute source, and therefore creative, of all finite reality, of all participation in the truth.

III

These considerations can help in understanding the role devolving on the "school" in the matter of philosophy, as well as the sense and import of the doctrinal renewal pursued by neo-Thomism.

The results of our inquiry can throw some vivid light on the declaration of Mercier that we make use of the names of Plato, Descartes, Leibniz, Kant, Fichte, Hegel, Wundt, as fully perhaps and as certainly and sincerely as those who range us in the camp opposite to theirs. If we differ from them, it is that we excommunicate no genius, merely because of the age in which he lived, from our zeal to study him.[5] The results of our inquiry can equally help us to understand why one is never satisfied with the philosophic writings of the past: one studies these writings, but one always publishes others, even when one regards himself the faithful disciple of a master. Each thinker has the conviction of having something to say which was never said before, or at least not in similar fashion, and he feels the need to "reveal" this truth which he knows in the way he knows it.

What then is the task of the Thomist?

First of all, he will attach himself to St. Thomas as to a master. Is one to wonder at such an attitude? Surely not. However, it may not be futile to recall a few banal truths on this subject.

Taking him in general, man has hardly changed since classical antiquity. His anatomical structure and physiological functions have remained the same. Has the heart of man been modified to the point where he can no longer know the meaning of the emotional life of the ancients? It seems not, for today we thoroughly enjoy the literature of their epoch. Similarly, we seem to discover ourselves in their ideas, notably in their philosophic conceptions. Despite individual differences, the essential structure of man has remained intact.

Therefore, thinkers of the past may have succeeded in discovering, with regard to man, truths which have lost nothing of their value, on the precise supposition that these truths concern man as he has remained through the course of centuries. What is more, it appears probable that every important thinker has likewise succeeded. Even those who have strayed on some essential points have something to teach us, be it ever so little as Cardinal Mercier took delight in saying: "In every error there is a soul of truth."

We know that the conceptions of philosophers do not contain the same coefficient of truth. Doubtless no thinker has brought out in an exhaustive manner the whole philosophic truth. But it is possible that one or another may have discovered the principal traits of the structure of the real and that he has grasped its fundamental meaning. This being so, it would be rash to contradict it. On the contrary it would be real wisdom to take it into account in further research. But the Thomist is convinced that the philosophy of St. Thomas possesses such a degree of truth, and that is why he holds it as the support of his own personal effort of philosophic research.

It is natural that the Thomist take St. Thomas as a model to be imitated. The Angelic Doctor is a magnificent example of a Christian devoting himself to philosophic research within the framework of his experience as a man who believes. In this respect it is necessary to underline the love of truth which animated St. Thomas, his sincerity in research, his loyalty and humility which induced him to inform himself of all that could help him in his study, and notably to read and study the writings of authors, Greek and pagan, Jew and Arab, as well as Christian, and with sincerity to acknowledge all patches of truth he found. He applied loyally the principle *"amicus Plato, sed magis amica veritas."*—I am much attached to Plato [and above all to Aristotle], but the truth is more dear to me still. However, to have the right to call oneself a Thomist, it does not suffice to take St. Thomas as a model in the sense described. For in the same sense one could just as well call himself Suarezian, Kantian, Hegelian, Bergsonian, etc. . . . But the characteristic of a Thomist is that he pursues his philosophic work in the prolongation of the theories of St. Thomas.

How should such a task be conceived?

We may recall that in every philosophical system, as we have indicated, one can distinguish two elements: on one hand, the logical elaboration of the *ensemble*, and on the other, the inspiration, the spirit, whose creative effort is operative from the start, from the source, and whose vivifying influence invades all the philosophic construction. It is a fundamental experience that procures this source of inspiration. The philosopher's awe has been aroused by this experience and that is why research has been embarked upon. This experience never abandons him; it is in its light that the research progresses. The philosopher ceaselessly refers to his original experience as to a source of light that projects its rays on the *ensemble* of the real and as to a center of attraction which retains and groups the development of thought, at the same time putting a sign upon its movement. It is thus that the philosopher takes the road that leads to the foundations of the real.

To rediscover the living thought of St. Thomas, to recognize its content and import, the Thomist has to rediscover, so far as he is able, the fundamental experience commanding the activity of philosophic thought of the Angelic Doctor. That is not as easy as it appears. Without doubt, St. Thomas is distinguished by the perspicuity of his conceptions and the clarity of his expositions, by his economy of language and his limpidity of style. But all this is accompanied by a profound humility: St. Thomas effaces himself behind the objective truth he exposes; and there he disappears to the point where it is difficult even to envisage the man who constructs this philosophy. A certain shyness prevents him from speaking of himself, of the personal experience that nourishes his philosophic conceptions. Whenever he finds himself constrained to speak, he is satisfied with a passing allusion.

On this point St. Thomas differs a great deal from most thinkers of today. These never weary of dwelling upon the personal experience which sustains their thought. Be that as it may, it is permissible to regret that the Angelic Doctor has not left us a description—let us call it a phenomenological one—of the living basis of his theories. This basis he has at his disposal throughout his philosophic work. St. Thomas draws upon fundamental ideas, "categories," which he himself has abstracted, starting from his personal experience. It was he who gave them their content. This content he knows perfectly and knows whence he has drawn it. Besides, the Angelic Doctor maintains contact with his basic experience. He constantly refers his categories to it, either to give an exact account of their content, or complete them, or deepen them, or, as the need arises, correct them.

Too often Thomists have inherited abstract categories which they themselves have not abstracted and which they employ without referring them to any personal experience. The result is that their philosophic activity unfolds itself only on the levels of a logical analysis of concepts and of the reasoning connected therewith. In addition the categories employed risk having a content devoid of much density or flexibility.

To rediscover the living thought of St. Thomas, one can start from different articulations of the system. A convergent orientation of theses will indicate the place where the fundamental experience lies; however, this orientation could not work except by a study that is pushed as far as doctrinal nuances. Some fleeting indications contained in the texts help to recognize the way. Here is a laborious enterprise, demanding patience, reflection, and penetration.

Of course, it is not the authentic experience of St. Thomas that one will discover, since that is personal and therefore incommunicable. But the Thomist who surmises the nature and place of the master's experience, strives to form a similar experience. This experience is also quite personal and therefore joined to the temporal and spatial situation of the man who makes it. St. Thomas has evolved the fundamental structure of men and of the world. The Thomist is a philosopher who, starting from his own experience, discovers the categories and essential theses of the master's doctrine and who endeavors thereafter to develop his thought along the lines of this doctrine.

As this experience of the Thomist is personal and bears the mark of the man who makes it, it remains infallibly linked to the intellectual and moral atmosphere, especially to the philosophic climate, of the epoch. It is no wonder that the Thomist of today raises problems which were not posed *ex professo* in the time of St. Thomas (e.g., in epistemology), that he has to impose a new orientation on the doctrine (e.g., in cosmology), or that he manages to acquire greater doctrinal density (e.g., in psychology, and notably in questions bearing on "existence"). Possibly metaphysics will least undergo modifications, for more than any other discipline, it deals with really invariable structure, everywhere present and decipherable. But even here the accent can be shifted and produce the impression of real renovation.

One could give examples to illustrate these remarks. It would be fascinating to show on what experience the doctrine of "being," which inspires in such a personal way the whole metaphysics of St. Thomas, is founded; or on what experience the doctrine of the substantial unity of man is grounded, since the Angelic Doctor developed it with such daring insistence. But that would lead us far afield. At any rate, the conclusions we have reached lack neither interest nor importance.

NOTES

Reprinted from *The Review of Politics* 20, no. 1 (January 1958): 3–20.

1. *Revue Néo-Scolastique,* I (1894): 14.
2. Ibid.
3. *Revue Néo-Scolastique,* VII (1900): 320.
4. Ibid.
5. *Revue Néo-Scolastique,* I (1894): 14.

CHAPTER 19

The Thinker in the Church
The Spirit of Newman

FRANK O'MALLEY

Frank O'Malley (1909–1974) was born in Clinton, Massachusetts. He received both his Bachelor's and his Master's degrees at the University of Notre Dame, and stayed on to help the university develop its English curriculum. O'Malley also became one of the first editors of The Review of Politics, *along with Waldemar Gurian. Much of his career focused on studying and teaching the literary and philosophical foundations of the Catholic faith, and his classes at Notre Dame drew vast numbers of students. An active member of the Democratic Party, O'Malley was a vocal proponent of social welfare programs. His involvement in politics as well as his teaching and intellectual life were all informed by his understanding of humanity's relation to God. For O'Malley, this relationship was best realized when Jesus Christ's suffering and love become the end of all human concerns.*

Recent reports reach us from England that a notable element in support of the cause of Cardinal Newman's canonization is the unusual extent of American devotion to him and to his thought. Certainly the name of Newman is great among us. Most American Catholic thinkers would agree with Otto Karrer, writing in April 1947, for *The Review of Politics* on Newman and the spiritual crisis of the Occident, that Newman is probably "the most illustrious religious mind in the modern Anglo-Saxon world."[1] It is clear that he is the truly great eminence at the start of the Catholic intellectual renascence of the past hundred years. In our devotion to him and in our praise of him as a foremost thinker in the Church, it is well to consider what is the justification for the esteem in which we hold him.

What was the spirit of this man who is with us a constant reference and a standard and a sign? We need to determine it carefully because even in the moment of using his name and imprinting it upon a cause or action or point-of-view, we may not actually understand the being who bore the name, and we may not realize the true qualities of the mind and heart of the man we revere and acclaim. Not really understanding him, we can and do readily take his name in vain, abuse the name of one of the greatest modern Englishmen, attach it to enterprises and activities he would surely have abhorred. So we misrepresent Newman. We cry up his name, and do not really care what he said or what he meant or what he was so long as we can comfort ourselves under the splendor of his distinction. Thus, while blessing ourselves with him, we are only confusing ourselves and others, and hardly honoring the human being whose greatness becomes a stereotype, a monumental but hollow word. What, then, was the quality of Newman? What was the real wonder of his humanity, of his spirit as a thinker in the Church, as a man, a teacher, and a prophet? Using Newman's own words as much as possible, we shall try, if not fully at least implicitly, suggestively and quite personally, to answer the question.[2]

I

We can say first that his spirit was liturgical, that is, the spirit of Newman moved within the spirit of the liturgy, the liturgy thought of in its most significant sense as the very rhythm of Christian existence, stirred and centered by the life of Christ. Newman absorbed the liturgical character of existence. He lived by the liturgy. Specifically, applying the words of Romano Guardini, himself a Newman type of thinker in the twentieth century, he was "led by the rule and love of the Holy Ghost to a life in Christ and in Him for the Father." The liturgy is not, as some say, aestheticism. It is real. It demands self-subjection, the disciplining of the inner life, never the flagrant and chaotic cultivation of the ego in the arbitrary and capricious. The liturgy is reality, physical and metaphysical. Neither thought nor emotion, it is "a process of fulfillment, a growth to maturity." It involves not the selfish universe of the individual but all creation: "Under Christ the Head, the Church gathers together 'all which is in Heaven, on Earth, and under the Earth.'" In *The Church and the Catholic and the Spirit of Liturgy*,[3] Guardini explains that in the act of worship directed towards God, everything is linked and "as a whole embraced in the relation with God established by prayer; the fullness of Nature, evoked and transfigured by the fullness of grace, organized by the organic law of the Triune God, and steadily growing according to a rhythm perfectly simple yet infinitely rich; the vessel and expression of the life of Christ and the Christian—this is the liturgy. The liturgy is creation redeemed and at prayer because it is the Church at prayer." This sense of Christ-in-time, of Christ-in-the-universe, of every age flowing and of every man growing in His Great Body—this Incarnational view—Newman had profoundly and it affected and controlled his attitude towards time and man and the problems of time and human society.

These are some very few of the words of Newman, expressing the spirit of the liturgy. Christ, he says, "left His Father's courts, He was manifested, He spake; and His voice went out into all lands. He has taken to Himself His great power and reigned; and, whereas an enemy is the god and tyrant of this world, as Adam made it, so, as far as He occupies it, does He restore it to His Father. Henceforth He is the one principle of life in all His servants who are but His organs. The Jewish church looked towards Him; the Christian speaks and acts from Him. What is prior to Him is dark, but all that comes after Him is illuminated. The Church, before His manifestation offered to Him material elements 'which perish with the using'; but now He has sent His spirit to fill such elements with Himself, and to make them living and availing sacrifices to the Father. Figures have become means of Grace, shadows are substances, types are Sacraments in Him. What before were decent ordinances and pious observances, have now not only a meaning but a virtue. Water could but wash the Body in the way of Nature; but now it acts toward the cleansing of the soul. 'Wine which maketh glad the heart of man' and 'bread which strengthens man's heart' nay, the 'oil which maketh him a cheerful countenance' henceforth are more than means of animal life, and savor of Him. Hands raised in blessing, the accents of the voice of man, which before could not symbolize the yearnings of human nature, or avail for lower benefits, have now become the 'unutterable intercessions' of the Spirit, and the touch, and the breath of the Incarnate Son. The Church has become His Body, her priests His delegates, her people His members." This, Newman appends, is what Christ has done by His coming.

In another passage he declares: "Christ Himself vouchsafes to repeat in each of us in figures and mystery all that He did and suffered in the flesh. He is formed in us; born in us, suffers in us, rises again in us, lives in us; and this not by succession of events, but all at once; for He comes to us as a spirit, all dying, all rising again, all living. We are ever receiving our birth, our justification, our renewal, ever dying to sin, ever rising to righteousness. His whole economy in all its parts is ever in us all at once; and this divine presence constitutes the title of each one of us to heaven; this is what He will acknowledge Himself, and His image in us, as though we reflected Him, and He, on looking roundabout, discerned at once who were His; those, namely, who gave back to Him His image."

Newman also notes that, while Socrates wished to improve man, "he laid no stress on their acting in concert in order to secure that improvement. On the contrary, the Christian law is political as certainly as it is moral. Why is this? It arises out of the intimate relation between Him and His subjects which, in bringing them all to Him as their common Father, necessarily brings them to each other. Our Lord says, 'Where two or more are gathered together in My Name, I am in the midst of them.' Fellowship between His followers is made a distinct object and duty, because it is a means, according to the provisions of His system, by which in some special way they are brought near to Him. . . . The almighty King of Israel was ever, indeed, invisibly present in the glory above the Ark, but he did not manifest Himself there or anywhere else as a present cause of spiritual strength to His people; but the new King is not only ever present, but to every one of His subjects individually is He a first element and perennial source of life. He is not only the Head of His kingdom, but also its animating principle and its centre of power."

Finally, we must cite Newman's famous description of the marvelous Action of the Mass, the central act of worship in the Church: "The Mass is not a mere form of words,—it is a great action, the greatest action that can be on earth. It is not the invocation merely, but if I dare use the word, the evocation of the Eternal. He becomes present on the altar in flesh and blood, before whom Angels bow and devils tremble . . . words are necessary, but as means, not as ends; they are not mere addresses to the throne of grace, they are instruments of what is far higher, of consecration, of sacrifice. . . . Each in his own place, with his own heart, with his own wants, with his own thoughts, his own intention, with his own prayers, separate but concordant, watching what is going on, watching its progress, uniting in its consummation;—not painfully and hopelessly following a hard form of prayer from beginning to end, but, like a concert of musical instruments, each different but concurring in a sweet harmony, we take our part with God's priest, supporting him, yet guided by him."

II

Because Newman's spirit was liturgical—here it has been recorded—it could not have been rationalistic, that is, Newman's vision could not have stopped with the limits of logic, with the walls of the world. The doctrine of the Incarnation, he observes, must be regarded as "the announcement of a divine gift conveyed in a material and visible medium, it being thus that heaven and earth are in the Incarnation united." The universe to Newman, because of his consciousness of the Incarnation, was unfinished. Christ had entered into it and it could never be closed again. The supernatural had touched the natural and the mind of man could not, tidily and categorically, shape it and control it as if it were utterly of itself and by itself. The narrow eye of a narrow reason could see the universe as finished, as perfectly and neatly manageable. But Newman's wide, insightful eye could see it as wide-open to the "effluences of His grace." Yet the civilization in which he lived was essentially rationalistic, just as ours is, narrow, superficial and arbitrary, moving along the surfaces, descending into the depths of the spiritual underworld only in its rarest men, like Blake, Hopkins, Kierkegaard, Dostoyevsky, Solovyev (once termed a Russian Newman), Bloy, and Newman himself. These thinkers, of course, bring to mind the older Pascal and the ancient Augustine. Newman especially, living in the spirit of the liturgy, could not have abided the rationalistic temper of the time. But, note well, that *it was not against reason* that Newman inveighed, only against its usurpations and abuses, the narrowing of the range of human vision into technical formulas, the confinements of logical propositions, and the complacencies of analysis. It is no credit, Newman says, for any man to deal with only what he considers rational. There is much beyond. "No analysis," he remarks, "is subtle and delicate enough to represent adequately the state of the mind under which we believe, or the subjects of belief, as they are presented to our thoughts." Of logical analysis, he says again, that it is but an account of the progress of reasoning: "it does not make the conclusion correct; it does not make the inference rational. . . . It does but give [a man] a sustained consciousness, for good or for evil, that he is reasoning. How a man reasons is as much a mystery as how he remembers." He further says, "While we talk logic, we are unanswerable; but then on the other hand, this universal living scene of things is after all as little a logical world as it is a poetical. . . ."

Newman describes the action of rationalism as follows: ". . . it is rationalism to accept the Revelation, and then to explain it away; to speak of it as the word of God, and to treat it as the word of man; to refuse to let it speak for itself; to claim to be told the *why* and *how* of God's dealings with us, as therein described, and to assign to Him a motive and scope of our own; to stumble at the partial knowledge which He may give us of them; to put aside what is obscure, as if it had not been said at all; to accept one-half of what has been told us, and not the other half; to assume that the contents of Revelation are also its proof; to frame some gratuitous hypothesis about them, and then to garnish, gloss and color them, to trim, clip, pare away, and twist them, in order to bring them into conformity with the idea to which we have subjected them." And Newman suggests what happens when we are content to look at the history of man through a rationalistic focus. "Christianity will melt away in our hands like snow; we shall be unbelievers before we at all suspect where we are. With a sigh we shall suddenly detect the real state of the case. We shall look on Christianity, not as a religion, but as a past event which exerted a great influence on the course of the world, when it happened, and gave a tone and direction to religion, government, philosophy, literature, manners; an idea which developed itself in various directions strongly, which was, indeed, from the first materialized into a system—a church, and is still upheld as such by numbers, but by an error; a great boon to the world, bestowed by the Giver of all good, as the discovery of printing may be, or the steam engine, but as incapable of continuity, except in its effects, as the shock of an earthquake, or the impulsive force which commenced the motions of the planets."

Newman compares the intellectual greatness of the philosophers of the world with the greatness seen in Christ and His Saints: "We know that philosophers of this world are men of deep reflection and inventive genius, who propose a doctrine and by its speciousness gather round them followers, found schools, and in the event, do wonderful things. These are the men, who at length change the face of society, reverse laws and opinions, subvert governments, and overthrow kingdoms. Or they extend the range of our knowledge, and, as it were, introduce us into new worlds. Well, this is surely admirable, so vast is the power of the mind. But, observe how inferior is this display of intellectual greatness compared with that which is seen in Christ and His Saints, inferior because defective. These great philosophers of the world, whose words are often so good and so effective, are themselves too often nothing more than words. Who shall warrant for their doing as well as speaking? They are shadows of Christ's prophetical office, but where is the sacerdotal or the regal? Where shall we find in them the nobleness of the King, and the self-denial of the priest? On the contrary, for nobleness they are often 'the meanest of mankind'; and for self-denial the most selfish and cowardly. They can sit at ease and follow their own pleasure and indulge the flesh, or serve the world, while their reason is so enlightened and their words are so influential. Of all forms of earthly greatness, surely this is the most despicable."

Let us repeat, however, that Newman was not indulging irrationalism or anti-intellectualism; he was not striking out against reason but only against its limitation to a narrow circle of light, the cribbing of its fullness and richness. Newman wanted to enlarge and enliven it in the total personality. In other words, he wanted to make reason ontological as well as logical. Newman lived in the mind; there can be no question of it. But, like Pascal, Newman lived in the mind entirely. His thought was alive with love and feeling; his whole being animated his mind and his utterance. And as with Henri Bergson, Newman was attempting to renew the importance of the intuitive, the knowledge of the heart in an age in which knowledge by logic had made man skeptical. Let us remember, too, Newman's cardinalatial motto: *cor ad cor loquitur.* Newman desired that the mind be capable of the experience of spiritual reality, from which the surface movements of mental acts often estrange it. Christopher Dawson (whose *Spirit of the Oxford Movement* remains a classic of interpretation) has tried, in his *Enquiries into Religion and Culture,* to describe this essential capacity of the soul: "Underneath the surface of our ordinary consciousness, the sphere of the discursive reason, is a deeper psychological level, 'the ground of the soul' . . . this is the domain of the spiritual intuition, the 'summit' of the mind and the spiritual level which is naturally directed towards God."[4]

Newman, somewhat in this vein, has used the term *spiritually-minded* which means "to see by faith all those good and holy beings who actually surround us, though we see them not with our bodily eyes; to see them by faith as vividly as we see the things of earth—the green country, the blue sky, and the brilliant sunshine. Hence it is that, when saintly souls are favored with heavenly visions, these visions are but the extraordinary continuations and the crown, by a divine intuition, of objects which, by the ordinary operation of grace, are ever before their minds." Briefly, Newman wished to reunite the mind and spirit, the mind and man's complete being, a unity destroyed by the rationalistic and aridly academic domination of modern thought.

The fact is that Newman's mind was fixed at the awesome point of Christ, the stitch in history, to employ Claudel's phrase, that cannot be undone. For him, as for Theodor Haecker, a spiritually lustrous Catholic inheritor of both Kierkegaard's and Newman's thought in the twentieth century, writing in his *Journal in the Night*: "Reflection, recollection and turning back to contemporaneity with Christ, is a requirement of *Christian thinking.* And if that capacity is lacking, a man may be a thinker of genius, where thoughts are concerned, but in the strict sense of the word he is not a *Christian* thinker. The life of Christ among men of every kind and position is so full, so complete, that in spite of the difference between life in those times and life today, every man can find a situation in which he can in all seriousness ask the question: what should I have done in that case?"[5] Newman, whom Haecker once characterized as "saintly," would have fitted Haecker's conception of the spiritual man as different from the intellectual man, "though naturally presupposing and including him: he has a whole dimension more, he is the complete man, according to the idea of God, a perfect unity, an incomparable totality, desired by God, and, as *anima naturaliter Christiana*, longed for by man." Haecker might well see in Newman not merely the demonstrator but the communicator, with pulsing power and wondrous style, of the truth of existence. He might see in him the embodiment of the unity of spiritual life and spiritual thought, which does not signify living or thinking without the body or even against the body; it signifies living and thinking hierarchically: "Christianity aims to educate man spiritually; it is hierarchical." But man remains, grandly and warmly, in all the strength of the deep and far-flung stretch of his personality, in all the immensity of his human and eternal possibilities. Newman the *spirituel*, the spiritually-minded, hoped and struggled valiantly to redeem the time of man and to restore the world of the fallen to the purity of its creation by God.

III

Newman's interest in the deepest realization of the personality suggests that his spirit was not just anti-rationalist but positively *humanistic*. Newman was a humanist—in the best sense. His was a Christian humanism, the humanism of the Incarnation, Maritain calls it in *True Humanism*, saying: ". . . the creature will neither be belittled nor annihilated before God, his rehabilitation will not be in contradiction to God or without God, but *in* God. There is but one way of progress for the history of the world, that is, for a Christian order, however, it may be otherwise: that the creature should be truly respected *in* his connection with God and *because* he is totally dependent on Him; humanism indeed, but a theocentric humanism, rooted in what is radical in man: integral humanism, the humanism of the Incarnation."[6]

Newman understood thoroughly that to submit the human intelligence to the service of Christ the King, to use Etienne Gilson's good phrases, was not to deny the intelligence but to cherish it and complete it. Yet, as Gilson comments in *Christianity and Philosophy*, ". . . the everlasting protest of the world against Christians is that they scorn it, and that by scorning it they misunderstand what constitutes the proper value of its nature: its goodness, its beauty, its intelligibility. That explains the ceaseless reproaches directed against us, in the name of philosophy, of history, and of science. Christianity refuses to take the whole man, and, under the pretext of making him better, it mutilates him, forcing him to close his eyes to things that constitute the excellence of nature and life, to misunderstand the progress of society throughout history and to hold suspect science which progressively discloses the laws of nature and those of societies. These reproaches, repeatedly flung at us, are so familiar as to cease to interest us; nevertheless it is our duty never to cease replying to them and above all, never to lose sight ourselves of what is the reply to them. Yes, Christianity is a radical condemnation of the world, but it is at the same time an unreserved approbation of nature; for the world is not nature. It is nature shaping its course without God."[7] It is clear from these statements by Gilson that Newman could have made them too. And Newman could have subscribed to Gilson's further remarks: "What is true of nature is eminently true of the intelligence, the crown of nature. . . . There is a love of the intelligence, which consists in turning it towards visible and transient things: that belongs to the world; but there is another which consists in turning it towards the invisible and the eternal: that belongs to Christians. It is, therefore, ours; and if we prefer it to the first, it is because it does not deny us anything the first would give us, and yet it overwhelms us with everything which the other is incapable of giving us." This is a great way to indicate the mystery of the Christian man and his attitude towards life. The Christian can "love the work of God while hating sin which deforms it."

This was the real import of Newman's approach to reality. Having had a grasp of the spirit of the liturgy, Newman also had truly the finest sense of the nature of man, as delineated by Maritain in *Education at the Crossroads*: ". . . man as an animal endowed with reason, whose supreme dignity is in the intellect, and man as a free individual in personal relation with God, whose supreme righteousness consists in voluntarily obeying the law of God; and man as a sinful and wounded creature called to divine life and the freedom of grace, whose supreme perfection consists of love."[8] Newman had the deepest understanding of man and the problems of man. He knew that man is not to be taken "for what he is not, for something more divine and sacred." He knew that it is not the way of the world to see man or to have man as man regenerate but rather as the natural man. Newman's own definition of man has an admirable realism: "Man is composed of body and soul; he thinks and he acts; he has appetites, passions, affections, motives, designs, he has within him the lifelong struggle of duty with inclination; he has an intellect fertile and capacious; he is formed for society and society multiplies and diversifies in endless combinations his personal characteristics, moral and intellectual. All this constitutes his life. . . ." Again, Newman describes man: "Man is a being of genius, passion, intellect, conscience, power. He exercises these gifts in various ways, in great deeds, in great thoughts, in heroic acts, in hateful crimes. He founds states, he fights battles, he builds cities, he ploughs the forest, he subdues the elements, he rules his kind. He creates vast ideas, and influences many generations. He takes a thousand shapes, and undergoes a thousand fortunes. . . ." Also, "He pours out his soul in fervid poetry; he sways to and fro, he soars, he dives, in his restless speculations; his lips drop eloquence; he touches the canvas, and it glows with beauty; he sweeps the strings, and they thrill with an ecstatic meaning. He looks back onto himself, and he reads his own thoughts, and notes them down; he looks out into the universe, and tells over and celebrates the elements and principles of which it is the product. Such is man. . . ."

Over this natural man, however, Newman did not despair. As a Catholic, he could not. For the wounds of nature, the mortalities of time, the Catholic believes, can be restored by the grace of Christ, the Creator and the Redeemer of nature and time. In one of the majestic and moving sermons that remain the great clue to his spirit, Newman declares: "The regenerate soul is taken into communion with saints and angels, and its life is 'hid with Christ in God' . . . And while it obeys the instinct of the senses, it does so for God's sake, and it submits itself to things of time so far as to be brought to perfection by them, that, when the veil is withdrawn and it sees itself to be, where it has ever been, in God's Kingdom, it may be found worthy to enjoy it. It is this view of life, which removes from us all surprise and disappointment that it is so incomplete: as well might we expect any chance event which happens in the course of it to be complete, any casual conversation with a stranger, or the toil or amusement of an hour. . . . Why should we be anxious for a long life, or wealth, or credit, or comfort, who know that the next world will be everything that our hearts can wish, and that not in appearance only, but truly and everlastingly? Why should we rest in this world, when it is the token and promise of another? Why should we be content with its surface, instead of appropriating what is stored beneath it?"

For this reason Newman could not have plunged himself into darkness and despair in the face of his own or of mankind's failures. Even though he observed and experienced personally the weaknesses of man's mortality and of man's civilization, the spirit of Newman was in general not tragically tormented, not shatteringly disturbed. In this he was not quite like those men who are to be remembered with him: Kierkegaard, the Danish poet in effect and perhaps the greatest Protestant religious thinker of the nineteenth century; Brownson, the fabulous American fighter for the life of the Church, for the things that are not Caesar's; and Hopkins, the poet in fact, the seer, the spiritual son of Newman, and actually born just the year before Newman's conversion. Newman's spirit had a quiet grandeur, like the quiet ocean rolling rhythmically or like great fields moving in winds that are even. Contrastingly, the spirit of Hopkins is sometimes like the upsurging of the ocean in cliffs of tumult or like the terrible sharp pain of scythes and knives, cutting into the very grain, the vein of the soul. Newman's spirit, it seems, is more exactly akin to that of Maritain, Gilson, Guardini, Dawson, Haecker, Pieper, Marcel, or to that splendid trio of French priest-thinkers in the Church, Danielou, de Lubac, and Bouyer, the last himself a priest of the Oratory and a lifetime as well as preeminent student of Newman's life and spirituality. At any rate the vision and the realization are always acutely there but the suffering is less apparent than in a Hopkins or a Kierkegaard or a Bloy.

IV

Newman realized that the Christian *had to be* in the world, and face the demands of the world, even though he was not of it. This is why it is hard to understand Sean O'Faolain's statement, in tracing Newman's way, that he was tainted by "a sense of man's pitiable weakness" before God and destiny.[9] Among other implications here is man's inadequacy to face the realities and mysteries of life. But in the sermon last cited, Newman emphasized that "the regenerate soul must submit itself to things of time so far as to be brought to perfection by them." Man possesses the strength and the grace to deal with the things of time and to improve his mortal lot. In dealing with the things of time and the problems of the world, Newman showed himself to be wonderfully sympathetic, comprehensive and variously-minded; not only could he deal with theological and philosophical subjects, but he turned his mind also to historical and political and social questions, to the problems of literature in the modern world, and, notably, to the problem of the education of a man through the humanities in a civilization preoccupied with matter. In an important essay, done for *The Review of Politics* in April 1945, Alvan S. Ryan reveals the development of Newman's political thought and compares it with that of contemporary Catholic thinkers like Maritain and Don Luigi Sturzo.[10] He concludes that Newman was "keenly alive to one of the major problems of our time," the problem of "the Church, the State and the human person in their mutual relations" and that Newman's ideas on this difficult subject have even today "real pertinence and validity." But perhaps Newman's most striking work was his attempt to create a Catholic University, a place where his engrossment with the relationships between human and divine wisdom, his celebrated devotion to the unity of knowledge and the unity of intellect and spirit, would have an impress upon young Catholics and enable them to become true thinkers in the Church. The "failure" of the Catholic university has been duly discussed. But, as Fergal McGrath properly points out in *Newman's University: Idea and Reality,* the record of Newman's work for the university must be seen as "the inspiring effort of a great mind to establish a perfect synthesis of the puzzling pattern of human existence, and to honor it as an ennoblement of the concept of man's destiny."[11]

In a certain sense, Newman's effort has received its recognition and justification not only in Ireland but in the United States. He would have been interested in and pleased by the extraordinary edifice of the higher learning built by American Catholics. Still he would have been distressed by our inveterate instinct, in the fashion of the day, to materialize rather than to spiritualize the intellect, to plunder the treasures of the soul by turning the wonderful and mysterious mind inside out in the adulation of bald facts, figures, and formulas. In times past our Catholic colleges may have tended to stress religion at the expense of intellectual development. Today infected by the rationalism of the American intellectual climate, they dedicate themselves as fervently as the next to the achievement of "soul-lessness," and the need to reunite the intellect and spirit is generally unrecognized. He would have been distressed by our too often programmatic, organizational, business-like, and bureaucratic rather than personal, reverent, and organic approach to the problems of the instruction of our youth. Indeed he appositely and wisely remarks: "An academical system without the personal influence of teachers upon pupils, is an arctic winter; it will create an ice-bound, petrified, cast-iron University, and nothing else." Do we not recklessly multiply the rigors of an arctic winter and thus create a cast-iron rather than a warmly and dynamically intellectual Catholic education? He would have been dubious about the prevailing belief that, through mere system and industriousness rather than through the free release of the spirit, we can develop first-rate excellence in our students. Discussing the formation of a Catholic literature in the English language as one of the special objects which a Catholic university ought to promote, he goes directly and sensibly to the heart of the matter. First-rate excellence in all matters is "either an accident or the outcome of a process; and in either case demands a course of years to secure. We cannot reckon on a Plato, we cannot force an Aristotle, any more than we can command a fine harvest or create a coal field."

In the variety of his humane concerns, he has been said to have shown exceptional talent in music. He wrote verse (more significant for its revelation of the mystery of Newman than anything else) and fiction. No matter how far removed from his own realm of life, he could always respect and appreciate any nobility of intellect, spirit and achievement. One of his contemporaries, James Anthony Froude, reminiscing about the high church revival, wrote of Newman justly: "Newman's mind was world-wide. . . . He had studied modern life and modern thought in all its forms. . . . He was interested in everything. . . . Nothing was too large for him, nothing too trivial, if it threw light upon the central question, what man really was and what was his destiny. . . . He seemed always to be better informed on common topics of conversation than anyone else who was present. He was never condescending with us, never didactic or authoritative; but what he said carried conviction along with it. When we were wrong he knew why we were wrong and excused our mistakes to ourselves, while he set us right. Perhaps his supreme merit as a talker was that he never tried to be witty or say striking things. Ironical he could be, but not ill-natured. Not a malicious anecdote was ever heard from him. Prosy he could not be. He was lightness itself—the lightness of elastic strength . . . we had never seen such another man . . . he was careless about his personal prospects. He had no ambitions to make a career, or to rise to rank and power. Still less had pleasure any seductions for him. His natural temperament was bright and light; his senses, even the commonest, were exceptionally delicate. I was told that, though he rarely drank wine, he was trusted to choose the vintages for the college cellar" (quoted from W. F. Stockley in his *Newman, Education and Ireland*[12]). This, then, is a portrait of a highly civilized as well as a genuinely distinguished person, a man of grace, sensibility and control.

V

Because he was what he was, Newman could not abide the Philistine, the creature who is, in Arnold's terms, vulgar in beauty and taste, coarse in morals and feeling, and dull in mind and spirit. He could not comprehend the bourgeois mind, the enemy of light and the children of light. His spirit was hierarchical and aristocratic in the finest way, that is, he was anti-mediocre, hostile not to the people but to mob-judgments and mob-standards, hostile to the complacency, the pharisaism, the traps of routine and the spirit of dead-leveling, the lack of order and distinction in modern civilization. He understood, like Kierkegaard, Bloy, Peguy and Bernanos, how essentially unheroic, undistinguished the spirit of modern man is, how fearful of taking real risks, how desirous of comfortable physical security, how indifferent to the true comfort of the soul—in his own word, how *tepid*. Newman says of small souls: "They who are ever taking aim, make no hits; they who never venture, never gain; to be ever safe is to be ever feeble." And he advises against bourgeois prudence: "Calculation never made a hero"; "Every great change is effected by the few, not the many; by the resolute, undaunted, zealous few," that is to say, by those who are not mediocre, not tepid, who are willing, right in the spirit of Christ, to give themselves for others.

But the warm, vibrant spirit of Christ and His Church does not prevail in the cold, mechanic reaches of modern civilization. Instead the spirit of The Public flourishes and overwhelms, a spirit brilliantly described by Kierkegaard, in *The Present Age*, as a gruesome abstraction: "the public is neither a nation, nor a generation, nor a community, nor a society, nor these particular men, for all these are only what they are through the concrete. No single person who belongs to the public makes a real commitment . . . a public is a kind of gigantic something, an abstract and deserted void which is everything and nothing . . . a public is something which everyone can claim . . . the most dangerous of all powers and the most insignificant: one can speak to a whole nation in the name of the public and still the public will be less than a single real man, however unimportant." Kierkegaard adds: "More and more individuals, owing to their bloodless indolence, will aspire to be nothing at all—in order to become the public." Similarly but more moderately, Newman reflects upon the public in terms of public opinion, which he says he would not be so irrational as to despise. Still, he expresses the feeling that "too often it is nothing else than what the whole world opines, and no one in particular. Your neighbor assures you that everyone is of one way of thinking; that there is but one opinion on the subject; and while he claims not to be answerable for it, he does not hesitate to propound and spread it. In such cases, everyone is appealing to everyone else; and the constituent members of a community one by one think it their duty to defer and succumb to the voice of that same community as whole."

In an era, then, that has succumbed to "the public," in an age of massification, what happens to the Christian and the Christian nation? Kierkegaard bluntly replies in his *Attack upon "Christendom"*: "We are what is called a 'Christian' nation—but in such a sense that not a single one of us is in the character of the Christianity of the New Testament. . . . The illusion of a Christian nation is due doubtless to the power which number exercises over the imagination." Likewise, Newman summarizes the real life situation of most men known as Christians: they "would go on almost as they do, neither much better nor much worse, if they believed Christianity to be a fable. When young, they indulge their lusts, or at least pursue the world's vanities; as time goes on, they get into a fair way of business, or other mode of making money; then they marry and settle; and their interest coinciding with their duty, they seem to be, and think themselves respectable and religious men; they grow attached to things as they are; they begin to have a zeal against vice and error; and they follow after peace with all men. Such conduct indeed, as far as it goes, is right and praiseworthy. Only I say, it has not necessarily anything to do with religion at all. . . ." These men called Christians "venture nothing, they risk, they sacrifice, they abandon nothing on the faith of Christ's words." The Christian man, the Christian mind is "religious morning, noon, and night; his religion is a certain character, a mould in which his thoughts, words and actions are cast, all forming parts of one and the same whole. He sees God in all things; every course of action he directs towards those spiritual objects which God has revealed to him; every occurrence of the day, every event, every person met with, all news which he hears, he measures by the standard of God's will. And a person who does this may be said almost literally to pray without ceasing." The Christian mind is one "ever marveling, and irreligious men laugh and scoff at it because it marvels." Out of the wonder of the Christian mysteries, the faithful and prayerful mind will be raised, refined, made reverent and expectant.

Yet Newman discerned the rarity of such men and minds in the midst of progressive modern civilization. It cannot be said that Newman did not understand the need for civilization. He realized and said that civilization is the state to which man's nature points and tends; it represents the "use, improvement, and combination of those faculties which are his characteristic; and, viewed in its idea, it is the perfection, the happiness of our mortal state." But the civilization of his experience, with its neglect and omission of the Christ-form in human thought and action, with its frustration and misuse of the graces and purposes of Christ's Church in history, simply was not contributing to the perfection and happiness of our mortal state. It was contributing only to the death of spirituality. So there rises from the very soul of Newman the absolute anguish—not normal for him—caught into the overpowering pressure of this unforgettable utterance, a cosmic cry of pain, where he wonders what will ever now, in civilization itself, help to arrest the onward course of willful and perverse human nature. He writes: "Starting then with the being of a God (which, as I have said, is as certain to me as the certainty of my own existence, though when I try to put the grounds of that certainty into logical shape I find a difficulty in doing so in mood and figure to my satisfaction) I look out of myself into the world of men, and there I see a sight which fills me with unspeakable distress. The world seems simply to give the lie to that great truth, of which my whole being is so full; and the effect upon me is, in consequence, as a matter of necessity, as confusing as if it denied that I am in existence myself. If I looked into a mirror and did not see my face, I should have the sort of feeling which actually comes upon me, when I look into this living busy world, and see no reflection of its creator. This is to me one of those great difficulties of this absolute primary truth, to which I referred just now. Were it not for this voice, speaking so clearly in my conscience and my heart, I should be an atheist, or a pantheist, or a polytheist when I looked into the world. I am speaking for myself only; and I am far from denying the real force of the arguments in proof of a God, drawn from the general facts of human society and the course of history, but these do not warm me nor enlighten me; they do not take away the winter of my desolation, or make the buds unfold and the leaves grow within me, and my moral being rejoice. The sight of the world is nothing else than the prophet's scroll, full of 'lamentations and mourning and woe.'"

The very complication and prolongation of the texture and structure of this remarkable sentence carry the intense and complex passion of the suffering and heartfelt mind of Newman: "To consider the world, its length and breadth, its various history, the many races of men, their starts, their fortunes, their mutual alienation, their conflicts; and then their ways, habits, governments, forms of worship; their enterprises, their aimless courses, their random achievements and acquirements, the impotent conclusion of long-standing facts, the token so faint and broken of a superintending design, the blind evolution of what turn out to be great powers or truths, the progress of things, as if from unreasoning elements, not towards final causes, the greatness and littleness of man, his far-reaching aims, his short duration, the curtain hung over his futurity, the disappointments of life, the defeat of good, the success of evil, physical pain, mental anguish, the prevalence and intensity of sin, the pervading idolatries, the corruptions, the dreary hopeless irreligion, that condition of the whole race, so fearfully yet exactly described in the Apostle's words, 'having no hope and without God in the world'—all this is a vision to dizzy and appall; and inflicts upon the mind the sense of a profound mystery, which is absolutely beyond human solution."

All this does not mean that Newman rejected nature or civilization. It means only that he could not endure a world going its own defiantly irreligious and irreverent way. It means that Newman, the Catholic, the sensitive realist and "imperial intellect" could not help being dizzied and appalled by the debased and debasing features of modern civilization. As the magisterial and spiritually-minded thinker in the Church, completing himself within the spirit of the liturgy, Newman had ever to be against progressing with the untoward spirit of the age. Unfortunately, too many of us as members and thinkers of the Church in America move against this spirit, even while using Newman's name. We are daily capable of demonstration, systematization, "objectivity," analysis, examination and self-examination, not to mention administration. But we are not capable of Newman's power of "communication," of his "realization," of transforming by our touch all that comes before us in human existence. We do not live in the reality, the self-subjection of the liturgy. We live by formulas and slogans and calculations. We weave arguments and wield propositions but we lack spiritual vision. We are not people of heart, people of love. We are, as any occasion requires, narrow and partisan and prejudiced. We are unwilling honestly and dynamically out of our own resources and values provided by the Church to deal with the problems of time, in politics or education or literature or science, because we tend to regard our light and our truth as inferior, as inadequate; we do not respect it enough; so we are afraid that it will fail. We are not proud of it and we will not try it. We are "reflective," in the Kierkegaardian meaning. We mirror, echo, reflect our environment instead of returning to Christ His image. We merely imitate the ways of the world and provide little light or "eternal form" to it. We are not really too sure about what man is or man's society. In our conception of order and discipline, we are Calvinists. We do not really regard man as regenerate, as open to grace though wounded. We rush into darkness and despair when failure befalls our enterprises. Or, mediocre in spirit, we do not attempt anything at all lest our set ways be altered seriously. We make progress only in routine or in things that are external. We like our realities to be huge, statistical and public. We seem incapable of true inwardness as well as openness, of "marveling." We work hard to organize and mechanize the spirit, to destroy its standards and values and hierarchies. We level the spirit and bury it and, in unmarked graves, we bury ourselves with it. Our poor spirit is clearly not the rich and full spirit of Newman. It is instead the spirit of the age. But we are pharisaical. We breathe the name of

Newman and incinerate his being. On the earth that is moving onwards we live by our wits—and on the verge of nothing. Intellectually and spiritually—and humanly—we perish. And we perish in pathetic poverty.

NOTES

Reprinted from *The Review of Politics* 21, no. 1, Twentieth Aniversary Issue: II (January 1959): 5–23.

1. Otto Karrer, "Newman and the Spiritual Crisis of the Occident," *The Review of Politics* 9, no. 2 (April 1947): 230–46.

2. In the present essay, the pattern of Newman's spirit is drawn through his words, most of them long familiar to his American readers. They have been chosen chiefly from the following volumes, listed in order of appearance in the text: *Lectures on Justification*; *Parochial and Plain Sermons* IV, V; *Discussions and Arguments; Loss and Gain; Oxford University Sermons; An Essay in Aid of a Grammar of Assent; Essays Critical and Historical; Sermons on Subjects of the Day; Meditations and Devotions; The Idea of a University; Historical Sketches III*; and *Apologia Pro Vita Sua*. [When this article appeared, O'Malley indicated that it would be followed by a second set of reflections. These thoughts were published as "The Thinker in the Church II: The Urgencies of Contemporary Catholic Thought," *The Review of Politics* 25, no. 4 (October 1963): 451–59. Ed.]

3. Romano Guardini, *The Church and the Catholic and the Spirit of Liturgy* (London: Sheed & Ward, 1935). [In this note and in subsequent ones, I provide bibliographical information about O'Malley's references but not exact page numbers because he does not include them in the text. Ed.]

4. Christopher Dawson, *Enquiries into Religion and Culture* (New York: Sheed & Ward, 1933).

5. Theodor Haecker, *Journal in the Night*, trans. by Alexander Dru, 1st ed. (New York: Pantheon Books, 1950).

6. Jacques Maritain, *True Humanism* (New York: C. Scribner's, 1938).

7. Etienne Gilson, *Christianity and Philosophy* (New York: Sheed & Ward, 1939).

8. Jacques Maritain, *Education at the Crossroads* (New Haven: Yale University Press, 1943).

9. Sean O'Faolain, *Newman's Way* (London: Longmans & Green, 1952).

10. Alvan S. Ryan, "The Development of Newman's Political Thought," *The Review of Politics* 1, no. 7 (January 1945): 210–40.

11. Fergal McGrath, *Newman's University: Idea and Reality* (New York: Longmans & Green, 1951).

12. W. F. Stockley, *Newman, Education and Ireland* (London: Sands & Co., 1933).

CHAPTER 20

Human Estrangement and the Failure of Political Imagination

GLENN TINDER

Glenn Tinder (1923–), the youngest contributor to The Review of Politics *in this volume, was born in California and received his PhD from the University of California at Berkeley in political science. He spent most of his career teaching at the University of Massachusetts. Tinder places himself in the existentialist tradition of Karl Jaspers, Søren Kierkegaard, and Gabriel Marcel, though he considers Plato and Kant to be the philosophers who influenced him the most. His thinking was also shaped by Russian authors, particularly novelists such as Fyodor Dostoyevsky and Boris Pasternak. Tinder's writings are based on a Christian perspective of philosophy, history, social concerns, and especially politics. He has argued that political order is best attained not through all-encompassing ideologies like Marxism, but instead through Christianity's more accurate understanding of the potential and limitations of human beings. Tinder has advocated what he calls a "prophetic stance," in which human beings recognize the limits of political community in contradistinction to the Kingdom of God. At the same time, he has argued for the importance of rectifying injustice and holding out hope for the formation of a just polity and a true human community.*

It is a well-known human tendency to continue applying remedies after the problem for which they are suitable has been solved. Concentration on a particular difficulty becomes habitual to such a degree that its disappearance may not be immediately realized. And new problems may take its place for some time without being noticed.

One wonders whether a condition of this kind does not prevail at present in the politics of Western nations. For one thing, are not the traditional issues of political controversy losing their power of compelling attention and arousing emotion? For a period of roughly a century prior to the outbreak of World War II there was intense political activity and excitement; this was due above all to the conditions of life which early industrialism imposed on the working classes. Proposals for governmental intervention in the economy caused heated disputes; socialist doctrines were evolved and contested; and the rise of trade unions caused fierce altercations. While these questions are still discussed, they do not give rise to the bitterness they once did; it is probably not going too far to say that most people no longer care greatly about the alternatives involved. At the same time, if there has been a waning of those emotions associated with the old political issues this hardly represents the attainment of a new confidence and serenity. On the contrary, uneasiness is perhaps more profound and widespread than it has been for centuries. As old disputes become less intense, fear for the very foundations of civilization grows. Phenomena as diverse as Hitlerism, nuclear weapons, and juvenile delinquency are among a host of unfamiliar specters. Finally, however, despite an apparent slackening of the furor surrounding old controversies and the emergence of new fears, the terms of political debate do not seem to have been substantially altered. There are of course new questions, such as those concerning atomic energy, and new forms to old questions, especially in the sphere of foreign policy. Yet at the center of political life there still continue the old disputes regarding the proper role of government in the economy, the merits of socialism, and the appropriate power of unions. Those concerned with politics still in many cases define their basic philosophies—whether "liberal" or "conservative"—in terms of the positions they take with respect to these issues.

The consequence is that one may feel that most political debate is not very enlightening. Social reformers and party managers may seem often to be pursuing arguments which fail either to ignite former emotions or to give utterance to those now prevailing. To what extent the challenges of a generation or two ago have been mastered, and what the causes are of the present disquietude, the various political disputants, embroiled in old debates, may not help one to discover.

There is reason, then, to ask whether our political imagination is not captive to passing problems, and perhaps oblivious to others appearing in their place.

I

That there is at present a maladjustment of some kind between imagination and reality in the sphere of politics seems highly probable in view of the fact that political spokesmen and leaders, on the one hand, and many of the most sensitive writers and thinkers, on the other, are apparently not worried by the same realities. It is, in very different ways, the business of both to understand and illuminate their society's troubles. Now, however, they seem in many cases hardly to occupy the same world. The gulf between those who rule and those who receive literary and philosophic respect—between the powerful and the perceptive—is in numerous instances so wide that the two cannot be brought into the same realm of discourse without one's experiencing a sense of absurdity. Is there, for example, any point of contact between the worlds of President Eisenhower and Albert Camus? Such a question is not ridiculous in view of the fact that both are leading figures in what is supposedly a single civilization. Even a fairly cursory comparison of the attitudes present in what may be called, for the sake of brevity, the political and literary minds will make clear a disquieting distance between them.

First, what are the major ideas and values among political men at present? In view of the variety of situations and problems which Western nations confront it might be assumed that there can be no simple answer to this question; and it must be granted that no generalization can totally comprehend twentieth-century political life, in all of its complexity. Yet if one endeavors to view the forest as a whole, a rough configuration seems to emerge. The leading issue of recent times has certainly been that of economic and social inequality. This issue was posed by the working class early in the industrial revolution; and it is at the heart of such controversies as those over the proper extent of governmental economic activity and the due prerogatives of labor unions. A century ago, and even a few decades ago, the challenge of inequality was doubtless more intensely felt than at present. It gave rise to European socialism, and it underlay, in America, the New Deal and all the political turbulence surrounding it. Much of the impact of the Bolshevik Revolution in 1917 was due to its claim to represent the one adequate way of destroying the unjust privileges of the upper classes.

It is to be emphasized, however, that the issue of inequality still dominates the political imagination. After all, the socialists still constitute the major reform parties in Europe; "liberals" in America still derive their spirit and aims from the New Deal; and the sole ideal significance of the Soviet Union, as well as some measure of its power in the world, is due to its continuing to stand, however hypocritically, for an ending of the class inequalities supposedly involved in capitalism. It is assumed, in Great Britain, in most Continental countries, and in America, as it has been assumed for decades, that progressive political leaders will devote themselves to effecting a more equal distribution of wealth and to removing inequities from which the common people supposedly suffer. Even the problems of international politics, colored as they are by the struggle between communist and free-world ideologies, reinforce this concern. Probably, as suggested above, the passion behind the old words has lessened greatly; and the most discerning of contemporary political leaders are more troubled and less certain than were their counterparts a few decades ago. Nevertheless, if one can imagine a blending of all recent political utterances does he not hear emergent above the babble of voices the promise that the masses of people will receive greater wealth and will be removed from the sway of unfair privilege?

It may seem that this describes the imagination of reformers but not of political men in general. In the first place, however, political imagination is presumably exercised to a greater degree by reformers than by other parties. Conservatives are avowedly less imaginative and more satisfied with what is or has been. In the second place, conservatives have to a great extent been forced to follow the lead of reformers. The Republican party in America, for example, accepted and even extended New Deal measures; Conservatives in Great Britain made clear to the electorate their acceptance of most Socialist-established institutions. Thus one is justified in saying of the contemporary political imagination in general that in its light the great problem of human society is that of bringing economic and social justice to the common man.

Yet this does not at all correspond to the insights of a great many contemporary writers and thinkers. It would of course be impossible adequately to summarize in brief compass the various literary assessments of the present situation. Yet if one selects names at random from twentieth-century writers he is apt to be struck by the fact that, while many of them paint present life in somber tones, they are relatively unconcerned with the supposed social and economic oppression which excites political minds. For example, the people delineated by Sherwood Anderson in *Winesburg, Ohio,* suffer deep anguish; but this anguish has no apparent relationship to class structure or to economic conditions. The desperation experienced by the characters in Hemingway's *The Sun Also Rises* is apparently unrelated to the problem of inequality. It is generally thought that Franz Kafka's novels contain penetrating accounts of the human experience in the twentieth century; but whatever may be the central theme of Kafka's obscure and disturbing books it does not seem to be the need for equal justice among classes. These are only random examples, but the roll could be almost indefinitely extended. One thinks, for example, of Thomas Wolfe, Scott Fitzgerald, and John P. Marquand; of Albert Camus and Boris Pasternak. Among writers of nonfiction, too, there are many who seem little concerned with the problem of class inequality. An example from among the most serious works of social analysis in this century is Ortega y Gasset's *The Revolt of the Masses*. More recently, David Riesman has described conditions which have seemed to many profoundly threatening to human society but which are apparently unconnected with exploitative class relations. John Kenneth Galbraith's *The Affluent Society* is a current example of the literature which identifies problems extremely serious but largely distinct from the traditional preoccupations of political life. This list too could be far extended; Irving Babbitt, Waldo Frank, Walter Lippmann, Karl Jaspers, and Gabriel Marcel are some of those whose names might be added to it.

On the basis of so heterogeneous a compilation of names one obviously cannot infer very much concerning the positive convictions of contemporary writers and thinkers; one can, however, begin to see the contours of the chasm which separates the political from the literary and philosophic mind. The latest generation of writers is particularly noteworthy in this respect. In almost every part of the world are heard the voices of young people who, viewing afresh the life about them, feel a deep repugnance for it but find little that rings true in the reformism of their fathers. John Osborne, among Britain's "Angry Young Men," is as little attracted to the institutions of socialism as he is to the monarchy and the Established Church. In America Jack Kerouac has expressed a revulsion from traditional patterns of social life which, however distasteful in some of its manifestations, is apparently genuine, widely shared, and altogether uncontainable in the old-fashioned forms of political protest. In France, the novels of Françoise Sagan, while at once lucid and feminine in comparison with Kerouac's, express, both in their desperate hedonism and in their total political detachment, a state of mind not altogether unlike that of the "Beat Generation." And from beyond the "Iron Curtain" has come *The Eighth Day of the Week* in which a young writer, Marek Hlasko, expresses the disgust of Polish youth for both the works and the ideals of the communistic older generation.

Candidates for public office, and various socialist and liberal spokesmen, continue to avow the primal importance of providing for the common man in greater abundance and fairer measure. How many writers of stature would endorse this emphasis? A few, perhaps; but not many. The artistic and philosophic imagination of this age is filled with dread and foreboding; but it is difficult to perceive that these feelings are in any way caused, consciously or unconsciously, by inequality in the relations of classes.

Some might argue that variance between the insights of writers and the views of political leaders is to be expected and should not cause concern; artists and thinkers, it may be asserted, must always have more intense experiences and thus draw more extreme conclusions than other people. But the disparity between the literary and the political imagination is not simply one of emphasis; it seems to be a difference in basic orientation and meaning. Furthermore, there is so much evidence that civilization is in serious trouble that complacency before the anguished testimony of contemporary literature is difficult. In the nineteenth century, men secure within the structures of Hegelianism or aggressively confident in the tenets of positivism, men in a world without great wars and living in the expectancy of endless progress, could dismiss Nietzsche as rabid and eccentric; they could ignore Melville's strange tale of an old sea captain who neglected business and chased a white whale to his own and his ship's destruction; they could remain unaware of the tortured works of Dostoyevsky and Kierkegaard. These were solitary and incomprehensible cries. But they are not solitary any longer; a great many have taken them up. And they are not incomprehensible; multitudes have experienced the moods which produced them. It seems the obvious duty of political men to look again at our situation and to see whether there are not realities to which they have been blinded by obsolete slogans and outworn commitments.

II

One fact which might be revealed by such a reexamination is that the problem of class conflict and mass oppression has, within the industrially advanced nations, been largely solved. This is due mainly to the immense and expanding material wealth which modern industry produces. It is true that even in America there remain pockets of poverty. But these affect small minorities only; and while they are indefensible, they obviously constitute a condition far different from the exploitation of the masses which occurred under earlier industrialism and which did so much to shape the sensibilities of liberals and socialists. In addition to this lingering poverty among minorities, there are many remaining inequities which do not perpetrate actual hardship. It is not to defend these inequities, however, to observe that they do not constitute the grave social ills they might in less affluent societies. The average person in the industrialized West enjoys an astounding abundance as compared with his counterpart in all earlier ages. The American or British wage earner may lack many things which the examples of the opulent and the enticements of the advertisers have caused him to desire. But doubtless Aristotle, and most Greeks of his time, would say that he possesses vastly more than he needs in order to live well.

The rather indiscriminate fervor of many liberals and socialists for the extension of welfare measures can appear highly ludicrous if one reflects on the degree of welfare which almost everyone already enjoys. This is not to imply that there should be no further increase in our welfare, but only that its indefinite extension is not a goal properly to excite the passions of reformers.

But one may question whether the ancient problems of economic oppression can be so casually set aside. After all, human beings are not easily satisfied. "The naughtiness of men is a cup that can never be filled," wrote Aristotle; "it is the nature of desire to be infinite." It must be admitted that the maturing of industrialism does not make the ending of class conflict automatic or inevitable. But it seems to render it very possible. It is not simply that industry provides a great quantity of wealth; this quantity is usually expanding. Thus the demand for more is not necessarily a demand for redistribution. In addition, industrial advance is apt to entail not only the production of ever greater quantities of goods but also the increasing refinement of techniques for entertaining and distracting the general population. The newspapers, magazines, sports, and television programs of the present day would perhaps be tranquillizers potent enough to quiet class animosity even in the absence of the multitudinous comforts which serve the same end. One who doubts the logic of this argument, however, may confirm at least its conclusion empirically. Class conflict and mass oppression are facts of primary significance in very few Western nations at present. Socialists may deplore the ebbing of class consciousness; but they can hardly deny it.

Some students of modern society would admit that the development of industrialism has made anachronous the notion that the primary form of social injustice is the oppression of the proletariat by the owners of property; they would argue, however, that new and equally sinister dominations have come to prevail. The most famous statement of this theme is perhaps that contained in James Burnham's *The Managerial Revolution*.[1] The author views mid-twentieth century society as involved in a revolution as decisive in regard to the distribution of power as was the process of industrialization which enthroned the industrial bourgeoisie. A more recent argument that there exist new controlling groups is contained in *The Power Elite* by C. Wright Mills.[2] This sociologist asserts, with considerable elaboration and detailed illustration, that Americans at the present time are ruled by cliques which include not only capitalists, but also politicians and military men. If, then, the conclusions of these studies are valid, old patterns of mass oppression are simply being replaced by new ones.

One point which may be made in regard to these arguments, is that even if men now are under the domination of new elites, these elites are certainly not equivalent to and probably do not even include, in their highest circles, those who can be accurately termed "managers." So far as single economic enterprises are concerned, it is a commonplace embodied not only in Burnham's book but in many others that the control of the managers is increasingly displacing that of the owners. It is not made out by Burnham, however, that the aims of the managers differ from those of the owners; and it is acknowledged that if they come to do so in any particular case the owners may replace the managers. In view of these considerations the decline of owner control seems less significant for the distribution of power in single industrial organizations than it may at first seem to be. With respect not merely to individual enterprises but to society as a whole, Burnham's argument is even more questionable. Both German Nazism and the American New Deal are treated as exemplifying, and carrying through, the "managerial revolution." But this depends on the drastically implausible assumption that both Franklin D. Roosevelt and Hitler are to be regarded primarily, not as skilled mass leaders, but as managers or agents of managers. There can be no doubt that the power of managers has in some ways greatly grown in recent decades. But there is considerable doubt that the managers can be viewed as a new ruling group, predominant over capitalists and politicians, and having the power to control and exploit the masses. Mills may be cited in this connection. Studying the American power structure a decade-and-a-half after Burnham, he does not include managers as such among the supreme holders of power.

But what of Mills' wider elite? Are we ruled, if not by managers, then by capitalists, politicians, and soldiers? Are these actual or potential exploiters of the masses? The point to be made here is of a different order from that concerning Burnham's book. Mills' argument is far less extreme than Burnham's, and it would be difficult to deny that it is valid in attributing considerable powers to a relative few. In the context of this essay, however, what is noteworthy is the extent to which these few must please the masses. Political, industrial, and military leaders in the various Western nations can do many things; but they cannot, with impunity, abuse the masses or even allow themselves any great latitude of indifference to mass desires. The politicians, despite loose talk to the contrary, are moved almost exclusively by their anxiety to please the multitudes who elect them; if they are irresponsible, it is by virtue of groveling submission, not callous inattention, to the wishes of the people. Perhaps more widely suspect than politicians are the capitalists. Yet surely it is plain that despite the shocking injustices of the early years of industrialism, the industrial owners have, through both ballot and market, been brought within boundaries tolerably in accordance with mass welfare demands. This is indicated not only by the strength in all Western countries of socialist and welfare-oriented parties; it is shown also by the triumph within most parties of a more or less egalitarian ideal of social and economic justice. The popularity of a twentieth-century Malthusianism, with deductions as ruthless as those drawn by dominant groups in the nineteenth century, is unthinkable. The subservience of capitalists to mass desires is reflected even in the behavior of American industrialists. These are among the most powerful and unrestricted in the world; yet, as the most casual look at American society shows, whatever they are doing to the American people they are not, in the usual sense of the word, exploiting them. "Our normal position," asserts a prominent automobile manufacturing executive recently, "is one of abject prostration at the feet of our customers." One has to agree, even if regretfully, that this is probably true. As for military men, it seems hardly to need saying that however great their powers in some directions are, they do not include the power to outrage or to ignore the expectations of the masses as interpreted by politicians and capitalists.

On these grounds it appears that the concern of political leaders for the economic and social standing of the multitudes is somewhat irrelevant. These multitudes have in various ways become dominant in most modern societies in the West. Capitalists, politicians, and managers must all, in various ways, serve them. This is not to imply that no injustices remain and that there are no men and groups receiving more than their share. Such conclusions would be absurd. The point is that these injustices no longer affect the very foundations of the society; they can continue only on the sufferance of the masses who are subject to them.

If mature industrialism thus elevates and gratifies the multitudes, how is it to be explained that throughout the West leaders in various reformist groups and parties persist in the search for inequities and in the announced determination to bring about a more equal justice? One reason is simply that numerous wrongs are still to be found, and that those who find them fail to understand that they are now grievances of detail rather than essential elements in the social system. It is to be noted, furthermore, that there is political profit in this misunderstanding;

there are greater prospects of popularity in promising more to the masses than in telling them that they already have all, and perhaps more, than they need. But the persistence of the reformer's sensitivity to mass exploitation is due in part to factors lying much further back in history. For over two millennia there have been thinkers who have defined injustice primarily in terms of class oppression. As early as Thucydides, *stasis* was identified as the great threat to just society, and this view was a commonplace of political speculation in the era prior to that of industrialization. The horrors of the early factory system merely recast and confirmed it. The industrial revolution was a very misleading event. The fact that the earliest industrialists coerced and impoverished their workmen made it difficult to foresee that in time, due not only to the pressures of electoral and market demands but also in order to have a willing and competent laboring force, they would be compelled to educate and enrich those under them.

This may appear to be a very "conservative" line of argument. But, in ultimate intention, it is not. For if the evils many seem to discern in present society are not really there, others as threatening to human dignity and perhaps harder to counter have taken their place. The fault of the contemporary political imagination lies not simply in its bewildering alertness to a passing danger, but in its blindness to a menace now very much at hand.

III

This menace, like the class antagonism which has long dominated political imagination, is a kind of disintegration. But it does not set group against group, and its workings are not usually spectacular or sanguinary. Its corrosions may spread beneath appearances of cohesion and harmony. Its ultimate effect is to leave men feeling cheerless and abandoned; but this effect is often produced with such unobtrusiveness and tact, as it were, that those subject to it may at first be unaware of it or even welcome it. To distinguish it from *class* disintegration, it may be termed "*mass* disintegration."

The spread of some kind of social decomposition other than that represented by antagonism between classes was obvious in the early stages of the industrial revolution, especially in England. Workingmen were not only divided from owners; they were torn from their places of birth and their ancestral occupations, and were denied satisfactory relations with their fellow workers, their families, and the products of their work. Their energies and lives were consumed by a process ruthlessly indifferent to their true potentialities. Mass disintegration has appeared at various times in history and possible causes are diverse. That which now prevails, however, was most violent in its incursions during the early period of industrialization.

Men could not avoid being aware of it. Those most conscious of its virulence, however, tended to attribute it to the oppression of workingmen by the owners of industrial property. The disruption of the laborer's organic relationships with his fellow men and the world was regarded merely as part of the maltreatment which he underwent at the hands of his industrial masters. Thus *mass* disintegration was reduced to *class* disintegration. Broadly speaking, the whole socialist movement followed this line; equality was made the overriding concern. Karl Marx, for example, described acutely the effects of machinery and factory discipline on the personalities, homes, and skills of the workers; but he assumed that these conditions would pass when the oppression of the proletariat by the bourgeoisie was ended. This attitude, in various forms, became fundamental in the reformist political mentality.

As the conflict of classes gradually dies away, however, it becomes apparent that mass disintegration is not simply a function of class disintegration. Despite the fact that the distinctions and animosities between proletariat and bourgeoisie are becoming less marked men are not more perfectly integrated with society and the world around them. On the contrary, to direct one's attention to some of the plainest characteristics of contemporary life is to perceive that almost every basic relationship into which a human being might enter has been dangerously attenuated.

(1) A disjoining of man and nature has taken place through a twofold movement which has shifted peoples not only into cities but also indoors. These two movements are not necessarily connected; city life in the ancient world was to a great extent an outdoor life. In the chief nations of the Western world today, however, most persons live in cities and spend the greater part of their time, both in work and play, indoors. A complementary and recent development is the spoilage of rural and natural places. Through the spread of suburbs, country areas are becoming residential; with the growth of population and the increasing swiftness of travel rural towns are being urbanized; and places at one time wild now are often heavily populated with vacationers. In perfecting his technological mastery man seems to be closing the gates between himself and the rest of creation. It would be rash to assume that through gardening and golf, and movement to the suburbs, these gates can again be opened.

(2) Distinct from, although often closely allied to, his attachment to the natural world is man's capacity for growing roots in a particular place. This capacity is beautifully represented by the Greek scholar A. E. Zimmern in a passage in which he attempts to evoke the feeling for his city of a boy in ancient Athens:

He loved every rock and spring in the folds of her mountains, every shrine and haunt within the circuit of her walls. He had watched every day from his childhood the shadow creeping slowly across the market-place and the old men shifting their seats when the sun grew too hot. He could tell the voice of the town-crier from the other end of the city, and had made a special study, for private performance, of his favourite butt of the comedian in his last year's play. . . . He never forgot the festival of a god or a hero. . . . He was never tired of listening to his father and his uncles telling stories of raids and battles against the men beyond the range. . . . And when his city brought forth not merely fighters and bards, but architects and sculptors, and all the resources of art reinforced the influence of early association and natural beauty, small wonder that the Greek citizen, as Pericles said, needed but to look at his city to fall in love with her. . . .[3]

It would be difficult to estimate what percentage of the population in present Western nations has suffered the loss of roots of this kind, or has been denied the possibility ever of forming them. But the percentage is certainly high; and it represents not only the havoc of warfare, but the less sanguinary effects of the mobility which modern industrial society imposes on most of its participants. The "Displaced Person" only experiences in its most painful form a condition which affects many persons, even among the outwardly fortunate. It is, furthermore, a condition which often cannot be avoided simply by resolving to remain settled; one is apt to discover that the place where he is established is being transformed about him. Thus modern men, either because they must themselves move, or because all about them is in movement, find homelessness forced upon them.

(3) How far and with how little recognition the process of disintegration has gone can be discerned in the relationship of men to their possessions. It is generally assumed that property, at least in articles of personal use, is highly valued in the Western world; it is supposedly only in communism and in extreme forms of socialism that the desirability of personal ownership is denied. In actuality, however, the connection of the individual with the physical objects about him is becoming more and more purely external and utilitarian. (This is true especially

in America. But through the very refinement of industrialism which is offensive to many, America reveals prospects lying before all societies.) Everyone is familiar, from the arguments of Locke as well as from personal experience, with the possibility of embodying oneself in physical objects; there is a certain kind of community between a human being and articles which he has made or has for a long time used. But this community, like others, is being destroyed. The property of many persons today is made up largely of standardized units manufactured for any one of millions of possible purchasers. Many of these units are designed soon to be obsolescent; they are bought on credit, and may be sold again before they are fully owned. To say in these circumstances that a high value is set on personal ownership is obviously somewhat misleading. Contemporary peoples have the use of a great many things; but there is a sense in which they own less than people have owned in most periods of history.

(4) One is capable of establishing bonds not only with nature, with place, and with the instruments of his daily life, but also with the past and the future. It is possible in appropriate circumstances to gain a sense of historic continuity, which involves understanding and respect relative to the lives of preceding generations and a consciousness of carrying forward the meaning contained in those lives. This constitutes a kind of rootedness in time. But largely because of the speed of technological change it is almost impossible today for the ordinary person to understand sympathetically the lives of past generations; even those of his parents and his grandparents may seem foreign. And due not only to the swiftness and unpredictability of these technological changes, but also to the portents of world catastrophe which they contain, the future is plunged in darkness. Thus contemporary man is uprooted in time, as well as in space; sundered both from the past and the future, he leads an existence which—to him—is historically meaningless.

(5) Mass disintegration inevitably has an important effect on the relations among persons. It is possible here only to mention some of the most conspicuous manifestations of this effect. In the first place, some of the conditions described above have repercussions in the relations of men. Mobility, for example, necessarily entails an attenuation of personal relations; and the severance of men from past and future involves not only a dividing of living generations but the loss of a kind of historic community which can extend far into the past. In the second place, there are conditions not already cited which have adversely affected human relations. Marx long ago called attention to the "cash nexus." Despite the changes which have occurred since Marx wrote, societies as preoccu-

pied with manufacturing and selling as are most of those in the West today necessarily give many relationships monetary foundation or color. Specialization is another facet of contemporary life which, while it is inescapable and facilitates a certain kind of personal development, is a significant obstacle to the attainment of community. Finally, modern totalitarianism is a systematic effort to destroy, on a wide scale, true communication and to establish in its place all-inclusive patterns decreed by the leader. Of course even in conditions which are most corrosive fragments of community endure; thus in most contemporary societies, enclaves of friendship can be built up and guarded. But these are apt to be constricted and beleaguered achievements.

These are the major reasons for believing that contemporary society is subject to a dissolvent process not yet recognized within the scope of the political imagination; Gabriel Marcel refers tellingly to a "broken world." The individual facts cited here are well-known. They obviously do not constitute a complete description of the process of disintegration, nor do they explain its ultimate causes. They do, however, make it appear that almost every contact which human beings desire and value has been weakened or broken. The enjoyment of nature is difficult and occasional; one's roots in a place are taken up or not allowed to form; possessions stand in a largely outward and merely instrumental relationship to the personality; the past is obscure and the future almost totally darkened; the more deep and satisfying contacts among persons, always difficult, have become more fragile. These circumstances of course vary greatly in their impact on persons, vocations, and peoples; but relatively few in the West can altogether escape them.

To comprehend the nature of mass disintegration, however, it is insufficient merely to note the objective characteristics of the process; it is necessary also to perceive its ultimate meaning in the subjective life of the individual.

IV

The eventual result of the separation of man from nature, place, possessions, past and future, and fellow man is that those subject to the process feel themselves strangers in the universe. They become conscious of a cosmic homelessness. One may protest that this is an awareness simply of the human situation, and that man feels estranged, not because of social conditions, but due to his melancholy ability to perceive the ultimate precariousness of his position in the universe. There is some validity to this protest; the present period has made us more aware of our cosmic, as well as our historic, fate. Yet if men must live on the edge of the abyss, they have found it in many ways more tolerable to do so as it were encamped together. It is these encampments which are being ravaged, and individuals are left solitary and filled with terror.

Is this not the experience—ignored in most political circles—which is reported by many of the most sensitive writers and thinkers? According to Albert Camus, for example, being is absurd and man's fundamental condition is one of alienation. Camus' first novel, which has become widely known, is aptly entitled *The Stranger*.[4] Similar insights are readily found in a great deal of contemporary fiction. Joseph K., in Kafka's *The Trial*, is in a basic sense a stranger; most of those who move through *The Sun Also Rises* and *Winesburg, Ohio*, are strangers. Anyone familiar with recent fiction can add titles to this list. On the side of philosophy, it may be said that the entire existentialist movement, with all of its diversities, has grown from an intense realization of human estrangement. Some existentialist writers find new homes, while others call for an acceptance of homelessness. But most of those classed among the existentialists share a conviction that the old structures, which have given form to human relations and meaning to the universe, have collapsed, leaving men desolate and exposed.

There is an heroic response to this situation: let man affirm his own insular integrity and attain grandeur through the courage which this requires. Nietzsche, for example, demands men strong enough to overcome the nausea felt on realizing the absurdity of the world and able to assert themselves gloriously in philosophy and art. Camus calls for the resolute patience of Sisyphus.

Perhaps a few (however, as Nietzsche insisted, not more than a few) have this strength and ability. But the present process of dissolution renders individual integration, even on the part of the most gifted persons, exceedingly difficult. For example the volume of knowledge makes it impossible even for those who devote their lives to learning to be acquainted with more than a small segment of reality. Correspondingly, the vocational specialization which in one way or another is forced on almost everyone entails the selection and development of only a portion of an individual's potentialities. And the demands of large-scale organization may lead to the abandonment even of that fractional integrity which is attained through specialization; this happens when engineers advance in the corporate hierarchy, when doctors become hospital administrators, and when professors give up teaching to enter university administration. Another way in which mass disintegration invades the domain of inward order is brought out by Erich Kahler, in *The Tower and the Abyss*, when he comments on the disintegrating effects of the huge volume of unrelated impressions and scraps of information one receives through modern media of communication. A comparable result, in the realm of impulses and interests, may come from the superfluity of instruments which modern industrialism bestows. People surrounded by great wealth are apt to lose their sense of purpose and do simply what their various possessions prompt them to do. Thus in industrial societies the heterogeneity of the industrial product may be reproduced in the personalities of individuals.

These are only examples. They suffice, however, to bring into focus the fact that mass disintegration does not leave standing even the single individual. The heroic integration of the self is, at least for most persons, altogether impossible. One tends to be reduced to a luminous center, distinct both from a meaningless world and from his own faculties and emotions. This predicament is powerfully delineated in the philosophy of Sartre. And the existentialists in general, in rediscovering the self, have found, not a full organic individual, but an isolated center of freedom. "All that's left," remarks one of the characters in Pasternak's *Doctor Zhivago*, "is the naked human soul stripped to its last shred."

There is nothing surprising in the fact that a world of strangers is also a world dominated by large organizations and by the spirit of adjustment to the group. Men who are uprooted are in many cases ready material for bureaucracies, advertisers, and the leaders of mass movements. They are sufficiently lost to be attracted by specious promises of unity; the deprivation of purpose which their isolation may entail enhances their willingness to subordinate themselves to the group. Accordingly, the various studies which point out the growth of organization and the spread of ideologies of "togetherness" are not in conflict with those works which emphasize the fact of estrangement.

But men are not, for the most part, truly brought together by the organization and conformity so conspicuous in the modern world. The unities effected are largely objective; they are not communities. Far from counteracting estrangement, the pressures of organization and mass opinion may actually deepen it. By hindering one from being what he really is they necessarily destroy, at the same time, the possibility of true contact with others. Thus men outwardly alike and working in harmony may inwardly feel forsaken and alone. David Riesman dramatically caught this truth in the title of his well-known book, *The Lonely Crowd*.[5]

A summary view of the state of affairs so far sketched suggests a multiple paradox. Various political leaders and their supporters still speak as though the chief social problem were the possibility of the multitudes being unfairly treated by upper class groups. In actuality, the antagonism of classes is increasingly

submerged beneath the sovereignty of mass opinion and the power of large organizations. As this mechanical fraternity replaces the warfare of classes, however, the individual underneath, neither beset by class divisions nor truly integrated within his society, is solitary and desperate.

V

It is "the stranger," far more than the proletarian, who now demands understanding on the part of those with political power. A century ago men's imagination
needed awakening to the justice and power behind the claims of the proletariat.
But in the Western countries this awakening has been largely accomplished.
There is, of course, still a massive proletariat in the world beyond the Western nations; and it is true, as is often argued, that this host will in time bring disaster on
mankind if their dissatisfactions do not find a remedy. But the challenge which
the backward and non-industrial countries present is not a good reason for trying to postpone meeting the equally serious challenge implicit in the condition
of estrangement. It is doubtful that "the stranger" will indefinitely wait.

The alienated, no less than the proletariat, are potential world destroyers.
Estrangement gives rise to the sense of a meaningless world. What can one do
in the face of such a world? One possibility is suicide; thus Albert Camus' argument that being is absurd is at the same time a meditation on suicide. However,
another possible response to absurdity is, in Dostoevsky's phrase, to "launch a
curse on the world." Instead of destroying the self, the attempt is made to destroy
the world which condemns the self to isolation. This entails, in contrast to the solitude and silent despair of self-annihilation, the fanaticism of mass-movements.
If this seems wildly conjectural one should consider, on the one hand, Sweden,
with its fulfilled socialism and its soaring suicide rates, and on the other hand
the destructive fury of Hitlerism.

In other words, the ultimate peril implicit in the condition of estrangement
is that of nihilism. When *class* disintegration was viewed as the major form of
injustice, it was both logical and natural to fear civil conflict. However, as the antagonism of classes gives way to *mass* disintegration, the threat of civil conflict is
replaced by that of nihilism. In the last century three great writers were, in various ways, prophets of nihilism: Dostoyevsky bespoke the "underground man,"
and "the possessed"; Nietzsche proclaimed the "death of God," and the duty
thus imposed of demolishing the old framework of values; and Melville depicted

Ahab's vengeful effort to kill the white whale. In the present century we have in many respects been struck by the prescience of these writers. It is not fanciful to fear the prophetic accuracy of their nihilistic visions.

In this situation the alternatives and prospects outlined in the prevailing political imagination have little meaning. "The stranger" is indifferent to the choice between capitalism and socialism; he has little interest either in "conservatism" or in "liberalism." These alternatives derive from the old problem of factional conflict, and have little relevance in societies pervaded by mass disintegration and threatened by nihilism. The projects of reformers, furthermore, are apt to be irrelevant or even harmful. For example, the indiscriminate enhancement of material well-being, which tends to ensue from the politics of the welfare state and the policies of the more "progressive" capitalists, may work to solidify patterns of disintegration. Even the protection and widening of civil liberties is in present circumstances of less significance than many suppose. For example, if there is any cause now in America which would seem to be worth all the support which can be given it this is the according of equal rights to the Negroes. Yet one who has fully taken cognizance of the realities of mass disintegration cannot feel confident that if all present trends continue, including those which are equalizing opportunities among races, the Negro will, a century-and-a-half in the future, be a more truly fulfilled human being than he was a century-and-a-half in the past. This does not imply that there is any justification for maintaining inequality among races. It simply reflects the profound ambiguity which attaches to the latter-day destruction of ancient injustices.

It is not only in matters of internal policy that commonplace attitudes are invalidated or impaired by obliviousness to mass disintegration. A great deal of the thought at present devoted to international relations almost certainly would be more fruitful were it more alive to the possibilities of nihilism. The importance of world politics today derives above all from the peril of total war. While it is generally acknowledged that war of any kind is an evil, it is the present threat of war carried to the end of total destruction which makes politics among nations a subject of urgent attention and thought. But why is there a danger of total war? Partly, of course, because of the possibility, implicit in the possession of weapons of unusual destructive power, that an accidental collision of national interests will kindle a conflict which is all-consuming but not really intended by any of its participants. The peril of total war can hardly be dissociated, however, from the capacity of men to be moved by a will to total destruction. The problems of total war and nihilism are closely related. Mankind might destroy itself with no one wishing it; but this seems unlikely. Probably, if such an event comes to pass it will be because some men willed it. So long as we are oblivious to mass disintegration, and to the nihilistic proclivities which may arise from it, the imagination of those who deal with international relations is necessarily to some degree crippled.

Simply stated, the essential weakness of the contemporary political imagination lies in its insensibility to the ultimate questions of political life. These have to do, not, as the title of a popular book on politics has it, with "who gets what, when, and how," but with the nature of the good life. They have to do not merely with the apportionment of means, but with the discovery and pursuit of valid ends. This is not a newfangled view; it is the classical conception of political thought. Plato's greatest work is indistinguishably about politics and morals; and Aristotle's inquiry into the nature of the good life, his *Nicomachean Ethics*, is a kind of preface to his *Politics*. It is true that certain events since the time of Plato and Aristotle—above all, the rise of the Christian Church—have given us an altered conception of the scope of politics. But government still is inescapably concerned with many problems bearing on the quality and ends of life; for example, with what is taught and to whom, with the bestowal of honor, and with beauty of environment. The idea that politics touches only the relatively secondary problems of physical security and economic distribution is in part a reflection of the failure of political imagination which is the subject of this essay.

This failure is part of the price paid for the appalling forms of class disintegration which developed with the industrial revolution. The inequities of the early factory system were so shocking that the attention of those whose thoughts and energies ran in political lines was riveted to problems of material distribution. Thus arrested by the task of providing for all persons a share in the new industrial wealth, the question as to the ultimate purpose for which this wealth should be used was not very seriously asked.

The condition of estrangement, however, cannot be ameliorated merely by redistributing material goods. The demand of men who are alienated is not for greater affluence, but for values which command loyalty and for a way of life which fulfills potentialities. Estranged men are not reconciled merely by the equalization of economic and social status; their need is for a rediscovery of meaning, and for a restoration of integrity to a "broken world." These demands and needs are not apt to be met unless the political mind moves to deeper levels of imagination and thought than those to which it has, during the past century or two, become habituated.

NOTES

Reprinted from *The Review of Politics* 21, no. 4 (October 1959): 611–30.

1. James Burnham, *The Managerial Revolution* (London, 1941). [James Burnham (1905–1987) was a former Trotskyist who broke with communism, worked with the Office of Strategic Services, and later gained attention as a conservative author and commentator. Ed.]

2. C. Wright Mills, *The Power Elite* (Oxford: Oxford University Press, 1956).

3. [Tinder is likely referring to Sir Alfred E. Zimmern, *The Greek Commonwealth* (Oxford: Oxford University Press, 1931). Ed.]

4. [Camus' novel, *The Stranger*, was originally published in 1942 as *L'Étranger*. Ed.]

5. David Riesman, *The Lonely Crowd* (New Haven: Yale University Press, 1950).

CHAPTER 21

Common Good and Common Action

YVES R. SIMON

Yves Simon (1903–1961) was born in Cherbourg, France. He completed his doctoral thesis on the Aristotelian-Thomist tradition at the Institut Catholique de Paris, where he first encountered Jacques Maritain. He was also influenced by the works of Pierre-Joseph Proudhon whose commitment to social justice he admired, even while rejecting his anarchist politics. With the outbreak of conflict in Europe, Simon came to the United States to lecture and teach, holding positions first at the University of Notre Dame and then at the University of Chicago. Although he was reluctant to allow his personal faith to intermingle with his philosophical writings, Simon became recognized internationally for his adaptation of the teachings of leading Catholic thinkers, such as Aquinas, to contemporary concerns such as opposing fascism and promoting democracy. He was a strong believer in the idea that democratic citizenship requires an education in basic values. While an interest in practical issues ran through all of his scholarship, he also displayed an ability to comment on a dazzling array of basic philosophical issues, including the nature of free choice, the limits of reason, the pursuit of happiness, and mind-body problems.

Anarchy is rarely or never upheld with consistency. In the pedagogy of Rousseau, there is a set purpose to let the child be guided by natural necessity rather than by human command, and to let him learn from the experience of physical facts rather than by obedience. "Keep the child solely dependent on things; you will have followed the order of Nature in the process of his upbringing. Never oppose to his unreasonable wishes any but physical obstacles or punishments resulting from the actions themselves—he will remember these punishments

in similar situations. It is enough to prevent him from doing evil without for-
bidding him to do it . . ." (*Emile*, II). Remarkably, the theory that the method of
authority is a poor substitute for the pedagogical power of nature has been accepted, in varying degree of enthusiasm or reluctance, by most schools of pedagogy and has demonstrated lasting power. Yet the authority of parents and tu-
tors is present throughout pedagogical theories, even when it is passed over in
silence. Childhood is the domain where the suppression of all authority is obviously impossible. The most radical constructs of anarchy, as soon as they rise
above the level of idle rhetoric, admit of qualifications so far at least as the im-
mature part of mankind is concerned. Anti-authoritarian theorists, with few
exceptions if any, do not mean that authority should disappear or that it can
ever cease to be a factor of major importance in human affairs. What thinkers
opposed to authority generally mean is that authority can never be vindicated
except by such *deficiencies* as are found in children, in the feeble-minded, the
emotionally unstable, the criminally inclined, the illiterate, and the historically
primitive.

The real problem is not whether authority must wither away: no doubt, it
will continue to play an all-important part in human affairs. The problem is
whether deficiencies alone cause authority to be necessary. It is obvious, indeed,
that in many cases the need for authority originates in some defect and disappears when sufficiency is attained. But the commonly associated negation, that
authority never originates in the positive qualities of man and society, is by no
means obvious and should not be received uncritically. The supposition that authority, in certain cases and domains, is made necessary not by human deficiencies but by the very nature of man and society—this supposition is not evidently
absurd. To hold, in some *a priori* way, that it does not deserve examination would
merely evince wishful thinking of the least scientific kind. The truth may well be
that authority has several functions, some of which would be relative to deficient
states of affairs and others to such features of perfection as the existence of
human communities, their actions, and their achievements.

If any functions of authority originate in nature and plenitude rather than in
deficiency, it can be reasonably conjectured that they are relative to common existence and common action. Granted that in many cases authority merely substitutes for self-government, the theory that it also has essential functions must
be tested first in the field of community life. But the definition of this field presupposes an inquiry, no matter how brief, into human sociability.

I. Grounds and Forms of Sociability

The Needs of the Individual

It is obvious that the needs of the individual call for the association of men. Yet significant implications of this proposition are commonly ignored. For one thing, the notion of individual need is often restricted, in most arbitrary fashion, to needs of a biological, physical, material character. The necessity of mutual assistance and division of labor in the fight against hunger and thirst, cold, wild beasts, and disease is more commonly expressed than the immense and almost constantly increased service that society renders to individuals in intellectual, esthetic, moral, and spiritual life. Any improper emphasis on the physical needs served by society suggests that the purposes and the requirements of social life are contained within a sphere of material goods. Concomitantly, it is often taken for granted that the goods of the spirit are altogether individual and that their pursuit is an entirely individualistic concern. Thus, human life would be split into a part socialized by material needs and a nobler part distinguished both by spirituality and individual independence. To dispose of this construct, just think of what a beginner in the sciences owes to the daily assistance of society. A comparison between a student in our universities and a man self-educated in the wilderness would involve a good deal of fiction, but we have all the data needed to compare, with regard to proficiency, students separated by a few generations. In the fields where the social life of the understanding is most successful—mathematics, physics—the men of the younger generation can solve with the resources of ordinary intelligence problems which were hardly treatable for geniuses of earlier ages.

By another unwarranted restriction of meaning, it is often held that a need is necessarily self-centered. In fact, the notion of need expresses merely the state of a tendency not yet satisfied with ultimate accomplishment. Among the tendencies which make up the dynamism of a rational being, some are self-centered and some are generous; all admit of a state of need, and the need to give is no less real than the need to take. Consider the grounds of friendship and the ways in which a man is related to his friends. A young fellow, uncertain about what he is and what he wants to be, with little background, no estate, no steady position, with much anxiety, will be looking for friends in a context of self-centered needs. No ethically unfavorable connotation attaches to the notion of a need centered about the self. Whether the center of a need is within the self or beyond it depends upon the nature of the tendency involved and is antecedent to moral use. Needs relative to such goods as food and shelter are self-centered by nature and remain self-centered in the most disinterested man despite all the generosity which enters into his way of satisfying his needs and of relating their satisfaction to further ends.

But some needs have their center beyond the self; a man whose personality features contrast with those of the young fellow described just above still needs friends. He does not depend on the help of friends for food or shelter, for his fortune is already made; he is not in the least motivated by the expectation of physical care in case of disease, for he is in good health and anyway has little fear of disease and death; neither does it occur to him that he may need friendly attention to soothe him in case of emotional disaster, for his nervous balance is well assured; and he does not feel that the company of friends is necessary to him as protection against boredom, for he does so well in the company of his ideas, his memories, his books, and familiar belongings that the threat of boredom is not felt. We are describing a distinguished instance of mature development, strength of character, soundness, dominating indifference, freedom. Yet this accomplished person needs the company of loved ones, inasmuch as his very state of accomplishment intensifies in him every generous trait and every tendency to act by way of superabundance. He needs to give. True, the center of the act of giving is found in the beneficiary of the gift, and the gift is primarily designed to satisfy a need in the receiver. Yet the gift satisfies also a need in the giver. Such a non-self-centered need may attain a high degree of intensity. The accomplished person whom we are considering would be unhappy if he knew no children to please with Christmas presents, and his homecoming from happy journeys would be gloomy if no one expected him to bring jewelry or dresses from the remote land. His knowledge would give him little joy if he had no chance to impart it to eager intellects, and the very firmness of his character would seem to him a tedious advantage if it should never result in a friend's achieving greater mastery over himself.

For the sake of clarity, we have used the example of a firm and accomplished person to describe other-centered needs. In such persons generosity is most obviously noticeable. However, other-centered needs exist in all; they secretly move the last of men. To appreciate the power and the social significance of other-centered needs in everyone, it suffices to remark that in case of frustration the tendency to act generously becomes the most redoubtable of antisocial drives. Men would rather stand physical destitution than be denied opportunity for disinterested love and sacrifice.

The Common Good

The question now arises whether the needs of the individual are the only cause of human association and whether, correspondingly, society has no purpose beyond the satisfaction of individual needs. The word "individualism," which so often is made worthless by confusion, admits of a precise sense insofar as it designates the theory that the single purpose of society is the service of the individual. The individualistic interpretation of sociability appeals to souls trained in humane disciplines and possessed of an exacting sense for the human character of everything that pertains to society. As soon as it is suggested that the purpose of human effort lies in an achievement placed beyond the individual's good, a suspicion arises that human substance may be ultimately dedicated to things as external to man as the pyramids of Egypt. In all periods of history, voluminous facts signify that under the name of common good, republic, fatherland, empire, what is actually pursued may not be a good state of human affairs but a work of art designed to provide its creator with the inebriating experience of creation. The joy of the creator assumes unique intensity when the thing out of which the work of art is made is human flesh and soul. The artist's rapture is greatest when he uses as matter of his own creation not marble and brass but beings made after the image of God. "The finest clay, the most precious marble—man—is here kneaded and hewn...."[1] True, the common good conceived as a work of art and a thing external to man is merely a corruption of the genuine common good. In this world of contingency, every form or process admits of imitation; in human affairs, the most dreadful counterfeit is often so related to the genuine form that it appears, with disquieting frequency, precisely where the genuine form is most earnestly sought. An inquiry into the common good must involve constant awareness that its object may, at any time, be displaced by deadly counterfeit.

To answer the question at the beginning of this section, we must turn our attention, first, to the limitations of individual plenitude. Then we should be able to understand, just by glancing at the daily life of human communities, how these limitations are transcended.

Individuals are narrowly restricted with regard to diversity, and inevitable circumstances hold in check the desire for totality which belongs to rational nature. In terms of essential causality, there is no reason why one and the same man should not be painter, musician, philosopher, captain of industry, and statesman. In fact, personalities developed excellently on more than a very few lines are extremely rare, and significant limitations can easily be found in Leonardo da Vinci and

Goethe. The rule to which all men are subjected in varying degree is one of specialization for the sake of proficiency. This rule entails heavy sacrifices even in the most
gifted. A man highly successful in his calling accomplishes little in comparison
with the ample virtualities of man. He has failed in a hundred respects. Only the
union of many can remedy the failure of each. But of all the restrictions inflicted
upon the boundless ambition of our rational nature, the most painful concerns
the duration of individual achievements. Within the temporal order we would feel
hopeless if the virtually immortal life of the community did not compensate for
the brevity of individual existence. Death is known to be particularly hard and surrounded with anxiety for those who end their days in individualistic loneliness.

These are the familiar facts referred to by a well-known text of Aristotle, or-
dinarily summed up in the following words, "The common good is greater and
more divine than the private good."[2] "Greater" expresses a higher degree of perfection with regard both to duration and to diversity. "Divine," as translating the
Greek *theion,* does not designate so much a godlike essence as a participation
in the privilege of imperishability. In this world of change, individuals come and
go. The law of generation and corruption covers the whole universe of nature.
This law is transcended in a very proper sense by the incorruptibility of the species and the immortality of human association. The masterpiece of the natural
world cannot be found in the transient individual. Nor can it be found in the species, which is not imperishable except in the state of universality; but in this state
it is no longer unqualifiedly real. Human communities are the highest attain-
ments of nature, for they are virtually unlimited with regard to diversity of perfections, and virtually immortal. Beyond the satisfaction of individual needs the
association of men serves a good unique in plenitude and duration, the common
good of the human community.

Partnership and Community

Before we examine the problem of authority, we still need to inquire about the
basic forms of association. The main patterns of human societies are the mere
partnership and the community. Of course, these two types may combine, but the
obscurity of mixed realizations just renders more valuable the understanding of
typical forms. Let us first consider familiar examples. A merchant succeeds in convincing an owner of capital that money invested in his business would bring nice
dividends. By the terms of their contract, any profits will be divided according to
a definite ratio.

Then the merchant goes to the market, and the money-lender sits back and awaits the event. Their "common interest" was celebrated in expectant toasts, but they are not engaged in any common action designed to promote any "common interest." The merchant works by himself or with his employees; he does not work with the money-lender, who remains a silent partner. Where there is no common action, there is no common good. These two men do not make up a community. What they call their "common interest" is in fact a sum of private interests that happen to be interdependent.

In contradistinction to mere partners, the members of a community—family, factory, football team, army, state, church—are engaged in a common action whose object is qualitatively different from a sum of interdependent goods. Whereas the contractual relation is normally the sufficient rule of the mere partnership, our problem is precisely to decide whether the community normally calls for the kind of rule known as authority.

To conclude this preliminary inquiry, let us remark that contract and community can be related in diverse ways. (1) The association established by contract may be of such nature that the relation between the associates remains exclusively contractual. The money-lender and the merchant exemplify such a case. (2) The association founded by contract may be of such nature as to involve a common action. When they sign a contract, partners may be entering into a society which is not a mere partnership. Such is the case, for instance, in the hiring of labor. Production demands that manager and laborer act together, and neither has the character of a silent partner. However, communities of this type can, in most instances, be dissolved at will, or according to terms specified by the initial contract. (3) The community founded by contract may not be dissoluble at will. It may even be of such nature as not to be dissoluble at all. Because the contract is the only rule of the mere partnership, it is commonly assumed, by unwarranted inference, that persons associated by contract necessarily remain mere partners and can dissolve their association. The relation between man and wife involves a character of stability determined by the very nature of the man-and-wife community. Yet this community was founded by contract.

If nothing abnormal occurs, the need for authority is never felt in a relation of mere partnership. The contractual arrangement which, as such, is absolutely equalitarian, suffices. A decision by authority will be necessary only if the working of the contract is impeded by such accidents as misunderstanding, bad faith, or unforeseen conjuncture. Thus, if all human societies were mere partnerships, authority would never be needed except on account of some fault or accident. The deficiency theory of authority would be entirely vindicated.

II. The Unity of Common Action

Assuming now the features proper to the kind of association described as community, let us examine the problem of united action. Every community is relative to a good to be sought and enjoyed in common. But, by the very fact that a community comprises a number of individuals, the unity of its action cannot be taken for granted: it has to be caused. Further, if the community is to endure, the cause of its united action must be firm and stable. Since rational agents are guided by judgment, the problem of bringing about unity in the action of men resolves into the problem of insuring the unity of their practical judgment. For example, the family community would cease to exist if each member did not judge, for one reason or another, that he ought to reside in this particular locality and in this particular house. A farm would soon be ruined if those engaged in the production of wheat did not all judge, again for one reason or another, that these fields ought to be put into wheat this year. A factory could not operate if the members of its personnel did not all judge that a definite schedule ought to be observed. A deliberating assembly is indeed a community designed to stand disagreement, yet in order that it should exist at all, there must be some agreement regarding the place and time of its meetings, regarding the rules of procedure, and regarding some principles. In these and all similar cases, unity of judgment cannot be procured by rational communication. The believers in a social science which would, under circumstances of perfect enlightenment, eliminate the decisions of authority—and those of freedom as well—assume that the kind of necessity which makes demonstration possible extends to the particulars of social practice. But, clearly, such propositions as "It is good for us to live in this house," and "It is proper that our assembly should meet at noon," admit of no demonstration. Philosophical prejudice alone may cause failure to perceive the contingency in which such propositions are engaged. United action demands a principle that works steadily amidst the overwhelming contingencies of perishable existence. Rational communication, which is bound up with essential necessities, is not such a principle.

Does it follow that unanimity is under all circumstances an uncertain and precarious principle of unity in action? This question requires that we consider a community whose members are, without exception, ideally virtuous and enlightened persons. Unanimity is well known to be a most precarious achievement in communities afflicted by such common deficiencies as ignorance, prejudice, selfish interest, and the like, but our purpose is to decide whether authority is ever needed independently of deficiencies. Accordingly, we must bear in mind a group free from stupidity and ill-will. If such a group were a Utopian fiction, it still could play a part in the understanding of society. In fact, there exist groups whose members are all intelligent and morally excellent; that these groups are very small makes no difference for the purposes of rational analysis.

Rational Communication and Affective Communion

Since unanimity cannot be established in these practical matters by the power of demonstration, the ideally clever and virtuous members of a community cannot be unanimous in more than fortuitous fashion unless a determined course of action is demanded by the virtuous inclination of their hearts. Whenever wisdom has to find its way in the midst of circumstances contingent and possibly unique, the certainty of its judgment results from its agreement with honest inclination. An ethical issue that is universal in character—say, a general problem of justice—can be answered, as St. Thomas puts it, in either of two ways, the way of cognition and the way of inclination. In the way of cognition, the answer proceeds from principles by logical connections. This is how the moral philosopher is supposed to answer questions, and no other method is acceptable in philosophy, because no other method procures certainty in knowledge as knowledge. But an honest man unacquainted with deductive processes may find the answer intuitively and in incommunicable fashion by feeling that such and such a way of doing things pleases or revolts his sentiment of justice. Provided his is a genuine virtue, as distinct from emotional counterfeits, and is sufficiently developed, the judgment dictated by such a sentiment of agreement or aversion is certain. By love for what justice demands the heart of the just is shaped after the pattern of justice, and his inclination is one with the requirement of his virtue. To say that a will is virtuous is to say that its movements coincide with the demands and aversions of virtue itself. Between the ethically good appetite and ethical goodness there exists a unity of nature, a connaturality, which constitutes a dependable source of practical truth. Because the just will corresponds in all its movements to the object of justice, the inclinations experienced by the just are like statements uttered by the object of justice. Here, according to the words of John of St. Thomas, "Love takes on the role of the object."

It is entirely accidental that we can demonstrate so little about the requirements of justice or chastity, considered in their intelligible universality. But it is not by accident that no one can demonstrate what the rule of justice consists in under individual, historically-conditioned, absolutely concrete, and possibly unprecedented and unrenewable circumstances. Here the rule of justice is not uttered by an essence and cannot be grasped by the demonstrative power of the intellect. It is uttered by the love which is the soul of the just and it can be learned only by listening to the teaching of love. Take for instance the problem of ownership in case of extreme necessity. Our sense of justice acknowledges that a starving person, without money and without liberal friends, has a right to save his life with food that he cannot pay for. No doubt, such a proposition can be demonstrated, and St. Thomas successfully designated the middle term of its demonstration when he remarked that in case of necessity all things become common.[3] But the argumentation will never establish a logical connection between the theory of property and the answer that *I* am looking for when, already weakened by hunger, I wonder whether my case is actually one of extreme necessity. A man in need will know for sure whether his necessity is extreme or not if and only if he is so just as to feel how far the right of his neighbor and his own right go, so temperate as not to mistake an accidental urge for a real need, and so strong as to fear neither the sufferings of hunger nor the resentment of his illiberal neighbors.

Thus, whereas a question relative to an ethical essence can be answered both by way of cognition and by way of inclination, the way of inclination alone can procure an answer when a question of human conduct involves contingency. This holds for the rules of common action as well as for those of individual conduct. Political prudence is no less dependent upon the obscure forces of the appetite than prudence in the government of individual life. However, with regard to unity of judgment among men, there is a significant difference between individual prudence and any prudence concerned with the conduct of a community. The prudence of the individual normally involves something singular and peculiar— it would almost be appropriate to say "eccentric." In their hopeless search for guidance amidst the obscurities of action, men easily assume that problems of individual conduct are the same for all, or at least for many, and that the rule which led one to a happy solution can be confidently followed by others. This assumption works sometimes, when problems are not significantly modified by individual circumstances. Yet it is false, and may at any time bring about disastrous effects, for, in the broad field that lies beyond determination by ethical essences, it never can be said *a priori* that individual features are irrelevant. A life of moderate work and strict parsimony may be precisely what a certain family needs, but misfortune may befall a neighboring home unless the line followed is one of rather lavish expenditure at the cost of strenuous work. In still another case real wisdom may paradoxically require liberal spending, an abundance of leisure, and willingness to go into debt. Of such contrasting rules of action, some may prove sound in a great number of cases and some may prove harmful save for rare exceptions. Yet it is never possible to know in advance—prior to an investigation of whatever unique features a case may comprise—that the rule required in this individual case is not precisely the one which would prove unsuited to nearly all other cases. Because of the possible relevance of unique features in the determination of individual prudence, each man is threatened with the contingency of having to make his decisions in utter solitude and to act like no one else. The anguish of such solitude is more than most men can stand, hence the tendency to take refuge in uniformity and conformity, even though precious features of individual destiny may be destroyed by adherence to common practice.

When the prudence of men is concerned with the welfare of one and the same community—their community—individual features have, in principle, nothing to do with the making of a wise decision. Among the most significant data, some are, indeed, strictly unique, but they pertain to the community's unique history and thus tend to cause agreement rather than diversity of judgment. Any common pursuit, on no matter how humble a level, is a welcome remedy to the anguished solitude of individual prudence. To be sure, science is a factor of human unity, but it is in a world of abstraction that it causes men to elicit identical judgments. In common action alone does concrete existence, with all its determinateness, with its character of totality, its location in time, and its contingency, tend to procure unity among men. Assuming that our community is made entirely of clever and well-intentioned persons, whatever is needed for its welfare is the object of unanimous assent. Affective communion achieves what cannot be expected of rational communication: it brings about unanimity of judgment in the life of action. Again, every certain judgment concerning what we have to do under concrete circumstances is dictated by an affective motion and owes its certain truth to its agreement with dependable inclination. But when the pursuit is that of a common good, the part played by affective and secret determinants is no longer an obstacle to unity of judgment among men. Wills properly inclined toward the same common good cannot but react in the same way to the same proposition, if what this proposition expresses is definitely what the common good demands. In groups small enough not to involve much error and bad will, the adherence of all to decisions that are necessary though indemonstrable brings about marvels of united action. As to larger communities—say, cities or nations—where all sorts of evils and deficiencies are inevitable, situations resembling unanimity and entailing most of the effects that unanimity would entail are a comparatively frequent occurrence. Consider the case of a nation attacked by a neighbor eager for territorial expansion. That resistance is better than appeasement cannot be demonstrated, and many citizens do not have the civic virtue which would procure indefectible adherence to what common salvation demands. Yet history shows that spontaneous unity often characterizes the reaction of peoples in this predicament. If there were a question of polling opinion, it would be impossible to speak of unanimity. There are traitors, collaborationists, neutralists, abstentionists, honest men deceived by overwhelming illusions, and passive citizens without an answer to a question that never actually reached their minds. But these disrupters of unanimity are comparatively few, and they carry so little weight as to make little difference. Practically and for all significant purposes, the situation is about what it would be if unanimity were realized.

Now that we have recognized the marvels that unanimity, or quasi-unanimity can work, it is important to note that *unanimity is a precarious principle of united action whenever the common good can be attained in more than one way.* All that has been said in the foregoing about the power of unanimity simply makes no sense except when the way to the common good is uniquely determined. If the common good can be attained in more than one way, neither enlightenment nor virtue, but only chance, can bring about unanimity. Accordingly, if unity of action is guaranteed by no other principle than that of unanimous agreement, it becomes an entirely casual affair, the result being either stalemate or divided and destructive action. Circumstances may be such that the happy life of a man-and-wife community can be easily attained either in Washington or in New York, but if one member of the community prefers, with the best of intentions, Washington, and the other, with an equally virtuous disposition, New York, the principle of action by unanimous agreement determines the separation of these well-meaning spouses.

There is nothing wrong with a man who, so far as he is concerned, likes to drive on the right hand side of the road, and nothing wrong with the fellow who, if he had his own choice, would drive on the left. Thus traffic rules cannot be decided by the unanimous consent of enlightened and virtuous drivers. Assuming that all good citizens are agreed that the public budget cannot be cut below such and such an amount, it is obvious that the money needed for public purposes can be gathered, without injustice or particular harm, in a diversity of ways. Citizens may, without there being anything wrong with their intelligence or intention, take diverse stands with regard to such methods of taxation as sales tax, gross income tax, or a combination of both. In military operations, either of two plans of attack may provide a reasonable chance of victory, but defeat is certain if the attacker's power is split between the two plans. Among the most experienced and dependable leaders, some prefer one plan and some the other. There is no reason why they should be unanimous, since each plan, insofar as those things fall under human providence, is a way to victory. Among the many ways of playing a concerto of Bach, several satisfy the requirements of great music, and highly qualified musicians will clash as to how the fourth Brandenburg Concerto should be played. Yet the members of an orchestra cannot be allowed conflicting interpretations of a concerto. In fact, any conceivable instance of common action, if considered in all its modes and particulars, admits of being carried out according to one or another of several methods, all leading to the common good.

Knowledge and Freedom

Some observers object to the proposition that authority, as the cause of united action, exercises an essential function, a function made necessary not by any evil or deficiency but by the nature of common action. They contend that any multiplicity of ways leading to a common purpose is an illusion that social science, if better developed, would dismiss. The problem involved here is that of choice, and it pertains to the subject of liberty more directly than to the subject of authority.

When the theory of liberty is not enlivened by some sort of ethical enthusiasm, it often is surrounded by a cloud of misgivings, as if liberty could be preserved only by cherished ignorance and should yield to unique determination as soon as the truth is known about the proper way to our end. Indeed, everyone's experience tells of deliberations that bear on illusory as well as genuine means. If proper information comes before decision is made, and excludes the illusory means—the lines of action which, in spite of appearances, do not lead to the end but to failure and perhaps disaster—everything is better in all conceivable respects. Considering that a wholesome simplification takes place whenever an illusory means is ruled out, we sometimes dream of carrying simplification down to the state of unique determinateness, and we like to imagine that in perfect acquaintance with the real state of affairs the lines of action originally listed as means would, with but one exception, be identified as so many illusions. It is easy to see that this postulate expresses aversion to the mystery involved in free choice as well as to the darkness of contingency. Relations characterized by sheer determinateness, without contingency and without freedom, offer an average type of intelligibility which has been constantly preferred by rationalism. Indeed, any feature of contingency is a restriction on intelligibility, but the world of reality may be such as not to be intelligible in all respects. It is, after all, a question of fact, and we must be ready to accept whatever conclusion is reached by the scientific and philosophic description of the world. Freedom, on the other hand, if there is such a thing, would involve extraordinary plenitude of being, causality and intelligibility. But the more intelligible is not always the more easy to understand. In all scientific disciplines there are admirably simple views and methods which remain inaccessible to all but a very few scholars. Why are these things so hard to grasp? Not because they lack intelligibility, but rather because they are so excellently intelligible that only the best intellects are proportioned to them. With a mind open both to the restricted intelligibility of things contingent and to the secrecy of freedom, it is possible to inquire into the meaning of choice without begging any question. Let the problem be stated in these simple words: Is choice necessarily narrowed down to one genuine and one (or several) ungenuine means? Is choice necessarily between one good and one (or several) evils? *Is there such a thing as a choice among goods?* Can there conceivably be several means to an end? In a comparison of agents, should it be said that some are restricted to one or few means and that others have a wide variety of means at their disposal?

As soon as these questions are posed without any prejudice relative to the intelligibility of things, experience supplies the basic answers. Several diets can maintain the health of a healthy man, but a diseased organism may need, as a *sine qua non* of survival, what everyone calls a strict, uniquely determined, diet. An ordinary student, to attain proficiency in mathematics, needs all the complex system worked out by academic societies, such as teachers, textbooks, treatises, discussions, and tutorials. But in the case of genius, alternative means make it possible to dispense with much of the academic apparatus. It has been remarked that when a new pedagogical method is tested by a born teacher, success proves nothing, for born teachers are known to achieve success with almost any method;

in order to know how good a method is, it is better to have it tested by an undistinguished teacher who depends heavily on the quality of the method used.

A man trained in one craft and unable to do any other job has to work in uncongenial conditions; the man with many skills can afford to be more particular about the circumstances of his employment. No one would say that the broader choice open to the man with many skills originates in ignorance and illusion; clearly, it results from a greater power and presupposes more and better knowledge. An industrial enterprise with little capital must produce only that which will surely bring immediate returns; the privilege of contributing extensively to diversity and novelty in the market belongs to firms better financed. It is a commonplace of American history that waste of natural resources was determined initially by an acute shortage of manpower. The only ways of development open to a young community placed in natural abundance were the wasteful ones. We judge more severely the habits of waste in the later generations which, owing to great numbers, firmer establishment, more advanced techniques, and many other forms of increased power, have choices that the early settlers did not have. A nation with no navy, a very small army, no financial stature, and declining population, if offered the alliance of a powerful neighbor, has to accept it albeit at the cost of heavy sacrifices and historical resentments; but given great bargaining power, a nation can choose its allies. In all conceivable circumstances, power increases choice. The proper effect of enlightenment, accordingly, is twofold: improved knowledge rules out illusory means and, insofar as it entails greater power, multiplies the genuine ones. To destroy the illusion of a means is not to cut the amplitude of choice, for, insofar as it extends to illusory means, choice itself is but an illusion. In an ideally enlightened community, authority would be spared the unhappy task of directing the common effort, in the darkness of illusion, along a possibly disastrous line. But, inasmuch as an excellent condition of knowledge implies greatly increased power, social science at its perfection would multiply genuine means and broaden real choice. *It would, consequently, increase the need for authority as a factor of united action in the cases where the plurality of the genuine means renders unanimity fortuitous.*

Strikingly, it is a better understanding of freedom which first discloses the essential character of the need for authority in common action. But why is it that whenever we think of diverse ways leading to the common good we are so strongly tempted to attribute their diversity, and the corresponding variety of preferences, to our ignorance of some relevant features or circumstances? A stubborn objection holds that if men were omniscient, unanimous adherence to the end would necessarily entail unanimity regarding the means. Let us briefly inquire into the cause of this belief.

In all domains of understanding and interpretation, whether trivial or lofty and subtle, we are inclined to transfer the properties of the better known subjects to subjects that are not so well known. This is why Aristotle, or some follower of his, says that it is unreasonable to seek at the same time the science of a subject and the method of this science.[4] Unless the method is known in advance, albeit in the most rudimentary fashion, we shall inevitably force upon the new study dispositions acquired in previous studies, for example, apply to medicine dispositions which proved excellent in mechanics, or consider ethics with the bias of a mind trained in theoretical science.

Notice, at this point, that the things pertaining to cognition are better known than the things pertaining to appetition and volition. Every time we turn to some aspect of appetitive and volitional life, we carry with us frames of mind and schemes of interpretation developed in our endeavor to understand cognitive life. We are inclined to reconstruct appetition after the pattern of cognition. But cognition is not free from deficiency unless it is strictly determinate. If the problem is to know what the things are, nothing is worse than perfect indifference, the state in which a proposition appears just as plausible as its contradictory. Things are somewhat better if one part of the alternative is more probable than the other, but so long as one of the two is not excluded by unqualified necessity, cognition remains defective. With regard to facts and to essences as well, the faculty of choosing, at will, between assent and dissent is not an asset but expresses an entirely negative state of affairs. Accordingly, the understanding of cognition results in a pattern where perfection strictly coincides with uniqueness. But appetition is, in a way, the opposite of cognition. Whereas the known is attracted into the knower, the lover is attracted toward the beloved, and whereas the true exists in the mind, the good exists in the things.[5] This basic contrast reverses the meaning of uniqueness, plurality and indifference, when inquiry moves from cognition to appetition. A plurality of possible assents with regard to one and the same subject evidences failure to attain truth with certainty; the indifference of the uncertain mind is made of inachievement, indetermination, potentiality, passivity. On the contrary, a plurality of means with regard to one and the same end evidences mastery, domination, actuality, activity, superdetermination. The myth of a perfect knowledge which would eliminate authority and liberty rests upon a crude confusion of two kinds of indifference: the passive one, which results from potency and inachievement, and the dominating one, which results from excellence.

An Essential Function of Authority

The existence of a plurality of genuine means in the pursuit of the common good excludes unanimity as a *sufficient* method of steadily procuring unity of action. To achieve indispensable unity in common action, one method is left, which can be described as follows: whether we prefer to live in Washington or in New York, whether we prefer to drive on the right or on the left side of the road, whether we prefer sales tax, gross income tax, or their combination, whether we prefer a richer or a more austere orchestration of Bach, everyone of us, insofar as he is engaged in the common action, will accept and follow, as rule of his own action, one judgment thus constituted into rule for all. This rule of common action may coincide with my own preference, but this is of no significance, for the common rule might just as well be at variance with my liking, and I would be equally bound to follow it out of dedication to the common good, which cannot be attained except through united action. *The power in charge of unifying common action through rules binding for all is what everyone calls authority.* It may be a distinct person designated by nature, as in the couple and in the family. It may be a distinct person designated by God, as in the cases of Saul and Peter. It may be a distinct person designated by the people, as in the case of David. It may be a distinct person designated by birth and accepted by the people. It may be a distinct group of persons designated by heredity or by election or by lot. And it may be no distinct person or group of persons, but the community itself proceeding by majority vote. The problem of the need for authority and the problem of the need for a distinct governing personnel have often been confused: at this point, it is already clear that they are distinct and that the argumentation which establishes the need for authority, even in a society made of ideally enlightened and well-intentioned persons, leaves open the question of whether some communities may be provided with all the authority they need without there being among them any distinct group of governing persons.

Thus, authority does not have only substitutional functions. In other words, it is not made necessary by deficiencies alone. We know, by now, that in one case at least the need for authority derives not from any lack or privation but from the sound nature of things. Given a community on its way to its common good, and given, on the part of this community, the degree of excellence which entails the possibility of attaining the good in a diversity of ways, authority has an indispensable role to play, and this role originates entirely in plenitude and accomplishment. The deficiency theory of authority is given the lie. An ideally enlightened and virtuous community needs authority to unify its action. By accident, it may need it less than a community which, as a result of ignorance, is often confronted by illusory means. But by essence it is more powerful than any community afflicted with vice and ignorance, and as a result of its greater power it controls choices involving new problems of unity which cannot be solved by way of unanimity but only by way of authority.

III. The Form and the Matter of the Common Good

Because we are engaged in the pursuit of a common end, we deliberate about ways of insuring the unity of our action. These may be the steady ways of authority or, should it prove impossible to embody the principle of authority in an appropriate agency, the precarious ways of unanimity. But the problem would not arise if we were not already intending in common a certain end. Underlying any problem relative to the unity of common action, there exist problems relative to the end of the action to be united. The next step in the theory of authority concerns the end willed in common, as presupposed by the question of the way to unify action toward this end. Let this problem be posed as follows: granted that authority has an essential part to play in the unifying of action toward the common end, does it have any essential part to play with regard to the common end itself?

The precise vocabulary worked out by Aristotle (*Ethics* 3) and improved by Aquinas (II-II, 6 ff.) can supply much valuable clarity. In perfect accord with the best usage of common language, philosophers describe "volition" as the act by which the will adheres to its end. If the end is considered, not absolutely as a thing good to attain, but more precisely as term of a means or series of means, the act of the will is called "intention." "Choice" deals with a diversity of means relative to the thing intended and willed. Thus, after having established that authority has an essential function in the order of choice and means, we are asking whether it has, by reason of the nature of things and not merely by accident, anything to do with the volition and the intention of the common good explicitly considered as an end.

To say the least, appearances strongly suggest that any function of authority concerned with the end is merely substitutional. It looks very much as if, in a community made exclusively of enlightened and virtuous persons, the volition and intention of the common good should be fully insured by the qualities of the persons. Whoever disregards the common good is not virtuous but selfish, and whoever is dedicated to genuine virtue is, by the very efficacy of his virtue, ready for any sacrifice that the common good demands. It seems that ideally enlightened and virtuous persons would be adequately related to the good of their community by their enlightened virtue. In societies such as the cities and states of our experience, where selfishness and ignorance prevail, persons have to be constantly directed and often coerced toward the common good. Men of ill will seek their own advantage and ignore the good of all, and many whose will is honest and even generous happen to place the character of common good where it does not belong. But suppose that both ill will and error are removed: the need for authority, insofar as the common good itself is concerned, seems to disappear. Authority, in an ideal community, would have no essential function, except with regard to the unity of common action when there exists a plurality of genuine means.

Sometimes, a very simple analysis suffices to bring into focus difficulties hidden by familiar appearances. In a discussion of authority with regard to the end of common action, it is decisively important to bear in mind the meaning of the polar opposition between form and content within the object of volition and intention. Consider this object, the end willed (as a thing absolutely good) and intended (as a term of means). It can be willed and intended in two ways. I may will and intend what is good without knowing *what the thing is* that is good. The daily life of a man of good will is made of problems of content stated on the basis of a satisfactory answer to a problem of form. The man of good will, by definition and hypothesis, wills that which is good, and firmly adheres to the form of goodness. If only he knew *what the thing is* in which the form of goodness resides, he would do the good thing and all would be perfect. There is an evil harmony in the sinful will which adheres to evil things known to be evil—known to bear the form of evil[6]—and there is a blessed harmony in the good will which, for the sake of goodness, adheres to things that are actually good. And between these two harmonies there is the daily problem of the man of good will who indeed adheres to the form of the good but feels uncertain about the thing in which this form resides, in other words, the matter or content of this form.

So far as community life is concerned, the problem of matter and form within the end can be posed as follows: Is it desirable that the common good be willed and intended, both with regard to matter and with regard to form, by private persons acting in a private capacity? In order to be sure that we reach the root of the issue, let us consider the case of a society with no distinct governing personnel. Here are a few hundred farmers who gather periodically into a people's assembly, and this assembly is the only government of their community. Assuming that the order of virtuous intentions obtains, I recognize in each farmer a dual capacity. Between the sessions of the assembly, he is Philip or Bartholomew, a private person, the husband of Ruth or Patricia, the father of these children, and the owner of this particular land unmistakably distinguished by a fence from the rest of the world. His duties are unique. A good neighbor and companion, he wants all fields to bear abundantly; yet he is responsible, in a unique way, for the plowing of the field described as his. A good-hearted man, he is ready to help any child that God places in his path, yet there would be dire subversion of order if he did not show special dedication to the children who are his, and prefer them, in intention and in action, to other children who, though equally lovely, are not in equal degree entrusted to his love.[7] In the relation of man and wife, a dedication unique in all respects is the essence of indissoluble marriage.

When the assembly meets, every citizen is expected to assume a new capacity. A man who yesterday was admired for his industry on his family farm would today be blamed if his devotion did not belong entirely to the community. Between the private and the common welfare, the relation is often one of harmony. But conflicts may arise at any time and a public person, say, a member of the people's assembly, is bound to uphold the public welfare, regardless of how his private interest is affected. For instance, a certain method of taxation, plainly beneficial to the community as a whole, may cause serious difficulty to the kind of enterprise that he is managing. If a member of a popular assembly is known to have opposed a taxation law for no other reason than the threat of increased difficulty for his own enterprise, we consider him, according to the seriousness of the circumstances, either a weak person or a despicably bad citizen. At any rate, this accident of private interest interfering with public service in the discharge of a public function is inconceivable in the community of virtuous and enlightened persons which remains the principal subject of our inquiry. Considering, thus, the citizen of a direct democracy who, by the very fact that there is no distinct governing personnel, is the bearer of two capacities—the public and the private, according as the people's assembly is or is not in session—and assuming, further, that this person acts blamelessly in each capacity, I recognize in him two relations to the common good, and I wonder precisely what difference there is between these two relations.

The problem would be overlooked if we were satisfied with the contrast between the private and the common. Again, this virtuous citizen is dedicated to the common good at all times, whether or not the assembly is in session, and, unmistakably, the difference that we are trying to express concerns, not the common good and its opposite, but two relations to the common good. The private person, inasmuch as he is morally excellent, wills and intends the common good, and subordinates his private wishes to it. He may not know what action the common good demands, but he adheres to the common good formally understood, to the form of the common good, whatever may be the matter in which this form resides; as far as content or matter is concerned, it is his business to will and intend private goods. But the public person is defined by the duty of willing and intending the common good considered both in its form and in its matter. And because the service of the common good normally involves an arrangement of things private, and sometimes requires the sacrifice of private interests, the subject of the public capacity exercises authority over the private person, whose business it is to look after particular matters.

In spite of appearances, the essence of authority and that of obedience are integrally preserved in a community practicing government by majority vote without any distinct governing personnel. The decisive question is not whether the content or matter of the common good is entrusted to distinct persons; it rather is whether, by reason of the common good's primacy, the volition and intention of *that in which* the common good resides must be expressed by a rule of action binding on all. The citizens of a direct democracy are inclined to boast of having no other masters than themselves.[8] This attitude may mean merely that they like to do without a distinct governing personnel. But the same boastful words may express the will to eliminate, through constitutional contrivance, the essence of authority and that of obedience. The soul of the system is revealed by the interpretation of majority, minority, and opposition. A citizen who, whenever the assembly meets, finds himself in the majority, may believe that he obeys only himself. But how is he going to feel when the majority votes against his preference? If he considers that the law he voted against is just as obligatory, and for the same reasons, as any law that he voted for, he is a law-abiding and obedient citizen for whom personal preference is altogether accidental. But if a person considers himself free from obligation to a law which he opposed, we understand that he has always been a rebel. True, he gave no signs of rebellion so long as the law was to his liking; but his later attitude discloses that having his own way has always been for him the thing essential, and obedience to the law a mere appearance.

The Most Essential Function of Authority

Thus, bringing about unity in common action is not, among the functions of authority, the only one which should be described as essential. Again, the problem of how to unify action, whether by unanimity or by authority, arises only on the ground of an already determinate volition and intention of the common good. Such volition and intention involve an antecedent function of authority, and this function, inasmuch as it is relative to the very end of common action, is more essential than anything pertaining to means. *The most essential function of authority is to issue and carry out rules expressing the requirements of the common good considered materially.*

This theory implies that two capacities are normally and desirably distinguished in every community. With reference to the best known case, that is, that of the body politic versus its components—individuals, families, and the like— these capacities have been called public and private. But in the present inquiry they should rather, by the rule of strict appropriateness, be designated as common and particular. Indeed, the capacity thus far called public exists in all communities, whether actually public, like a township, a county, and a state, or private, like a family. On the other hand, we shall soon see that the basic opposition is not between the common and the private but, more precisely, between the common and the particular. For privateness is but one mode of particularity. *The common capacity is defined by a relation to the common good considered not only in its form but also in its matter or content.* As to the particular capacity, it involves a relation to the form of the common good but not to its matter. Clearly, if the particular capacity were related to both the form and the matter of the common good, it would cease to be particular; the problem of authority would disappear, as far at least as the volition and intention of the common good are concerned. The whole theory truly stands or falls upon the answer to this simple question: Is it desirable that there should exist, in every community, persons whose business it is, within the order of material consideration, to look after goods particular rather than after the common good? It almost irresistibly seems that a disposition concerned with the form of the common good but not with its matter is just about half of a virtue. A person determined to serve the common good but unconcerned with the matter of its requirements seems to stop half way, and it looks very much as if a "full measure of devotion" would extend to the matter of the common good as well as to its form.

Let us refer, once more, to a community governed by a majority vote. According to a project under deliberation, a certain road, so far a very quiet one, would be paved and opened to fast-moving traffic. Large families live on this road, and the parents are worried about increased danger to their children. But, in spite of the risk involved, the good of the community demands that the road should be paved, and worried fathers, acting as members of the people's assembly, support the project. By the terms of the preceding description, these good citizens, exercising the capacity of particular persons between the sessions of the assembly, should oppose the project as dangerous to their children, with a firm determination, however, to abide by the decision of the majority. Here, the twofold capacity described in the foregoing seems irrelevant. These citizens, though lovingly concerned with danger to their children, will and intend the form of the common good. Consequently, they refrain from any rebellious act against the decision to pave the road, although they do their best under all circumstances to reduce the danger. *If these good people can do so much, why should they not do a little more* and, without waiting for the emergence of a new capacity at the assembly's session, confess that the road should be paved? The construct of a community made of ideally enlightened and virtuous persons seems to imply, over and above adherence to the common good formally considered, the determinate volition of the things that the common good actually requires or contains. But then, the volition and intention of the common good, both with regard to form and with regard to matter, are adequately guaranteed by enlightened virtue. As far, at least, as the volition and intention of the common good are concerned, an ideally perfect community seems able to do without authority.

Thus, according to a plausible hypothesis, the perfection of virtue causes the capacity described as particular to disappear into the common capacity. A single capacity is left, which is altogether relative to the common good. *The particular capacity, by taking in hand the matter of the common good, has indeed become common.* Such transmutation is precisely what was suggested when we voiced the conjecture that excellent citizens, fully prepared to make all sacrifices required by the common good, should take one more step and, without assuming any new capacity, should will and intend the common good materially considered. *It remains to be decided how the common good itself is affected by the disappearance or impairment of the particular capacity.*

The Function and the Subject

Let us first break down particularity into its main types. Every community exercises several functions—in the case of the state, justice, defense, diplomacy, public works, and the like—and in relation to the whole life of the community each function obviously has the character of a part. But in what specific sense does the notion of particularity apply here? Take, for instance, national defense. It is aimed at protecting all the national territory, all its wealth, all its counties, townships, families, and citizens. This function is altogether relative to the common good, yet it retains the character of a part inasmuch as its object is not the total good of the community but only one aspect of it. The object of a function is a certain aspect of a whole, and this is what defines particularity in the case of the function. The subject whose good is sought may be an individual organism. Indeed the concept of function is basic in biology; it may be a person, and it may just as well be a community of any rank and description. Whether the subject considered is an organism, a person or a community, the successful exercise of one function is only an aspect and a part of its good condition; if other functions are defective, disaster is not ruled out. A function may be public in an unqualified sense, as in the case of the functions pertaining exclusively to the body politic, without ceasing to be particular, inasmuch as its object is but one aspect of a complex good.

In sharp contrast to the particularity of the function, a good may be particular by reason of its subject. Consider the activities involved in the upbringing of a child. Taken together, they intend the whole good of the child, not one aspect of it. But because the child is part of the community, his is a particular good. Private communities, as the family, and such public communities as the township, the county, and the units of a federal organization are also related to the larger communities of which they are members as particular subjects. The state is the community which is so complete and self-sufficient that its good is not that of a particular subject—individual, family, township, and the like—but, unqualifiedly, the common good of men assembled for the sake of noble life.

We now turn to the question of the excellence of the particular in the two ways of particularity just defined. Familiar experiences suffice to show how desirable it is that functions should be clearly distinguished, and that each of them should be exercised with a special eagerness for what is unique about it. It is good for the community that military men be devoted with a passion to national defense, bridge builders to the building of bridges, foresters to the preservation of forests, physicians to public health, and classicists to the study of the classics. The particularity of the function removes confusion and opens the way to the advantages of specialization. It is hardly possible that both the task of building bridges and that of conserving forests should be successfully fulfilled by the same persons; but even if a team happened to be expert both in bridge building and in forestry, a division of social labor would still be necessary with regard to place and time. One reason why we keep rereading the *Republic* of Plato is that it expresses better than any other book the ideal of a community from which confusion is removed, and in which justice is achieved, through wise division of labor and dedication to specific tasks. A most enjoyable clarity pertains to the distinctness of the function, for every function is relative to an object, and, in human affairs at least, every object is definable. When the object of a social function no longer can be defined, the function itself becomes meaningless: this is when reformers step in. The administration of justice, the conduct of foreign relations, the management of public finances, and the like, are so many functions defined by perfectly intelligible objects.

Since functions are concerned with distinct aspects of the common good, functional diversity causes a need for an agency relative to the common good as a whole. Bringing about order among functions is the job of this central agency. What ratio of public funds can be allocated to agricultural projects without jeopardizing national defense or public health? This is an issue on which the function of promoting agriculture, the function of defending the national territory, and the function of procuring good health conditions have nothing to say, except in purely preparatory and indecisive fashion. Decision pertains to a power which, inasmuch as it is responsible for order among the functions, necessarily controls all of them and commands all the functionaries.

The particularity of the function, as ground of authority, has a negative feature of major significance: it does not, in any essential manner, set limits to the authority that it grounds. In fact, authority is commonly restricted, and often crippled, by the resistance of its functionaries; but this is an entirely accidental occurrence. Such resistance is foreign and opposed to the concept of function. True, it may be held desirable that functionaries be possessed of some autonomy, and it may be a matter of fact that they always are. But their autonomy is caused by a particularity which is not that of the function. This simple remark sums up many products of political theory as well as many facts pertaining to the history of government. Because the functionary, as such, is an instrument, the particularity of the function is a thing that despots do not dread. They know that, all other things being equal, the clear division of social labor into functions increases the efficacy of their power.

Does the particularity of the subject possess an excellence of its own? No doubt, it helps to remove confusion. A good way to make sure that every farmer knows what piece of land he is supposed to till is to divide the land into homesteads. This is indeed a result of considerable value, and it may constitute an everlasting argument in favor of private ownership. However, the power of removing confusion does not belong to the particularity of the subject in strict appropriateness, since it also belongs to the particularity of the function. A factory where rigorous discipline obtains and whose workers, for the most part, can be easily replaced, has but minimum recourse to the particularity of the subject. The feats of order accomplished by the modern organization of industry have given a new appeal to the old ideal of a state which would keep free from confusion without releasing the suspicious energies of such powers as privately owned land, privately conducted schools, strongly organized families, and citizens protected by inalienable rights.

The decisive fact is that the particularity of the subject, in all its forms and degrees, involves autonomy. To use a simple example, let us imagine that all the parts of a vast plain, by reason of homogeneity in all relevant respects, produce the same crops. Within such functional unity, farming can be administered according to the diversity of the tasks (plowing, fertilizing, sowing). Then it is a public affair, entrusted, say, to a branch of the Department of Agriculture. But the cultivation of this plain can also be entrusted to a multiplicity of farms each of which is governed by its individual proprietor. For the comparison to be meaningful, we must, of course, assume that other things are equal. Under definite circumstances, one system of management may insure a much higher yield than the other. On the assumption that the production is about the same in either system, let us ask whether it is better that the job be done by a multitude of self-ruling agents or by mere instruments of a central agency.

To ask this question is like asking whether there is more perfection in life than in lifelessness, in activity than in mere instrumentality, in plenitude than in emptiness. Clearly, a whole is better off if its parts are full of initiative than if they are merely traversed by an energy which never becomes their own. Much can be learned from the fact that social thinkers and metaphysicians conduct, on the subject of plenitude versus vacuum, parallel dialogues. William James's book, *A Pluralistic Universe*, forcefully expresses the metaphysical sentiment that genuine plurality in the world of our experience is the condition of meaning and plenitude.[9] A totality which does not admit of autonomous parts disappears into the vacuum caused by its imperialistic arrogance. But the particularity of the subject in the social as well as in the metaphysical world harbors mysteries that are extremely uncongenial to the rationalistic mind. Whenever it has its own way in social affairs, rationalism exalts the clarity of the function and crushes the particularity of the subject.

To be sure, contingency often makes it impossible to vindicate in an entirely rational fashion the distinction between communities of the same functional type.

What reasons could we bring forth if we had to explain why two states or nations remain separated by a borderline instead of merging into one unit? The notion of natural boundary is not absurd, and sometimes a fence built by nature serves quite reasonably to distinguish one community from another. Spain is south of the Pyrenees Range and France north of it. But in many other cases, the most famous of which is the great East European plain, nations remain stubbornly distinct although they cannot claim any natural boundary. Sometimes language supplies reasonable principles of unity and diversity, but it also happens that people refuse to merge in spite of linguistic unity (the French-speaking Swiss and Belgians do not want to be one nation with the French) and it also happens that the unity of a nation (Switzerland) is in no way jeopardized by diversity of language. After having probed all such causes of unity and diversity let us yield to the accidents of history, for theirs is the final power of decision. Whatever is accidental is, as such, unexplainable, but in the world of action a thing can be significant, worthy, treasurable, without having any character of essentiality or intelligibility: it just is, it has been, it tends to keep being, and this is why it is significant, without any further explanation. The precise location of the borderline between Canada and the United States is, in a number of places, entirely conventional, but, by the decision of history the community centered about Ottawa is something else than the community centered about Washington, D.C. Again, there may be no good reason why the borderline between Colorado and New Mexico should be where it is rather than a few miles farther north or south. Yet it is hardly questionable that the community whose main centers are Colorado Springs and Denver is, by the decisions of history, different from the community whose main centers are Santa Fe and Albuquerque. Any rationalist, if in the position of philosopher-king, would erase the borderline between Colorado and New Mexico and reduce the fifty States to a smaller number of more rational units. Such operations, which would sweep away a great deal of mystery, would also destroy much historical substance and, in a number of cases, leave only deceptive clarity where there used to be historical plenitude. No doubt, existent particularities may be dead remnants and their suppression may prove beneficial. But it also happens that the works of the past, no matter how contingent, are so full of life that their disappearance would involve great destruction. In a profound sense a "survival" is a thing which maintains in the present some of the life which was that of the past. Such life is not clearly intelligible, for an important part of it results from the successful management of contingent occurrences over a long time.

The Person

The best way to understand the relation between the mysteries of contingency and those of free choice is by examining the individual subject of human existence. As a member of a species, distinguished within the species by the material components of his being, a human subject is more properly designated as an individual. Considered as a complete substance which owes to its rationality a unique way of being a whole and of facing the rest of the universe, he is more properly designated as a person. The fortune of "personalism" in the ideologies of our time is clearly traceable to the promises held by the notion of person, as distinct from that of individual, in the working out of difficulties which, though of all times, have assumed extraordinary significance in the last generations. Indeed, the word personalism often stood for doctrines and attitudes that "individualism" would designate with equal or greater accuracy. Such a confusing change in expression bears witness to the power that the idea of person came to possess in minds confronted by problems which, some time before, were not held so obvious and momentous. Many, who would have been satisfied with the language of individualism half a century ago, were necessitated by the spirit of the age to speak a personalistic language. But what is it that caused, in such a large variety of doctrinal contexts, the decline of individualistic rhetoric, and a new attention to the meaning of the person? With due allowance for profound diversities among the so-called personalistic schools of thought, it can be said that the displacement of "individualism" by "personalism" generally expressed the following insights:

(1) As we have seen, the philosophy of individualism implies that whatever is called common good is merely useful, that things common are but means, and that the character of end belongs exclusively to the individual. "Means" and "end" must be understood here rigorously: a mere means is a thing which has no desirability of its own and which would not be desired at all if it did not lead to a thing desirable in its own right. The mere means, in other words, the thing, that is merely useful, is just traversed by the goodness of the end. To treat the common good as a thing merely useful becomes the *critical* periods, but as soon as the possibility of a new *organic* period[10] is strongly felt, to represent the common good as sheer utility without any dignity of its own is unbearably paradoxical. Only the pressures and appeals of a critical period can make men blind to the character of the common good as autonomous good, *bonum honestum*, and to the primacy that it enjoys as long as the common and the particular are contained within the same order. When such pressures and appeals have become things of the past, the sense

for the eternal worth of the human individual is not necessarily weakened, but why should we keep the language and the ways of a philosophy committed to treating the common good as a thing with no excellence of its own?

(2) Another aspect of classical individualism concerns the role of material causality in human affairs. The features involved belong both to economic and political theory. The individualism of the economists proceeds, in part, from the stubborn belief that the best state of affairs is brought about by the independent operation of ultimate units, the independent money-maker, the individual supplier of labor-force, the individual consumer, the individual organizer, and the like, all moved by the power of individual well-being. Likewise, some democratic polities embody the postulate that what is best for the state is steadily brought about by the solitary determination of its individual components. These polities, famously associated with the teaching of Rousseau and with Jacobinism, strive to maintain the isolation of the citizen. The best state would emerge from the sheer multitude of its citizens and be confronted by nothing but such a multitude.[11] Again, we are dealing here with a disposition marked by the characteristics of the critical periods.

The use of the word *organic*, as in "organic period," suffices to conjure up the danger of attributing to society a unity of *primary* character. Likening society to an organism may be useful as long as we remain in control of our analogies and understand that society is not one after the fashion of an organic body. Its individual members are not organs or cells but primary subjects of human existence. What we need is a concept expressive of the unique way in which an individual exercises membership in a set when the set is a community of intelligent beings. This concept is that of person rather than that of individual. True, the person is sociable by essence and it is capable of playing the role of part (the persons who make up the Senate are parts of the Senate), and the individual, inasmuch as it is a thing "undivided in itself and divided from all the rest,"[12] implies a character of wholeness and separation. But when the being which is an individual and a person is considered *as a member of a set* (and this is the relevant way of considering it in the theory of society, for the unity of society is that of an ordered set), the concept of person restricts the character of part whereas the concept of individual expresses no such restriction. *As a member of a set* the individual is purely and simply a part. But because personality, in every possible connection, expresses a universe of reason and freedom, emphasis on the person implies emphasis on the privileges of this universe. In its most intelligent forms at least, personalism, with all its ambiguities, had the merit of tracing to the unique kind of totality which results from rationality and liberty effects that the individualism of the critical period used to trace to the spontaneity of the part. If atoms were persons, their arrangements would account for many wonders that Epicurean imagination leaves unaccounted for.

(3) Above all, the autonomy of the individual man, as fact of nature and as moral requirement, is incomparably better expressed by the notion of person than by that of individual.[13] Just as it is desirable, in all respects and most precisely in relation to the common good, that the affairs of the state be not managed by the federal power but by the state itself, and the affairs of the county by the county, and the affairs of the township by the township, and the affairs of the family by the family, so it is ultimately desirable that the affairs of the individual man, as long as he is free from important deficiency, be managed by himself. But when the individual man is precisely considered as a being possessed of integrity and rationality, when he is considered as an agent in control of his destiny, when he is considered as an agent which contains its own law not merely by way of natural constitution, but also and principally by way of understanding, voluntariness and freedom, the aspect brought forth is that of personality. On the level of individual existence, autonomy belongs to the person more properly than to the individual. Such greater propriety makes much difference both in terms of explanation and in terms of appeal. The most valuable contribution of personalism is the general theory that the particularity of the human individual, in ultimate contradistinction to that of the function, is a privilege of personality.

Indeed, it is historically absurd to speak of personalism in the singular, as if the various personalistic movements were possessed of doctrinal unity. Endless variety is found in the positive content of their programs, and, whereas each of them is marked by sharp opposition to some general feature of the modern world, the objects of their oppositions may not coincide and may even contrast with each other. Yet there is more unity in the aversions of the personalists than in their assertions, and of all their aversions the most steady concerns the predominance of function in the order of society. If the use of one word to designate such a variety of doctrines, attitudes, inspirations and moods can be justified at all, it should be justified by the central significance, in all personalistic movements, of the conflict between person and function.

The Subject and the Person

Accordingly, in terms of most essential necessity, authority is needed because it is desirable that particular goods should be taken care of by particular agencies.

Some of these agencies are defined by their functions, others are constituted by subjects of various kinds. Along the line which goes from the broader to the more narrow, a particular subject may be a state in a federal union, a county in a state, a township in a county, a family in a township. The ultimateness of the individual is accompanied by the emergence of significant features: this whole, the individual man, is possessed of substantial unity, whereas the other subjects, state, township, family, are not. And by reason of its rational nature, this whole, the individual man, is, in a way, all things, adheres to the absoluteness of the good, and thereby achieves mastery over its own acts. Extreme amplitude arises just when the most narrow unit is attained, for it is not in a merely metaphorical sense that a complete substance of rational nature is said to be a universe. As soon as this is understood, a new light is shed on the particularity of the antecedent subjects. A family, for instance, is not just a smaller group within a township: each of its members is, all things; a family is a whole made of universes, each of which is in control of its own operations—a perfection that no solar system can achieve. Owing to the unique character of totality which belongs to the individual substance of rational nature, the whole system of the subjects is transfigured: a family, a township, a county are particular subjects, they are particular after the fashion of the subject, they are parts indeed, but of these parts the ultimate components are wholes which in a way comprehend all things. At all levels of human association the presence of the person causes the energies of totality, rationality, and liberty to be present.

Looking again at the series of the particular subjects, but from the opposite standpoint, let us now remark that the most particular of them, the person, comes to exist, by virtue of its own sociability, in subjects that are less and less particular, up to the level of a community describable as complete.[14] With regard to the social character of the person, much confusion would be spared if some attention were given to the difference between (1) sociability as such and (2) the tendency to exist in a society as a part in a whole. To be sure, the notion of person expresses wholeness and opposes the character of part, just as the notion of freedom expresses dominating indifference and opposes contingency, and just as the notion of being expresses actuality and opposes potency. But just as finite being cannot exist without an admixture of potency, and just as our freedom cannot exist without harboring a passive indifference, so the person of man, by reason of all the limitations which place it at an infinite distance from absolute personality, demands to exist in a community as a part in a whole. Yet, certain features of sociability belong to the human person *qua* person, and in all the system of human relations, nothing is more determining, more decisive, more distinguish-ing and more final than the acts traceable to the sociability of the person con-sidered as such. In the small area of concentrated energy where these acts take place, the disinterestedness of tendencies and the other-centeredness of needs are more than facts of nature: they involve a commitment of the self in its dis-tinct existence. No doubt, disinterested tendencies and other-centered needs are present in animals, but so long as the reason is not at work the individual agent contributes only a tendency toward its own satisfaction. Disinterestedness and other-centeredness are contributed by nature; in other words, they are caused by a dynamism antecedent to individual activity. The experience of human disor-der shows that a tendency which, by nature, is disinterested and which, in fact, serves another subject, may involve no generosity on the part of the agent. Thus, some mothers love their children in a selfish way; out of selfish love they would do many things beneficial to the child, expose themselves to great dangers and inflict upon themselves great sacrifices. Here, other-centered needs are satisfied and some acts demanded by disinterested tendencies are elicited. But the way of acting remains interested and self-centered. Effects of generous love are brought into existence without generosity. Much is given, and yet action does not *proceed by way of a gift*. When the devotion of a mother to her child bears these charac-teristics, it is commonly interpreted as an animal passion, and thereby we mean that it is nature—that is, a dynamism antecedent to reason and voluntariness—which places the effect of love in another rather than in the acting self. It is only where reason, voluntariness, and free choice are at work that the subject takes care of transcending its subjectivity. Then actions that are gifts also *proceed by way of a gift*. Such disinterestedness, which concerns both the content and the ways of action, originates in rationality, but inasmuch as it implies the actual transcending of the self by itself, it is traceable, in strict appropriateness, to the way of subsisting and to the way of acting which belong to a complete substance of rational nature. In short, it is traceable to personality. Qualities are transcended and the relation of friendship is established on its true basis. As long as it is di-rected to qualities, friendship remains uncertain: it achieves complete genuine-ness only when it exists between person and person, regardless of what hap-pens to the qualities of the beloved. Then, the question *why* one loves is best answered—if this can be called an answer—by pointing to what is unique and unutterable about a person. This state of affairs is powerfully described in a cele-brated essay of Montaigne. "If I am entreated to say why I loved him, I feel that this cannot be expressed except by answering 'Because it was he, because it was I.'

Beyond all my discourse and whatever I can say distinctly about it, I do not know what unexplainable and overwhelming force is instrumental in such a union."[15] In all likelihood Pascal was commenting on Montaigne when he wrote the words:

> But if one loves another one because of his beauty, does he love him? No: for smallpox, which kills the beauty without killing the person, will put an end to love. And if one loves me for my judgment, for my memory, does one love me? No, for I can lose these qualities without losing myself. But where is this self, if it is neither in the body, nor in the soul? and how would it be possible to love the body and the soul, except for these qualities, which do not constitute the self, since they are perishable? should one love the substance of the soul of a person abstractly, and regardless of the qualities in it? that cannot be, and that would be unfair. Thus, one never loves any person, but only qualities.[16]

The last sentence will be misunderstood unless it is held to express the sorrowful perplexity of a man who does not see the answer to a question that he has stated with extreme keenness. Pascal knows that the object of genuine love cannot be anything else than the self. Then, perhaps with some bitterness, he turns to the fact that people are liked and loved because of their qualities, which seems to imply that they never are loved genuinely and that they are bound to remain unhappy. Both in terms of natural possibility and in terms of justice, he sees no way out of this fateful state of affairs. Apparently, he is not unaware of the difference between "being an object of love," and "being a ground of love"; on the one hand, he speaks of loving a person *because of* his beauty, *for* his judgment, *for* his memory; on the other hand, he speaks of loving qualities, not persons.

To get more out of the distinction between ground and object of love, let us see in what sense friendship can make itself independent of its own grounds. Indeed, the only thing that human love cannot do is to create out of nothing the goodness, the desirability of its object. Divine love alone causes the beloved to be good, independently of any goodness antecedent to love. In order to be an object for the love of a creature, a thing must already be good: in that sense it is true that no one is loved or liked by his fellow man except for his qualities. But, although many of these qualities are subject to destruction—Pascal's first example is beauty—a human being will never be totally devoid of qualities. There will always be in him a ground, or a multiplicity of grounds, for disinterested love. Even though a lady has been loved for her beauty, smallpox does not necessarily cause her to be neglected. Under the worst of circumstances, the excellence of human nature, considered in actual existence and in relation to its end, would still be a perfect ground for loving a person without measure. And this excellence of man becomes an infinitely more powerful ground of love when man is considered in the mystery of his supernatural relation to God. Pascal seems to have missed, at least in the present fragment, this ability of love to transcend qualities and be concerned with persons. But without such ability, the other-centered needs which bind men together would be sheer facts of nature and in no way pertain to reason and freedom. Friendship would be impossible. And civic virtue would be impossible.

To sum up this argument, let us imagine again that the members of a community, in a supreme act of boundless dedication, resolve to will and intend, under all circumstances, the matter of the common good as well as its form. By this resolution the particular capacity is abolished. From now on, it will be up to the common capacity to take care of the most particular business.

As far as the function is concerned, the disappearance of the particular capacity results in a loss of order, and among the forms which make up order those are more directly and seriously damaged which are rational in character. As far as the subject is concerned, the disappearance of the particular capacity entails also a loss of order, and this damage is greater where order is mostly made of historical settlement. If the particularity of the subject alone were impaired, and its ordering power transferred to the function, as in the *Republic* of Plato, whatever is historical in the arrangement of the state would be replaced by a rational disposition, and this would make a great deal of difference, for any impairment of particularity, in the case of the subject, entails a loss of autonomy.

The excellence of autonomy vindicates the particularity of the subject and whatever forms of authority are needed for the preservation of this particularity. Familiar contrasts are transcended, authority and autonomy do not conflict with each other and do not restrict each other. They cause and guarantee one another. But no rebel perceives the great unity, the great peace which obtains at this very deep level. Autonomy implies the interiority of the law, a condition which, for human agents at least, is not native, but has to be achieved through arduous progress. Rebels hate the sacrifices that the interiorization of the law requires. It is bad enough for them that the law should exist outside man, and hover around after the fashion of a threat. Autonomy will never lead them to the understanding of authority, for their notion of autonomy is itself a counterfeit.

Notes

Reprinted, with omission of some discursive notes, from *The Review of Politics* 22, no. 2 (April 1960): 202–44.

1. Friedrich Nietzsche, *The Birth of Tragedy* (Garden City, NY: Doubleday, 1956), 24.

2. *Eth.*, I, 2, 1094b7.

3. *Sum. Theol.*, II-II, 32, 7 ad 3.

4. *Met.* 2.3.995a13.

5. *Met.* 6.4.1027b25.

6. Evil is a privation, not a form, but this privation is understood after the pattern of a form and cannot be understood otherwise.

7. According to a well-known remark of Aristotle, the natural order of excellence may be reversed by a condition of emergency. To philosophize is, absolutely speaking, better than to make money. But for the fellow who is in dire poverty, to get money is better than to philosophize. Likewise, the order of love which requires under ordinary circumstances that I should provide my own children with advantages that many other children do not have, also requires that in an emergency (e.g., flood, epidemic, war, revolution), I should deprive my own people of goods that are not needed for their survival in order to insure the survival of children who are not mine.

8. There are, in the history of mankind, only a few communities governed exclusively by the methods of direct democracy. But every democracy, no matter how important the part that a distinct personnel plays in its operation, embodies direct democracy in some of its political processes

9. William James, *Pluralistic Universe.* Hibbert Lectures at Manchester College on the Present Situation in Philosophy (New York: Longmans, Green, and Co., 1909).

10. These Saint-Simonian expressions (*Exposition de la doctrine de Saint-Simon,* ed. Elie Halévy and C. Bougie [Paris: Rivière, 1924], p. 127) are used here without the connotations implied by the Saint-Simonian philosophy of historical causality. For the Saint-Simonists, the great facts of change as well as the great facts of permanence in human history are determined by ideas, and especially by religious beliefs. [The followers of Henri de Saint-Simon (1760–1825), who were far more influential than their namesake, constituted a quasi-religious sect that sought to bring an autocratic, industrial elite to power. Ed.]

11. Proudhon was a firm opponent of democracy so understood. (He called it "democracy" with no further specification.) In his 1848 pamphlet *Solution of the Social Problem,* a subtitle attracts the attention of the philosophers: *Democracy is materialistic and atheistic.* In Jacobin democracy he recognized the traditional picture of the Epicurean universe where all things result from the encounters of particles, without patterns of wholes, without plans and with-out final causes: "Universal suffrage is a kind of atomism by which the legislator, being unable to make the people speak in the unity of its essence, invites the citizens to express their opinion by heads, *viritim,* just as the Epicurean philosopher explains thought, will, understanding, by arrangements of atoms. This is political atheism in

the worst sense of this expression. How could a general thought ever result from the addition of any number of votes?" (A. Lacroix, ed., pp. 62–63) [Pierre-Joseph Proudhon (1809–1865), was one of the leading leftist intellectuals in Europe in the nineteenth century; an anarchist, who opposed all forms of private property and profit-making, he had a major influence on Karl Marx. Ed.]

12. *Sum. Theol.*, I, 29, 4.

13. When individuation originates in matter, as it does in all composite substances, man included, to speak of the "autonomy of the individual" involves a degree of inappropriateness. To be sure, individuals are possessed of autonomy, but the principle of their autonomy is not the same as the principle of their individuality. Matter is that which has no law of its own. In a composite substance all that has the character of a law comes from the form. But the form is specific and consequently all the law of the material individual is the law of its species. In order to reach the principle of a norm concerned with what is unique in the individual substance, we have to turn to the concept which results from the union of *completeness* in substantial constitution and *rationality in* specific nature: this is, by the celebrated definition of Boethius, the concept of person. Among the many writings of Jacques Maritain on the person, see in particular, *The Person and the Common Good* (New York: Scribner's, 1947).

14. It is obvious that no human community is unqualifiedly complete. But insofar as the most comprehensive of our communities remains incomplete, we keep struggling toward something beyond the least incomplete of the existent communities

15. *Essays*, Bk. I, ch. 27.

16. *Pensées*, frag. 323 (New York: Modern Library, 1941), 109.

CHAPTER 22

Is the Intellectual Life an End in Itself?

JOHN U. NEF

At about the time I received my first faculty assignment at Swarthmore College, an obituary notice of an old and admired professor made a deep impression on me. The subject was L. T. Hobhouse, the distinguished English sociologist and lifelong liberal.[1] He had been one of the intellectual pillars upon which the Webbs and a few others had constructed the London School of Economics. I did not know Hobhouse well. But his obituary notice was written by a man I much admired, who was in a way *my* intellectual father: R. H. Tawney. You perhaps know him as the author of *Religion and the Rise of Capitalism,* but he was much better known then as a moral force in the British Labour party. To some of its members Tawney's *Acquisitive Society,* first published in 1921,[2] seemed to offer a fresh charter of liberty, giving a kind of spiritual sanction, missing in Marxian philosophy, to the struggle to overcome misery and poverty with the help of political action. Tawney is alive today and has passed the age at which Hobhouse died. When he wrote this older man's obituary he was not much younger than I am now.[3]

As nearly as I can remember these were for me the words in that obituary notice which had an effect on my life: "Knowledge is such an excellent thing in itself that one has no right to ask for more. Nevertheless one's heart goes out to a person like Hobhouse who is prodigal in the giving of it."

These sentences reveal a confidence in the value of knowledge that is no longer as firmly held. It was then believed, as it still is to some extent, that the methods of inquiry employed increasingly in all domains of learning since the scientific revolution of the late sixteenth and seventeenth centuries provide glimpses at pieces of truth, small and partial though these pieces are. But there has been a great change since 1930, and especially since 1900, in the nature of the hopes men derive from scientific truth.

From the late seventeenth and eighteenth centuries until the beginning of the twentieth it had been more and more widely believed, especially in the so-called

Anglo-Saxon countries of Europe and America, that the more we knew scientifically the better for the characters of men and women. Something of the sort seems to be present in Tawney's words "knowledge is . . . an excellent thing in itself." They emerge from his own integrity as a man, which has been close to absolute. But the words also emerge (as did to some extent his integrity) from his Victorian background. For it seems to have been pretty generally assumed in the Victorian era both in Great Britain and in North America that there is a connection between knowledge and virtue. I write from my experience as an early twentieth-century child, whose father, a distinguished chemist, transmitted this idea to me. And the writings of many Victorians, both in Great Britain and in North America, support this view. In his essay on Machiavelli, written in the mid-nineteenth century, Macaulay comments on the great change in this matter of associating virtue with the life of the mind, which had come about since the Renaissance, since Machiavelli wrote his principal works at the beginning of the sixteenth century:

> Habits of dissimulation and falsehood, no doubt, mark a man of our age and country as utterly worthless and abandoned. But it by no means follows that a similar judgment would be just in the case of an Italian of the Middle Ages. On the contrary, we frequently find those faults, which we are accustomed to consider as certain indications of a mind altogether depraved, in company with great and good qualities. . . . The character of an Italian statesman seems, at first sight, a collection of contradictions. . . . We see a man whose thoughts and words have no connection with each other, who never hesitates at an oath when he wants to seduce, who never wants a pretext when he is inclined to betray . . . yet his aspect and language exhibit nothing but philosophic moderation.[4]

By Tawney's time brilliant young Englishmen, Maynard Keynes and others of the Bloomsbury group among them, were adopting a view in which the divorce between virtue and knowledge was as complete, in new ways, as the divorce between virtue and conduct described by Macaulay in connection with the Italians of the Renaissance. But Tawney stood aside from that movement in the arts and sciences which was to lead persons in our time to take it for granted almost that a moral life and a life devoted to art and letters are separate. I was conversing recently with an American woman, who has tried her hand at writing poetry, and who has had some acquaintance with professional writers from the times of the First World War, while retaining an active life as wife and mother. I asked her what characterized a poet, an artist. I discovered he was for her a person unreliable in keeping engagements, who drank to the point of becoming an alcoholic, who practiced numerous irregularities in matters of sex, in short a person, as Macaulay might have expressed it, utterly worthless and abandoned. While she may have gone too far, and while this judgment of hers might not have extended to university writers, by her time this connection between knowledge and the good life, which Tawney believed in, had been largely forgotten. It is not so much that learned men are now notoriously bad as that almost no one thinks of them in connection with the good as such.

As the assumed connection between knowledge and the good has disappeared since 1930, the number of the learned, and the subsidies granted to them by rich individuals, by foundations created by rich individuals, and above all by governments, has increased overwhelmingly. I can remember a time when my father, as a scientist, was greatly touched by a three-year grant of $3,000 per annum which enabled him to employ two research assistants in his laboratory. But I was recently told by a scientist who is my contemporary that the equipment and support a man like him needs today to carry on his research requires an endowment which seems to me, at least, overwhelmingly large. This scientist told me that a million dollars invested to yield 4% is only enough to buy the equivalent in necessary equipment of what he called "peanuts." Since the beginning of the twentieth century the investment of the Western countries—especially the United States—in knowledge and the arts (but especially in science) has multiplied almost beyond recognition. This has happened during a time when confidence in any necessary connection between the life of the mind and a virtuous life has been all but obliterated.

In an age when statistics and categories frequently take the place of thought and the search for beauty, our contemporaries often find a convenient shorthand in tags. One such tag is "intellectual." The word has come to be applied to all persons who are supposed to concern themselves with knowledge and the arts. Professors of history, like myself, are included with all professors as intellectuals. Persons who publish books or articles, and persons who take doctor's and even master's degrees are all "intellectuals." They become a kind of class in the sense in which members of labor unions or business executives form classes. They hold in all the cities of our country increasingly frequent and increasingly large conventions in big hotels, sandwiched in between the Colonial Dames, the insurance executives, and the Daughters of the American Revolution. They travel on expense accounts to the centers of government.

It is no wonder, therefore, that the number of "intellectuals" has become prodigious. The more the numbers have swelled, the more the members of this category are presumed to have in their keeping possessions of an esoteric nature from knowing which the general public are excluded. Our friends outside the gild, as well as the other persons we meet more casually, take it for granted that we have arrived at knowledge they cannot understand. Gertrude Stein, who used to be charged with unintelligibility, once said she was writing for herself and strangers. We resemble her mainly in that we omit the strangers.

This absence of an understanding audience increases the public's and also the intellectuals' loneliness. It sometimes arouses a sense of inferiority in our contemporaries outside the gild, and also among those within it. The more sensitive are dismayed to find themselves unable to participate with those outside or unable to reach the uninitiated within, except, up to a point, the students who follow their courses and take down in notes a portion of the words that issue from their throats. The communion between members of the gild itself diminishes as the gild is split into ever more numerous specialties.

One of my younger friends, a charming woman who has six children, is the daughter of a learned professor of anthropology, who recently died. Not long ago her father said of her, "Susan is intelligent but she is not an intellectual." She told me she was "shattered" by his comment.

As I remarked in answering her I could not understand why she should be. An intelligent person is now better equipped, it seems to me, to lead an interesting life than an intellectual, unless he happens to be intelligent and to cut some of the ties which bind him to the gild. This is because the intellectual lives, however intensely and however absorbingly, in a specialized arena where his knowledge is mainly of value to himself or, at the most, to a very few colleagues, and, in the case especially of the natural scientist, to businessmen and to government officials because of the bearing their researches have on the technology which, allied with science, in the hands of enterprising organizers, has made over the material world.

"Intellectual," in this sense, is very remotely related to the "knowledge" Tawney seems to have had in mind when he wrote Hobhouse's obituary some thirty years ago. He meant partial truths that could be transmitted widely to the general enrichment of the knowers, knowledge which was food for the inner, the moral and spiritual, lives of human beings. The distinction Tawney drew was between the man who transmitted this only through his books and formal lectures, and the man who, like the Hobhouse he depicted, shared it informally and without premeditation with his students and colleagues and with an intelligent public. At that time an intelligent public was still believed to make the opinion that was taken seriously and that counted with the great newspaper editors of the period who guided statesmen. Hobhouse, in fact, used sometimes to write leading editorials for the *Manchester Guardian* under the famous editorship of C. P. Scott, and the influence of both the *Guardian* and the *Times,* or in our country the old *New York World* and the *Baltimore Sun,* on men like Asquith and Woodrow Wilson is a matter of history. It was not that Hobhouse or Scott or Cobb, the great editorial writer of *The World,* joined the government; they would have never thought of doing that: they told men in the government how they might act, and sometimes changed their thinking.

It was not simply a fiction in those times that knowledge contributed to the good life, to a better life than there could have been without it. Is this true now? And what has our answer to such a question to do with the main question of this paper: "Is the intellectual life an end in itself?"

Unless a person cares more for something that transcends him, and that is good, something that is bigger than himself, he can never achieve the happiness that comes from being better than he is. I have always remembered a passage of an eighteenth-century French writer who is frequently thought of as light— Marivaux. In a book that was then most influential, *La Vie de Marianne,* he writes: "You have to be better than you are to be great; to be small you need only re-main what you are."[5] If one believes, as I do, that the extraordinary world in which we find ourselves today, different from any world that has existed before on this planet, needs as never before men and women who are better than they are, it becomes a matter of great practical as well as great spiritual importance for each of us what the intellectual life is. What is it for our students? What is it for us as teachers? What is it for those who do research? What is it for artists?

By filling ourselves with a life of study and research, by writing or by painting pictures, are we contributing to something that is bigger than ourselves as individuals? Do our lives enable us to serve a higher purpose? Do they raise us up to more nearly resemble what we would like to be in those moments when we are our best selves? In the face of the unparalleled challenge that we face as human beings in this second half of the twentieth century, the great weaknesses of art and of science are that neither have done much to overcome the evil, the moral softness, the jealousy and hatred inherent in human nature. Therefore we ask, did even the Victorians at their best go far enough in their quest for the good as such?

They assumed that by pursuing to the best of their capacities the work of the mind, they would contribute to virtue. But it has so often proved otherwise. And here Machiavelli and some moderns were perhaps more realistic in their outlook than Macaulay and other Victorians. But is it now enough to be realistic? In a world where we expect soon to have some of our fellow men hurtled through space to other planets, must we not transcend realism, in our quest for the good? To me it seems that the supreme goal God offers men and women is to reach Him through their love and compassion for one another. If you accept for the purpose of this paper the hypothesis that this is the hope for human beings, what relation has it to the intellectual life as this is pursued in the twentieth century?

For me at least there seems to be only one way of trying to answer such a question. That is out of my own experience, and out of the experiences others have shared with me on the intimate terms of friendship—others who are classed as "intellectuals." My experience in this matter is the experience of the historian; the experiences others have shared with me are mainly the experiences of the artist and the man of letters.

Please let me begin with one of these experiences, before I submit a few sections of my own intellectual autobiography. The experience emerges from a conversation which took place some fifteen years ago over Sunday luncheon in my Chicago apartment. The luncheon was for Marc Chagall, the painter, who has twice been a visitor to the Committee on Social Thought. The night before I was called up by a foreign professor whom I scarcely knew. He said he wanted to see me. When I suggested we meet at my office on Monday, his voice showed disappointment. This is what he said, "Je sais que Chagall déjeune chez vous demain. Je voudrais vous observer que je suis très bien avec Chagall." ("I know Chagall is coming to your home tomorrow and I want to tell you that Chagall and I are on excellent terms.") So, without verifying this information as a historian should, I quickly made what was not wholly an intellectual decision. I asked the foreign professor to join us at luncheon.

He rather monopolized the conversation. His theme was that all great men are bad characters—"des salauds." The nearest English equivalent I can think of for this word is sons-of-guns. His is a familiar theme. He offered us two examples to prove his case. One was Lenin (whose historical importance has been somewhat eclipsed recently by the excitement over Stalin and Khrushchev). The other was the celebrated philosopher Henri Bergson. I had never known Bergson, let alone Lenin, but I cannot say that the visiting foreigner made a notably convincing case against either. I remember Chagall's contribution to the discussion. At the time he was not himself widely considered a great man. He spoke out of his experience and he suggested that to be great, as an artist at any rate, a person must have at least a minimum of decency. Of course much depends on what we mean by decency and by great. If we consider Hitler, for example, to be great, then Chagall's thesis falls to the ground. And there is a chapter in the *City of God* in which Augustine strips Alexander the Great of basic decency.[6] However we are considering not the political but the intellectual life.

In that my own experience coincides with Chagall's. And I want to tell you how my efforts to be a historian helped me to understand why I think Chagall was right.

As a young student at Harvard I had the good fortune to know pretty well as friends two of the great historians of an older generation—Turner and Haskins.[7] Neither were politicians in any sense. Turner played almost no part in what can be an insidious form of politics: university politics. If the stories that were told in my time, years after the event, were true, Haskins barely missed having to play a big part. For he might have been president.

This reminds me of the story of another "intellectual" who did not escape the dangers of political office as Haskins did. I am thinking of Woodrow Wilson. One of his daughters gave a delightful account of an episode in that great man's life. It occurred after his election in 1912, but before his inauguration in 1913. Wilson felt it would be appropriate if he paid his respects to some members of his family who lived in North Carolina. Among them was an aunt he had not seen since young manhood. She had attained an advanced age and become extremely deaf. When Wilson called on her he was taken upstairs to her room. She recognized him and greeted him with a question that rather took him aback. "I am glad to see you, Tommy," she said, "what have you been doing with yourself all these years?" His response was perhaps more intellectual than witty.

"Aunt Jennie," he said, "they've elected me president."

"Eh, what's that?" she asked. His words were lost on her deaf ears.

"They've elected me president!" He tried several times, screaming each time louder into her long ear trumpet, so loud that all the servants in the house heard and were a little dismayed by the ordeal this famous man was being put to.

Finally the old lady heard him. "Well Tommy, that's fine," she said, "president of what?"

So I should explain that Haskins was almost elected president of Harvard in 1909, according to the reports which lingered on many years later when I was his pupil. And in Massachusetts being president of Harvard is often treated as the next thing to being president of the United States. The Harvard Corporation, which had the final choice, was made up of five men. Two of them voted for Haskins and three for Lowell, at least that was the story. Consequently Haskins was freed, up to a point, at the age of about forty to lead an interesting and in its way an inspiring intellectual life. He was a great teacher. And he used to give at Harvard a graduate seminar in Historical Bibliography and Criticism. It served as a kind of model for all such seminars set up in other universities in the United States. The object was to offer more or less mature students, who were in the process of trying to become historians, instruction in how to gather materials and how to subject the materials to scientific scrutiny in the interest of accuracy. It was a seminar to teach how to write history.

I did well enough in it—had praise from Haskins written on my term paper. But what strikes me now, as I look back, was how little I really learned about writing history from this best of teachers, who was one of the most interesting and cultured of professors. When I set out to become a historian I had to learn everything for myself.

This led me to a tentative conclusion, which has grown stronger with the years. When we are concerned with excellence and originality, and you cannot have excellence without originality, one can't teach a person how to be a historian, to be an artist painter, or even to be an inspiring teacher. It is only by trying to write history, trying to paint, trying to teach—and falling in love with the doing of these things, with the subject matter and the ways of presenting it, so that they absorb one's life—that one can hope to be a little bit good at them. Along the way it is interesting and stimulating to talk over the issues with masters like Haskins or Turner, to discuss with them particular problems as these arise, to have them discuss with you their own problems. But even the greatest masters cannot tell you how to become a master. That you can do only for yourself. Matisse is said to have given up teaching because all his pupils imitated him. He was a wise master. Masters can encourage you by telling you are on the right road, they can help you towards the discriminative enthusiasm essential to creative work. So, at any rate, it seems to me.

I had, as I say, what is regarded as a respectable training for a historian, in what is regarded as not the worst school of learning in this country. Now what was it that decided me to embark on my career, what led me to choose a particular historical subject, and how did the subject take on the meaning for me that I tried to give it for others in the first book that I wrote? I hope these questions have a bearing on the intellectual career, and on the question how far it is properly an end in itself.

I seem to remember that, when I was a student at Harvard College following the First World War, one of the matters that interested me was the conditions behind a nation's greatness. Great Britain had emerged outwardly as a great nation with colonies all over the globe. A lot was written in the newspapers at the time about the British coal industry. I remember talking over with Professor Taussig,[8] with whom I took an advanced course in economics, my interest in coal as a factor in Great Britain's economic strength. He was interested in guiding me; with several other professors I knew at Harvard—Haskins and Turner among them— Taussig encouraged me in my desire to go abroad to begin my career. He suggested I read Adam Smith on the subject of coal, which I did. When, by singular good luck, I was able to go abroad under what were ideal conditions for a young man, I consulted Tawney, partly because he had been one of the members of a famous commission—the Sankey Commission it was called—which inquired into the state of the coal industry following the war. Tawney was also a historian; he suggested that a history of the coal industry had never been written, and that I start out about the middle of the eighteenth century, since efforts to exploit coal before that in Great Britain were of all importance, though the earlier history might perhaps be worth a brief introductory chapter.

It was here that I had my first lesson. Everything which is really worth finding out about a historical subject one has to find out for oneself. Tawney was certainly regarded at the time as one of the persons who knew the most about the history of British coal. But, as I began to rummage about the British Museum in search of material bearing on the subject, I discovered that he really knew very little about it. I discovered further that all the most learned English historians were, as it seemed to me, more ignorant in this matter than Tawney.

Then I began working with manuscript materials. I came on sets of documents in the Public Record Office that had never been carefully examined before: port book records of the shipments of coal to and from British ports from the beginning of Elizabeth I's reign, some from an even earlier time. They covered especially the period from 1550–1700. There were hundreds of books containing the coal entries at various ports for particular years between those dates. The trouble was that the shipments of coal were mixed in with many other items and never totaled. The job of doing this in those days, when no one brought into the Record Office any instruments more mechanical than a pencil, was rather formidable. It meant, as I soon found out, weeks and months of labor. Yet, from running through some of the books, I could see that it was going to provide statistical proof of what I was already beginning to understand from other less statistical evidence: that there was an expansion of coal mining and the coal trade in Great Britain during the sixteenth and seventeenth centuries of dimensions no one had dreamed of, that this expansion was related to a hitherto neglected expansion of other industries, and that the changes effected in industrial life constituted a kind of early industrial revolution.

These were for me very exciting discoveries. I felt like a mountaineer ascending a peak which no one had climbed. I saw I might blaze a new trail.

I pressed on into other kinds of documents, among them the records of different law courts, with the testimony of witnesses, often hewers and carriers of coal, sometimes seamen on the coal boats. I found out many other things that were new (e.g., how the exceptionally heavy demand for coal in the Elizabethan Age and after, encouraged rich landlords and traders who had made large fortunes in the English towns, above all in London, to consolidate small holdings of peasant farmers into large estates). I saw that it was partly the pressure which produced what was called the "enclosure movement" in England, which made the country a natural place for great landlords with poor tenants.

How could I convey all these parts of truth to others? I found here that the training I had had at Harvard in historical bibliography and criticism was not much help. There we had been set subjects like: Who was the real author of this or that Federalist paper? I seem to remember working at that puzzle. I had found it an interesting exercise. But I could see that it had little relevance to the problems that confronted me looking over this ocean of new information which had come into my hands. No one could set the problems for me because no one else knew what I knew. I had to formulate for myself the questions that needed to be answered. The research methods we were taught offered no general principles applicable to all problems of research. The real matter I dimly realized was what was important for man. And here I had no guide. It is only out of a rich and difficult life that one sometimes discovers these things, if one discovers them at all, and one must be as wary of thinking one has found them as one must be wary of thinking one has found wisdom. I was then only on the threshold of life, living by great good luck during those years abroad under conditions which made it seem worth while to try to be a historian but which did not tell me how.

In formulating questions for myself I had an extraordinarily wide range of choice, partly because of the wide general culture one could still derive from the European experience, lived moderately and healthfully. I also had a wide range of choice because I had not had inculcated in me any of the set formulas concerning historical evolution, such as the stage theory of history. The only formula which had made an impression upon me was the notion that capitalism had brought about the world in which we live, partly at least a Marxian notion which had been adopted then by almost all economic historians. I think now as I look back that the notion has its uses, largely if one goes beyond it and sees that it by no means offers a final solution for the researcher into economic history to discover what made for the rise of capitalism. In fact it is only now, almost thirty years after I finished my book, that the implications of what I was finding are taking on what seems to be a more important meaning. The quest for the origins of large capitals in industrial organization now seems to me in many ways a blind alley for those who are trying to understand the historical forces which have created the world with which we have to deal.

What was most difficult of all for me was the writing of a book. Trying to tell in written words what I thought ought to be told, for I obviously knew much more than I could tell. And even if I found—as I had to try to find out—what it was I wanted to tell, how could I tell it accurately and honestly as a part of history, for here in connection with general history I knew so much less than I needed to know? I discovered how easy it would be to cheat. And this brought with it, fortunately for me, the realization that if I cheated, the person I would be cheating most of all would be myself.

So I learned from an experience of the intellectual life over a period of ten years, pursued both abroad and later in the United States (to which I returned and got a university job), I learned the value of factual honesty, of telling what is so as precisely as one can. And I found out how difficult it is to do this even when you want to very much.

This kind of search for truth is something that the coming of modern scientific inquiry since the late sixteenth and seventeenth centuries has strengthened in the world. Accurate observation and experiment. Accurate measurements. Accurate statements of new mathematical propositions. Matter on which firm agreement is possible about tangible things. I find myself drawn to emphasize the *importance* of this discipline, partly because I have since learned and emphasized in papers of mine the *limitations* of science. Those are very real. And in the new world of the intellect and the conscience, which we may hope will emerge in years to come, and help our successors to interpret and improve the new world of machinery, automation and movement through space, I think we shall have to find new ways of searching for truth. These will be ways that recognize, and at the same time transcend, both scientific accuracy and the limitations of scientific accuracy.

Learning to tell the truth, whether it is agreeable to do so or not, for no other reason than because it is true, is a great lesson. But the lesson is only partly learned if it is kept an intellectual lesson, a scientific lesson. The great need is to have telling the truth become a part of life. One can almost always play intellectual tricks when the matter under consideration is of importance, because then there is not one truth but many truths. The price of living well is to work one's way through the maze of many truths in the direction of Truth.

It is difficult to say just when, but mainly after I had finished that first long book of mine (though the problem arose dimly in my mind when I was writing it), this larger problem in the matter of truth confronted me. What I was finding out about coal in history, what I was able after many false starts and many rewritings to give was perhaps (at least I had to hope so) a pretty true account of one aspect of history, and it was turning out to be related to more of history than others had supposed. But it was I who formulated the questions, and while I thought (and still think) that this was better than fitting the material into grooves ready-made by my predecessors, I did load the dice by the choices I made. The penalty of not loading them somehow would have been not to write at all. How small was my story in relation to history as a whole. It would have been easy to say, "The rest doesn't concern me; that isn't my job." But I have found out increasingly that this is not a satisfactory way of meeting the problem. I had been concerned with one side of Britain's history. Comparisons with French and German history and with the history of the Low Countries were helping me to see the weakness of treating even a single side of British economic history by itself. And then, beyond Europe, I could see other parts of the world. Europe, after all, when you look at it, is only a spot on the map. Also there was a past, before the subject I had chosen began, a past stretching back endlessly, it seemed, among persons who had lived in different places on the planet. How was what I was trying to tell related to that past? And then there was what had happened since, in the period Tawney had assumed in the beginning I was going to write about—the two centuries and more since 1700, that followed the establishment of coal as a vital part of the economy of Great Britain. How was what I was trying to tell related to that future?

These speculations have led me on to universal history. How did a picture of the past derived from my new starting point differ from that of the universal historians who were cropping up in my time? There was H. G. Wells for instance, now little thought about by historians, though Haskins used to point out, I remember, that Wells's span of historical inquiry had a future. There was Spengler who was being enormously read in Germany while I was writing my coal history. And then finally Toynbee who, assisted without his planning it by *Time* magazine, became the first popular authority on the subject. I found the rest of history was not irrelevant to what I had done, and to my reconsideration of what I had done, and that out of this there emerged a picture of universal history fundamentally different from the one presented by the universal historians, one of whom— Toynbee—I know pretty well, for he has lectured for the Committee on Social Thought on three occasions.

I began to reflect too that the very way I had begun, along with many others, to search for historical truth partly determined what we wrote, and that this enabled us to tell a particular story of the past, and to leave readers without any inkling of other stories of the past which might, for all we knew, be more important. An accidental choice of documents had guided me. And even though my choice of documents was justified by the search for truth, and I think that it was largely justified by the kind of search for truth that I set out to make, the documents that the past has left behind are largely accidental. I mean this in more than one sense. Documents are at the mercy of circumstances—personal decisions of their authors as to what to preserve, fires and destruction of all kinds. I remember going to Cambrai in 1936 with a list of documents I wanted to consult which had once been there and been catalogued, to find that during the War of 1914–18 all of them had been wiped out. The Germans had set fire to the town hall when they retreated, and what they had not destroyed, the Canadians in taking the town had drowned in water in their effort to put out the fire. On top of all that there is much that is humanly important—sometimes what is humanly most important—that is never written down. History after all is the history of human beings, and so a history interpreted from documents is necessarily only a partially true history, because the most precious matters for human beings are seldom, if ever, recorded.

So I have discovered many things about the intellectual life in the process of having tried to live it. The enthusiasms of my youth were not unjustified because a number of conditions which were no merit of mine led me to want not to cheat, to try to find out the truth. But to rest on those enthusiasms would not have been justified, when I was finding out the limitations of the search based on those enthusiasms. The larger matter of historical truth as such, which in its turn is only a part of truth as such, and to which we human beings have access only if it *is* true, through Christ, that we *are* children of God, must always partly escape us. Historical truth and truth are both, in a final sense, matters of faith. We need to have the humility to know this and to breathe it into our works.

I hope I shall not be misunderstood. The rigorous discipline involved in the establishment of historical facts is an excellent thing. The attention directed towards it during the past four centuries is a result partly of the rise of the modern natural sciences. The danger in this quest is that persons become so enamored of this scientific search for truth that it becomes an end in itself. Some of the best intellectuals are seduced by the honesty of their search. They delude themselves into thinking this search absolves them from the search for Truth itself. So, at this critical time in history, when in science the search for partial truth can produce universal disaster, what we are doing is not enough.

The intellectual life can be cultivated *effectively* for the truths it contains only if one falls in love with it to such an extent that it is *cultivated* as an end in itself. And yet—which seems at first sight a contradiction—one can only cultivate the intellectual life for all it is worth if the love it generates becomes more important than the problems one is trying to solve; until love matters more than the problems; until the problems become problems of love. For then a person is led on to see all tangible problems as part of bigger more important problems still.

In making the intellectual life an end in itself, a person is being what he is. And as Marivaux said to be small you have only to be what you are. The road to something more than that, which to follow is to edge as individuals a little closer to truth, is the road towards disinterested love, which has its greatest test in the temporal world in our love for another human being. If one grows to learn this, one will love the intellectual life knowing that the greatest good for man is to love. This can help one to keep the particular intellectual problem to which one addresses oneself in its place. It can help one, without discouraging the search, to recognize the limitations contained even in the most perfect solution.

It is not the intellectual life, it is love that is an end in itself.

NOTES

Reprinted from *The Review of Politics* 24, no. 1 (January 1962): 3–18.

1. [Leonard Trelawny Hobhouse (1864–1929) was a British Liberal politician and the first sociologist to be appointed to a professorship at a British university. Ed.]

2. This small book incorporated Tawney's earlier pamphlet "The Sickness of an Acquisitive Society" which first appeared in the *Hibbert Journal*. See R. H. Tawney, *Acquisitive Society* (London: G. Bell and Sons, 1921).

3. [R. H. Tawney was a leader in the Christian Socialist movement and a prominent economist. Ed.]

4. Thomas Babington Macaulay, *Critical and Historical Essays*, I (London: Longman, Brown, and Green, 1843), 83–84.

5. Marivaux, *La Vie de Marianne*, Part III. [Pierre Carlet de Chamblain de Marivaux (1688–1763) was one of the most important comedic playwrights of eighteenth-century France. A recent edition of *La Vie de Marianne* is published by Gallimard (Paris, 1997). Ed.]

6. *City of God*, Bk. IV, chap. iv.

7. [The historian Frederick Jackson Turner (1861–1932) is best-known for his studies of the American frontier; Charles H. Haskins was one of the early American scholars of the Middle Ages. Ed.]

8. [Frank William Taussig (1859–1940) was an economist and one of the first theorists of international trade. Ed.]

DATE DUE

HIGHSMITH 45230